T0143304

Using Metering to Perform Energy Management: Performing Data Analytics via the Metering System

RIVER PUBLISHERS SERIES IN ENERGY MANAGEMENT

Series Editors

MICHELE ALBANO
Aalborg University,
Denmark

The "River Publishers Series in Energy Management" is a series of comprehensive academic and professional books focussing on management theory and applications for energy related industries and facilities. Books published in the series serve to provide discussion and exchange information on management strategies, techniques, methodologies and applications, with a focus on the energy industry.

Topics include management systems, handbooks for facility management, safety, security, industrial strategies, maintenance and financing, impacting organizational communications, processes and work practices. Content is also featured for energy resilient and high-performance buildings.

The main aim of this series is to serve as a useful reference for academics, researchers, managers, engineers, and other professionals in related matters with energy management practices.

Books published in the series include research monographs, edited volumes, handbooks and textbooks. The books provide professionals, researchers, educators, and advanced students in the field with an invaluable insight into the latest research and developments.

Topics covered in the series include, but are not limited to:

- Facility management;
- Safety and security;
- Management systems and solutions;
- Industrial energy strategies;
- Financing and costs;
- Energy resilient buildings;
- Green buildings management.

For a list of other books in this series, visit www.riverpublishers.com

Using Metering to Perform Energy Management: Performing Data Analytics via the Metering System

George "Buster" Barksdale
GES, Inc. Huntsville, Alabama, US

Kecia Pierce
K. Pierce Consulting, LLC., Madison, Alabama, US

Routledge
Taylor & Francis Group
NEW YORK AND LONDON

Published 2024 by River Publishers
River Publishers
Alsbjergvej 10, 9260 Gistrup, Denmark
www.riverpublishers.com

Distributed exclusively by Routledge
605 Third Avenue, New York, NY 10017, USA
4 Park Square, Milton Park, Abingdon, Oxon OX14 4RN

Using Metering to Perform Energy Management: Performing Data Analytics via the Metering System / George "Buster" Barksdale and Kecia Pierce.

Routledge is an imprint of the Taylor & Francis Group, an informa business

ISBN 978-87-7022-838-1 (hardback)
ISBN 978-87-7004-098-3 (paperback)
ISBN 978-10-4001-089-1 (online)
ISBN 978-1-003-46711-3 (ebook master)

While every effort is made to provide dependable information, the publisher, authors, and editors cannot be held responsible for any errors or omissions.

Contents

Preface

The book was written as a textbook to support anyone studying meter data. My partner, Kecia Pierce, and I have been working together for six years, training students in using the meter data and the best practices for performing analysis. Kecia has provided sanity to the insanity and kept us focused as we worked on this project. We have benchmarked and analyzed over 7000 buildings on numerous campuses.

The data analytics work started with basic benchmarking and EUIs but has morphed into a significant analysis area. Two major areas of analytics have been discovered that are monumental in data analytics. The first is the value from the base load and how that impacts solution sets' decisions. The second is the scatter plot and how it provided all the energy subsets that precipitated data breakdown into energy systems.

We will show how meter data can be utilized at all energy manager (EM) experience levels. This book should prove helpful for supporting many functions that EMs do every day. Each chapter is designed to streamline the EM's job and guide them to tools that can save them time and make their life easier.

Many friends and colleagues worked with us to develop this product. We appreciate their friendship and comments to help get this book over the finish line. Eric Oliver was a great sounding board for ideas, and he read through most of the booklet providing invaluable guidance and thoughts on how to present the information. As an installer, Joe Arian's insights effectively ensured that we were technically correct when we addressed meter issues and the network. Our teammate Carolyn Bakke was meticulous in her data work and reviewed our information on data connectivity and quality. Her background in meter data from the utility industry provided us with a sanity check on how we validate meter data. For the detailed analytics, we thank Jim Wajciechowski for providing some examples of comprehensive analytics from Cimetric's projects. Finally, thanks to Jim Plourde for assisting with meter hardware and installation issues.

List of Figures

List of Tables

List of Abbreviations

AC	Air conditioning
AEE	Association of Energy Engineers
AFB	Air force base
AFDD	Automated fault detection and diagnostics
AHS	Air-handling system
AHU	Air-handling unit
ASHRAE	American Society of Heating, Refrigerating and Air-Conditioning Engineers
BAS	Building automation system
BEDES	Building Energy Data Exchange Specification
BMS	Building management system
BN HQ	Battalion Head Quarters
BOS	Building operations and support
BTU	British Thermal Unit
CBA	Comprehensive building analytics
CBECS	Commercial Buildings Energy Consumption Survey
CC	Cooling coil
CDD	Cooling degree day
CDH	Cooling degree hours
CEM	Certified energy manager
Cf	Cubic feet
CG&SV	Consulting groups and software vendors
CHLR	Chiller
CHW	Chilled water valve
CHWRT	Chilled water return temperature
CHWST	Chilled water supply temperature
CMMS	Computerized maintenance management system
COF	Company Operations Facility
COP	Coefficient of performance
CPU	Central processing unit
CT	Current transformer
CTS	Compliance tracking system

CV	Constant volume
DAT	Discharge air temperature
DDC	Direct digital control
DOE	Department of Energy
EA	Exhaust air
ECM	Energy conservation measure
EER	Energy efficiency ratio
EIA	Energy Information Administration
EISA	Energy Independence and Security Act
EM	Energy manager
EMS	Enterprise management system
EPA	Environmental Protection Agency
EPAct	Energy Policy Act
ERDA	Energy Research and Development Administration
ESCO	Energy Services Company
ESPC	Energy savings performance contract
EUI	Energy use intensity
FDD	Fault detection and diagnostics
FH	Fume hood
FV	Face velocity
GHG	Greenhouse gas
HDD	Heating degree days
HOA	Hand-off-auto
HTHW	High-temperature hot water
HVAC	Heating, ventilation, and air conditioning
IES	Illuminating Engineering Society
IRR	Internal rate of return
JACE	Java Application Control Engine
KPI	Key performance indicator
LBNL	Lawrence Berkeley National Laboratory
LED	Light Emitting Diode
M&V	Measurement and verification
MAT	Mixed air temperature
MBCx	Monitoring-based commissioning
MCx	Monitoring commissioning
MMBTU	Million BTUs
MMS	Meter management system
NREL	National Renewable Energy Laboratory
O&M	Operations & maintenance
OAT	Outdoor air temperature

OPEC	Organization of Arab Petroleum Exporting Countries
PHC	Preheat coil
PNNL	Pacific Northwest National Laboratory
RCx	Recommissioning
REM	Resource efficiency manager
ROI	Return on investment
SA	Supply air
SEED	Standard Energy Efficiency Data
SEER	Seasonal Energy Efficiency Ratio
Sf	Square foot
SOO	Sequence of operations
SysE	System efficiency
UEC	Unit energy consumption
UEPH	Unaccompanied Enlisted Personnel Housing
UESC	Utility energy services contract
USACE	United States Army Corps of Engineers
VAV	Variable air volume
VFD	Variable frequency drive
XML	Extensible markup language

1

Introduction

Abstract

This chapter serves as an introduction to using metered data for performing data analytics to support energy management. This book provides tools that assist the energy manager (EM) in managing energy utilizing a monitoring system. These data analytics tools empower the EM to become more efficient and effective.

1 Introduction

This chapter will introduce us to the data analytics transition over the last 50 years as it increased for the EM and the EM's capability to manage energy. This data and the analytic capabilities evolved slowly over time and then mushroomed into many facets, providing the EM with many options to manage their programs. The slow evolution and data increase provided EMs with various options for best managing their programs. This grew into the eventual use of metering data and how that can be used in energy management. In this chapter, we will learn the following:

- Introduction to meter management systems

- Evolution of energy management

- Evolution of available energy data

- Building management systems

- Implementing a successful MMS

- Data analysis

1.1 Introduction to Meter Management Systems

This book will cover the data generated by meter management systems (MMSs) and how it can be incorporated into data analytic tools and processes to successfully assist energy managers (EMs) in executing their energy programs. These tools and the corresponding techniques offer opportunities for EMs to expand their capabilities while optimizing their time. The MMS, if optimized, will allow an EM to reduce field time significantly. Comprehensive data analytics from an MMS will enable them to perform most of the energy management pre-analysis, benchmarking by building and by energy system, fault detection analysis, and data analysis, all remotely from their office. In many cases, the MMS data will allow them to complete the task of performing a virtual energy audit. This book covers many instructional areas that are – for the most part – currently only offered by a portion of consulting groups and software vendors (CG&SV) as data analytic services. We will show how many of these CG&SV services can be covered by the MMS, especially in smaller buildings. While utility metering does not address all areas of energy management, it provides a strong foundation of the analytics associated with that data. The CG&SV groups offer their services for fees and, therefore, do not typically publish their concepts or best practices for others to use, which are provided in this textbook. These CG&SV companies offer various hardware and software analytics whose capabilities are addressed as we describe solutions in Chapters 1 and 2. An EM may still require analytics beyond the capabilities of an MMS. Many analytic companies will take MMS and enterprise management system (EMS) data and other data to provide those additional analytics or services we require. This book lets EMs expand their current analytics knowledge by viewing other practices.

Other CG&SV groups offer services like MMS but in more detail in related areas such as basic benchmarking, detailed data analytics, and monitoring-based commissioning (MBCx). These services are considered essential energy management and are generally used as on-site services. Their cost will vary depending on the level of effort, with the most expensive being MBCx, which is more costly than monitoring commissioning (MCx) (which will be covered in Chapter 15). MCx, in contrast to MBCx, is purely done at the monitoring level and allows us to manage the critical energy measures that comprise the majority of the savings but without getting into the detailed testing.

Benchmarking is easily performed by basic power meters, and this will be covered at a deeper level in the book as we show how to benchmark each system in a building. The benchmarking chapters show how to automatically analyze each system's usage into categories, including base load, lighting,

AC systems, and fan/pump systems. These systems have benchmarks; so EMs can compare by campus, category type, climate zone, etc. We also introduce other benchmarking strategies that enable the EM to utilize many tools to determine their buildings' performance and which systems require their greatest attention. These numerous data analytic functions are all combined into tools to produce results that establish potential energy savings criteria prioritized by savings for each system. These services are considered essential energy management and are performed remotely via the cloud.

1.2 Evolution of Energy Management

Energy management has changed exponentially over the last 50 years. Understanding the progression requires reviewing the history and covering the drivers in this process. Energy management became a required skill set due to energy-related crises in the 1970s. Several significant issues were already being researched for clean energy during this time. On October 6, 1973, it became pivotal when the Yom Kippur War broke out in the Middle East. Due to the US support for Israel, the Organization of Arab Petroleum Exporting Countries (OPEC) declared an oil embargo on October 17, 1973, sparking the first "energy crisis." As a result, the Department of Energy evolved from its predecessors, the Federal Energy Administration and Energy Research and Development Administration (ERDA). On August 4, 1977, President Carter signed the Department of Energy (DOE) Organization Act to replace the Federal Energy Administration and ERDA. Officially, DOE was activated on October 1, 1977. It brought together a score of organizational entities from a dozen departments and agencies; the new department was also responsible for the nuclear weapons program [2].

The Association of Energy Engineers (AEE) was founded in 1977 by Energy Engineer Al Thumann in response to the need for critical training and certifications to support the new normal that had evolved over the previous four years. This booming industry needed more expertise to develop a written policy; so with much collaboration, President Carter wrote and signed the National Energy Act on November 9, 1978. This included the National Energy Conservation Policy Act, the Power Plant and Industrial Fuel Use Act, the Public Utilities Regulatory Policy Act, the Energy Tax Act, and the Natural Gas Policy Act [2].

1.3 Evolution of Available Energy Data

During these early days of energy management, we needed more data to make decisions on energy in facilities. All data during that time was based on monthly utility bills and analyses based on building audits or modeling. Building HVAC controls were pneumatic or electric. There was real-time data once campuses started transitioning from pneumatic to electronic controls, and those controls were tied into a rudimentary front end with little power or connectivity. This transitioned quickly to more powerful direct digital controls (DDC), allowing the EMS to monitor while the DDC maintained local control. Chip evolution increased the ability of DDCs at building levels to perform independently and report at intervals to the EMS. This was the first stage of fundamental data analysis. The enterprise servers monitored DDC or other HVAC endpoints that provide the critical data information for analysis along with the sequence of operations of control applications.

All these data endpoints were now available in one location, and people began learning how to use them effectively on the EMS to perform energy management and enhance their data analytics. Shortly after that, meters started being added to the EMS, but people needed to understand how to use the meters as effectively. While meter analytics should be a part of the total energy management analytic solutions, EMs did not become effective with meter analytics until meters were integrated into the EMS. And even then, most EMs depended on the limited data analytics packages provided by EMS because this information overload meant they could not use all the data effectively. The integration of the various systems drove the industry to higher capabilities from an analytics perspective. However, there were few good analytic packages in EMS and few trained analysts. The mix of metering and other data analytics was not utilized to its full potential.

Therefore, the US Federal Government determined that adding meter systems into buildings was vital. While the following guidance primarily applies to federal facilities, it establishes a solid minimum baseline for commercial facilities. With the associated rationale, we will show where to use these minimum baselines in a program and how or why to increase their usage.

The Energy Independence and Security Act of 2007 (EISA), the Energy Policy Act of 2005 (EPAct), and March 19, 2015, Executive Order – Planning for Federal Sustainability in the Next Decade have established that agencies are to install electricity, natural gas, steam, and water meters on all federal buildings. They must also incorporate the usage data into federal energy tracking systems and make the data available to federal facility managers. Specifically:

"Each agency shall use, to the maximum extent practicable, advanced meters or advanced metering devices that provide data at least daily and that measure at least hourly consumption of electricity in the Federal buildings of the agency." The deadline for this action was October 1, 2012 [5].

Since 2005, agencies have developed data management systems for tracking metered data. Executive Order 13963 requires agencies to enter monthly energy and water data for facilities into the Environmental Protection Agency's (EPA) ENERGY STAR Portfolio Manager (herein referred to as Portfolio Manager) to enable performance management and benchmarking. The Executive Order addresses the goal of "incorporating, where feasible, the consensus-based, industry-standard Green Button data access system into reporting, data analytics, and automation processes" to facilitate energy data analysis and management. Agencies must also post and update building performance data in the US Department of Energy's (DOE) compliance tracking system (CTS). A facility is one that an agency has designated as subject to the requirements of section 432 of the Energy Independence and Security Act of 2007 (Pub. L. No. 110-140, as codified at 42 U.S.C. section 8253(f)), which requires agencies to designate covered facilities comprising at least 75% of their total facility energy use [1].

DOE guidance identifies what buildings are appropriate and a subjective criterion for prioritization. The previous guidance was superior as it set 10,000 sf as the minimum and provided an alternative to prioritizing by an economic analysis related to a prescriptive 5% savings target as the stipulated savings. We are finding that it is a low estimated number, with the actual number exceeding 20% for institutional buildings. We recommend an EM decide on a criterion based on the economics of a reasonable percentage of savings with a 10-year simple payback. Our experience has seen the savings for institutional buildings exceed 25% and commercial at 15%. Therefore, the return on investment can be estimated by determining the cost of a meter's installation divided by 25% of the cost of electric usage for electric meters. Generally, buildings with more than 10,000 sf economically justify an electric meter, and those around 30,000 sf justify a gas meter. Water meters can be justified based on our experience of approximately 20,000 sf; however, if we have trouble tracking breakages, any issues might explain the need for meters to check for leaks.

As we exceed this sf minimum, the guidance is not prescriptive for additional meters. This gives a false sense of security in the single meter, and we see a need for meters on systems and sections of facilities as they increase over 20,000 sf. This is also a simple economic decision and should be pursued in the same manner as described above. The analysis in this book will address approaches for a single meter on a building and give guidance related to that type of construction. As we add more meters, we can monitor each system more accurately. In contrast, one meter requires calculations or proportioning to assess end-use consumption, such as adding a meter for each air conditioning system when a building contains multiple units. For industrial processes, EMs prefer that every piece of equipment be metered for all commodities so that the charges for each system can be calculated directly for accounting purposes.

Benchmarking was critical enough for DOE to establish Energy Star Portfolio Manager for benchmarking federal agencies' buildings. Portfolio Manager is an online tool developed by the EPA specifically to allow benchmarking of all federal government facilities. It also allows other facilities to be added to the benchmarking tool. EPA claims it is the most used energy management and tracking tool for commercial buildings, with almost 25% of US commercial buildings space already tracked. This book extensively covers benchmarking, providing more details and options with an MMS [4].

DOE uses benchmarking data to report to Congress on energy use in facilities. A portfolio manager can track the energy use intensity of a campus or across buildings in similar geographic zones. All energy use streams, such as natural gas, chilled water, etc., must be entered into Portfolio Manager. The values can be estimated if metered values are unavailable for all energy use streams. If a building is also metered for water use, the water data must also be included in Portfolio Manager. Portfolio Manager is available for commercial buildings, but the limitations by category within Portfolio Manager do not allow us to be as accurate in benchmarking as we can be within a business' portfolio (entire inventory). If an EM does not have a portfolio, then Portfolio Manager is the next best solution to benchmark against [1].

1.4 Building Management System

Although a building management system (BMS), sometimes called a building automation system (BAS), may seem like a new concept, these have been around for 50+ years. Although available, their computing capacity was drastically inferior to that of today. The energy industry and building management closely followed the exponential growth of the computer chip, which increased computing power and, thus, capabilities. With increased capabilities came advanced data and the analytics of that data. The analytics increased exponentially as we had real-time access to data and computing power to analyze multiple scenarios and situations.

Traditionally, a BMS is a computer-based control system installed in a building or a portion of a building and used to monitor and regulate its mechanical and electrical systems. These systems may include lighting, ventilation, power, elevator, and security. The BMS has evolved throughout the years with the rise of BMS technology, especially within the commercial market. This has resulted in the three classifications of BMS that this chapter will address: single-integration BMS, partial integration BMS, and fully enabled BMS (integrating multiple BMS and other systems) [3].

Single-integration BMS has been utilized within the commercial industry for decades to increase operational efficiency and reduce energy costs. However, small- and medium-sized commercial buildings have experienced minimal cost benefits due to the limited interconnectivity the single-integration BMS provides. This traditional BMS can be one of multiple disparate subsystems installed within a building office. Each has its IT infrastructure, and only building/facility management staff are granted access to these systems. All the disparate subsystems in a building, such as HVAC and lighting, remain disconnected and are managed separately by manual intervention [3].

As subsystems grew and became more complex and integrated across campus into an EMS, there arose a need for improved energy efficiency and integrated building management solutions. Control manufacturers integrated these systems through gateways, but this provided a partial integration from the 1990s through the 2010s. This integration was expensive and had drawbacks in communication and control. The Internet of Things (IoT) for buildings developed around 2010 and quickly became a game-changer. The term "Internet of Things" describes the myriad of machines, equipment, and sensors connected to the Internet and, therefore, can all communicate with each other.

As a result, integrated BMS systems were adopted, combining individual subsystems that could now communicate with one another. For businesses, this meant the rise of remote monitoring, condition-based maintenance, and automated labor scheduling. These interconnected IoT technologies became valuable to facility management staff through data collection, analysis, and automated control. In these systems, the maintenance staff would receive a notification of "no occupancy," and the personnel at the system desk would then turn off the lights. The highest classification involves a fully enabled EMS and other systems interacting and making decisions based on multiple inputs. They exhibit a higher level of real-time decision-making and a deeper focus on tenant experience. The technology provides real-time data on how interactions between people, processes, and connected equipment influence assets such as lighting and HVAC. While this is the ultimate goal with an overlay of some degree of data analytics, this is a long way off for most buildings, especially institutions. Our coverage in this book will concentrate on the analytics available from the simplest data acquisition from the MMS [3].

1.5 Implementing a Successful MMS

An MMS is only successful if the metered data is used to save energy or to improve operations. After the data is available, the interaction between the EMs and the campus maintenance personnel or shops and their capabilities is the next critical piece of the puzzle. The personnel who work in engineering and maintenance are needed to install, maintain, and operate the MMS. Then someone must analyze the metered data and implement the analysis results. There are five single points of failure in an organization, and the associated processes that can occur in that sequence and personnel need to be appropriately trained and afforded the necessary time to operate and maintain the metering equipment and system. All these points must be working correctly to gain the benefits of the metering system [1]. Those five single points of failure are as follows.

1. **EM training**. Training is essential, but a good EM should already have a broad skill set. The EM must understand the energy efficiency objectives to focus on the aspects of their program that have the greatest potential return on investment (ROI). The EM and the shops need to jointly have a strong understanding of energy systems and how to assess energy data when it is available. Certified energy manager (CEM) training offered by AEE is an example of the training that would provide both organizational and building EM with the knowledge needed to improve energy operations.

2. **Organizational cohesion**. The ability of the organization to work together to emphasize maintenance while resolving energy issues is critical to the mission's success. We want to have a core thread of continuity across the organization based on the ROI to ensure the success of an MMS and the associated energy program.

3. **Technical support**. The technical issues may require outside support from various on-campus experts or outside contractors such as utility providers, the IT network, cybersecurity, complexities of HVAC systems, and, in most cases, the control systems.

4. **Interconnection design**. Connecting the meter to a data management system introduces additional security concerns. Cybersecurity concerns will need to be addressed regarding whether the data can be transmitted over existing network systems or if a separate communication system will be required, which means that energy professionals will need

to engage agency cybersecurity professionals early in selecting and installing metering and related communication systems.

5. **Designed for maintenance**. Designing, developing, and maintaining an MMS is challenging and expensive. Data must be consistently evaluated, and meters and MMS must be maintained to capture and analyze the data. One starts with a simple spreadsheet or database tool generated internally and transitions to complex, commercially available software packages. Choosing the appropriate system that is flexible and can transition to meet one's needs and requirements of the campus is crucial. Automating as much of the process as possible minimizes data entry errors, data loss, and management costs. We want a robust system to grow as we expand to the requirements and knowledge base [1].

1.6 Data Analysis

"What level of data analysis is required?" That is a question of what data we can acquire and then maximize the analytics based on available data. Then increase that level of data input as we can justify the economics. We will perform a monthly data analysis during the earliest stages to identify efficiency opportunities. Before we can perform any analytics on a building or meter, the data within the MMS needs to be verified, checked for gaps and errors, cleaned, and organized. We cannot waste time analyzing data that is wrong. EMs need training on what to look for and how to fix these occurrences. We will cover that training in Chapters 6 and 7.

The next question is, "what data should be analyzed"? We initially start with a basic standard of techniques to use. For the basic level, they will include:

- Annual energy use intensity (EUI)
- Monthly EUI
- Interval data analysis
  - Seasonal load profiles
  - Weekly load profiles
  - Daily load profiles
  - Granular time-interval analysis

Government agencies have been working to improve their metering data collection, management, and analysis efforts over the last two decades (since EPAct 2005). They will continue expanding these capabilities as new requirements and data needs emerge. This does not have a simple solution as most federal facilities' level of implementation of BMS is limited, which means the EMS-integrated system coverage for data analysis offers limited solution sets. As federal agencies continue to expand their capabilities to use MMS data and we grow their data analysis capability, data will become more accessible and usable. The commercial world is more advanced, but we will use the federal standards as a baseline example for requirements and build on that [1].

What we have seen in data analysis over the years is more than equipment control. As an EM, we desired data to analyze and make intelligent EM decisions. From the early days, we preprogrammed those decisions. Preprogramming helped but did not allow for all circumstances. We were limited to known parameters like schedule and temperature. Decisions were related to outdoor air temperature (OAT), space temperature, and occupancy schedule. We could do various analytics with these three parameters, but the controls in the early days did not allow us to use more data than those factors. As we evolved to a higher capability with central systems, the ability to interact and use more data increased our control systems usage. This grew drastically when DDC controls gained additional capacity, and controls could work remotely in full control mode but be monitored by a remote system. As discussed above, this is the first level of BMS, which is currently the highest level attained in institutional systems. Many buildings in institutions are still on stand-alone DDC controllers. This limits the amount of usable data and direct management of those systems.

Regardless of the level of the BMS, we can enhance the usable data by tapping into the data provided by the metering system. This book will show how to use the meter data effectively to the maximum extent possible. An EM can then augment the meter data with whatever level of control system data is available, starting from the simplest with DDC only, progressing to first-level BMS to a whole second-level BMS system. These chapters will show various tools we can employ to enhance meter analytics effectively. At the advanced level, we may have a data analytics tool that overlaps the BMS and the MMS, giving an advanced analytic tool to make more informed decisions.

References

[1] Federal Metering Data Analysis, Needs and Existing Tools; JW Henderson, KM Fowler; July 2015; Prepared for the U.S. Department

of Energy under Contract DE-AC05-76RL01830; Pacific Northwest National Laboratory; Richland, Washington 99352

[2] Timeline of Events: 1971 to 1980 | Department of Energy; https://www.energy.gov/lm/doe-history/doe-history-timeline/timeline-events-1971-1980; Office of Legacy Management History DOE History Timeline; Timeline of Events: 1971 to 1980; October 1973: The First Energy Crisis

[3] The Evolution of Building Management Systems, from Limited Control to a Fully Integrated Digital Twin; by Carly McLeod17, JUN 2020

[4] (n.d.). Benchmark Your Building Using Energy Star® Portfolio Manager®. Energy Star. https://www.energystar.gov/buildings/benchmark

[5] Energy Policy Act of 2005 (EPAct)

2

What is Important About Managing Meter Systems?

Abstract

This chapter will cover how data acquisition has evolved and the use of data in energy management. This will show how to use the data sources available and how the ability to be effective in analysis improves as the data increases. Each data source explains the synergies of tying those sources together. This chapter will also show how to use the data to roll into other tools useful in analytics.

2   What is Important About Managing Meter Systems?

This chapter will dive into more detail on the meter data related to the other data sources. The EM must learn which data is essential and can be utilized by this type of organization to implement energy conservation projects successfully. This will also show which data is valuable in different types of analytics, how analytics have been used over time, and how they have advanced with the increase in data availability. The chapter will cover the following:

- Evolution of data

- Where do we source data?

- What types of data can be pulled into the analysis?

- How much data analytics can meters provide in this universe of data?

- How do we add meter data to other tools?

2.1 Evolution of Data

As stated in Chapter 1, an EM desires to use as much data as is available to contribute to the analysis process. Historically, data availability has changed

13

drastically over time. In the 70s, the only data available was basic data that came from billing. As a result, the breakdown of fuel data from the monthly deliveries was translated into an EUI. Data analytics were only possible for electricity if we had the local utility measuring and billing per building. When EM's responsibilities covered a campus, then they generally only had one meter for the campus. In most cases, realizing consumption by the building was not available. Getting electricity broken down in this way required a temporary meter, an audit dependent on one or more temporary meters, or the development of a simulation model. This could take a week or longer to analyze one building. If we were modeling in the 70s, it also required us to send off the modeling data to be processed at a separate location.

Managing data was a complex process, and even the most straightforward step of an EUI calculation would take weeks; therefore, determining the best solution required building surveys over multiple seasons. Since controls were pneumatic or electric, an EM would manage the set-points as a part of recurring maintenance programs, and significant energy conservation measures (ECMs) were dealt with in groups for seasonal implementation.

The desire was to expand control systems and the information that flowed into a central database. Building energy analytics was envisioned early on to impact facility and property management. The goal was to drive operational processes and even capital investment decisions based on the data analysis. If we could harness the data adequately, we no longer had to make uninformed decisions because we could process the information the data provided [1].

We traditionally concentrated on HVAC controls for data, as that was required for temperature and comfort control. Once we tried to tie these together, it provided a better opportunity of bringing in data throughout the 70s and 80s. Later, the ability to incorporate other control systems was developed. Even into the 80s, we generically called all controls "HVAC controls," even though the technology evolved from pneumatic and electric controls to a minicomputer, which became the first BMS.

The next system evolution was achieved by expanding into localized DDCs and eventually a central EMS that tied into all the DDC systems on campus. BMS was initially described as a single building with one or more DDC within that building. EMS was defined as a central location on campus that tied many BMSs together. Now these terms are interchanged regularly, although they may mean different things. Most DDCs and BMSs were legacy systems with proprietary protocols that transmit the data to the EMS front end. Standard protocols were developed for data transmission, and most HVAC systems used BACnet and LonMark. These communication protocols are used throughout the industry for HVAC and sometimes Modbus. The shortfall of BACnet and LonMark is that it becomes proprietary upon entering the controllers limiting the integration options from a cost perspective. While other systems use the Modbus protocol, which was open at all stages, those systems are primarily electric, meaning we cannot use it in most cases with HVAC systems. These markets precipitated the next generation of integration, which required middleware, web services, and the cloud. This is the era we are in now that involves a lot of various systems, such as middleware to communicate or where software analytics packages tie directly into controllers to interpret the data from multiple sources [2].

We will now define data analytics within three "pillars" or "requirements" for implementation:

1. Technology

2. People

3. Buildings

2.1.1 The Technology Pillar

The technology pillar is generally seen as the only tool for data analytics; therefore, most property managers try to throw a lot of technology into a property, assuming that alone will solve their problems. They often find themselves disappointed in the results as technology alone cannot deliver a solution, nor does it inspire action. In most cases, technology needs to be more utilized.

First, the building must be equipped to handle the technology. That means the equipment must be compatible with the controls or software (assumed in most cases). The controls must be set up correctly on the network to communicate with an EMS. The sequence of operations (SOO) must work with the equipment and operate within the required parameters (design intent) for the equipment and the controls. This SOO must be programmed within the equipment tolerances and match the schedule of the occupants [1].

The technology pillar is complex and can grow exponentially if one does not plan effectively and efficiently. The integration of systems can be expensive and bulky. The reason is shown in Figure 2.1. Multiple automation systems will, in many cases, use different protocols. Integrating them requires individual gateways at the controllers or middleware to convert into a common protocol before entering the EMS. Those gateways or middleware add a lot of cost to the integration efforts. Figure 2.1 shows a simple diagram

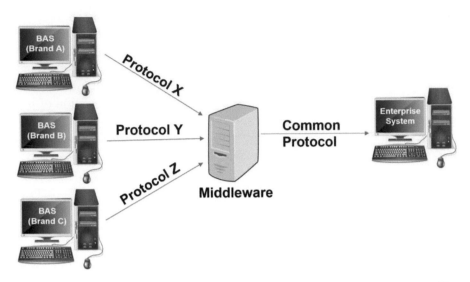

Figure 2.1   Various BMSs/BASs coming into an enterprise management system with different protocols.

but realizes the connections may need to travel long distances and through many interconnections in the local network to the EMS.

While technology solutions will deliver us the data, they may not be as easily accessible as we would like. Hardware must be added with expensive middleware and/or software in various places to bring that data together. The level of effort can be quite expensive regarding how we integrate it from multiple sources. In the simplest form, we may have 2–10+ BMS platforms in buildings around the campus. The most extensive integration we have seen was over 20 BMSs integrated into an EMS. Those may have different proprietary software communicating across BACnet and LonMark. These proprietary systems require a gateway or integration into some middleware at each building. This equipment cost can be high, and the consulting services to integrate are specialized and also have high cost. Sometimes the simplest is hardware middleware, such as Tridium or connecting directly to the source code through a third-party box, to bring that in and then display that on an EMS. That still requires some middleware, but the hardware is less, and the integration services are less intensive and more straightforward [1].

In addition, as we expand the data requirements, we will need to bring in other systems. In Figure 2.2, the complexity rises as we interconnect the BMS into other systems, such as maintenance management, lighting, security, occupancy, and real property systems.

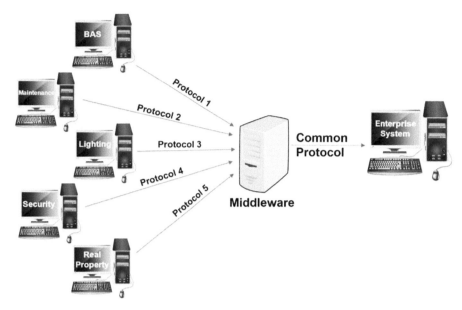

Figure 2.2 Various other systems coming into an enterprise management system with different protocols.

The increased available data enhances the analytics capability, enabling and expanding a perpetual commissioning process as the data input increases. This will be discussed in detail in Chapter 15 on monitoring commissioning. This commissioning will eliminate faults since, as data is made available, the system reviews and analyzes the data and processes the data points as they occur. These faults are identified initially through access to HVAC and other critical systems data.

So as the amount of data increases, the number of fault detection points also increases, thereby eliminating faults soon after they are detected. This fault detection and elimination is a natural extension of expanding data analytics.

The basis of all fault detection analytics is a set of energy engineering rules which identifies the problems as a fault and flags the user when they occur. The rules for analytics are straightforward in some respects but get more complex as the level of benchmarking rises or the complexity of the control's sequences increases. Our goal in this book is to keep the rules simple and align those with the various solution options available, as there are generally no absolutes when generating data and the accompanying analytics. Energy management is premised on the fact that it is based on standard economic analysis. Economics throws a different situational awareness on most processes where there will be and often are exceptions. The application of rules assumes that every building behaves within specific parameters. We have found exceptions to almost every parameter. We will strive to provide the types of exceptions, how to catch them and evaluate them accordingly as we move through the different analytic options throughout this book [1].

There are hundreds of building analytic companies that proclaim they provide energy analytics. This can be confusing as various levels of analytics could be provided. The industry is young in many senses, but there appears to be a trend that separates analytics companies into four categories. Those are:

1. Dashboards

2. Platforms

3. Services

4. Operational

These categories are helpful as they allow users to match their current circumstances to a contractor or service provider that best fits their situation or need.

Dashboards:
Dashboard companies provide a web-based user interface to the user, often with all data summarized onto one screen. Most dashboard companies do not offer data-gathering tools but collect and comprehensively present existing data points. Dashboards are the simplest solution in that they provide a customized visualization of energy use and, in some cases, highlight energy patterns and alarms. This solution puts most of the analytics on the EM. It easily supports EMs capable of generating visual references but only requires a few pre-canned queries or tools for their day-to-day operations. This is used where the campus maintains higher-level oversight by talented people who only desire to review the key performance indicators (KPIs).

Platforms:
Platforms are software tools that are very flexible and allow an EM to build a collection of many different tools to do their job. A platform enables an EM to add rules for finding faults and establish many capabilities from gathered data. With this option, the EM is required to have directly or indirectly many integration skills. This category is for an advanced EM with the skills and capability to build their own rules for data analysis.

Services:

Services are an extension of basic EM services where the EM directs the service provider to perform specific custom tasks. The service provider determines what the EM wants and develops the rules to determine the faults and tools to perform those tasks.

Operational:

Operations are focused on the shops' actions themselves. This is the controls contractor and the HVAC maintenance contractor who are involved in changing programs. They support us in ensuring the control systems are working properly and correctly integrated into the equipment.

Summary:

Equipment, as was shown, is the most significant emphasis today. Equipment requires training and expertise to make that a viable option unless we outsource that whole portion related to the equipment. That is generally easier to do if we outsource all aspects. The primary takeaway is that this is costly, but there is a payback that often covers these costs. The payback may be in direct energy savings or product quality. Go away assured that there are services that can cover the equipment and services discussed here if we desire this level of sophistication.

2.1.2 The People Pillar

The people component or organizational structure of operations is one of the most difficult ones. This aspect requires the campus to modify its organizational or management processes to adapt to the new technical approach. If utilizing an unknown technology, then training is required to implement it. The training may require the maintenance shops to change the way they do business. That requires a different approach and change management in the shop's processes of how they do business. In some cases, that goes against years of learned techniques. Senior leadership involvement may be required to communicate these process revisions effectively through the management levels to accomplish the change management process required.

The "people pillar" is essentially a function of the operations staff, focused on the continuing analysis of control systems. For example, a contract may call for a specific task to be performed that is related to making sure the HVAC systems or other systems operate correctly. A campus may have one or more of these categories. For example, a campus may have a controls contractor to ensure the control systems function correctly. Yet, a service contractor will establish faults and perform data analytics to determine if the buildings are operating correctly. In another example, an end user may contract a platform provider to integrate multiple BMS and hire an analytics group to determine if their buildings are correctly optimized and work with the shops to ensure they are adjusted based on those data analytic recommendations. At some point, these various components must work together. Will that be managed by one of the components, the campus EM, or another third-party contractor? [1]

2.1.3 The Buildings Pillar

The third pillar of data analytics is called the "buildings pillar," but it is more than simply the structure itself. It covers an organization that is committed to changing its overall approach. That means the leadership supports those objectives and wants to transition to a forward-thinking process in data analytics. The organization must be oriented to perform maintenance in a proactive manner vs. a reactive manner. Reactive maintenance is pervasive throughout institutions and is based on waiting for breakage or a call, and that is the opposite of a data analytic approach. Upper management must change the expectations and incentivize the operations personnel to avoid situations and prevent energy loss. This means everyone is a stakeholder in the process and benefits from preventing waste.

Once we understand these factors within the organization, we must look hard to determine if we have the resources and experience to accomplish the desired results. Many organizations do not have the organizational structure to support the analytics or the money to hire a third-party data analytics firm. A third-party analytics group will only succeed if the management structure supports its efforts.

Many firms try to make technology their solution, which is a wasted effort if we cannot do the analytics internally or come up with an approach but cannot execute the solutions. As indicated above, just having the right platform does not guarantee the results. The right platform is less important than the organizational wherewithal and commitment to execute the results. Plenty of good analysts and companies perform in such a way, but this must be teamed with an organization that is capable and desires to execute [1] [3].

2.2 Where Do We Source Data?

Let us look at data from the variety of available sources. There are levels of data at those sources, and a specific approach is required for each of those levels. Those levels of sources are:

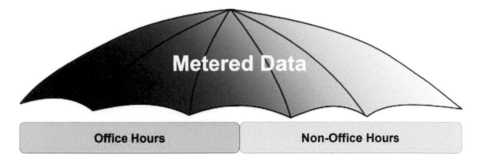

Figure 2.3 Breakdown of utility data into two time periods: office vs. non-office.

- Utility data
- BMS
- EMS
- Real property data
- Equipment
- Data analytics tools

This section will analyze the universe of data available on campus. The umbrella encompassing utility data provides the boundaries for all other data sources. It identifies the total usage for that building, and everything else must fit within. All the data must fit within those parameters or boundaries. We certainly have the fullest extent covered. Based on the date and time stamp for a facility of the utility data, we can also allocate that usage data into time periods, allowing us to distribute it against specific systems. The two most critical time periods for EMs are depicted in Figure 2.3. The universe of usage data can be broken into two time periods: office hours and non-office hours. Knowing this tells a lot about how the systems operate and how much savings are immediately available.

The following breakdown in Figure 2.4 shows that the umbrella of utility data can also be broken down into four system groups. This will be covered in detail in various chapters (10, 11, 12, and 13) later in the book. We have found that the usage timing breaks down into energy subsets. Those subsets can only have certain functions or systems functioning during that time. If we measure that, we can understand what systems are being used during that time and apportion their energy use based on rules of energy management applied to the system being used in that energy subset.

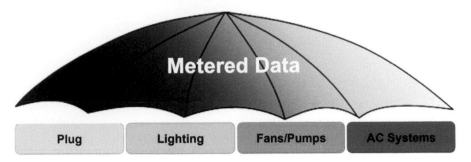

Figure 2.4   Breakdown of umbrella of utility data into four systems.

That generates four energy systems of usage under the umbrella of the total universe of utility consumption:

1. Plug

2. Lighting

3. Fan/pump systems

4. AC systems

This approach is excellent in general for understanding the usage of the systems, especially when we have only one unit (a piece of equipment) in a system. Still, the values become harder to allocate as we get more than one unit in a system. So, for example, if we have five rooftop air-handling units in a facility, then the energy usage attributed to the AC system is the sum of all the units, and it is not easy to attribute the load for a particular piece of equipment. At the same time, this limitation is generally not a problem in smaller facilities, as we will discuss. Even when we have this limitation, values can still be gleaned.

Data analysis from this top-down approach can accurately attribute the energy to systems in smaller buildings using just one building-level meter. Additional systems usage can be estimated somewhat based on equipment proportions. Still, we cannot break them down accurately if system sizes are the same or if the number of systems increases above two unless we provide additional metering beyond the building meter. If we estimate that the average single system services buildings sized between 10,000 and 20,000 sf, then as a building size goes up, we might see a need for a submeter for every additional 20,000 sf. The addition of other meters and the loads they monitor must be planned carefully before the installation.

Data analytics can be managed to a certain extent using just utility data. What is essential is the ability of the organization to use the data to make the recommended changes. In the last section, we addressed each decision level and impact, indicating that a balance is required. If the organization is currently well-served by the organizational structure, then we probably do not need to provide additional data analytics. This means we probably have a small building with one meter and a proactive maintenance force, or every system is metered combined with a proactive maintenance force. The second influx of data comes primarily from the control system endpoints. Those sensors, temperatures, actuator positions, and/or other endpoints on the HVAC systems are covered in the next section. Still, they can be pulled from the EMS or directly at each building, depending on the middleware.

Adding this output data into the analytics mode adds all the data from the endpoints of two systems, for example. These outputs for a fan/pump system and an AC system have all the data points required to generate the usage for those systems. It requires more equipment or building information, such as system type, etc., to map the data to sizes, capacity, volume, etc. This approach, coupled with the meter data, can match the data up first to validate the numbers from the meters and second to fill in the details by the system. The primary value of having the output from the endpoints of these systems is to give us that extra granularity. This is especially important as we assess buildings larger than 20,000 sf. Buildings of over 100,000 sf become easier to analyze with a detailed breakdown from submetering for all systems, the data from the endpoints, or both. Including submeters at the equipment level is especially required where we need precision control or high-energy intensity equipment.

The next dataset is more parallel systems that control other system inputs or bring in detailed data inputs. Parallel systems include management, fire, lighting, etc. Data points for additional stored information include real property data such as systems, size, ratings, etc., which are essential for magnitude, and tracing the benchmarks for each type of system.

The level of impact for additional systems on the EM analytics will look something like Figure 2.5, where the single-meter system is suitable for buildings up to 20,000 sf with one system. Then the energy analytics is still reasonable at 40,000 sf or two systems, but then the effectiveness drops quickly and flattens off.

The following approach starts with a single meter at the lower level and then adds submeters for each significant system over 20,000 sf. Figure 2.6 shows where we can have the best of all worlds with meter and endpoint data.

This book will cover the details of the meters and how to utilize the data from those meters to the maximum extent possible. We will sometimes reference the need for additional data from the endpoints but will try to keep that to a minimum in case we do not have the opportunity to collect data at

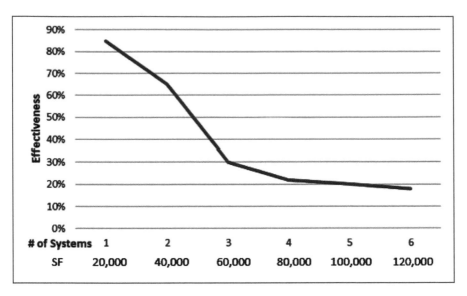

Figure 2.5   EM effectiveness with a single building meter goes down as the number of systems or sf increases.

the input and output points. There will be occasions when we can incorporate utility input data from a separate system to test output theories or to break down the output from equipment so that we can solve a problem. We will try to indicate those as we go through all the meter input scenarios.

We want to bring in all available data and then determine what specific portion, or call it level, of our data universe and the particular data analytics it supports. An EM desires everything in the sense of having all the data, but we must live with what we have and to what extent of analysis an EM can glean from that data to accomplish their job [4].

2.3 What Types of Data Can Be Incorporated Into the Analysis?

The data will be categorized according to the sources in Section 2.2. We break down the first source as utility or meter data. That can come in at various levels if we look at it hierarchically, as described below.

Hierarchical utility or metered data:

1.   *Campus or main utility metered feed* (may be more than one feed into a campus).

2.   *Meters for substations* to drop voltage and distribute into loops.

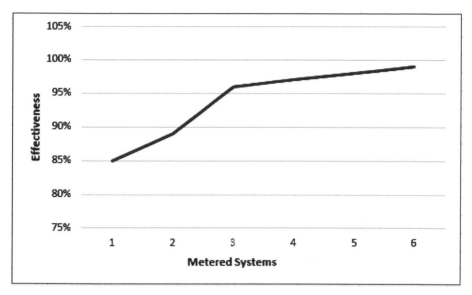

Figure 2.6 EM effectiveness increases as meters increase proportionately to the number of systems or 20,000 sf increments.

3. *Building (main) meter.* There will be one or more panels in the building depending on how many sections of the building were designed with separate electrical entrances or if this building was modified later and a main panel was added for convenience and/or cost.

4. *Submetering* in a building to break down that building into sections. This could also be applied by building sections or by major pieces of equipment.

5. *End-use or equipment meters* are meters that measure specific equipment that is under a submeter.

The meters in this hierarchy will be used to cross-check each other to validate the data's usage and the quality of the data. This allows us to sum up the parts based on all submeters to the next level of accumulating meters and finally to the master building meter. This provides a check on meters to validate their outputs, thus ensuring they stay accurate. The same can be applied from building meters through substations to the campus meter.

The next stage is to use the building meter data. The building meter can pick up any of the following data points:

1. Kilowatt hours (kWh) intervals

2. kWh usage

3. Power factor (including individual power factors for a phase of a three-phase meter)

4. Frequency

5. Demand average

6. Demand peak

7. Reactive power

8. Voltage (including individual voltages for each leg of a three-phase meter)

9. Current (including individual currents for each leg of a three-phase meter)

As discussed in the previous section, we could add more meters with the same parameters if we needed to analyze multiple systems or a larger building. The meters do not have many data points, but as discussed previously, we can break that down sufficiently by the system when we have single units of systems within a building. As we go to multiple systems, we can add additional meters to distribute that exact breakdown in energy subsets.

The next set of data points comes from the HVAC systems as our data source. We will look at the many systems listed below as primary systems that each have datasets of endpoints. Then we will look at a representative set for one system of endpoints to show the variety of endpoints. The main system datasets are:

1. Air-handling units (AHUs)

2. Fan coil units

3. Energy recovery units

4. Boilers

5. Pumps

6. Terminal units or boxes

7. Supply and exhaust fans

8. Cooling towers

9. Air-cooled chillers

10. Heat exchangers

11. Water-cooled chillers

12. Direct expansion air condition units

13. Economizers

14. Air compressors

These are the main ones for typical facilities. If an EM goes into a representative set of endpoints for an AHU system dataset when he requires additional data, then he could have points like the following:

1. Fan airflow rate (ft^3/min)

2. Motor power (amps, voltage)

3. Cooling coil pressure drop (Delta *P*)

4. Cooling coil performance

5. VFD data

6. Control valve control logic

7. Coil entering temperature

8. Coil exit temperature

9. Chilled water delta *T*

These represent a system dataset; the other datasets have similar endpoints and/or other data endpoints. As we indicated, numerous data points become available from the HVAC systems. This additional data will allow complete data analysis of all the systems and cross-check that data against the overall metered usage, which is a nice double-check and validation of many of the data analytic rules. The additional data is designed to identify the root cause of the problem and validate the data analytical rules [4].

Now, let us discuss other datasets that can be used. The next set includes the basic real estate data, such as the type of facility, square footage, location, campus, climate zone, etc. This specific information is usually fed directly from a real property data file and will be input into the database, whether against a meter or HVAC system. The following dataset is the equipment specifics, including the size and equipment type. This will typically be in a data file maintained by the maintenance staff. This data should consist of all pieces of HVAC equipment, including capacity in HP, cfm, tons, etc. It will also include the systems used, such as VAV, rooftop, split, chiller, etc. Finally, we look to maintenance data, which could consist of the number of calls, type of calls, frequency of unscheduled calls, etc. All of these can be rolled together with data analytics; so the predictive analytics can determine if and when it will require replacement, the costs, etc. The remainder of the book will address the use of meter data and how to maximize that data analytics as the EMS data can and will be added to provide more details that can increase the accuracy and predictability of all data analytics [4].

2.4 How Much Data Analytics Can Meters Provide in this Universe of Data?

What portion of data can meters provide in this search for analytics? As discussed above, the single-meter data will be the top-down look that encompasses and is the boundary for all usage data from all other sources. That means all the data for the facility is wrapped into the total usage. How we break that down into times, systems, and specific usages is where we make this data useful. The first and most crucial piece tied to meters is benchmarking. Benchmarking is essential to know where we stand measuring a building against itself, over time, and against others (comparing buildings). The meter data is best used for developing tiers of benchmarking building data and all the associated analytics and for benchmarking the individual systems. The benchmarking can be compared to the portfolio, the campus, the category type, and the climate zone. All these give us a strong ability to rank buildings against each other to determine which buildings need the most emphasis to drive an audit or modeling. This can also be used against the same building to see how it changes from year to year. Single-meter data also allows the ability to establish new benchmark analytics for base load and percent of base load. These benchmarks and their value will be covered in detail in the four chapters on benchmarking (10, 11, 12, and 13) in this book.

Single-meter data also provides a method for determining if the system(s) have been overridden. This is critical as that is the priority for any project on a facility. It also provides the highest return on investment (ROI) over any other project. This ECM alone is the highest priority for resolution.

We can often determine if recurring or preventative maintenance was performed correctly. We certainly know if the efficiency of an AC system drops or gets better over time. Also, we can determine if maintenance was performed improperly in some instances.

2.5 How Do We Add Meter Data to Other Tools?

Once we have the abovementioned meter data, we can use it in other analytical tools to simplify the EM's job. Several tools will allow us to perform basic analytics in several areas. Those include audit templates, project summaries, scatter plots, and others.

These tools can easily incorporate meter data and produce a result that helps define and decide how to prioritize the next ECMs. We can also roll this basic data into other tools. We can roll it into a third-party audit platform (Chapter 8) with services as one good option. Audit platforms can be self-populated by the basic MMS data. It can also break down usage into different time periods, such as office and non-office hours. It can break down the usage by systems, which is one of the largest time-consuming tasks for EM. That requires some involvement by the EM but generally requires much less hours than most of the other options.

Another tool is the ability to generate project ECMs (Chapter 18) based on usage. Usage is divided based on the time of use in the energy subsets discussed previously. From that, we learn how to apportion the usage against the total usage. This tool separates the system excess usage based on excess from overridden systems first and the remainder of the energy apportioned for each energy system. At that point, we can determine what energy and, thus, potential dollar savings are available for each system. This is a quick project audit tool that allows one to quickly prioritize where there are potential savings and concentrate the EM's time effectively. Finally, we can break down the usage for each system by energy subset so that we know what energy is used in each time period by the system. This feeds into the project tool and the audit tool. These tools will be addressed in detail in later chapters.

Another option for using data in other analytical tools is packages and/ or templates the DOE developed specifically for EM use. These are general information, but these require a lot of involvement by the EM, so be aware as we move forward.

A list of federally developed tools potentially useful for federal agencies can be found below. All of these tools are free and available for public and federal agency use. Benchmarking using Portfolio Manager is a requirement for all federal covered facilities; however, other benchmarking tools may offer additional insight into a building's performance improvement opportunities.

ENERGY STAR Portfolio Manager [5]:

Portfolio Manager is a peer benchmarking tool developed by the EPA. The tool tracks monthly energy and water performance and provides benchmarking and target projections. The tool requires metadata such as square footage, number of personal computers, building type, year constructed, location, percent heated and cooled, and number of occupants.

Labs21 [6]:

Labs for the 21st century (Labs21) were developed by the Lawrence Berkeley National Laboratory (LBNL) to offer a laboratory benchmarking tool. Labs21 "allows laboratories to compare the annual energy performance of similar buildings within the database" and "requires similar meta-data (but less) to Portfolio Manager."

Commercial Building Asset Score [7]:

DOE's Commercial Building Asset Score is "a national standardized tool for assessing commercial and multifamily residential buildings' physical and structural energy efficiency. The Asset Score generates a simple energy efficiency rating enabling building comparison and identifying investment opportunities in energy efficiency upgrades."

BEDES [8]:

The Building Energy Data Exchange Specification (BEDES) is a building energy data dictionary. It offers a "dictionary of terms, definitions, and field formats created to help facilitate the exchange of information on building characteristics and energy use. It can be used in tools and activities that help stakeholders make energy investment decisions, track building performance, and implement energy efficient policies and programs."

SEED [9]:

The Standard Energy Efficiency Data (SEED) Platform™ is an open-source software application developed by the DOE to help agencies and organizations manage large datasets for groups of buildings about energy performance. The SEED Platform™ allows users to combine, clean, validate, and share data from various sources and is described as flexible for a wide range of potential purposes.

Building Performance Database (BPD) [10]:

LBNL developed the BPD under the direction of the DOE. The tool provides the nation's largest dataset of information about the energy-related characteristics of commercial and residential buildings. The BPD allows users to create and save custom peer group datasets based on specific variables including building types, locations, sizes, ages, equipment, operational characteristics and more.

Green Button Grapher [11]:

The Green Button Grapher is a webpage interface that "allows users with Green Button Data to chart their usage and experiment with how reducing power consumption could impact their power bill."

BuildingSync [12]:

Led by the National Renewable Energy Laboratory (NREL), BuildingSync was developed by a working group of industry partners, organizations, and other national laboratories. In the form of an XML schema, BuildingSync is a standard language for commercial building energy audit data "that can be utilized by different software and databases involved in the energy audit process. It allows data to be more easily aggregated, compared and exchanged between databases and software tools. This streamlines the energy audit process, improving the data's value and facilitating greater energy efficiency."

OpenStudio [13]:

OpenStudio is a free, open-source, cross-platform (Windows, Mac, and Linux) set of tools developed by NREL and DOE for building energy modeling. In 2008, OpenStudio was initially created as a geometry creation plug-in for EnergyPlus. Since then, the tool has developed into a robust software development kit that helps automate functions associated with creating and modifying energy models.

References

[1] Automated Diagnostics and Analytics for Buildings Editor Barney Capehart and Michael Brambley River Publishers, 2020, Chapter 3, Perspective on Building Analytics Adoption, Tom Shircliff and Rob Murchison, Intelligent Buildings.

[2] Energy Analytics BIG DATA and Building Technology Integration, John J. "Jack" Mc Gowan, River Publishers, 2020

[3] Automated Diagnostics and Analytics for Buildings Editor Barney Capehart and Michael Brambley River Publishers, 2020, Chapter 4, Delivering Successful Results from Automated Diagnostics Solutions, Its Not Just About the Technology, Paul Oswald

[4] Data Driven Energy Centered Maintenance, 2nd Edition of Energy Centered Maintenance: A Green Maintenance System, Fadl Alshakhshir, Marvin T. Howell

[5] (n.d.). Commercial Buildings. Energy Star. http://www.energystar.gov/buildings

[6] (n.d.). Welcome to the Laboratory Benchmarking Tool. Laboratory Benchmarking Tool. http://labs21benchmarking.lbl.gov/

[7] (n.d.). Building Energy Asset Score. Office of Energy Efficiency & Renewable Energy. http://energy.gov/eere/buildings/building-energy-asset-score

[8] (n.d.). Building Energy Data. Office of Energy Efficiency & Renewable Energy. https://www.energy.gov/eere/buildings/building-energy-data

[9] (n.d.). Standard Energy Efficiency Data (SEED) Platform. Office of Energy Efficiency & Renewable Energy. https://www.energy.gov/eere/buildings/standard-energy-efficiency-data-seed-platform

[10] (n.d.). Building Performance Database. Berkeley Lab. https://buildings.lbl.gov/cbs/bpd

[11] (n.d.). Green Button Data for 123 Sample St Berkeley CA 94707-2701. Green Button Grapher. https://mtmckenna.github.io/green-button-grapher/

[12] (n.d.). BuildingSync. BuildingSync. https://buildingsync.net/

[13] (n.d.). OpenStudio. OpenStudio. https://openstudio.net/

3

Fault Detection

Abstract

This chapter shows EMs the fault detection and diagnostics (FDD) concept and how that can be implemented in MMS. There are many capabilities in MMS, and performing the basic functions of FDD is core to most MMS. This section will cover the importance of FDD and how MMS can perform many of those functions. We will show the limitations of MMS for being effective based on the size and complexity of the building. MMS can be very effective for smaller buildings and simpler energy systems in FDD.

3 Fault Detection

This chapter will introduce the concept of FDD. We will learn the following:

- Introduction

- What is fault detection?

- Can we use MMS to do fault detection?

- Additional functionality

- Summary

3.1 Introduction

We have found over our careers that energy savings between 20% and 40% can be realized in commercial and institutional buildings due to faults in the EMS and local control systems. Many companies have software applications to identify those faults so that the EM can rectify the situation and save energy losses. These software and hardware applications are called fault detection and diagnostic (FDD) systems. We will show how to use the MMS to do many of these functions and then supplement it with other FDD systems as the benefits present themselves. The ultimate goal would be to transition to automatic fault detection and diagnostic (AFDD) systems, which provide a layer of automatic correction to the fault.

3.2 What is Fault Detection?

Fault detection is a term used to identify an anomaly within a system. Identifying the anomaly and the level of detail for that anomaly can vary and is based on the complexity and precision of the software or equipment that is highlighting the issue. These systems that identify those anomalies are called FDD systems. An anomaly is a deviation from the normal or design intent. Many systems perform these functions in the commercial world. We discussed some of these functions in general in Chapter 2 and will discuss them further in Chapter 4. This chapter will discuss what faults can be detected and if we can diagnose the cause.

FDD is the process of identifying a deviation from the design intent. Design intent is discussed in detail in Chapter 15 as the way the building is currently operated or should be operated to satisfy the occupants' needs for comfort and operations. At the same time, the space has times when it is occupied and not occupied. Once a fault is identified, there is a diagnostics process to evaluate or diagnose the cause of the problem.

In practice, FDD in buildings is usually applied against heating, ventilation, and air conditioning (HVAC) systems. It is more specifically applied to the control systems as they drive the operations and thus most of the savings. We can, however, apply FDD to all systems in the building. With MMS, we can use the umbrella of the usage to determine what systems have produced a fault from design intent and produce an option of solution sets. While knowing there is a fault is easy with an MMS, the probability of an accurate diagnosis is dependent on several factors.

The overall umbrella of the total utility savings will be broken down into energy subsets in subsequent chapters. With that knowledge, we set benchmarks in Chapters 10, 11, 12, 13, and 17 to establish the baseline for fault detection. Those chapters will also give detailed guidance on what the benchmark is and what it should be so that the user can alarm the fault condition. Those alarms could be sensor failure, energy consumption thresholds, an error in the sensors, economizer position, ventilation rates and schedule, fan/pump system schedule, and lighting schedule.

Then, there is the diagnostics side of FDD that an MMS can show; it can also identify equipment degradation or efficiency change (Chapter 13), fault prioritization, energy impacts, energy cost impacts, meter data analytics for other statistics, time series visualization of intervals, key performance indicators (KPI) tracking and reporting (Chapters 16 and 17), benchmarking (Chapters 10, 11, 12, 13, and 17), and project cost of resolution and payback (Chapter 18).

The FDD process is core to other processes such as monitoring commissioning (Chapter 15), remote audits and virtual assessments (Chapter 8), enterprise monitoring, continuous savings estimation (Chapter 18), and energy anomaly detection.

EMS comprises several tools and services that analyze, monitor, and control commercial building equipment and energy use. These systems, on many occasions, include some FDD tools. Sometimes an EMS is augmented by other commercial products that provide FDD analytics to some extent. Some commercial products link all systems, MMS, EMS, and a higher level FDD together through the FDD software to bring more information to the equation so that better analytics are included to diagnose the cause and solution. Coverage of systems and faults is driven more by site data availability than by product offering. However, a complex set of interrelated informational, organizational, and technical solutions must be addressed to realize the full potential at scale. As we go through this textbook, we will show that the basic level of information from the MMS is more complex than most EMs can manage. The MMS can very successfully manage buildings under 20,000 sf. As a system gets larger or the complexity of the system is expanded, additional FDD is required to manage the processes or building systems effectively.

It is estimated that 5%–30% of the energy used in commercial buildings is wasted due to faults and errors in the operation of the control system [1], [2], [3]. Tools that can automatically identify and isolate these faults offer the potential to improve performance greatly and do so cost-effectively [4].

Buildings are becoming more information intensive. There is the basic data from MMS for the overall umbrella of consumption and when it is used. Next, there are analytic tools, such as an EMS and many local systems that do not roll up into the EMS, and now, we add FDD tools on top. FDD tries to roll many of these systems together to translate large amounts of time-stamped data into actionable information to achieve energy and non-energy benefits. Data analytics adoption and technology innovation will precipitate more involvement as users become aware of reliable cost–benefit data and become educated on deployment options. As the author of this study notes, FDD tools tied into EMS achieved 9% and 3% median annual energy savings, respectively. The median base cost and annual recurring cost for FDD are $0.06 per square foot (sf) and $0.02 per sf, and for EMS are $0.01 per sf and $0.01 per sf, respectively [5].

Some commercial vendors, as well as several government papers, encourage going from an FDD tool to an AFDD. This is a tool that continuously identifies the presence of faults and efficiency improvement opportunities and interacts with the BAS via automated analytics to resolve the fault. All FDD tools inform operators of building operational faults, but they require human intervention to correct the faults to generate energy savings. Fault auto-correction integrating directly into EMS with commercial FDD technology offerings can close the loop between passive diagnostics and active control. In these cases, algorithms automatically correct faults and improve the operation of large HVAC systems, focusing on overrides, control hunting, rogue zone, and set points being off. While this sounds attractive in some situations, we caution against widespread acceptance. One must carefully weigh the risk of the action and determine if the liability is worth the specific programmed action. No life safety or high-cost actions should be included in auto-correction. The savings of the differential in response time must be weighed against the risks and liability [6].

Another paper addresses the importance of cost and case studies of results. This paper addresses the question of what today's users of FDD are saving and spending on technology. They assessed 26 organizations that use FDD across 550 buildings, and 97 M sf achieved a median savings of 8%. For the cost, they assessed 27 FDD users. They reported that the median base cost for FDD software, annual recurring software cost, and annual labor cost were $8, $2.7, and $8 per monitoring point, respectively. The median implementation system size was approximately 1300 points.

They reported one case with an annual energy cost savings of $18,400 and FDD installation costs of $94,500 at one building in the United States. Another case study showed an 18.5% reduction in annual electricity consumption between 2009 and 2015 after Microsoft deployed the FDD-based Energy-Smart Buildings Program campus-wide. In another case, they indicated yearly savings of 8%–20% in electricity and 13%–28% in gas for FDD implementations [7].

3.3 Can We Use MMS to Do Fault Detection?

There are many categories where an EM would want some fault detection capability. MMS can do many of those directly and some indirectly. We will cover those for the EM so that he can determine if that covers the needs or if a secondary service is required to cover the remaining FDD for the EM's purposes.

An MMS can cover basic applications, which account for most of the savings. This applies to buildings with a 1 or 2 HVAC systems ratio to the building size. That occurs generally when there are smaller buildings. Our experience is that a building may have 1–2 systems up to 20,000 sf. An EM can easily calculate the impact based on the system ratios with 1–2 systems in that mix. As a building grows larger in square footage, more systems complicate the ratios and, thus, the calculations. It is possible to have two systems for a 40,000-sf building. If that is the case, then the ability to proportion the load between systems is manageable. As a building grows past that point in either square feet or several systems, the ability to manage with an MMS becomes limited, especially for the more complex tools that MMS employs. Adding additional meters or an FDD to give better viability and fidelity would be encouraged in the larger building cases.

Let us divide the information an MMS can provide into sections. In an FDD scenario, three data types are valuable: overrides, equipment, and consumption.

3.3.1 Overrides

The first data type is broad in that every piece of equipment could run during non-office hours when the design intent is for that system to be off.

That will affect:

1. Fan schedules

2. Pump schedules

3. AC systems

4. Heating system components

5. Exhaust systems

6. Cooling system components

7. Supply air systems

8. Outdoor air dampers

9. Valves

10. Lighting

This is one of the primary areas where the MMS can identify faults. The MMS can easily determine when systems are on during non-office hours. The limitation is the number of systems. Generally, when the building is small, 20,000–40,000 sf, we can easily identify that the systems are on during non-office hours. If there is more than one system or equipment that supports that system, it may be tougher to break down which piece of equipment is not performing to the design intent. If the system sizes differ, we can calculate the system based on an overridden energy ratio. These types of faults are covered extensively in Chapters 10, 11, 12, 14, and 17. This identification can be simplified by additional meters. When a building is larger than 40,000 sf, breaking down the equipment is much more difficult. We can identify a fault, but we may not be able to identify the specific equipment or system that is generating that fault in the building.

3.3.2 Equipment

This is the ability to understand if a piece of equipment has failed or the efficiency has changed. Of the categories of faults detectable, the following are the categories of faults that the MMS FDD tool can detect and potentially diagnose. The fault categories included in this framework include:

- Sensor errors/faults

- Energy consumption (explicit energy threshold fault)

- Economizers and ventilation (position/amounts)

- Heating system (boiler, heat exchanger, furnace, etc.)

- Cooling system (chillers, towers, rooftop, etc.)

- Equipment cycling

- Pump and fan systems

- Scheduling (out of design intent)

- Lighting or other end uses

Note that problems such as mechanical failures and departures from set point or intended sequences may be included under multiple fault categories in the list above.

FDD methods in MMS may be model-based or based purely on process history data. Generally, we see model-based methods rely upon knowledge of the underlying processes of the system being analyzed. History-based approaches do not rely upon engineering knowledge for modeling but may leverage some degree of engineering knowledge for processing historical data. This is especially relevant when comparing faults for changes in condition such as efficiency.

3.3.3 Consumption

Consumption can be easily flagged as a fault in the MMS. Generally, we will look for any fluctuations in consumption that will trigger a fault for evaluation. For example, if a building's electrical consumption was 10% higher this month than last year, corrected for weather, then the EM should evaluate the cause. This would apply to all commodities, and the intervals can be triggered for extremes. A water meter on any day would trigger if the consumption doubled, indicating a leak.

This can be applied to energy systems such as lights or AC systems. Lighting system consumption might trigger a fault at night, indicating they were left on. An AC system might increase its energy usage by 20% daily after weather correction. That might indicate the system being overridden. The MMS can also check to validate if the system was overridden. Then the system might look at the AC system efficiency. An efficiency change would indicate something has gone wrong with the equipment that requires the maintenance shop to respond and evaluate. In general, the MMS can identify probably 80% of the items required for FDD on smaller buildings and most of the larger buildings. Still, an issue on a larger building will be limited in pinpointing the specific HVAC unit itself.

3.4 Additional Functionality

Other features that can be easily included in an MMS FDD tool, which are not represented above, may include the following:

- Detection of equipment degradation
- Fault prioritization
- Assessment of energy impacts
- Conversion of energy impacts to cost impacts
- Meter data analytics
- Interval history visualization and plotting

- KPI tracking and reporting

- Internal and external benchmarking (within a given portfolio or via ENERGY STAR Portfolio Manager)

3.5 Summary

Many software systems provide various levels of FDD. We hope an EM takes away that an MMS can provide a basic level of FDD, and it will be exceptional for small buildings at a much lower cost than traditional FDD. As we get into larger (greater than 40,000 sf) and more complex structures, the ability of an MMS in this area drops significantly. We can remedy that by adding more utility meters into MMS or overlaying a commercial FDD system to take advantage of the MMS while tying into the EMS. This is especially important and necessary for industrial facilities.

References

[1] Roth, K. W., D. Westphalen, M. Y. Feng, P. Llana, and L. Quartararo. Energy Impact of Commercial Building Controls and Performance Diagnostics: Market Characterization, Energy Impact of Building Faults and Energy Savings Potential. 2005. Report prepared by TIAC LLC for the U.S. Department of Energy.

[2] Katipamula, S., and M. Brambley. 2005. "Methods for fault detection, diagnostics, and prognostics for building systems – a review, part 1." HVAC&R Research 11(1): 3–25.

[3] Fernandez, N., Katipamula, S., Wang, W., Xie, Y., Zhao, M., & Corbin, C. (n.d.). Impacts of Commercial Building Controls on Energy Savings and Peak Load Reduction. Pacific Northwest National Laboratory. https:// buildingretuning.pnnl.gov/publications/PNNL-25985.pdf

[4] Granderson, J., Singla, R., Mayhorn, E., Ehrlich, P., Vrabie, D., & Frank, S. (n.d.). Characterization and Survey of Automated Fault Detection and Diagnostic Tools. Berkeley Lab Energy Technologies Area Publications. https://eta-publications.lbl.gov/sites/default/files/lbnl-2001075.pdf

[5] Lin, G., Kramer, H., Nibler, V., Crowe, E., & Granderson, J. (n.d.). Building Analytics Tool Deployment at Scale: Benefits, Costs, and Deployment Practices. MDPI Open Access Journals. https://www. mdpi.com/1996-1073/15/13/4858

[6] Pritoni, M., Lin, G., Chen, Y., Vitti, R., Weyandt, C., & Granderson, J. (n.d.). From fault-detection to automated fault correction: A field study. ScienceDirect. https://doi.org/10.1016/j.buildenv.2022.108900

[7] Lin, G., Kramer, H., & Granderson, J. (n.d.). Building fault detection and diagnostics: Achieved savings, and methods to evaluate algorithm performance. ScienceDirect. https://doi.org/10.1016/j.buildenv.2019.106505

4

Comprehensive Building Analytics (HVAC Systems)

Abstract

In this chapter, we will learn about case studies of detailed data analytics that are beyond the scope of the MMS. We will also look into doing diagnostics to determine the root cause of any fault discovered. The analytics discussed in Chapters 16, 17, 18, and 20 show trends in energy use for lighting, plug load, HVAC, etc., which can be categorized for deeper research and diagnostics. This chapter is dedicated to FDD on the HVAC system by looking deeper into the specific cause and correction of these energy conservation measures.

4 Energy Conservation Measures

This chapter will cover the following typical ECMs found in buildings using comprehensive building analytics (a term coined by Cimetrics for building analytics) as follows:

- Introduction

- Case Study 1: Simultaneous heating and cooling

- Case Study 2: Air-handler scheduling

- Case Study 3: Leaking chiller isolation valve

- Case Study 4: Fume hood face velocity

- Case Study 5: Sash position during occupied hours

4.1 Introduction

This chapter will give the EM a glimpse of a few case studies of issues that cannot be analyzed fully by MMS. This brings out examples where the MMS

43

will not cover every situation, and we will have to add an FDD to provide detailed analytics and diagnostics. This chapter will cover five case studies where we had to tie into the local control boxes to generate the data to analyze these critical problems. We are using one of the service vendors, Cimetrics, which adds a middleware to the local controllers to pull the data and read that back into their software platform to perform the FDD.

Their analysis, called "comprehensive building analytics" (CBA), looks into all HVAC control systems' monitoring and control points. It models the building operation and compares it with the design model to determine compliance with the design intent of the control system. For example, if a valve is requested to be open, is it indeed open? That is analyzed by valve position and entering and leaving conditions before and after the valve.

4.2 Case Study 1: Simultaneous Heating and Cooling

This section demonstrates airflow entering an air-handling unit (AHU) with a preheat coil heating the temperature above the design condition. This causes the cooling coil to do excessive work to cool the air back down to satisfy zone requirements. The zone does not realize that large amounts of energy are wasted within the AHU. The example in Figure 4.1 shows the actual savings of $64,080 per year. Utilizing the analytics and local facilities staff, we can determine what remedy would correct this problem. The diagnostics generate the following causes to evaluate:

- Faulty preheat valve and/or actuator

- Mixed air temperature sensor calibration

- Incorrect sensor location

- Incorrect programming for controller

- And maybe others as we perform deeper diagnostics

Since there could be several solutions, the problem will be tracked to see when it is corrected. This tracking is monitoring commissioning, which will be covered in detail in Chapter 15. It will be an iterative process to track the problem until the specific cause is identified and corrected. It also benchmarks every solution set; therefore, we can identify if any possible solution sets fail later.

Guide to above:

- CC – cooling coil

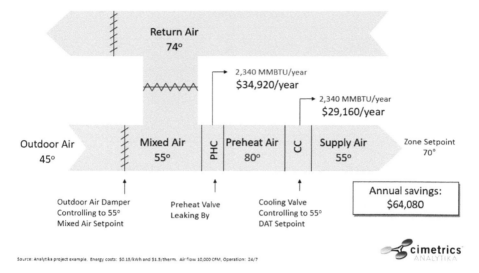

Figure 4.1   Cimetrics case study on simultaneous heating and cooling.

- PHC – preheat coil

- DAT – discharge air temperature

Figure 4.2, on the left, indicates the normal design of AHU – 04 heating and cooling the air. To the right, we see the preheat coil heating the air well above the design set point, resulting in simultaneous heating and cooling. This type of ECM goes unnoticed without having the data deep within the HVAC system to find savings opportunities. Two major benefits from finding these and correcting them are (1) energy savings and (2) potential for not meeting zone set point (when preheat overcomes cooling capacity).

Noted above are all the points utilized to determine this ECM opportunity:

- Outside air temperature (OAT)

- Mixed air temperature (MAT)

- Preheat discharge air temperature (preheat DAT)

- Preheat signal

- Cooling coil discharge air temperature (CC DAT)

- Discharge air temperature set point (DAT set point)

- Cooling coil valve signal (CC Sig)

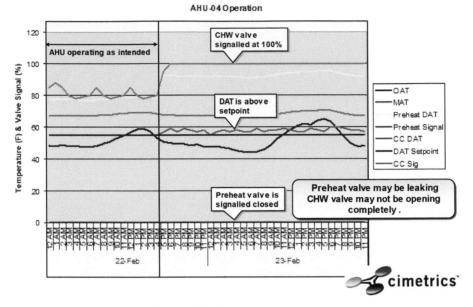

Figure 4.2   Cimetrics screen shot.

- Air-handling unit (AHU)
- Chilled water valve (CHW)

4.3 Case Study 2: Air-handling Scheduling

Case Study 2 shows the impact of having an operating schedule for each piece of HVAC equipment and tracking compliance with that schedule. We often see equipment running continuously when it is only required for a portion of that time. Excessive runtime is a major ECM opportunity identified in the example shown in Figure 4.3.

In this particular case, the savings are very large. All savings are actual and based on the horsepower of equipment and other fuel usage. The critical challenge is getting the equipment on the correct schedule and ensuring compliance by continuously monitoring and reporting deviation from desired results. This is addressed weekly or monthly to ensure the ECM is achieved in practical application. Anything less than that frequency results in excessive runtime, which wears out equipment prematurely and wastes energy.

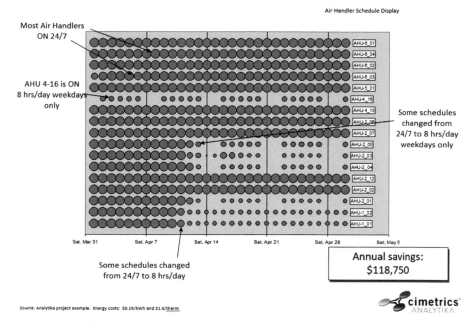

Figure 4.3 Cimetrics case study on air-handler scheduling.

4.4 Case Study 3: Leaking Chiller Isolation Valve

While most points monitored are automatic, we also have points such as isolation valves, which can be manually operated or automated. In cases of manual control, we also see significant saving opportunities in an ECM when failures occur. These failures can be mechanical in nature or operational.

Whatever the reason, we can see where an ECM to correct this waste of energy can make a significant difference to a facility. See Figure 4.4 for an example.

Guide to above:

- Chiller (CHLR)

- Chilled water return temperature (CHWRT)

- Chilled water supply temperature (CHWST)

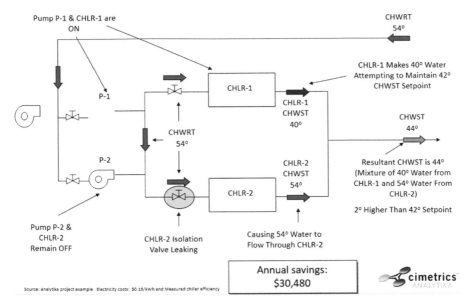

Figure 4.4   Cimetrics case study on leaking chiller isolation valve.

4.5 Case Study 4: Fume Hood Face Velocity

While many examples of ECMs are based on design, many are based on commissioning and balance quantities. When laboratory (fume) hoods are installed, they are designed with a face velocity for fume capture and safety. These airflow amounts are critical. With analytical monitoring of face velocities, we can provide compliance documentation for the safety and optimization of ECM performance.

Excessive face velocities will waste energy and should be logged, tracked, and optimized. See Figure 4.5 for an example.

Guide to above:

- Supply air (SA)

- Exhaust air (EA)

- Fume hood (FH)

- Variable air volume (VAV)

Note below (Figure 4.6) in the before and after analytics; we can see excessive 100% outside air on the left part of the graph and proper operation on the right, which is a significant difference.

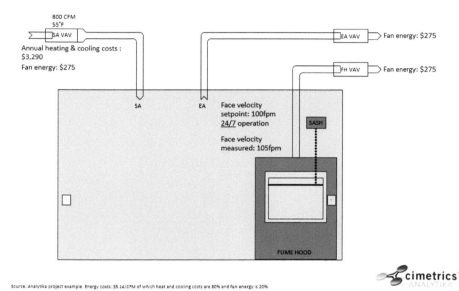

Figure 4.5 Cimetrics case study on fume hood velocity.

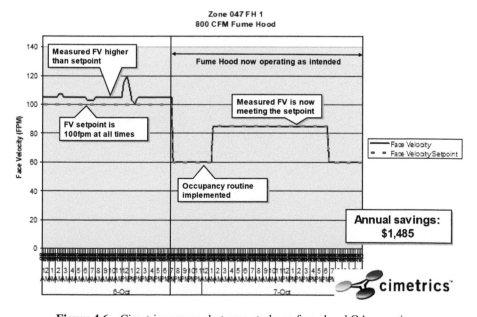

Figure 4.6 Cimetrics screen shot case study on fume hood OA operation.

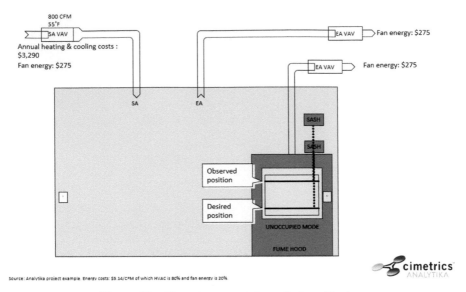

Figure 4.7   Cimetrics case study on Sash positioning.

Guide to above:

- Face velocity (FV)

4.6 Case Study 5: Sash Position during Occupied Hours

Case Study 5 has equipment similar to Case Study 4, with fume hoods as the ECM opportunity. In this case, it is not the balancing, commissioning, and setting up; it now involves the use and operation of the system.

Hoods must maintain the face velocity no matter where the Sash position stands. That is important if the Sash position is wide open as needed for access and use. The second position would be partially closed, while the third Sash position is closed. There is a significant ECM opportunity in both the second and third positions.

Most of this ECM is operational; so education, continuous tracking, and discipline are key to success. See the example in Figure 4.7.

Guide to above:

- Exhaust air (EA)
- Supply air (SA)
- Variable air volume (VAV)

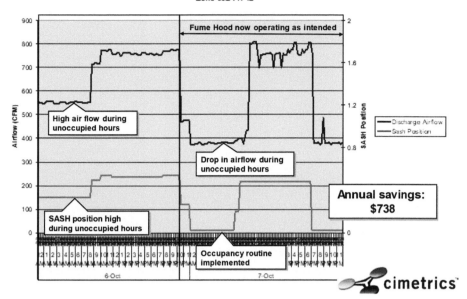

Figure 4.8 Cimetrics screen shot on case study on one hood ECM.

Figure 4.8 states savings for the ECM based on one hood. Rarely do we see one hood in practice. The range for similar facilities usually has 40–75 hoods; so the ECM savings are proportional to the number of hoods.

The five case studies are a small sample of what we encounter when providing an analytics system on campus. The system supports local staff and provides data to prioritize their resources in large campus applications. Most of the savings opportunities are low-cost and high-impact ECMs.

The typical connection is to terminal units, AHUs, pumps, fans, chillers, heating units, and lighting. This enables the analytics to work on 90% or more of the building usage.

Comprehensive building analytics is capable of providing enhanced commissioning during building start-up. It is also used as the main support for the data for MBCx (monitoring-based commissioning) and retro-commissioning.

References

[1] Cimetrics Analytika Case studies from actual jobs. Names of customers are redacted.

5

Setting Up Billing

Abstract

This chapter shows EMs how to create rate structures that will allow the billing of customers. These rate structures can be simple or complex, depending on the needs of the end users. This section will cover the three parts of the bill and ways to apply them to the end user building on campus. Then we will cover various billing methods to make this easy for the end user to understand.

5 Setting Up Billing

This chapter will introduce setting up customer billing. The EM will learn the following:

- Introduction

- Setting the rate structure

- Options on billing

- Summary

5.1 Introduction

This chapter introduces the EM to rate structures. All the utilities have many different rate structures. We will break them into three components: consumption, demand, and flat fees. The rate structure can also be broken down into a simple blended rate, used in most cases, or a complex rate structure, such as that billed by the utility. While the blended rate is generally used, we find that some EMs desire to pass along the impact of the demand to their end users. Since the complex rate is problematic for many reasons, several hybrid approaches ensure the demand component is shared and relevant to the end

53

user in their day-to-day actions. These then turn into a monthly bill that provides relevant information on billing details plus any graphs and charts that help educate the end users on the impact of their usage habits.

5.2 Setting the Rate Structure

The rate structure is usually a complex set of calculations. If we want to bill customers, we must address the legal aspects of billing users, the specification on meters, and the software required for billing in that state. Since that is an overly complex situation, we will only address that billing third parties generally requires very complex software to meet the state's requirements. The rate model will generally cost between $100,000 and $200,000 to develop the calculation model and its certification.

Most billing is simple since we are billing tenants tied directly to the organization. With that relationship, we can simplify the rate structures to something usable and billable. There are three types of rate structures:

- Blended rate

- Complex rate

- Hybrid

The blended rate is generally used for billing various components, and it is also used for budgets. A blended rate simply divides the bill's total cost by the total kWh. So, we will get a cost of around $0.085 per kWh across the US. The users are then billed based on how many kWh they use, and this does not consider any changes in the demand, other charges, etc. As this is the simplest rate structure, it is the most commonly used in billing within a campus environment.

The next rate structure available for users is a complex rate. This is difficult to break down, as discussed earlier. The main reason is that some of the line items on a bill do not translate over from a billing perspective based on the relationship between a specific building's usage vs. the campus usage at that point in time. Let us break down the bill into three components: consumption charges, demand or delivery charges, and flat charges. The consumption charges, sometimes called supply charges, are based on cost/kWh. In Table 5.1, the rate for consumption is $0.065/kWh. This consumption shown is distributed over 12 months. The next charge is demand or sometimes called delivery charges. This may be composed of many charges, but for simplicity, let us break it down to a unit cost of $4.00/kW, and it is set the same for the whole year. The highest demand usually sets this for the

Table 5.1   Single tier of charges on the simple rate structure.

Consumption Charge	Unit cost ($/kWh)	$0.065			
	# units (kWh)	277,000			
	Subtotal	$ 18,005.00			
Demand Charge	Unit cost ($/kW)		$4.00		
	# units (kW)		2,460		
	Subtotal		$ 9,840.00		
Flat Charge	Unit cost ($)			$550.00	
	# units (each)			1	
	Subtotal			$550.00	
		$ 18,005.00	$ 9,840.00	$550.00	$ 28,395.00

month, but this can vary drastically depending on the utility and that rate category. The third is a flat charge. The flat charge is a unitary charge for various services, such as a connection or billing fee. This charge is the same regardless of how many kWh are used. This can cover many things, such as meter charges, renewable surcharges, energy conservation charges, EV surcharges, and so forth, which are flat charges applied to every service. Note that we calculate the blended rate mentioned above from this table by dividing the $28,395 by 277,000 kWh to get a rate of $0.103/kWh. Table 5.1 covers a simple breakdown of the three components of the bill.

The previous table, Table 5.1, was the simplest form of one tier for the three components. A utility may have multiple tiers and even seasons, and this rate is called a time-of-use rate. Let us look at the multiple tiers of charges first. Table 5.2 breaks down the charges into three daily tiers against consumption and demand. The tiers are billing tiers, and there is a different rate for the commodity during each of those tiers. So, the tiers, in this case, are set up as 1200–1900, which is usually the highest cost period for most of the US. This tier can change somewhat in duration, but this is a good time period for discussion. The cost for the demand is also higher per kW during this period. This is proportionally higher in demand than the other periods. The other two periods are generally close in cost for consumption (kWh). Demand charges are usually very low for the other two time periods, and, sometimes, there is no utility rate associated with the other two periods for demand. From this table, notice a low rate for demand ($1.00/kW) in the morning tier and none at night. These can be even more complex as each time of use may have usage thresholds. So, the first 10,000 kWh may be a higher rate than the next 40,000 kWh. Everything above 50,000 kWh would be the lowest rate. This benefits larger users, but it makes billing more complex if billing a complex rate as a tool in MMS.

Table 5.2   Multiple tiers of charges on the complex rate structure.

	Consumption Charge			Demand Charge			Flat Charge	Total
Hours of Day	1200-1900	1900-2100	2200-1200	1200-1900	1900-2100	2200-1200		
Unit cost ($/kWh)	$0.095	$0.036	$0.058					
# units (kWh)	92,241	69,250	115,509					
Subtotal	$ 8,762.90	$ 2,493.00	$6,699.52					$17,955.42
Unit cost ($/kW)				$5.00	$ -	$ 1.00		
# units (kW)				1,845		615		
Subtotal				$9,225.00	$ -	$ 615.00		$ 9,840.00
Unit cost ($)							$550.00	
# units (each)							1	
Subtotal							$550.00	$ 550.00
	$ 8,762.90	$ 2,493.00	$6,699.52	$9,225.00		$ 615.00	$550.00	$28,345.42

The second aspect of the time-of-use on the complex rate structure is a different rate for summer and winter loading. This one is self-explanatory since winter would be low generally for both consumption (kWh) and demand (kW). Those rates indicate what utility costs are for the generation during that season. The summer will be higher in consumption costs in most cases and much higher in demand costs.

The last rate structure is a hybrid of blended and complex rate structures, hence the name. The blended rate is simple and easy to apply. The complex rate is extremely multifaceted and would not represent the real cost in most cases for the campus. That is without a complex algorithm, which is a major effort and cost.

How is this hybrid rate applied in billing in MMS? The blended rate is easy to produce. For this reason, it is used in most cases. The complex billing rate would make it difficult to calculate the real cost of doing business. Peak demand for a particular building on campus may not be coincident with the overall peak, thereby not representative of the cost of that facility vs. the others on campus. Calculating it at that same time period is an extremely complex formula. It requires an integration of all the buildings into a model to generate that contribution to the peak in each interval and spread it proportionately. That is difficult to measure precisely and distribute; so most people avoid that situation.

If we do not want the headaches of the complex rate but want to ensure each building has a monetary incentive to manage its demand, then the best solution is a hybrid billing rate. This can be achieved in one of two ways. One is by using their demand this month to set the rate for the next month. Many utilities apply this into a rolling 12-month ratchet-type billing. The other is to pull the cost of the aggregate peak for a month and proportion that by the

Table 5.3 Basic billing showing monthly usage and cost.

Building 101		April	May	June	July
Consumption Charge	Unit cost ($/kWh)	$0.065	$0.065	$0.065	$0.065
	# units (kWh)	277,000	357,000	406,000	455,000
	Subtotal	$ 18,005.00	$ 23,205.00	$ 26,390.00	$29,575.00
Demand Charge	Unit cost ($/kW)	$4.00	$4.00	$4.00	$4.00
	# units (kW)	2,460	2,790	2,460	2,460
	Subtotal	$ 9,840.00	$ 11,160.00	$ 9,840.00	$ 9,840.00
Flat Charge	Unit cost ($)	$550.00	$550.00	$550.00	$550.00
Total		$ 28,395.00	$ 34,915.00	$ 36,780.00	$39,965.00

highest one, three, or five peaks in the month (consolidated together). Having more than one peak day per time (billing) period forces people to do a better job lowering their daily peaks, not just for that one peaking day in a month. This causes a flattening to the peaking each day, which guards against inadvertent peaks. Some utilities also use this method, forcing a downward trend overall by flattening a larger group of their peak periods. This does make the EM's job harder, but we can easily set the peaks to consolidate by the number of peaks desired. We have seen consolidating five peaks become a good place to start, and it encourages better management by the building managers.

5.3 Options on Billing

Once we decide on the process for setting rates, the next step is deciding how to show the billing. Including the usage and the respective cost is a minimum requirement. This can be done simply by showing monthly usage and the cost, as shown in Table 5.3. This billing template gives the end user a better idea of consumption usage by showing 12 consecutive months of data. With this example bill, they can compare their usage across the year. We would also recommend adding the degree days for the month. That provides a basis for comparing the usage against an approved standard. Some people like to see a cooling degree day (CDD) adjusted value to compare their usage against that

Table 5.4   Complex billing showing monthly usage and cost.

Building 101		April				May			
Hours of Day		1200-1900	1900-2100	2200-1200	Total	1200-1900	1900-2100	2200-1200	Total
Consumption Charge	Unit cost ($/kWh)	$0.095	$0.036	$0.058		$0.095	$0.036	$0.058	
	# units (kWh)	92,241	69,250	115,509	277,000	118,881	89,250	148,869	357,000
	Subtotal	$8,762.90	$2,493.00	$6,699.52	$17,955.42	$11,293.70	$3,213.00	$8,634.40	$23,141.10
Demand Charge	Unit cost ($/kW)	$5.00	$ -	$ 1.00		$5.00	$ -	$ 1.00	
	# units (kW)	1,845		615	2,460	2,093	0	698	2,790
	Subtotal	$9,225.00	$ -	$ 615.00	$ 9,840.00	$10,462.50	$ -	$ 697.50	$11,160.00
Flat Charge	Unit cost ($)	$550.00				$550.00			$550.00
					$28,345.42				$34,851.10

value. We usually do that calculation in our heads, as it is relatively obvious. This is the EM's choice on how he depicts this for the end users.

As we try to bill for the complex rate (Table 5.4), it becomes a visually busy type of billing with the totals hard to follow. An EM can just go to the totals if they like. This also illustrates the difficulty of billing against a demand line item. Is the demand the real demand for the year or just the highest for the month for that building? This may not be coincident with the overall campus peak billing. So, one might collect more money than they have paid unless we look at the demand for the specific interval where demand occurred on the campus.

This hybrid rate in Table 5.5 is more manageable from a calculation perspective and an EM perspective of accomplishing the end goal. This rate encourages a more diligent look at lowering the peak impact across the board vs. just high usage times. Controlling the usage for one peak becomes a gamble, but averaging 3–5 peaks encourages a lifestyle change. The rate may change somewhat, as noted in the demand cost/unit, but that is due to the cost overall shifting to the number of units to equal the total demand. In most cases, this is complex, but when we involve the building managers, they can assist in understanding the problem time(s) and become part of the solution impacting the overall campus performance.

Other things that can be added are charts that outline the monthly overall usage for a year. Many things, including the cooling degree days for the month, help the user understand the impact of weather. Sometimes we see the consumption graph and a normalized graph for weather overlaid with the consumption. These are basic but easily understandable ways to portray the billing for all buildings on campus.

Table 5.5   Hybrid billing showing monthly usage and cost.

Building 101		April				May			
Hours of Day		1200-1900	1900-2100	2200-1200	Total	1200-1900	1900-2100	2200-1200	Total
Consumption Charge	Unit cost ($/kWh)	$0.095	$0.036	$0.058		$0.095	$0.036	$0.058	
	# units	92,241	69,250	115,509	277,000	118,881	89,250	148,869	357,000
	Subtotal	$8,762.90	$2,493.00	$6,699.52	$17,955.42	$11,293.70	$3,213.00	$8,634.40	$23,141.10
Demand Charge	Unit cost ($/kW)	$5.20	$ -	$ 1.05		$5.20	$ -	$ 1.05	
	# units for 5 highest peaks (kW ave)	1,765		630	2,395	2,103	0	670	2,773
	Subtotal	$9,178.00	$ -	$ 661.50	$ 9,839.50	$10,935.60	$ -	$ 703.50	$11,639.10
Flat Charge	Unit cost ($)	$550.00			$550.00	$550.00			$550.00
					$28,344.92				$35,330.20

5.4 Summary

Billing is a core function of MMS. An EM has to establish the rate structure before billing can take place. This can be a basic blended rate, which most people use, or a complex rate. Generally, a complex rate is too big of a burden from a cost and manhour perspective. A hybrid approach can be used if the EM finds that including the burden for the demand is important to share with building managers to get them vested in helping focus on that part of the bill. A couple of ways exist to bring the demand into the equation without making it overly complex. Actual reporting of the bill is a matter of communicating the demand and the usage costs to the end user in simple terms that meet their requirements. Do they want a simple bill or the details of the rate structure? Graphic charts are always helpful in portraying the annual usage and impact of cooling degree days.

6

Meter Data Connectivity

Abstract

This chapter discusses the overall importance of meter connectivity to the data's quality and usability. As EMs, we receive a lot of data and are asked to perform analysis on that data. First, we must assess whether the data is good enough to perform analytics. This chapter will address how connectivity affects our ability to use the data and what level or percent of connectivity is acceptable in using the data for analysis. We will also discuss ways to use portions of data and when to use those portions effectively.

6   Meter Data Connectivity

In this chapter, there will be a lot of discussion on meters, their connectivity, and how the connectivity impacts data quality. An EM will learn the following:

- Introduction

- Meter network options

- How to assess the connectivity of meters

- Different ways to track the status

- Meter connectivity and data quality

- Meter reporting trends

- How to use notifications for offline meters

- Overall impact

6.1 Introduction

This chapter will go into detail on understanding the value of the data received by the MMS. We will discuss how an EM can view the data to determine if the data is adequate to make an informed decision or to analyze the data. This requires understanding the data quality and how much connectivity affects the quality. That means there are two parts to evaluate on the usability of the data: the quality and the connectivity. If the meter is not connected, it is useless for the EM. If there is no connectivity for a large percentage of the time, then we cannot expect the EM to evaluate or use the data. There are levels of usefulness of the data, with the highest level enabling the user to perform data analytics. For example, if a meter is only connected on day 1 of a year and day 365, then we know the total consumption for the year. With only these two data points, we have the total consumption for the year. However, the lack of daily 15-minute interval data trends between day 1 and day 365 will prevent us from effectively benchmarking the building amongst other buildings when performing a detailed analysis. We will show those various levels of usefulness of the data and how much data satisfies a level of quality that can be useful for the EM to perform data analytics. Most EMs do not understand the complexity of meter connectivity or the various places in a system that can impact the network and data transmission. We will try to present these two chapters (Chapters 6 and 7) from the standpoint of the usability of the data for analytics. So, while the EM may not know the root cause for bad data, he will know if he can use the data after reviewing the topics and metrics covered in this chapter. Chapter 7 will continue this discussion to cover the additional issues that are pure quality issues and how they impact the usability of the data. For EMs who do not understand how the network works and how the meters are installed, we will cover the issues and how they present themselves and, in some cases, identify the root cause and solution.

6.2 Meter Network Options

The meter installation sounds simple, but the correct installation, configuration, and naming convention are critical for ensuring the meter data is connected to the MMS correctly. There are many steps and components involved in connecting the meters, and it is helpful to know the following for each type of meter that will be connected to the MMS:

- How is it connected?

- Is the data stored at the meter in case of a network connection drop? If so, how much data will it store?

- How often does the meter record the data intervals?

  ○ 15-minute

  ○ Hourly

  ○ Daily

  ○ Monthly (basically no storage, and readings are taken monthly to get the end readings)

- How often does the meter report these intervals to the gateway server or database?

  ○ Every few minutes

  ○ Hourly

  ○ Daily

  ○ Monthly

- And how do the answers to all these questions regarding the meter affect the value of the meter data to the EM?

Most people think this configuration and transmission of meter data is automatic and the same for every meter. We have seen various mixes of all these parameters on the same campus. This makes the analytical tools very complex and sometimes impossible to function properly. The connection can be by various mediums that will be addressed below. Still, the transmission of that data depends on how it is connected, as some meters send data every few minutes, while others store the data and send it in groups every hour or so at the intervals in which it is stored. Storing the data (store-it-forward) and sending it periodically eliminates congestion on the network and avoids data gaps where the network was down during that sending process. Storing it forward allows the meter to hold, say, 30 days of data (in a waterfall refreshing to maintain a constant 30-day look back) and then send it with the older data to ensure any gaps for whatever reason are filled to ensure a continuous refreshing complete set of data.

Reporting is also misunderstood, as most people think all meters are alike. Our rule is that electricity should be reporting 15-minute intervals. That allows us to do all EM functions mentioned in this book with the utility meters and most that an EM needs in other circumstances. If the meter is at 30- or 60-minute intervals, then the ability to do benchmarking suffers, and our ability to understand the peaking is completely diminished. Daily and monthly reporting intervals for electric means we can only use the data for determining an EUI. That is a serious limitation to any diagnostics that an EM normally performs.

We can usually use gas and water data at 60-minute intervals for analytics. If there is equipment that requires more precise analysis, then we have to modify this requirement. Daily and monthly for gas and water means we can only use the data for determining an EUI. Daily and monthly are generally difficult because the reading times vary; therefore, we even have trouble calculating the EUI accurately for those commodities, and it becomes an estimate to establish an EUI. If we look at annual EUIs, the accuracy is blended and will be within 1%–3%.

The last couple of paragraphs cover the recording increments but not how often the system reports. Systems can report in a variety of blocks of the increments mentioned before. So, data collected in 15-minute intervals could be transmitted every 15 minutes, 30 minutes, 60 minutes, 4 hours, daily, or monthly. The usability of this depends on when we run analytics and how close to real time we need those runs. EM functions can generally be performed with 4-hour pulls. Most analytics would be satisfied with a daily pull. Beyond that would impact the ability of the EM to do their job properly. If we are doing peak shaving, the interval for electricity has to be a minimum of 15 minutes, depending on how the local utility sets the peak load. In some cases, primarily industrial, the requirement is 1-minute intervals. This adds a load of traffic on the system network; so in this case, we want to run those on a separate network from the other data pulls. Gas and water are generally good with daily pulls.

Various methods can be used for the transmission of meter data. A campus can have a radio, Internet, Ethernet or cellular service network, or a combination. Figure 6.1 shows a radio transmission network. Figure 6.2 shows a cell network similar to the radio transmission network. The usability of each of these has advantages and disadvantages. Still, the driver will be the ability of each to handle the traffic and the security of the data to meet the local EM requirements. In a large building, network transmission usually goes over the Wi-Fi system. Government facilities recently started working with networks such as Wi-Fi and cellular, but Ethernet/Internet was the only approved medium for years. Utilities will transmit meter data by radio, cell, line carrier, or drive-by. Drive-by will only be picking up cumulative consumption readings for monthly reports.

The reporting reliability or connectivity depends on the transmission medium and the maintenance of the meters. Both depend on the maintenance program or each system and communication between the two shops performing that maintenance. For example, the facilities maintenance staff usually

Figure 6.1   Meters connected through radio network.

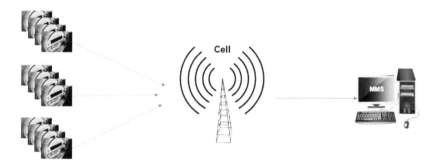

Figure 6.2   Meters connected through cellular service.

maintains the meters, while the IT staff usually maintains the network. The next issue with data connectivity is what happens when the data does not come through. Most systems can be set up to update the data for a certain period of time. If maintenance is adequate, then updates can be pulled for several days before the system locks down its smoothing process – which essentially fills in or cleans missing data. There is a limit on how long we can hold on running the smoothing calculations to some maximum time period. Otherwise, the system always runs updates, which cascades into many reports within the MMS, which is not feasible in execution. To remedy late reporting, we only need to have the ability to flag late data so that it can be run again manually in the MMS.

Smoothing is accurate if there is only one 15-minute interval missed. There are many algorithms to calculate the gap, but let us make it simple here and say it is the average between the before and after reading. There are many sophisticated algorithms for calculating smoothing, such as taking the hour before and after to the more complex that takes an average of readings for previous days at the same date time stamp for office or non-office hours as appropriate. Smoothing helps the EM do their job in the analytic process. The minimum is that it helps them visualize the usage and determine how and when the system performs. It is very accurate for a few missed data readings at a duration. The smoothing accuracy decreases considerably if that duration goes to days or more. The longer the duration, then the estimated usage depends on the part of the curve where it stops. If the data stops on the higher part of the curve, then the estimate will be higher and vice versa. After a few hours, most smoothing algorithms will flatten out, which makes it difficult to do any analytics during this time.

Data quality goes down as those data points are smoothed. Deciding whether it is usable is not always easy; so we use the 35% rule based on statistical checks of actual meters. We will show that in Chapter 7. Technically, if the data field was missing every other data point, the smoothing would probably maintain greater than 99% accuracy against the actual numbers. This scenario is generally not found as most are longer outages or groups of several days each.

6.3 How to Assess Connectivity of Meters

When assessing the connectivity of the meters, there are several aspects to understand: is it currently connected and reporting? How often has it been connected? If it is not connected or has been intermittently connected, what is causing the problem? There are many single points of failure for the reporting.

The points of connection in the system determine the number of points of failure. That includes the points that are imposed by the security on the network. Let us go through these with one example, as that will be sufficient to show the degree of impact and how to track it in a particular system. For this example, let us show a generic design in Figure 6.3 of a system going through the Internet.

So, here are the following connection points to check:

- Meter to JACE

  o Does the meter have power?

  o Is the meter connected to the JACE?

- Is the JACE connected?

  o Does the JACE have power?

  o Is the JACE connected to the internet switch?

Figure 6.3   Meters connected through the Internet.

- Internet switches
  - ○ Does the switch have power?
  - ○ Does the switch have the correct version of the software?
- Transmission at the correct priority
  - ○ What priority is the signal being transmitted?
  - ○ The traffic on a network determines what priority it requires to get the data through.
- In sync
  - ○ Does the transmission of the data match the receiving signal?
- Is the local campus server connected?
  - ○ Does it have power?
  - ○ Is it submitting the data properly?
- Is MMS reading correct values and correct meters?
  - ○ Are we reading kWh or voltage?
  - ○ Do we have a standard meter naming for the points we transmit?
  - ○ Are we reading the meters assigned to the correct building?

6.4 Different Ways to Track the Status

There are several ways to track the status of the campus meters. One way is visual with a GIS map showing meter locations and color-coded for its current connectivity status. This gives an immediate picture of the health and status of the meter connectivity at the campus level. Many systems allow us to click on a building to see how many meters are at that building location, the commodity of those meters, the connectivity status of each meter, and the date and time of the last meter reading received. Also helpful are the building details, including the building name and number, meter number, meter name, category type, description, square footage (SF), and construction date. This visual tool is also important for viewing the trends of meter outages. For example, a group of buildings in one sector where all meters are offline may indicate a network switch or that a line is down.

A tabular report can also accomplish this. The report can cover the same details as those listed above. At the portfolio level, one would usually see the complete list of meters and their status across the portfolio. We usually see sorting by commodity, region, campus, etc., to view issues to troubleshoot the situation.

Additional meter connectivity details provide more granular information to help resolve a problem with the meter connection. For example, we can have notes on the report showing a meter's maintenance status or the network components. These can be filtered to develop metrics for the reliability of the meters, the network, and the overall system. Consistency in meter data can be tracked in this report for durations of 30, 60, 120 days, and so forth. The longer a meter stays offline, the lower the reporting consistency percentage. Data quality indicators can also be shown in these reports, but we will cover that in the next section.

6.5 Meter Connectivity and Data Quality

This section will touch on the data quality to show the relationship between quality and the connectivity of the meter. The next chapter will address quality in detail; however, quality indicates an EM's ability to use the data effectively. There are levels to data quality, but for this section, we want to show the tie between how a lack of data affects the quality. This is straightforward from a commonsense perspective. From this perspective, we need to have enough data to use it. For example, if we have a meter reading at the first of the year and a meter reading at the end of the year, then we have a full year of usage. We know our consumption, assuming the meter registry did not roll over. But knowing a year's worth of consumption does not allow us to perform any useful analysis from an hourly analytics perspective. So how do we translate the lack of data to its impact on the data quality? We studied this for a long time as most people would like one factor to indicate a problem, that is, that the data is bad from a quality perspective. After looking at 10 factors, none could be tied directly with any degree of accuracy to predicting bad quality. So, we started comparing multiple factors against each other to determine if that would give us a quick predictability indicator. We found that the only decisive way to determine if a meter had good quality was by examining the interval graphs and analyzing the data. Other factors, such as benchmarks, were only predictive, and the highest probability of any of the other factors was a comparison between the amount of data provided from the meter and the total consumption.

Let us define this more clearly. An online meter does not necessarily mean it provides quality data to support energy management efforts. For the meter to pass the data quality, the following two criteria must be met:

- Greater than 35% of estimated usage of the interval calculations will fail the data quality algorithm, which considers repeated readings (for electric), missing readings, negative usage, excessive spikes, zero-meter readings, etc. We also refer to this as the smoothed rate. Some people refer to the smoothing process as cleaning the data.

- The ratio of the difference in end-to-end readings divided by the sum of the smoothed interval usage is within 15% tolerance. This is a measure of the accuracy of the smoothing against the actual data.

These numbers might seem a bit arbitrary, just as do raw numbers, but let us look at each one. The first is the smoothed rate. Many things contribute to the smoothed rate, as stated above, but we will concentrate on one, that is, missing readings. Some software uses repeated readings for missed readings, but for these purposes, we will show these as missed readings to discuss the impact of connectivity on the quality. We will address the repeated readings in detail in the next chapter.

We use a graphical report to visualize the smoothed data vs. the raw meter data, as shown in Figure 6.4. This report compares reported usage, raw meter usage, and estimated usage points for the last 30 days.

The meter reading information is included to provide further insight because the usage values are calculated from the readings. Also displayed in red are the estimated usage points for intervals that failed data quality. There is a summary in the legend below the graph of the total number of estimated usage points and the percentage of the displayed usage data that the estimated usage represents. A high number of estimated usage points and, thus, a high percent estimated usage is not good, as it indicates heightened periods of

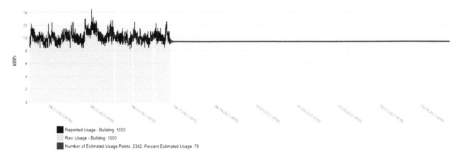

Figure 6.4   Graph of interval data with missing data shown in red points.

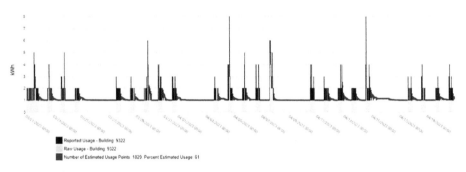

Figure 6.5   Graph of interval data with missing data shown in red points.

network interruptions for that particular meter. Suppose the percentage of estimated usage is greater than 35%. In that case, the accuracy of the usage data is unreliable based on statistical sampling of actual meters and, therefore, not usable by the energy manager. It is easy to see the flat line where connectivity to the meter was down. We will show in Chapter 7 that when this passes 35%, the probability of a meter where the data can be used for analytics is less than 15%.

Figure 6.5 shows a meter with sporadic connectivity. As we can see, the connectivity here is only 29%, which leads to excess smoothing and is less than the target of 65% connectivity (35% smoothing).

The consistency of meter data reporting is important to our energy use metrics and analysis. And the longer a meter stays offline, the more smoothing and interpolation are required to fill in missing data. Data gaps are usually acceptable if our consistency remains high (greater than 65%). We assess that if it is greater than 65% of the data present, we have an 85% probability that the meter data is good. If the consistency is lower than 65%, then there is an 85% probability that the meter data is bad. A large portion of the consistency

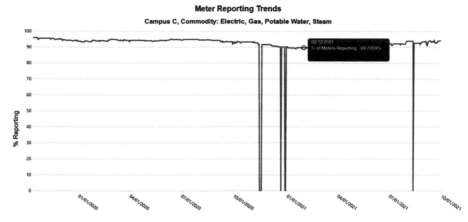

Figure 6.6 Meter reporting trends at the campus level.

is directly related to the connectivity; therefore, the connectivity, in many instances, drives the data quality.

6.6 Meter Reporting Trends

Another useful report to assess portfolio or campus-level meter connectivity shows meter reporting trends. This report (Figure 6.6) displays a graphical view of meter reporting trends for the selected portfolio or campus over time. This data is sourced from daily snapshots of the connectivity captured at the same time, say 24:00 every day. This report may be run at any organizational level to determine where connectivity is off and needs our attention. Any major dips indicate network disruptions, regardless of planned or unplanned outages. We can also see trends as this campus dropped by 5% over time but has been coming up over the last few months.

6.7 How to Use Notifications for Offline Meters

An effective way to follow these meter connectivity disruptions is to establish fault detection for offline notifications. Establish a defined time period for when a notification is sent – it could be 24 hours, three days, or even a week. These notifications are very useful, as we can send them to one or more people via text, phone call, or email so that they are aware and can troubleshoot the problems. If the problem persists, we can have our MMS follow up with another notification after seven days to ensure the problem is being worked.

From: no-reply@mms.com
Sent: Tuesday, May 23, 2023 3:00 AM
To: Energy Manager energy.manager@portfolioassociates.com
Subject: Offline Meter Notification

See below for offline meters at Campus C as of 5/23/2023.
Total Offline Meter Count for Campus C: 14

Meter: CAMPC_1234_METER1 last reading 12/23/2022 4:45:00 AM
Meter: CAMPC_1234_METER2 last reading 12/23/2022 4:45:00 AM
Meter: CAMPC_3325_METER1 last reading 1/12/2023 8:30:00 AM
Meter: CAMPC_9954_METER1 last reading 1/27/2023 1:45:00 AM
Meter: CAMPC_4475_METER1 last reading 2/16/2023 4:15:00 PM
Meter: CAMPC_4475_METER2 last reading 2/16/2023 4:15:00 PM
Meter: CAMPC_6595_METER1 last reading 3/22/2023 5:45:00 AM

Figure 6.7   Offline meter notification email.

An example of an email notification for offline meters is shown in Figure 6.7.

6.8 Overall Impact

One would expect a connectivity rate of 95% or greater for a campus network or a utility network. Anything less requires a review of our maintenance program on the facility and network side. We have seen connectivity rates as low as 50%. The connectivity can affect the quality of the meter data considerably. For example, if we have a 60% connected rate and the quality is 53% of the overall total, our quality is much higher than the numbers indicate. If we take the data quality of just the connected load, we have 88% of the data as good quality. For this reason, the first priority is ensuring we are connected and then connected more than 65% of the time. We may still have quality issues after we fix all the connectivity issues, but at least now we know the connectivity rate does not mask it.

7

Data Quality

Abstract

When we start data analytics, we start without knowing whether our data is good. This chapter will show users how to check the quality of the meter data reporting. They can determine if the quality is good enough for their analysis and for what occasions they can use the data depending on the associated problems. We will also cover a variety of problems with the data and, in some cases, the cause of those problems and a solution.

7   Data Quality

This chapter will detail how to check the quality of the meter data. This chapter will cover:

- Introduction

- How to do a quick check on the quality of the meter data

- What is the impact of repeated readings?

- What do zero readings mean?

- Should data readings increment upward?

- What is the impact of fluctuations in alternating readings?

- Does a reading's precision affect my analysis?

- Can the percentage of base load be a good benchmark for quality?

- How do we assess if the multipliers are off, and what is that impact?

- What happens when multiple issues affect a meter?

- What is the basic approach to check quality?

7.1 Introduction

When assessing the quality of meter data at any campus or site, an energy manager should ask themselves a few questions first. Is the data quality adequate to do the analysis that I need? Is the meter reporting enough to produce the quality we require? Is the data usable for our encrgy analysis? Many factors can affect the quality of the meter data, such as redundant data values, on/off fluctuations, meter multipliers, and multiple readings for the same date/time stamp, and there may also be multiple issues simultaneously affecting a meter, making analysis more difficult.

We have found approximately 10 indicators or tests that identify specific problem areas for a meter that indicate poor data quality. They do not guarantee bad quality but are good indicators. One indicator may show there is a probability that the meter is bad, but it is not a conclusive test. As there are more indicators, then the probability of poor data quality goes up. While one indicator only gives an overall probability of failure, the second increases that probability exponentially. The third instance almost guarantees a problem associated with the meter. These are the indicators we have identified:

1. Sum of the interval usage vs. end-to-end meter readings

2. Percentage smoothing

3. Percentage missing data

4. Percentage repeated readings

5. Is percentage base load in tolerance?

6. Percentage zero readings

7. Is data incrementing upward?

8. Is there flux behavior?

9. Is the multiplier correct?

10. Is the reading precision correct?

As discussed in Chapter 6, connectivity impacts many of these factors. Six of the above indicators are where the connectivity impacts partially or 100% of the data quality. Those factors are:

1. Percentage smoothing

2. Percentage missing data

3. Percentage repeated readings

4.   Percentage zero readings

5.   Data incrementing upward

6.   Flux behavior

We will address the impact of connectivity on each of these as we discuss the overall impact of these on data quality. As discussed in Chapter 6, maintenance is run by two or more groups. Usually, maintenance is performed by the IT group for all the connectivity issues and the maintenance for the meters, which the facilities group generally manages. Those two areas where maintenance intersects are where we connect into a JACE and at the campus-level storage server. The facilities group is responsible for maintenance on the meters and the JACEs in most cases. Some of the maintenance factors mentioned above can be caused by the meter on the network side, which shows the dilemma due to the overlap in boundaries, which affects our ability to identify the root cause of some of those above factors. For example, we have seen where the meters were disconnected from the network for some reason in the building.

Where is the breakdown of good data quality between the network and other data quality? We find that connectivity generally impacts around 80% of the data quality issues, whereas other factors at the meter impact the remaining quality issues.

7.2 How to Do a Quick Check on the Quality of the Meter Data

We defined quality as the ability of the EM to use the data effectively. That is a sliding scale in many aspects. For example, if the EM only needs the annual consumption, the only requirement is the beginning meter read point and the endpoint. If the meter readings are correct, those two-meter reading points will provide the annual consumption. Those two points provide minimal usefulness, but it is not useful for all the other things an EM requires for daily analysis. Good quality means that most of the points are there; so an EM can analyze how the energy is used throughout the day, including when it is used and the magnitude of that use. So, we look for a majority of the points so that the interval curves are visible and easy to follow. The only way to know definitively if the data is good is to look at the interval curves to see if it produces the appropriate curve. An appropriate curve would show a sine wave type curve with weekdays higher than weekends. There should be a pattern where a single shift operation has five distinct peaks, and the weekend is relatively flat or has smaller usage peaks if and when a facility leaves one or more

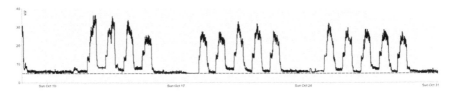

Figure 7.1   Graph showing weekday symmetric curves and flat weekend usage.

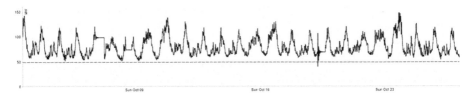

Figure 7.2   Graph showing weekday and weekend for dormitory.

systems on. In Figure 7.1, note that the weekday curves and the weekend flat usage are shown as we just discussed. Even dormitories have a distinct curve with seven peaks, as shown in Figure 7.2. A two-shift operation will have the same look as Figure 7.1, but the duration of the peak will be 16 hours vs. 8 hours. The second thing we look at is the start and end of the day. Are the starting and ending points for the wave duration matching the office hours?

Visual validation is not as practical as needed when doing data analytics via an MMS. After extensively analyzing different indicators, we finally concluded that one indicator alone cannot conclusively tell if the meter generates bad data. So, we determined that two indicators together can give us a high probability of success in predicting the meter's usefulness as an analytic tool. Those two factors are the amount of smoothing and the ratio of the smoothed usage to the actual endpoints. The smoothed data is sometimes called cleaned data. Smoothing is the process of interpolation for gaps or anomalies in data. Gaps due to transmission issues are common and will occur 5% of the time on good systems. Anomalies are situations with a spike in the system due to errant transmission or just glitches from the network. Those spikes are smoothed out. Smoothing formulas take on various forms, but at the simplest, it is just an averaging between the previous and the next point. Interpolations for one point or a few points will be very accurate. Sometimes we must smooth over longer periods and even fill in days of data. As the gap grows, the smoothing accuracy goes down regardless of your smoothing formulae. If the software smoothens for an hour or more, then this long gap will migrate to a straight line after an hour or so of smoothed points. Smoothing will thus

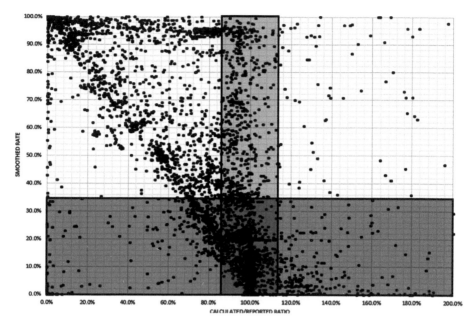

Figure 7.3 Scatter plot of effectiveness of interpolation vs. the smoothed rate.

depend on the position of the last read; so if high on a curve before the gap, the straight line will show higher readings, and if low on a curve, the opposite will be true. The EM must know the interpolation and how it affects your results.

To get a sense of the impact, we took a theory that the more the smoothing on the meter, the higher the probability that the meter could not be useable for data analytics and/or had bad data quality. That was inadequate to satisfy the statistical validity of meter quality; so we added another factor. We know the value of end-to-end points is valid as long as the meter register does not flip over. A flip in the registry would cause a negative value, which is obvious at that point. Making a comparison of the sum of the endpoint's consumption against the smoothed annual consumption value would show how close the smoothing is compared to the actual reading, indicating the effectiveness of smoothing in interpolating the values.

With those definitions, we combine the two values in a scatter plot to determine where the line will be drawn from a valid statistical perspective. The plot provides a visual in Figure 7.3, with the *x*-axis being the percent variance between the smoothed annual vs. the actual value to show the effectiveness of interpolation, and the *y*-axis being the percent smoothed rate of all the data. The black rectangle is set in the figure below to +/− 15% and the

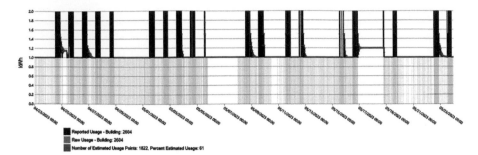

Figure 7.4   Interval data showing bad meter that is outside the rectangle.

smoothed rate at 35% in the red rectangle. We looked at the interval graphs to see if the meters were good at +/− 5% of each box to determine how many meters failed outside and inside that range. To simplify this analysis, we found anything outside the cross-section between the values had an 85% probability of being a bad meter. Everything inside the cross-section had an 85% probability that the meter was good. So, to make this easy for the EM, we fail those meters outside so that the EM does not waste time doing data analytics on those meters. At least if they do, then they understand the potential for failure, and we recommend they perform a visual evaluation on the interval chart if this test shows a meter is close to or outside the boundaries.

Figure 7.4 shows a meter that was outside the rectangle. A visual check shows that the meters are not performing correctly.

Figure 7.5 is a meter inside the rectangle, and your visual check reveals that it looks correct with a symmetrical pattern. The hours match the office hours; the smoothed rate is 6%. This would be a good meter to analyze against the building.

7.3 What Is the Impact of Repeated Readings?

Repeated (redundant) readings are conditions where the meter reading does not increment from one interval to the next. There are several reasons that this takes place. The first and most obvious is that there is no usage. Generally, an electric meter for a building will not retain the same meter value between 15-minute readings. We use this rule for electric meters only because they have the biggest problems and the largest impact on utility costs in most applications. We do not apply this rule to water or gas meters as there will be many opportunities with those meters when an interval does not change. There are enough loads on the plug loads that the electric meter will increment somewhat even on a small building during that 15-minute interval. So,

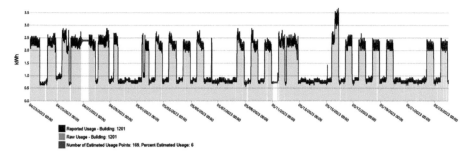

Figure 7.5   Interval data showing good meter that is inside the rectangle.

repeated readings are impossible except when a building is shut down at the panel. We have found that if the panel is not shut off, then there will be some vampire loads always showing usage. Another rare example where a building could have flat usage would be when there is power generation behind the meter on a building, such as photovoltaic solar that matches the usage load on the building. That may periodically happen on one reading, but very few readings of exact matches to zero usage would occur, and not in a series of readings. It is more likely to see a negative value than an exact repeated reading from a power generation source. The overwhelming scenario for a redundant reading is related to transmission loss and the local server replacing that current value with the previous reading. This appears to be the default setting for Metasys servers but optional for other EMS servers. We have seen this on all servers but primarily from Metasys. When this happens, it overshadows most other meter issues and factors that may also be occurring. We have found the redundant readings to be extensive. For electric meters, usage for redundant readings is smoothed (estimated), downgrading the quality. Redundant data values may indicate a problem with the priority of the data transmission. In some systems, the amount of data flow may impact the data getting through to the local campus server. If we see an amount that exceeds 10% of the data not getting through and is distributed across most of the site, then this could be the problem. In those cases, we may need to increase the priority of the transmission. The default setting for meter system data identifier for transmission is priority 3, but if there is a lot of traffic on the network from EMS, then increase that meter transmission authority to priority 2. This does not impact the overall transmission traffic since the meter represents a minor number of points on the network. That should solve any issues related to the transmission and the network defaulting to repeating the values. When we see more than 10% of these redundant readings overall, we have a major breakdown in the quality of the meter data. To understand

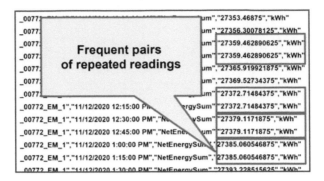

Figure 7.6   Meter data transmission file, showing repeated readings.

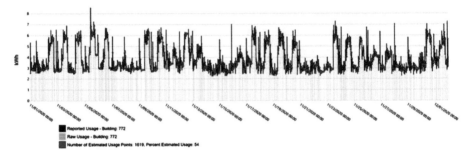

Figure 7.7   Interval usage quality graph showing repeated readings distributed evenly.

what this looks like in your meter data transmission files, see Figure 7.6. Any additional redundant readings are because meters are not transmitting up the network. In the example file of readings below, we have highlighted frequent pairs of repeated readings.

Another way to see this is by highlighting repeated or redundant values. Figure 7.7 displays the same time period and interval readings in an interval usage quality graph. The red points are the redundant values that have to be smoothed, and as can be seen, the percentage of estimated usage is at 54% of the points, which shows that it will be bad quality based on our previous guide. Here, note that the readings are distributed evenly across this month, which means that this is an exception due to the even dispersion of the missing points. Because of that, your likelihood of having good extrapolations is very strong. There is symmetry in the intervals for weekdays and weekends. This means the meter falls outside the rectangle but is an exception to the 85% rule due to the even distribution.

Any meter with greater than 35% smoothed (estimated) data indicates too much missing data to be reliable/usable. The 35% could be one period or

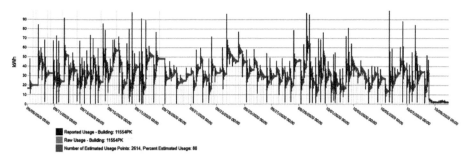

Figure 7.8   Interval data showing 88% of points interpolated.

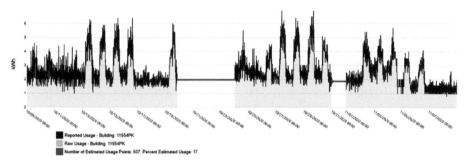

Figure 7.9   Same meter after fixing transmission issues showing good reporting except for two network outages.

every other missing reading and still be accurate for consumption. Still, the 35% breakpoint has been the best indicator to generate a secondary analysis for the EM before they use the data. Figure 7.8 is an example where there is high interpolated usage at 91%, and then the second graph, Figure 7.9, shows the results for the meter after the transmission priority issue was resolved, showing the interpolated usage is down to 18%, and that was due to two short network outage durations as indicated by the flat line.

7.4 What Do Zero Readings Mean?

A zero-meter reading will show up as a smoothed value, but we highlight this as a particular problem that can be identified and resolved. Meter readings are going to come in six or more digits. So, there will not be a meter reading of zero (0) except in extremely rare circumstances where a meter turns over the register, and the usage flips the reading to zero. That is a probability of 1 in 1,000,000, with only one value at zero. This problem is identified by a series of zeros instead of the normal multidigit meter readings. Receiving a zero means there was an error in transmission, and so a value was not received. The software from the local campus server gets a false signal from somewhere in the network and generates a false value of zero. Receiving a meter reading of zero is a failure regarding data quality, as this means there is a lack of connection from the meter to the local campus server. Meter readings will always be in values greater than zero for electric, gas, and water meters since we are looking for a meter registry reading. Readings of zero are a false output, as they are generated when nothing gets through on the network. It indicates connectivity that does not exist.

7.5 Should Data Readings Increment Upward?

Did you get any readings? The meter readings indicate consumption. So, the values will increase, showing consumption is increasing for all types of meters. If so, are your meter values incrementing in an upward direction (meaning that the consumption is increasing)? We should not have a reading that goes backward. The only situation where that should occur is where there is power generation (such as cogeneration or renewables) where the power generation input is located behind the meter. If there is no change in the reading, it is a conditional failure. If we do not get a reading, we cannot check it. The ability to check the readings is fundamental to showing the meter is working. This will be a negative value if the meter is incrementing downwards. All MMSs will show that as a bad value and interpolate (smooth) that value.

7.6 What Is the Impact of Fluctuations in Alternating Readings?

Up/down fluctuations (flux) are when the meter alternates go up and down every other interval or in the opposite direction every 15 minutes. The amplitude is usually approximately 25%–30% of the load; in most cases, they are consistently a similar amplitude change. Some intervals vary at different amplitudes every 15 minutes, but they have the same look regarding the blocks of the up/down fluctuations. While we are not sure of the cause, we know this is not normal behavior for meters. In Figure 7.10, shown in the interval kW benchmarking, the intervals look normal in November and December, with symmetry for the five days of the week and the weekends.

But upon drilling/zooming in on the intervals, the 15-minute up/down fluctuations become apparent in Figure 7.11. While they are generally consistent, the differences are in usage between those intervals. Our theory is that the transmission is out of sync between the JACE and the local campus server and therefore misses 15% of the transmitted readings in a 15-minute

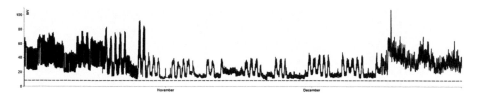

Figure 7.10 Interval data showing good symmetry but an underlying problem.

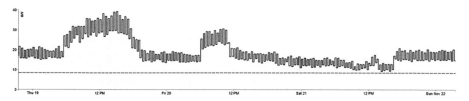

Figure 7.11 Interval data showing 25% flux every 15 minutes.

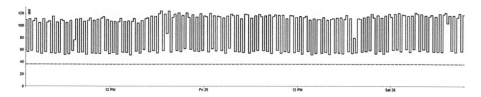

Figure 7.12 Interval data showing 100% flux every 15 minutes.

interval. That means 15% less on one 15-minute interval and 15% more on the following 15-minute interval (30% difference between usages). It appears to catch up at the next interval. We have been searching for an integrator to validate the cause and provide a solution for this issue. The overall usage is correct, and the meter responds properly, but we cannot use the intervals to determine the size or benchmark unless the values are averaged. In this case, the data can be used for a few analytics but only for a small percentage of the analytics the MMS was designed to accomplish.

Figure 7.12 is another example of the 15-minute up/down flux, but the amplitudes are much larger. This is 100% off; so there is no symmetry of the usage, and the data cannot be used for analytics.

7.7 Does the Reading's Precision Affect My Analysis?

The following examples show multiple cases of various precision issues. Precision issues could cause data metrics to be off on midsize buildings by 3% and 25% on small buildings. On a large building, it may not be as noticeable.

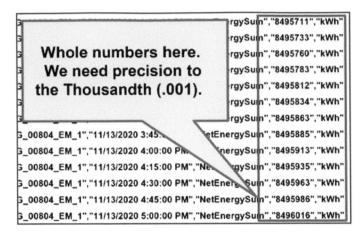

Figure 7.13   Meter readings that are truncated to whole numbers.

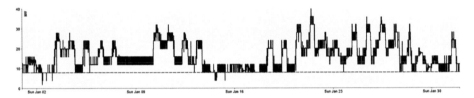

Figure 7.14   Meter readings that are truncated to whole numbers.

Our first example in Figure 7.13 shows readings of all whole numbers. For our meter data analysis to be more accurate, we recommend the precision to be to the thousandth (0.001) so that the installers do not have to evaluate and establish a standard for every size building. This example with whole numbers and no precision is the worst-case situation and can cause a small building to be off by up to 25% in certain situations.

Precision, in some cases, is dependent on the meter's capabilities. For example, we have been told by the EMs in the field that Shark meters only have six digits. So, if they set to 0.001 in significant digits, they only have three digits above the decimal point. That could cause a meter to roll over every 1–3 days. If a meter has this level of restriction, then use one significant digit or 0.1 for your display. That will cause a rollover of 4–8 months, depending on the size of the building. Figure 7.14 indicates how the truncation on a reading affects the analysis on an interval chart. This makes the data analysis difficult in those areas where the graph is boxy vs. a smooth flow of values. This particular one does not lose data as the numbers are large enough; so the values do not truncate to zero (0). The biggest problem occurs

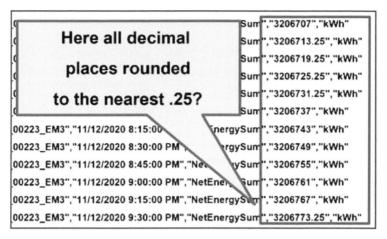

Figure 7.15 Meter readings that are truncated to 0.25 increments.

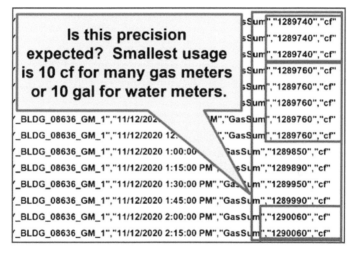

Figure 7.16 Meter readings that report in 10 cf increments.

when the values go to zero, cutting off the rounding; so the meter loses that data due to a rounding error.

In this next example, Figure 7.15 shows the decimal places are rounded to the nearest 0.25; so all values have readings with 0.25, 0.50, 0.75, and whole numbers. This is still not a reasonable solution for the EM.

Figure 7.16 asks, "Is this precision expected?" The smallest usage is generally 10 cubic feet (cf) for gas meters and 10 gallons (gal) for water meters. These could be pulse kits set to specific increments such as 10, 100, and 1000 cf or 10, 100, and 1000 gal; therefore, they accumulate until they

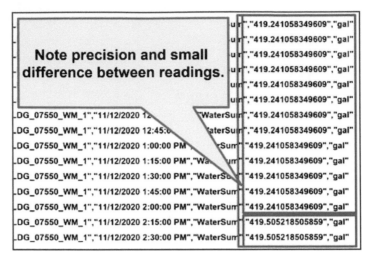

Figure 7.17   Meter readings for water indicating multiplier issue.

reach that threshold. This does not cause much of an issue in evaluating gas or water, but it could if it is a small building usage and the thresholds are larger such as 1000 cf or 1000 gal. The meter does not lose any data but limits data analytics.

In Figure 7.17, note the precision and the fact that there is very little difference between readings. This is a good indicator that it is probably a meter multiplier issue. There are many significant digits, but the movement is first shown at 0.25 gal over 3 hours, which is extremely small and unreasonable for even a smaller building. For this reason, we would see if this meter has a multiplier issue or if the meter is bad.

7.8 Can the Percentage of Base Load be a Good Benchmark for Quality?

We have found that the base load (Chapter 17) translated to watts per sf is a good metric to apply for all facilities. Each base load can be compared against the other benchmarks in that facility category type. The median for that category type does not vary much across the portfolio and is unaffected by climate zones. We also can generate this benchmark with a few days of data vs. waiting for a year's worth of data for an EUI-type benchmark. The base load is also a good indicator of when a building is out of tolerance. For example, if a base load is too large, then there is a high probability that the meter is bad for that facility. If it is too low, then we have the same scenario.

Generally, any building with a base load 2× the median has an 85% probability that the meter is bad. Any number less than 0.5× the median has the same probability on the lower end. This value does not help determine the underlying problem, but it is accurate as a benchmark for determining meter issues. These multipliers were determined by manually checking category type and annotating the overall difference from the median when the meter became bad. After looking at numerous meters in the various category types, the median across all the category types was 1.7× the median. We have taken the conservative route, that it is 2× the median, which is a good rule of thumb for all meters. The same method was determined at the bottom. That was consistent at 0.5× the median. We found that on the lower end, it showed a problem with those meters, usually related to a multiplier problem. Regardless, this method allows us to easily determine if a meter has a high probability of being bad without extensive analysis. This will be a core application for developing the Stop Light Charts addressed in Chapter 20.

A second way to use the base load is in its relationship to the overall consumption. We address this as a percentage of the base load. This is calculated by multiplying the base load by the number of 15-minute increments for the year. That number is the annual consumption for the base load, which is the constant (non-variable load) on a building. We then divide that annual consumption by the overall consumption of the building. Generally, that number comes out around 45% even though theoretical should drive it to around 8%–15%. We found that the largest number that can be theoretically achieved is around 75%. That means every light is left on 24/7, every pump and fan system is overridden, and anything else is left on as a flat load. To allow for the AC and fan/pump systems' variable load, the flat usage will max out at around 75% and sometimes lower depending on the building type. In most cases, the maximum should be much lower than 75%. We have checked that threshold extensively and found that there is probably a 90%–95% chance that any base load greater than 75% is a bad meter.

We look at the bottom in much the same way. We found that anything below 15% was a high probability that it was a bad meter. This is covered in Chapter 17 to discuss the details associated with that number and the exceptions to the 75% and 15% rule.

7.9 How Do We Assess if the Multipliers are Off, and What is that Impact?

Multipliers are usually applied at the meter to convert the meter signal based on the voltage and meter specification sheet ratio outlined for the current

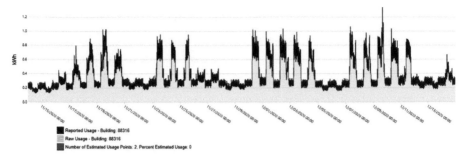

Figure 7.18   Meter multiplier off by 10×.

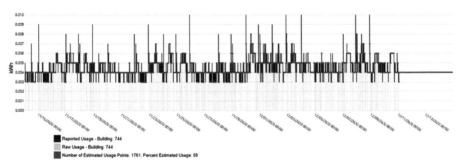

Figure 7.19   Meter multiplier issue and excessive estimated usage.

transformer. These are shown in the design and can vary in many different multiplier numbers. An EM can check this by pulling the manufacturer's specification sheet. The sheet should cover that, and an EM can check it in the display for the meter to ensure it was applied correctly. We have seen it applied incorrectly across the board at the local campus server or on submission to MMS erroneously by applying it as an MWh or Wh instead of kWh, which will skew all the values reported. In this case, the meter could be off by 1000× in either direction. Many meters are not configured properly and can be over- or under-reported in MMS. We have assessed that the meters that are under-reporting are doing so significantly. The graph for these issues in meters usually has a curve, varies consistently, and can be off by a factor of 2–1000. And this can mask other issues, especially if it is off by 1000×.

In Figure 7.18, shown below, the meter is probably around 10× off, which means it has to be corrected at the meter itself vs. at the campus server.

This next example in Figure 7.19 has two issues. The intervals are reading at 0.003 kWh, indicating the meter multiplier is off by 1000×, as none of our meters should be reporting values that are low. We can see a second problem over the estimated usage (smoothing) problem, given that the percentage

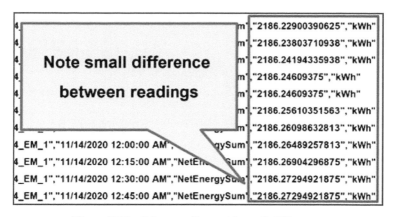

Figure 7.20   Meter readings with small difference.

of estimated usage is 59%, above our 35% threshold. In this case, it is dispersed evenly and may be fine as it does not appear to impact the symmetric curves. Still, we cannot tell since the multipliers are truncating the values, leading to a boxy look, making the analysis more difficult. We would guess this meter data might have good data once the multiplier is fixed, but we will not know until then.

In the example file of readings in Figure 7.20, there is a depiction of the readings showing the small values for each increment. Note the small differences between the readings in the meter file, indicating a multiplier issue.

7.10 What Happens When Multiple Issues Affect a Meter?

Some meters have multiple issues that need to be addressed. The usual indicator for this is that the usage does not represent a sine wave or symmetric curve. They could have redundant readings masking other issues, and there could be other issues as well. In Figure 7.21, note that there is no distinct pattern. That is always a first indicator of a problem with the meter. The pattern changes for all seasons and cannot maintain a pattern during a partial season. The base load also changes. There is also a change in the time of day when they start to have some symmetry in a few instances on the figure's right hand. In this case, the meter probably has more than one issue because we cannot even narrow the issues down to start troubleshooting. The first step would be to check the redundant readings. That is the easiest to check and can mask many other issues.

In Figure 7.22, we have zoomed in on almost a week's data for the same facility. There are multiple issues with this meter, but no indication of what

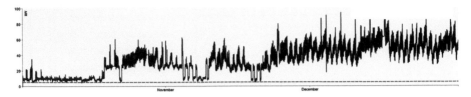

Figure 7.21   Meter intervals showing many issues to resolve.

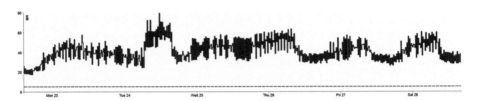

Figure 7.22   Meter intervals showing a combination of issues on weekly data plot.

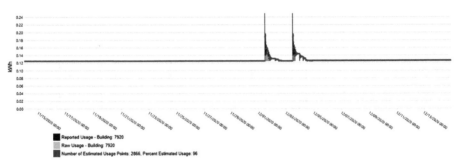

Figure 7.23   Meter usage showing only 4% connectivity and a multiplier issue.

those issues could be. It appears to have some visual indicators of flux, but it is sporadic. That gets us back to the issue of checking the redundant readings first, as the combination of that and the flux would probably generate this pattern.

In Figure 7.23, the meter is not connected enough to provide adequate data for the EM to use in any analysis. So, here, connectivity is reducing the EM's ability to troubleshoot throughout the year. In addition, the meter has a multiplier problem and is also under-reporting.

7.11 What Is the Basic Approach to Checking the Quality?

We recommend using the quick identification tool on data quality to ensure the EM is not wasting your time analyzing bad data. If this flags the meter as bad or on the borderline, visually analyze the interval data. This ensures that the EM uses their time effectively for the type of analysis that they need to perform. If this quick identification tool identifies many problems, then the EM must troubleshoot the issues. Generally, connectivity issues drive us to 80% or more of our quality problems. Redundant readings would then be checked to determine what the interpolated rate is for the meter. This usually is the largest cause of any problems with the meter quality.

We attack the issues based on what we see as the leading causes; so the next issue would be to determine if connectivity is impacted by the priority of our transmission from the meter to the local campus server. Those usually happen in groups; so finding regional problems on campus may lead to this issue. It also is more prevalent on campuses with high traffic on the network.

The next group we would review would be flux, which generally applies to multiple buildings. We have not found the cause and solution other than it appears to be a syncing issue. If someone can pass on their success in this endeavor, we will make it part of our training for others.

Bad multipliers may come in groups; so check for large differences (1000× or 0.001×) first to see if the local campus server causes it. After that, check for random numbers based on being out of the normal ranges covered in Chapter 17, but if most are off, then your installation team did not set them correctly. This can be difficult to fix unless the original drawings indicate the multiplier on the installed drawings. We would recalculate those by taking the meter specification sheet and applying the formula for the current transformer (CT) and voltage on-site to the formulae in the specification sheet to determine the correct multiplier. Then the maintenance shops can easily adjust the multipliers in the field.

The next universal step is to check the value applied to your significant figures. Make sure it is at least 0.1 and 0.001 if the meter has the flexibility with enough digits on the meter's registry.

All other meter issues will require you to evaluate each meter, determine the cause, and plan a solution.

8

Auditing Template

Abstract

MMS can bring things together to support other critical requirements. One task that energy managers routinely perform is an energy audit. An audit is required every four to five years for most buildings. We will show the EM how to set up a basic template in MMS where MMS information fills in data that supports the audit. This is one of many functions where the MMS data becomes an integral part of another program requirement.

8 Auditing Template

This chapter will cover information that should be used in an audit and how to use the MMS system to accomplish as much of that as possible. The reader will find the following topics covered:

- Introduction
- Summary of campus and facilities plan
- Facility systems' information
- Executive summary of the ECMs
- Commissioning component of recommendations
- Developing detailed ECMs
- Summary

8.1 Introduction

This chapter will lay out the basic format for an energy audit. The energy audit is a normal process performed by EMs annually. We will show the basic outline for an audit and how to evaluate ECMs for the facility. A checklist for

93

ECMs will be provided that concentrates on low-cost/no-cost solutions. This chapter will show how the MMS can support many of these ECMs with data and direct the EM to the best solution for that ECM. We will also cover an approach to consider the economics of a project for each building. There are many synergies between the MMS data and an energy audit. Our goal is to try to lay those out for the EM and allow the EM to save a lot of on-site time by gleaning as much data as possible from the MMS.

8.2 Summary of Campus and Facilities Plan

We first establish a section that covers your plan for the campus. A plan should cover auditing every major building once every four to five years. Generally, there are some commonsense rules applied. For example, we may want to target every building above 10,000 sf unless there are high-intensity smaller buildings. A second method is to audit the highest energy-consuming buildings, up to 80% of the campus' total energy. Either method focuses on facilities that use the most energy and those where the results will justify your effort.

This section should give details about the campus. For example, the campus has 380 buildings totaling 4,640,000 sf. Two grid inputs supply power, and the campus purchases power at high voltage. There is solar on roofs at 10 buildings behind the meter rated for maximum production of 1500 kW and a solar ground mounted at 5 MW. Gas is supplied to all buildings and powers a decentralized boiler for all but 10 buildings that a central plant services. Most buildings (80%) are on 10 hours/day for five-day shifts, except those indicated by annotation in Table 8.1.

We generate a table like Table 8.1 for the campus in general. The table lists each building, the sf, annual usage, hours of operation, etc. The EM can easily take this list and rank order by energy usage and then draw a line where the evaluations should stop. In this case, we would stop evaluating at 80% of usage. This general campus information will remain a permanent record in MMS until a change requires updating.

8.3 Facility Systems' Information

For each facility that will be audited, we will prepare a description of the type of building, hours of operation, energy systems, distribution systems, and lighting systems. For the base load, specifically the plug load portion, we need to understand the impacts of the larger loads on the plug load, such as data center closets, etc. These will be important later in differentiating the

Table 8.1 List of buildings on a campus.

Building	Square Footage	Primary Function	Annual Usage (kWh)	Baseload Benchmark kW	Hours of Operation
515	41,401	Office	245,508	7.431	0600-1700
821	46,608	Office	311,315	7.217	0600-1700
7441	81,581	Office	609,107	28.908	0600-1700
7591	23,595	Office	83,053	3.906	0600-1700
8591	23,595	Office	94,826	3.906	0600-1700
8502	18,967	Office	62,142	3.958	0600-1700
7702	18,967	Office	67,265	3.906	0600-1700
7512	18,967	Office	80,907	3.906	0600-1700
8512	18,967	Office	81,515	3.906	0600-1700
162	66,673	Office	321,462	15.747	0600-1700
262	87,254	Office	375,278	22.163	0600-1700
362	87,254	Office	386,909	19.480	0600-1700
462	54,621	Office	206,314	8.000	0600-1700
562	49,140	Office	248,549	8.000	0600-1700
8147	35,730	Office	195,590	9.955	0600-1700
4647	19,972	Office	130,832	7.960	0600-1700
9709	57,607	Office	253,048	11.793	0600-1700
7249	46,613	Office	273,161	9.994	0600-1700
7849	73,007	Office	366,444	14.463	0600-1700

energy systems' range of impact on a specific energy subset. That lets the EM know how the range affects the energy subset to determine where savings are available.

So, for example, we need to break down the equipment to determine the overall impact each has on their respective energy systems, similar to that shown in Table 8.2 for each building. An EM should know what systems are in each building. It is important to note if a building has two VAV systems at 30,000 cfm each with a 10-HP motor for each. We should know if the buildings have T8s, T12s, LEDs, etc. Also, we should know the building type, admin type A, and whether it is a two-story concrete block building with 40,000 sf. Knowing the use, such as the building being an administrative type of facility that operates from 8:00 AM to 5:00 PM, is useful. This information will remain the same until a project changes the equipment. So, this will remain as stored content until it requires changing, but the data is sustained as a part of the MMS database.

Table 8.2 List of building systems.

Building	Square Footage	Primary Function	Baseload Benchmark kW	On Chiller Plant	On Geothermal	On Heat Plant	On Steam Plant	Cooling + Package Tons	Air tons	Air CFM	Thermal MBH	Hydronic HP	Electric kW	System
515	41,401	Office	7.431	No	No	No	No	18		35,500	3,840	10		VAV
821	46,608	Office	7.217	No	Yes	No	No	86	1.5	15,000	16,365	22	5	VAV
7441	81,581	Office	28.908	No	No	No	No	224	5	9,900	4,980	9		CV
8502	18,967	Office	3.958	Yes	No	Yes	No	9			600	3		
7512	18,967	Office	3.906	Yes	No	Yes	No	10			600	3		
8512	18,967	Office	3.906	Yes	No	Yes	No	2	7.5		600	3		
162	66,673	Office	15.747	No	No	No	No	84	12	30,000	1,100	10	30	VAV
262	87,254	Office	22.163	No	No	No	No	90	9	30,000	1,940	10	30	VAV
462	54,621	Office	8.000	No	No	No	No	58	9		5,312	10	20	pac
8147	35,730	Office	9.955	No	No	No	No	98		35,000	1,860	26		VAV
4647	19,972	Office	7.960	No	No	No	No	22		21,500	1,500	9		CV
9709	57,607	Office	11.793	No	Yes	No	No	9			2,000	3,372	12	VAV

8.4 Executive Summary of the ECMs

Here is a list of commonly used ECMs that can be identified by MMS. These are available to review as we perform our audit through MMS. The following is a partial list of those provided by the ENERGY STAR® program as a "Checklist of Common Energy Savings Measures," which can be identified and validated by MMS.

8.4.1 Operations and maintenance [1]

Low-cost measures:

- What is on after hours that should not be?

- Optimize start-up time, power-down time, and equipment sequencing.

- Revise janitorial practices to reduce the hours that lights are turned on daily. Consider switching to day cleaning, which takes place while occupants are in the building and has also been shown to reduce complaints.

- Retro or re-commission the building to make sure it is running the way it was intended, and then set benchmarks in MMS.

- Identify areas where building systems have become inefficient over time and return them to peak performance.

- Repair leaking faucets and equipment.

8.4.2 Lighting

Low-cost measures:

- Turn off lights when not in use or when natural daylight is sufficient. This can reduce lighting expenses by 10%–40%.

- Use task lighting where feasible.

- Implement a regular lighting maintenance program.

- Remove unnecessary lamps (de-lamp) in over-lit areas. Check light levels against the Illuminating Engineering Society (IES) standards to see if areas are over- or under-lit.

Rapid payback measures:

- Replace old fluorescent and incandescent lighting with ENERGY STAR® certified LEDs, T-8 (or even T-5) fixtures, ENERGY STAR® certified LEDs, and other energy-efficient lighting systems that improve light quality and reduce heat gain. LEDs use up to 90% less energy than incandescent lighting and last 35–50 times longer.

- Install LED exit signs. These signs can dramatically reduce maintenance by eliminating the need to replace lamps and can save $10 per sign annually in electricity costs.

- Swap out incandescent light bulbs with ENERGY STAR® certified LEDs for desk, task, and floor lamps.

- Install occupancy sensors to automatically turn off lights when no one is present and back on when people return. Storage rooms, back-of-house spaces, meeting rooms, and other low-traffic areas are often good places to start. Occupancy sensors can save between 15% and 30% on lighting costs. And do not forget – even good equipment can be installed incorrectly; so do not install the sensor behind a coat rack, door, bookcase, etc. It must be able to "see" an approaching person's motion to turn on the light as they enter an unlit room.

- Examine the opportunity to switch from high-pressure sodium lamps to metal halide lamps in parking lots and consider upgrading LED lighting for outdoor signage.

8.4.3 Plug load: office equipment

Low-cost measures:

- Enable the power management function on office computers, automatically putting monitors to sleep when not in use. To learn how to enable this function, visit www.energystar.gov/powermanagement.

- Activate sleep settings on all printers, copiers, fax machines, scanners, and multifunction devices so that they automatically enter a low-powered sleep mode when inactive. Use the owner's manual to make the setting changes to ensure machines are configured to take full advantage of these features.

- Consolidate stand-alone office equipment to achieve a ratio of one device (typically a networked multifunction device) per 10 or more users. Typical cost savings can reach 30%–40% for electricity, hardware, consumables (paper, ink, and toner), and maintenance.

- Plug electronics into a "smart" power strip that designates which electronics should always be on and which do not need power when not used.

- Purchase energy-efficient products like ENERGY STAR® certified office equipment and electronics and establish a procurement policy for energy-saving products.

8.4.4 Plug load: food service equipment

Rapid payback measures:
- Purchase ENERGY STAR® certified commercial food service equipment. For example, certified refrigerators and freezers can save over 45% of the energy used by conventional models, which equals as much as $140 annually for refrigerators and $100 for freezers; deep fryers can save between $60 and $180 per year; hot food holding cabinets can save up to $280 per year; and steam cookers can save between $450 and $820 per year depending on fuel.

- For existing refrigerators, clean refrigerator coils twice a year and replace door gaskets if a dollar bill easily slips out when closed between the door's seals.

- Have large and walk-in refrigeration systems serviced at least annually. This includes cleaning, refrigerant top-off, lubricating moving parts, and adjustment of belts. This will help ensure efficient operation and longer equipment life.

- Consider retrofitting existing refrigerators and display cases with anti-sweat door heater controls and variable speed evaporator fan motors and controls.

8.4.5 Heating and cooling

Low-cost measures:
- Set back/up the thermostat in the evenings and when the building space is not occupied.

- Perform monthly heating and cooling equipment maintenance to guarantee efficient operations throughout the year.

- Regularly change or clean HVAC filters every month during peak cooling or heating season. Dirty filters cost more to use, overwork the equipment, and result in lower indoor air quality.

- Use shades and blinds to control direct sun through windows in summer and winter to prevent or encourage heat gain.

  o During the cooling season, block direct heat gain from the sun shining through the windows on the east and especially west sides of the facility. Depending on the facility, options such as "solar screens," "solar films," awnings, and vegetation can help. Over time, trees can attractively shade the facility and help clean the air. Interior curtains or drapes can help, but it is best to prevent the summer heat from getting past the glass and inside.

  o During the heating season, with the sun low in the south, unobstructed southern windows can contribute solar heat gain during the day.

- Make sure that the area in front of the vents is clear of furniture and paper. If vents are blocked, as much as 25% more energy is required to distribute air.

- Clean the evaporator and condenser coils on heat pumps, air conditioners, or chillers. Dirty coils inhibit heat transfer; so keeping coils clean saves energy.

- Keep exterior doors closed while running the HVAC. It sounds simple, but it will help avoid wasteful loss of heated or cooled air! If a building has revolving doors, encourage or require their use instead of swinging doors.

Rapid payback measures:
- Tune up the heating, ventilation, and air conditioning (HVAC) system with an annual maintenance contract. Even a new HVAC system, like a new car, will decline in performance without regular maintenance. A contract automatically ensures that the HVAC contractor will provide "preseason" tune-ups before each cooling and heating season. The chances of an emergency HVAC breakdown also decrease with regular maintenance.

- Install variable frequency drives (VFDs) and energy-efficient motors.

- Balance air and water systems.

- Install window films and add insulation or reflective roof coating to reduce energy consumption.

While the above list is not all-inclusive, it provides a great start to items that MMS supports. The MMS will readily indicate where the building has waste energy. That will show up in the base load and the overrides (through the non-office hour's percentage of usage). If a building profile indicates a high number for the base load, then use the list to determine what system is left on as a flat load and whether it is a plug load or a fan/pump system. The MMS will identify the excess usage by energy subset and energy system, giving us the tools to determine the likely contributors. In the audit summary of the building, the audit may discover a data center closet. The EM can attribute the kW load from the data center closet to see if that accounts for the total base load above the plug load. If not, see if the office space's remaining computer towers are left on at night. If that is not happening, then the EM can see if there is a supply fan or pump that matches the HP load on the system. The analysis for this is provided through the tools for base load and can be easily determined. See Chapters 10 and 11 for more details on how to manage the plug load.

The second issue that can apply to this checklist is the systems used during non-office hours. That is a substantial loading that the MMS system can easily chart. The MMS can show the magnitude of the usage during non-office hours. For example, a 20-kW peak during non-office hours will correlate to a chiller coming on for the majority of the building. A 2-kW peak means a small rooftop unit is coming on during non-office hours, and the larger system is working under schedule correctly. Turn to Chapter 10 to go into more detail on how to read these tools in MMS.

8.5 Commissioning Component of Recommendations

Audits have a commissioning component that was discussed somewhat in the last section. There will be levels of application of commissioning:

- Non-office constant base load

- Non-office hours variable load

- Total AC system (fan/pump systems and the AC system)

- Lighting systems

The pathway for these four listed applications is to accomplish this as a part of the above or through a monitoring commissioning (MCx) program, which will continue to monitor it in the future, as discussed in Chapter 15. These applications can be monitored by the MCx, with any discrepancies passed to the local maintenance shop to accomplish any low-cost ECMs. So, what ECMs above flow into these applications can be easily tied into and supported by MMS.

So, the first application mentioned is related to the base load, which is a constant load. So, let us split this into the plug and the remaining base load. We identify this in Chapters 10 and 11 as we focus on identifying the systems on a constant load and work with the shop to identify and resolve those systems. This may be some of those ECMs mentioned above. The MMS should effectively identify the magnitude of the constant load, whether a plug or a fan/pump system, and maybe even the type of system by size. Certainly, the magnitude can correlate to the specific equipment based on the data indicating the size of the motors, etc., for the building discussed in Section 8.4.

The second application is the variable portion of the non-office hours, which identifies the overrides for systems that are oscillating on and off during non-office hours. The MMS also shows these system overrides. Each of these systems can be identified by the MMS by the kW, and we can translate it to the system sizes identified in Section 8.4. So, with this, we can easily identify a system that is 2.5 tons of AC system coming on that is operating during non-office hours vs. the two 40-ton units. This is covered in Chapter 13.

The third application is to identify the efficiency of the fans/pump systems and the AC systems. This is a remote monitored data opportunity for the MMS to identify those changes in efficiency each year and compare them against the other years. This is covered in Chapter 13, where we break down the relationship between the fan/pump system and the AC system and the efficiencies benchmark. The EM can look at the overall system ratings for a building. MMS will only be able to identify the rating for a building AC system itself; so if the building has multiple systems, we may be unable to break it down by each system. A change between years may be easily attributable to a specific system if there are larger disparities between the system sizes in a building where we can proportion the loading based on size. Still, it may be difficult to correlate the change to a specific system. If we compare the annual increase or decrease, we can determine if the AC system has degraded and what the savings would be to bring it back to compliance. This identification will help focus on a systematic issue, not the specific problem system. The fan/pump systems will be the same approach.

Finally, the MMS can identify lighting system issues based on the watts per sf rating. This is discussed in Chapter 12. The scatter plot can identify the building rating for lights on a watts/sf basis. This allows the EM to determine if a building has T8s vs. LEDs, therefore, identifying buildings needing a more efficient lighting system. The MMS can only look at the aggregate building; so the MMS is looking at the building overall, similar to the approach in the previous paragraph for the AC and fan/pump systems.

8.6 Developing Detailed ECMs

As the ECMs get beyond the capability of the local maintenance shops, the EM will have to look at the development of projects or bring in a third party or an ESCO to develop projects. These projects are covered in a few places by MMS in this book, but the most direct approach is covered in Chapter 18, "Setting Up for Energy Projects." The MMS can list overarching opportunities where savings are highly supportive. Still, the EM will have to develop the specific ECM for that building or system indicated by the tool shown in Chapter 18. Chapter 18 can also be useful in identifying buildings that do not require an audit or where an audit would not be economical because a project would not have a reasonable payback.

8.7 Summary

In summary, we have identified several ways to outline the audit through the MMS. The EM will have to input the background for the campus and building information if it is not already in MMS. Once in MMS, the data is there for all future audits. The tools within the MMS can populate a large percentage of the analytical portion of the audit. Once the EM brings in the analytics, the only remaining requirements are to validate the findings with either the maintenance shops or by observation at the building. Once a routine has been established, the follow-up audits can be accomplished primarily from the EM's desk.

References

[1] (n.d.). Checklist of Common Energy-Saving Measures. Energy Star. https://www.energystar.gov/sites/default/files/tools/Checklist_of_ common_energy_saving_measures_2021.pdf

9

Using Metering for Measurement and Verification (M&V)

Abstract

This chapter shows users how to validate estimated savings from energy conservation measures (ECMs) using metering for measurement and verification (M&V).

9 Using Metering for Measurement and Verification (M&V)

This chapter will validate estimated energy conservation measures (ECMs) savings using metering for measurement and verification (M&V). This chapter will cover the following:

- Introduction
- Breakdown of approach
- Graphical interval usage
- Graphical annual usage
- Monthly usage
- Daily usage
- Interval usage
- Measurement and verification tool
- Summary

9.1 Introduction

Without a continuous diagnostic and a proactive energy management approach, energy usage will be 20%–40% higher than required to provide a comfortable and healthy indoor environment. Proactive energy management is the cradle-to-grave strategy that highlights facility energy use, pinpoints anomalies, tracks trends, benchmarks campus and/or building performance, identifies effective saving opportunities, and verifies energy savings.

We all do ECMs, from simple maintenance actions to full-scale construction projects. When we accomplish an ECM, we want to understand if it was successful. Did the ECM save the energy projected, and will it pay back the effort or cost to accomplish that ECM? This chapter will show how to validate those estimated savings from energy conservation measures (ECMs) using MMS for measurement and verification.

9.2 Breakdown of Approach

There are several ways to perform M&V depending on the level of detail required to support the results. For example, the simplest level is to know we have made a positive impact. That can be done visually from a graph in many cases. The best example is to compare monthly savings to a cost. That savings is somewhat limited to the metering level, as discussed later. So, let us first discuss the ways M&V can check in MMS. Those are as follows:

- Graphical interval usage query
  - Visual check to see if there are any changes
- Graphical annual usage report
  - Graphical check on overall numbers year over year
- Monthly usage report
  - Tabular check with monthly granularity (year over year)
- Daily usage report
  - Fine-tune the analysis and start dates to days vs. months
- Interval usage query (exported to Excel)
  - Tabular deeper dive with 15-minute detail
- M&V ECM report tool
  - Specifically designed to track savings of an ECM over time

We will break down each of these to provide an understanding of how the MMS can help an EM at each level.

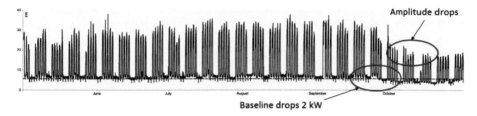

Figure 9.1 Graphic interval view of ECM impact.

9.3 Breakdown of Graphical Interval Usage

The first is a graphical look at the intervals to give us a quick visual check on the impact of the ECM. The intervals are usually 15 minutes, and we want to review the period before and after the ECM is accomplished. That generally means comparing the previous period (season) against the current season. The previous season's shoulder month will work if the ECM starts in a shoulder month. Figure 9.1 shows how the interval data should look before and after an ECM. This is a great example for a couple of reasons.

The first is a noticeable drop in the base load, as shown in the lower red circle. Base load definition and analysis are discussed in Chapters 10 and 11 in detail. That means a drop in the constant load on the facility. That drop is around 2–2.5 kW. The second visible change is the change to the variable load (upper red circle), as the peaks are consistently lower than the previous shoulder month. Remember, do not compare October to September; their load is completely different. If we compare the shoulder month of April and May vs. October, there is a noticeable difference in amplitude. This gives us a good understanding that we can see savings if we do a detailed analysis.

9.4 Graphical Monthly Usage

The second test is a quick graphical check to understand the magnitude of the difference in annual usage. Usually, we run the 12 months before the ECM was completed and then the 12 months after to compare the difference. In Figure 9.2, the usage before the ECM completion date is recorded. In Figure 9.3, the usage after the ECM completion is recorded. Breaking down the difference of 116,218 minus 76,075 leaves a difference of 40,143 kWh in savings per year. This is still a rough magnitude because we have to use months vs. the exact day an ECM is finished, which should not affect much, but it still must be accounted for.

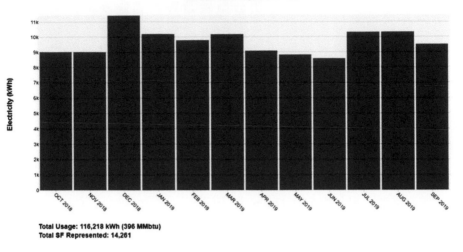

Total Usage: 116,218 kWh (396 MMbtu)
Total SF Represented: 14,261

Figure 9.2   Annual graphic view before ECM completion.

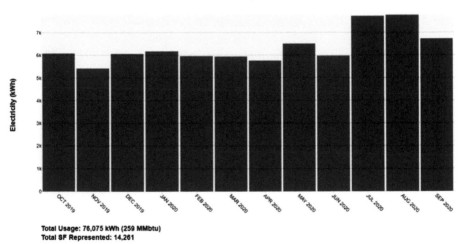

Total Usage: 76,075 kWh (259 MMbtu)
Total SF Represented: 14,261

Figure 9.3   Annual graphic view after ECM completion.

Now the key to M&V is the long-term viability of the project. In Figure 9.4, we have followed with the second year after ECM completion. We note that the usage is back to the same as before the ECM. This means that whatever had been accomplished to drop the constant load and the variable load has moved back to an overridden position.

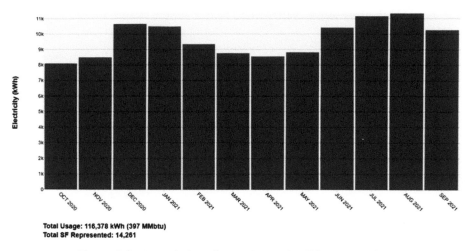

Total Usage: 116,378 kWh (397 MMbtu)
Total SF Represented: 14,261

Figure 9.4 Annual view of second year after ECM completion.

9.5 Monthly Usage

The monthly usage report, Table 9.1, is a tabular usage similar to the last section's graphical chart. Many people prefer tabular, and this is available in MMS, where a building can generate the data for the year before the ECM and the year after. Again, we are comparing months against the previous year as a quick check with monthly granularity.

9.6 Daily Usage

Now the daily usage report provides more granularity and narrows down the start dates on the ECM completion. This provides a higher level of detail than the monthly data. Table 9.2 covers this, and because it is a longer list of inputs, we always lay the years beside each other. These long lists are not always going to match in-line items. In those cases, we take the longer list and drop the extra lines till they are equal in the number of entries. This is done to ensure the number of intervals matches since the intervals are the consumption in kWh for that time period. There are generally few missing intervals, but any offsets will reduce the comparison accuracy; so we even up the intervals. In Table 9.2, we hid the middle of the year's worth of data to depict the beginning and end of the evaluation period.

Table 9.1   Two-year annual view after ECM completion.

Monthly Usage Report
Date Range: October 2018 - October 2020
Commodity: Electricity

Campus	Building	Category Type	Building SqFt	Month/Year	Commodity	Usage	Units	Usage MMBtu	Units BTU
Campus F	1021	Office N	14261	Oct2018	Electricity	9,010.47	kWh	30.74	MMBtu
Campus F	1021	Office N	14261	Nov2018	Electricity	9,004.27	kWh	30.72	MMBtu
Campus F	1021	Office N	14261	Dec2018	Electricity	11,415.30	kWh	38.95	MMBtu
Campus F	1021	Office N	14261	Jan2019	Electricity	10,189.72	kWh	34.77	MMBtu
Campus F	1021	Office N	14261	Feb2019	Electricity	9,783.56	kWh	33.38	MMBtu
Campus F	1021	Office N	14261	Mar2019	Electricity	10,179.90	kWh	34.74	MMBtu
Campus F	1021	Office N	14261	Apr2019	Electricity	9,085.60	kWh	31.00	MMBtu
Campus F	1021	Office N	14261	May2019	Electricity	8,826.06	kWh	30.12	MMBtu
Campus F	1021	Office N	14261	Jun2019	Electricity	8,579.13	kWh	29.27	MMBtu
Campus F	1021	Office N	14261	Jul2019	Electricity	10,318.90	kWh	35.21	MMBtu
Campus F	1021	Office N	14261	Aug2019	Electricity	10,321.11	kWh	35.22	MMBtu
Campus F	1021	Office N	14261	Sep2019	Electricity	9,504.42	kWh	32.43	MMBtu
					Total Usage	116,218.44			
Campus F	1021	Office N	14261	Oct2019	Electricity	6,079.31	kWh	20.74	MMBtu
Campus F	1021	Office N	14261	Nov2019	Electricity	5,412.80	kWh	18.47	MMBtu
Campus F	1021	Office N	14261	Dec2019	Electricity	6,057.52	kWh	20.67	MMBtu
Campus F	1021	Office N	14261	Jan2020	Electricity	6,171.10	kWh	21.06	MMBtu
Campus F	1021	Office N	14261	Feb2020	Electricity	5,955.41	kWh	20.32	MMBtu
Campus F	1021	Office N	14261	Mar2020	Electricity	5,935.44	kWh	20.25	MMBtu
Campus F	1021	Office N	14261	Apr2020	Electricity	5,752.70	kWh	19.63	MMBtu
Campus F	1021	Office N	14261	May2020	Electricity	6,507.67	kWh	22.21	MMBtu
Campus F	1021	Office N	14261	Jun2020	Electricity	5,971.13	kWh	20.37	MMBtu
Campus F	1021	Office N	14261	Jul2020	Electricity	7,729.97	kWh	26.38	MMBtu
Campus F	1021	Office N	14261	Aug2020	Electricity	7,777.84	kWh	26.54	MMBtu
Campus F	1021	Office N	14261	Sep2020	Electricity	6,724.44	kWh	22.94	MMBtu
					Total Usage	76,075.33			

% Usage Savings: 34.54%

9.7 Interval Usage

Now the interval (15-minute) usage graphic, Figure 9.5, was partially shown earlier in this book and is used to indicate the highest level of granularity before and after the ECM completion. This provides a higher level of detail than the daily or hourly. We did not show the hourly, but it follows the same approach as the daily depicted in the last section. We usually use the 15-minute intervals for our analysis as it is almost as fast and gives us the best data fidelity.

We take the data from Figure 9.5 and convert it into tabular form and compare four years of analytics to determine how the ECM has done over the four years. This data is depicted in Table 9.3. We show the data was high, 110,594 kWh in 2018, 116,211 kWh in 2019, and then the ECM hit on the first of 2020. This shows a 35% savings, but in 2021, the building somehow regressed to the previous state. This is a good example of why we perform

Table 9.2   Annual view with daily usage comparing before and after ECM.

Daily Usage Data
Date Range 10/1/2018 12:00:00 AM - 9/1/2020 12:00:00 AM

Campus	Building	Category Type	SF	Commodity	Timestamp	Usage	Units	Timestamp	Usage	Units
Campus F	1021	Office N	14261	Electricity	2018-10-01	333.18	kWh	2019-10-01	280.38	kWh
Campus F	1021	Office N	14261	Electricity	2018-10-02	363.16	kWh	2019-10-02	241.75	kWh
Campus F	1021	Office N	14261	Electricity	2018-10-03	276.67	kWh	2019-10-03	234.43	kWh
Campus F	1021	Office N	14261	Electricity	2018-10-04	304.71	kWh	2019-10-04	222.75	kWh
Campus F	1021	Office N	14261	Electricity	2018-10-05	246.51	kWh	2019-10-05	98.07	kWh
Campus F	1021	Office N	14261	Electricity	2019-08-21	407.24	kWh	2020-08-20	348.96	kWh
Campus F	1021	Office N	14261	Electricity	2019-08-22	407.81	kWh	2020-08-21	289.72	kWh
Campus F	1021	Office N	14261	Electricity	2019-08-23	372.44	kWh	2020-08-22	103.65	kWh
Campus F	1021	Office N	14261	Electricity	2019-08-24	165.34	kWh	2020-08-23	102.02	kWh
Campus F	1021	Office N	14261	Electricity	2019-08-25	167.19	kWh	2020-08-24	312.39	kWh
Campus F	1021	Office N	14261	Electricity	2019-08-26	414.09	kWh	2020-08-25	302.06	kWh
Campus F	1021	Office N	14261	Electricity	2019-08-27	398.48	kWh	2020-08-26	306.13	kWh
Campus F	1021	Office N	14261	Electricity	2019-08-28	400.14	kWh	2020-08-27	295.69	kWh
Campus F	1021	Office N	14261	Electricity	2019-08-29	404.00	kWh	2020-08-28	342.86	kWh
Campus F	1021	Office N	14261	Electricity	2019-08-30	356.09	kWh	2020-08-29	114.12	kWh
Campus F	1021	Office N	14261	Electricity	2019-08-31	148.69	kWh	2020-08-30	112.88	kWh
Campus F	1021	Office N	14261	Electricity	2019-09-01	150.19	kWh	2020-08-31	249.43	kWh
						Total Usage	106,864.23		Total Usage	69,350.91

% Usage Savings: 35.10%

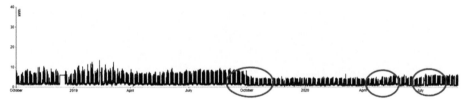

Figure 9.5   Multi-year view of 15-minute intervals graph comparing before and after ECM.

M&V. This should also be caught in the monitoring commissioning (MCx) program when it occurs.

We will perform the same analysis on another building where a lighting ECM was performed. Let us review this ECM that installed LEDs in late 2018 at campus T. We will review the analysis for installing LEDs for this campus. The first is Building A, and we will show the intervals and perform a visual inspection. In Figure 9.6, we show a drop in the amplitude of the peaks in late 2018 in the red circle. The drop has to be compared to a similar shoulder season, the previous Spring or Fall. It is much less than the Fall; so we also look at the previous Spring to compare similar situations with temperature, etc. Both shoulder seasons indicate a drop in lighting loading.

We will also review the second Building L from a visual perspective. This one is easier to see the drop in amplitude in Figure 9.7 in the red circle vs. the previous Fall and Spring.

Table 9.3   Four-year view of 15-minute intervals comparing before and after ECM.

Four-Year Comparison
Campus F, Building 1021 (14261 sf)

FY2018	Electricity	Units	FY2019	Electricity	Units	FY2020	Electricity	Units	FY2021	Electricity	Units	FY2022	Electricity	Units
2018-09-30 19:00	1.46	kWH	2019-09-30 19:00	1.22	kWH	2020-09-29 18:00	1.44	kWH	2021-09-30 18:00	1.63	kWH	2022-09-30 19:00	1.19	kWH
2018-09-30 19:15	1.46	kWH	2019-09-30 19:15	1.31	kWH	2020-09-29 18:15	1.38	kWH	2021-09-30 18:15	1.31	kWH	2022-09-30 19:15	1.00	kWH
2018-09-30 19:30	1.54	kWH	2019-09-30 19:30	1.28	kWH	2020-09-29 18:30	1.25	kWH	2021-09-30 18:30	1.44	kWH	2022-09-30 19:30	1.00	kWH
2018-09-30 19:45	1.56	kWH	2019-09-30 19:45	1.25	kWH	2020-09-29 18:45	1.25	kWH	2021-09-30 18:45	1.50	kWH	2022-09-30 19:45	1.12	kWH
2018-09-30 20:00	1.56	kWH	2019-09-30 20:00	1.32	kWH	2020-09-29 19:00	1.25	kWH	2021-09-30 19:00	1.62	kWH	2022-09-30 20:00	1.06	kWH
2018-09-30 20:15	1.56	kWH	2019-09-30 20:15	1.37	kWH	2020-09-29 19:15	1.37	kWH	2021-09-30 19:15	1.38	kWH	2022-09-30 20:15	1.13	kWH
2018-09-30 20:30	1.38	kWH	2019-09-30 20:30	1.31	kWH	2020-09-29 19:30	1.44	kWH	2021-09-30 19:30	1.62	kWH	2022-09-30 20:30	1.06	kWH
2018-09-30 20:45	1.44	kWH	2019-09-30 20:45	1.32	kWH	2020-09-29 19:45	1.31	kWH	2021-09-30 19:45	1.50	kWH	2022-09-30 20:45	1.00	kWH
2018-09-30 21:00	1.46	kWH	2019-09-30 21:00	1.31	kWH	2020-09-29 20:00	1.25	kWH	2021-09-30 20:00	1.63	kWH	2022-09-30 21:00	1.19	kWH
2018-09-30 21:15	1.54	kWH	2019-09-30 21:15	1.37	kWH	2020-09-29 20:15	1.31	kWH	2021-09-30 20:15	1.43	kWH	2022-09-30 21:15	1.00	kWH
2018-09-30 21:30	1.50	kWH	2019-09-30 21:30	1.38	kWH	2020-09-29 20:30	1.32	kWH	2021-09-30 20:30	1.44	kWH	2022-09-30 21:30	1.06	kWH
2018-09-30 21:45	1.43	kWH	2019-09-30 21:45	1.28	kWH	2020-09-29 20:45	1.31	kWH	2021-09-30 20:45	1.63	kWH	2022-09-30 21:45	1.13	kWH
2018-09-30 22:00	1.47	kWH	2019-09-30 22:00	1.28	kWH	2020-09-29 21:00	0.94	kWH	2021-09-30 21:00	1.43	kWH	2022-09-30 22:00	1.06	kWH
2018-09-30 22:15	1.63	kWH	2019-09-30 22:15	1.31	kWH	2020-09-29 21:15	1.37	kWH	2021-09-30 21:15	1.38	kWH	2022-09-30 22:15	1.12	kWH
2018-09-30 22:30	1.65	kWH	2019-09-30 22:30	1.38	kWH	2020-09-29 21:30	1.31	kWH	2021-09-30 21:30	1.62	kWH	2022-09-30 22:30	1.07	kWH
2018-09-30 22:45	1.50	kWH	2019-09-30 22:45	1.37	kWH	2020-09-29 21:45	1.44	kWH	2021-09-30 21:45	1.50	kWH	2022-09-30 22:45	1.00	kWH
2018-09-30 23:00	1.44	kWH	2019-09-30 23:00	1.32	kWH	2020-09-29 22:00	1.25	kWH	2021-09-30 22:00	1.69	kWH	2022-09-30 23:00	1.12	kWH
2018-09-30 23:15	1.41	kWH	2019-09-30 23:15	1.37	kWH	2020-09-29 22:15	1.38	kWH	2021-09-30 22:15	1.44	kWH	2022-09-30 23:15	1.00	kWH
2018-09-30 23:30	1.47	kWH	2019-09-30 23:30	1.34	kWH	2020-09-29 22:30	1.31	kWH	2021-09-30 22:30	1.56	kWH	2022-09-30 23:30	1.06	kWH
2018-09-30 23:45	1.50	kWH	2019-09-30 23:45	1.35	kWH	2020-09-29 22:45	1.31	kWH	2021-09-30 22:45	1.50	kWH	2022-09-30 23:45	1.13	kWH
	110,594			116,211			75,730			116,396			118,027	
				105%			65%			154%			101%	

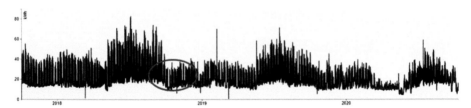

Figure 9.6   Lighting LED ECM in the Fall of 2019 indicated on interval graph for Building A.

Figure 9.7   Lighting LED ECM in the Fall of 2019 indicated on an interval graph for Building L.

Before we analyze these two buildings, we will look at the justification for the project. Table 9.4 shows the projected savings based on the number of fixtures to be replaced. This will set the baseline for the M&V that will follow. As shown on the chart, Building A was projected to have 85,851 kWh/yr, and Building L was 19,447 kWh/yr.

Let us analyze Building L in Table 9.5 to compare it to the projected savings that justified the project. First, we must clarify that a building meter will register everything accomplished in the building as both good and bad from a savings perspective. In most cases, we only implement one ECM at a time; so all the savings will be associated with that ECM. Just beware that any operational changes also impact the usage. So, let us review the lights

Table 9.4 Calculations for savings for the LED projects.

2017-2019 LED Lighting
Campus T

Building	Number of Fixtures	Average of Existing Fixture Wattage	Average of Proposed Fixture Wattage	Average of kW Savings per Fixture	Hrs/Yr from M&V	Existing Lighting with Total	New Lighting with Total	KW Savings	KWH/Yr savings	Approximate Install Date	Notes - office area unless noted
A	707	71.0	33.9	0.037	3,276	50,197	23,991	26.2	85,851	Aug-18	major HVAC reno 2018
B1	45	93.0	40.0	0.053	3,162	4,185	1,800	2.4	7,540	Summer/Fall 2018	
C	179	69.6	38.6	0.031	2,918	12,464	6,915	5.5	16,190	Summer/Fall 2018	
F	475	76.5	38.5	0.038	2,635	36,343	18,282	18.1	47,588	Summer/Fall 2018	
J1	71	62.0	27.0	0.035	4,119	4,402	1,917	2.5	10,236	Summer/Fall 2018	
J2	222	84.8	36.6	0.048	3,978	18,824	8,116	10.7	42,597	Aug-18	
J3	101	81.6	38.6	0.043	3,990	8,237	3,894	4.3	17,328	May-18	CDC
L	261	62.9	37.8	0.025	2,977	16,407	9,875	6.5	19,447	Aug-18	
O	27	62.0	40.0	0.022	1,927	1,674	1,080	0.6	1,145	Summer/Fall 2018	
R1	124	67.0	40.0	0.027	3,536	8,302	4,960	3.3	11,818	Summer/Fall 2018	
U	57	62.0	40.0	0.022	3,718	3,534	2,280	1.3	4,662	Summer/Fall 2018	CDC

over four years. The first year on the left side of the equation is partially metered; so we have to extrapolate the baseline. The year of implementation appears to be a partial year, as we only see a 5.3% savings over the baseline year. After implementation, the second year (third usage column from left) is a full year of savings and shows 25.2% savings. The fourth year shows a savings of 30.4%. The numbers at the bottom of the table below indicate the actual savings of 64,809 kWh vs. the projected savings of 19,477 kWh/yr shown in Table 9.4. So why were the numbers so far apart? One solution might be that the original estimate was off due to a miscalculation of operational hours. If the office hours were underestimated, then the savings would be larger. The second solution might be if the space made an operational change to their hours or the end user required fewer lights. Finally, the savings might be due to some change in the ECMs initiated during this period. The EM might presume that the lighting ECM for LEDs was the only ECM, but the maintenance shop may have fixed a VFD or some other maintenance issue that required a quick repair that impacted the overall savings. All M&V is difficult to focus aggregate savings on the specific ECM savings, but we use this as an indicator to guide the EM so that they can adjust if there are other factors. As stated above, there are normally no other factors, but the EM must be cognizant. In this case, that level of savings was probably increased because of activities the shops were performing on control system overrides.

We will look at the second building in Table 9.6 on Campus T for the change in usage before and after the LED ECM. That usage will be compared against the projected savings that the EM used to justify the decision to go forward on the project. We show the base year in the first highlighted column on the left from the four years shown. As discussed above, this required extrapolation in the first year. Some ask if it is skewed because of the seasonal

Table 9.5 Four-year view of hourly intervals comparing before and after ECM.

Four-Year Comparison
Date Range: 10/1/2017 12:00:00 AM - 11/1/2021 12:00:00 AM
Campus T, Building L (19762 sf)

Timestamp	Usage	Units	Timestamp	Usage	Units	Timestamp	Usage	Units	Timestamp	Usage	Units
2018-07-31 15:00	49.50	kWh	2019-07-31 15:00	52.50	kWh	2020-07-30 15:00	43.56	kWh	2021-07-31 15:00	15.48	kWh
2018-07-31 16:00	46.14	kWh	2019-07-31 16:00	50.28	kWh	2020-07-30 16:00	43.68	kWh	2021-07-31 16:00	17.70	kWh
2018-07-31 17:00	46.02	kWh	2019-07-31 17:00	44.40	kWh	2020-07-30 17:00	42.78	kWh	2021-07-31 17:00	17.22	kWh
2018-07-31 18:00	37.14	kWh	2019-07-31 18:00	35.34	kWh	2020-07-30 18:00	38.82	kWh	2021-07-31 18:00	20.70	kWh
2018-07-31 19:00	30.42	kWh	2019-07-31 19:00	30.96	kWh	2020-07-30 19:00	21.42	kWh	2021-07-31 19:00	19.38	kWh
2018-07-31 20:00	27.48	kWh	2019-07-31 20:00	25.74	kWh	2020-07-30 20:00	15.90	kWh	2021-07-31 20:00	19.56	kWh
2018-07-31 21:00	23.70	kWh	2019-07-31 21:00	21.48	kWh	2020-07-30 21:00	18.00	kWh	2021-07-31 21:00	16.74	kWh
2018-07-31 22:00	24.18	kWh	2019-07-31 22:00	22.32	kWh	2020-07-30 22:00	18.36	kWh	2021-07-31 22:00	17.40	kWh
2018-07-31 23:00	23.88	kWh	2019-07-31 23:00	20.34	kWh	2020-07-30 23:00	20.04	kWh	2021-07-31 23:00	15.12	kWh
	177,527.31			201,778.12			159,477.18			148,340.12	

intervals available	7296		baseline year	213,149.57		baseline year	213,149.57		baseline year	213,149.57
annual intervals	8760		less usage	94.7%		less usage	74.8%		less usage	69.6%
	83.3%		savings	5.3%		savings	25.2%		savings	30.4%
Extrapolated year	213,149.57								Savings kWh	64,809.45

Table 9.6 Four-year view of hourly intervals comparing before and after ECM for Building A.

Four-Year Comparison
Date Range: 10/1/2017 12:00:00 AM - 11/1/2021 12:00:00 AM
Campus T, Building A (59304 sf)

Timestamp	Usage	Units	Timestamp	Usage	Units	Timestamp	Usage	Units	Timestamp	Usage	Units
2018-07-31 15:00	118.02	kWh	2019-07-31 15:00	177.72	kWh	2020-07-30 15:00	125.94	kWh	2021-07-31 15:00	34.98	kWh
2018-07-31 16:00	115.14	kWh	2019-07-31 16:00	165.12	kWh	2020-07-30 16:00	127.02	kWh	2021-07-31 16:00	38.34	kWh
2018-07-31 17:00	106.92	kWh	2019-07-31 17:00	142.98	kWh	2020-07-30 17:00	123.24	kWh	2021-07-31 17:00	38.58	kWh
2018-07-31 18:00	97.86	kWh	2019-07-31 18:00	106.02	kWh	2020-07-30 18:00	93.48	kWh	2021-07-31 18:00	36.96	kWh
2018-07-31 19:00	83.22	kWh	2019-07-31 19:00	55.86	kWh	2020-07-30 19:00	55.32	kWh	2021-07-31 19:00	38.4	kWh
2018-07-31 20:00	74.28	kWh	2019-07-31 20:00	52.02	kWh	2020-07-30 20:00	45.36	kWh	2021-07-31 20:00	34.98	kWh
2018-07-31 21:00	68.52	kWh	2019-07-31 21:00	47.94	kWh	2020-07-30 21:00	45.24	kWh	2021-07-31 21:00	35.94	kWh
2018-07-31 22:00	65.52	kWh	2019-07-31 22:00	46.26	kWh	2020-07-30 22:00	43.2	kWh	2021-07-31 22:00	35.7	kWh
2018-07-31 23:00	61.02	kWh	2019-07-31 23:00	49.56	kWh	2020-07-30 23:00	41.76	kWh	2021-07-31 23:00	36.48	kWh
	444,700.71			528,390.79			493,305.43			492,638.48	

intervals available	7295		baseline year	534,006.61		baseline year	534,006.61		baseline year	534,006.61
annual intervals	8760		less usage	98.9%		less usage	92.4%		less usage	92.3%
	83.3%		savings	1.1%		savings	7.6%		savings	7.7%
Extrapolated year	534,006.61								Savings kWh	41,368.13

impact on the interpolation. Since we are interpolating the previous shoulder months, it will be a minimum impact but something to consider if we have to interpolate a summer or winter. From this analysis, there is a 1% savings in the first year; so as above, the ECM did not get implemented as expected to realize the full savings. In the third year of M&V, it was 7.6%, and in the fourth year, it was 7.7%; so the savings settled at around 41,368 kWh. The actual savings is about half the projected, shown in Table 9.4. This could be caused by overestimating the schedule that the lights were normally on or by a change in the usage since the ECM was installed. The increased usage could be caused by a failure or override in other systems causing the facility to use more energy than normal.

9.8 Measurement and Verification Tool

Finally, we will look at a simple tool to consolidate the above analysis for the ease of the EM. The tool shown in Figure 9.8 shows the analysis page

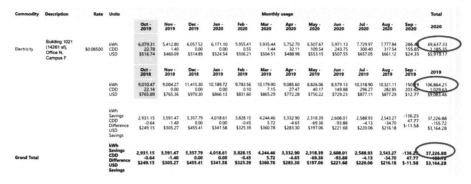

Figure 9.8   Summary of intervals comparing before and after ECM in the M&V template.

Figure 9.9   M&V template allowing the inclusion of manual meters if required.

for the building in the project. In the analysis, we show the base load usage per month and compare it to the actual usage for the current month. We can overlay multiple years in this analysis and the actual month for any future year against that same month in the base year. The value of a form allows us to compare multiple buildings under the same ECM. So, for example, the LEDs ECM mentioned previously covered many buildings. This consolidates those into one report and shows the overall savings for each building and the overall ECM. In the figure below, we only show one building summing to total savings for ease of the visual aid.

In Figure 9.8, we are looking at the meter contribution and the CDD to understand the impact of weather on each month. Figure 9.9 adds another factor for M&V: meters not included in MMS. In this case, add a manual meter where MMS does not cover a particular building or a system. This allows adding that usage onto the analysis, which is especially important when there are many buildings in an ECM where we want to sum the results,

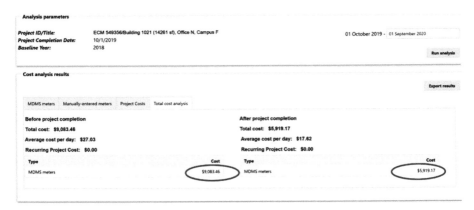

Figure 9.10 M&V template for project costs.

Figure 9.11 Summary template for the M&V total from each tab.

and the MMS does not cover all the buildings. In this case, add the usage during the base period and after the ECM was installed.

The next addition to the template is the inclusion of other project costs. Figure 9.10 includes a manual input for factors such as payments for the project manager, M&V costs, or even payment of the ECM. We can add anything the EM would like to compare against the savings. Many costs should be covered, especially if the EM wants to show that the project pays for the financing.

This final template summarizes all the tabs, as shown in Figure 9.11. In this template, we add the lines for all the costs associated with the ECM before and after the completion. This is a summary of all the elements.

9.9 Summary

This chapter has shown a buildup of various methods to analyze the M&V savings. We started by giving a visual but then transitioned to the broadest and quickest tool, a monthly analysis. This was followed by increasing granularity from monthly to daily to hourly to 15-minute intervals. Each was generated similarly with the additional layers of granularity.

Several projects were covered that provided good examples of savings and approaches. They also showed when an ECM reverted to the previous state, which is a primary reason for accomplishing M&V. Some ECMs did not match their initial estimates. Hence, the M&V led us to analyze the differences to determine why we were off in the initial estimates or if something else contributed to the difference.

These tools can be rolled into a template that tracks all ECMs for a building as an aggregate. The template can cover anything desired, including manual meters, project costs, etc. The outcome should be flexible enough to be usable by the EM to make their job easier.

10

Basic Benchmarking (First Level)

Abstract

This chapter covers the basics of benchmarking, starting with the base load of a building and how to determine that base load. Then we will discuss the composition of the base load, which includes the plug load and other equipment that comprise a constant load on the facility. The section closes with benchmarking various facilities' situations that may arise while performing analytics.

10 Basic Benchmarking

This chapter is the first in a four-chapter series on benchmarking building systems and system components. This chapter will address the following:

- Benchmarking guidance

- Basic plug loads

- Base load

- Resetting the base load

- Other building curves to benchmark

10.1 Benchmarking Guidance

Benchmarking buildings or systems against one another has been used in the energy management industry for years. It is defined as a mark or standard that can motivate the users to bring their facility into compliance or at least more consistent with other facilities by using less energy [1]. As stated, it was and is still used as a benchmark against itself as an early warning of a system's anomaly to allow early detection and correction, avoiding wasted energy [2]. The Department of Energy (DOE) and its labs have developed detailed benchmarking definitions. The DOE thought benchmarking was so important that they required all Federal facilities to be benchmarked if that building constituted at least the top 75% of the total campus energy use [3].

Benchmarking has many benefits, but we also explain the process by acknowledging the benefits. Benefits include (1) a baseline understanding of a building's energy use, (2) metrics to rank a building against others in the portfolio, (3) a better understanding of how their buildings' energy performance compares to peers, and (4) a basis of establishing an investment strategy from an energy management plan to drive continuous energy improvement [4].

Benchmarking originally started where we could only assess our building, or set of buildings, for a campus or across the entire portfolio. This process improved as we started comparing against published building data collected by the US Department of Energy (DOE) through the US Energy Information Agency (EIA). The commercial building energy consumption collection started on October 1, 1977 [5]; so we have data for almost 46 years. Those benchmarks and many others will be discussed in Chapter 11.

Approaches to benchmarks have taken many avenues. We will address a few here but expand those to a much deeper level and extent as we go into the various chapters. For example, one group calls approaches to "cross-sectional benchmarking" for comparing building energy performance to similar buildings. Benchmarking a specific building against its history is known as "longitudinal benchmarking" [6]. We have always called these "external" and "internal" benchmarking. As we get into more details, we will demonstrate hybrid methodologies, including comparing a system within a building against itself over time and against parameters established against the campus, category types, climate zone, and across the portfolio.

Benchmarking sounds complicated, but it is simply noting the energy performance metrics of the building. Over the next few chapters, we will benchmark more than overall building consumption, including energy systems and energy conservation measures (ECMs). The secondary implication of benchmarking is to compare one building to other similar building benchmarks or against a baseline for the specific building or a baseline year. We can then compare future years against the baseline year to gauge the program's success. It also provides a standard to determine if parameters need to be adjusted, which allows a building to reset the baseline and establish that as a point of reference to gauge success going forward. We can also use this benchmark to gauge or rank a building against the energy performance of similar buildings.

We can benchmark any value, such as consumption, but to analyze it in any external benchmarking requires it to be normalized to some relative comparison value. Benchmarks in the past were described as an energy use intensity (EUI) or annual usage characterized by total consumption per square foot (kbtu/sf) by most data compilers [7]; this will be discussed in Chapter 16, "Evaluating the Energy Use Intensity (EUI) Value to Energy Managers." We will show many other ways to benchmark the building or system, giving us more flexibility to assess the facility's energy usage. The US Federal Government must enter all benchmarks into a system, such as the Energy Star Portfolio Manager, for the building to be benchmarked in compliance with Federal requirements [8].

Benchmarking is the basic building-block energy management function for developing ECMs, or projects, for which we will use these two terms interactively as the same function throughout this book. Benchmarking is not an end in itself. It has a purpose for us to use the information to make engineering decisions related to energy usage in a facility. These decisions should be prioritized based on a return on investment (ROI). The highest ROI will consist of low-cost/no-cost investments covered primarily through various commissioning programs [9]. The highest return will be through monitoring commissioning (MCx). Benchmarking through the utilization of meter data will lay the foundation for those types of programs, which will be addressed in Chapter 15, "Monitoring Commissioning (MCx) Process."

We will start by iterating that all energy management is based on attacking any problem in a systematic hierarchical fashion. The hierarchy is based on economics. Economics is the driving factor or key differentiator for an energy manager vs. a design engineer. Everything is done based on economics, which will evolve somewhat to add a climate factor in the future or monetize to a cost of that impact on the climate.

From a cost perspective, we will concentrate on electric consumption primarily because electricity impacts most campuses that we have observed anywhere from around 70% of facilities cost to overall energy savings somewhere in the 80%–95% range for all the energy costs that are directly tied to the electricity usage. This is because electricity also controls the medium for thermal distribution systems in most cases. So, a fan or pump will move most of the thermal distribution. When we manage the electric system and the associated controls, we will automatically manage the distribution for the heating and cooling. As seen in Table 10.1, 65% of the total energy and 91% of the total utility cost [10] for a facility can be controlled by managing the electric system, the electric distribution system, and its associated controls. These are calculated from the EIA data for total energy to a facility. The "Other" column on the right is outside the meter borders; defined as external loads we do not usually see under the facility meter. The electric systems do

Table 10.1   EIA split of gas usage [10].

Release date: May 2016										
Table E2. Major fuel consumption intensities (Btu) by end use, 2012										
Major fuel energy intensity[1] (thousand Btu/square foot in buildings using any major fuel for the end use)										
		Space heat-ing	Cool-ing	Venti-lation	Water heat-ing	Light-ing	Cook-ing	Refrig-eration	Office equip-ment	Com-puting	Other
	Total										
All buildings	82	22.3	8.6	8.1	6.5	8.7	13.8	9.1	2.1	5.2	10.5
% of total		27.2%	10.5%	9.9%	7.9%	10.6%	16.8%	11.1%	2.6%	6.3%	NA
% energy not affected by Electric Distribution Mediums									35.9%		
% cost									9.0%		

not distribute the three columns; therefore, the only energy not affected or controlled by the electric meter are water heating, cooking, and refrigeration. We have 35.9% of energy outside the electric meter control. Electric energy costs are 4–5× the cost per MMBTU over gas. That calculates to 9% of costs outside the electric system's direct control or otherwise impacting 91% of the total utility cost.

10.2 Basic Plug Loads

To start benchmarking, we want to discuss how to approach a building's energy and the systems that use that energy. This chapter is the first of four that will address benchmarking systems. We will look at the energy usage in a building based on a normal breakdown of systems. The EIA supplies a table that breaks down all these systems as usages in electric consumption intensities in their benchmark data (Table 10.2). But if we take a closer look, there are four distinct definable systems for office buildings. Those systems are:

- Plug load

- Lighting load

- Fan/pump system load

- Air conditioning (AC) system load

Plug loads primarily consist of office equipment and computers. Sometimes we may see a small amount of consumption from the kitchen (cooking and refrigeration loading columns below).

Plug loads fall under and are primarily estimated in the EIA tables under office equipment and computing categories. The cooking and refrigeration loading (shown on the table) would be used during office hours and is

Table 10.2 Electricity consumption intensities [11].

Table E6. Electricity consumption intensities (kWh) by end use, 2012
Electricity energy intensity¹ (kWh/square foot in buildings using electricity for the end use)

	Total	Space heating	Cool-ing	Venti-lation	Water heat-ing	Light-ing	Cook-ing	Refrig-eration	Office equip-ment	Com-puting	Other
buildings Principal building activity	14.6	0.5	2.4	2.4	0.2	2.5	1.1	2.7	0.6	1.5	2.7
Education	11	0.5	2.5	1.6	0.2	1.9	0.2	1	0.5	1.9	1.6
Food sales	48.7	0.6	1.6	2.8	(*)	3.6	4.3	34.5	0.5	0.6	2.7
Food service	44.9	1.4	5.3	5	1.1	3	15.9	18.3	1.2	0.8	3.4
Office	15.9	0.6	2.2	3.9	0.1	2.7	0.2	0.6	0.7	3.1	2.4
Public assembly	14.5	1	5.2	1.3	(*)	1.9	0.5	1.5	0.4	0.9	3.8

variable; therefore, it is not included in the "base" plug loading. Most administrative buildings do not see these heavy cooking and refrigeration loadings. Still, they drive the usage up during office hours for retail space, merchants, and food sales, which weigh the total category heavily. By definition, the "Other" category (column on the far right) is related to usage outside the building, which is not measured by the facility meter in this book's examples.

If we remove the equipment measurements that do not apply to most buildings, we will get the four systems mentioned above. In Table 10.3, these four systems are broken down, showing the total plug load at 34.8%, including the kitchen loading. This gives a distribution shown in the pie chart in Figure 10.1. Remember that this was compiled in 2012 and will drop drastically in 10 years, as shown in the next chapter. Naturally, this is contingent on the fan/pump systems, as well as the related controls, working at design intent as we will find that in most institutional settings, those are overridden from design intent, making a large energy impact. These issues will be discussed in Chapter 14, "Understanding and Troubleshooting System Overrides."

In this chapter and the next, we will focus on plug loads and the base load easily identifiable in all usage graphs. This easily definable base load absorbs the plug loading as a component. We will break down the base load and show how the plug is identified. In Chapter 11, "Second-level Benchmarking," we will focus on the breakdown of the other loads within the base load and how each type of benchmark is valuable in its own right. Chapter 12, "Third-level Benchmarking," will break down how to benchmark lights and demonstrate how to generate another benchmark tool, the scatter plot. We can show how to calculate those usages and give a range for the benchmarks. The final benchmarking chapter, Chapter 13, "Fourth-level Benchmarking," will cover air conditioning (AC) systems and the fan/pump systems and present a way

Table 10.3   Calculating the system usage categories from EIA [12].

	Total	Cooling	Ventilation	Water heating	Lighting	Cooking	Refrigeration	Office equipment	Computing	Plug
All buildings	13.4	2.4	2.4	0.2	2.5	1.1	2.7	0.6	1.5	6.1
		17.9%	17.9%	1.5%	18.7%	8.2%	20.1%	4.5%	11.2%	45.5%
Office	13.5	2.2	3.9	0.1	2.7	0.2	0.6	0.7	3.1	4.7
		16.3%	28.9%	0.7%	20.0%	1.5%	4.4%	5.2%	23.0%	34.8%

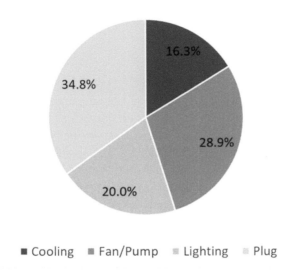

Figure 10.1   Four major components of usage calculated from Table 10.2.

to calculate the AC system efficiency based on the usage (easily identified in MMS) vs. the ratio of the usage divided by the output. Chapter 13 will also provide a complete system approach for the AC systems regardless of the system type and the ability to benchmark those systems against other AC systems. In concluding the benchmarking series of chapters, we will roll the energy into a waterfall of values for each of the eight energy subsets into their office or non-office hours and seasons.

10.3 Base Load

The easiest benchmark to calculate is a base load. The base load is the constant consumption level that is on (no variable loading). That means systems are always running to sustain that flat usage rate. A typical building energy consumption chart is shown in Figure 10.2. The normal usage pattern will be

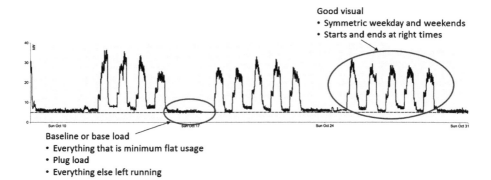

Figure 10.2 Interval kW graph showing areas of potential savings.

a sine wave type curve indicating a five-weekday single-shift usage pattern. The vertical axis represents kW, while the horizontal axis shows time. The base load is represented by the horizontal line drawn so that it "kisses" the bottom edge of the usage curve. It is usually consistent for all four seasons. There are only a few exceptions to this rule.

If a building is a one-shift operation or runs like a one-shift operation with the base load and with an increase in loading for usage during operations, it will appear similar to the curve shown in the above graph. This is a one-shift operation where we can see the five workdays with the rise and fall daily and the weekend dropping down to the base load. Each day will begin when work starts, say, 7:00 AM and end at 5:00 PM. The usage ramps up each day at that time, generally peaking around 2:00 PM and then dropping down to the baseline at 5:00 PM. The weekend should be flat on the baseline. Assuming a good meter, the pattern for each workday should be symmetrical, and the weekends almost flat. This is expected in any building that has regular hours of operation. We even see this same type of pattern in apartments. The usage pattern will increase when people come home from work and peak around 9:00 or 10:00 PM and then decrease to a base load for apartments. Even two-shift operation buildings will have symmetric patterns. One of the key indicators of a bad meter reading is a lack of symmetry.

Figure 10.2 shows a sawtooth pattern at night and on weekends. Night and weekends are not going to the usage baseline because some systems are using power during those non-office hours. Since administrative space does not have many varying equipment loads, the highest probability is that the AC systems are running. That means the AC system schedule is on or overridden, and the usage responds to the outdoor air temperature (OAT) requirement for cooling during the night and then OAT and solar loads during Saturdays and

Sundays. There may be a couple of other pieces of equipment, such as appliances coming on. Still, the only loads that will supply a noticeable loading will be cycling, such as refrigerators. Those do not vary much and will be minor chatter shown on the interval usage graph. A refrigerator uses a maximum of 0.8 kW [13] every 4–8 hours [14]; so this sawtooth usage effect is much more frequent than the refrigerator loading.

This base load can be set manually, or it can also be calculated automatically. We have found that calculating the 300 lowest non-zero numbers over the past 12 months will accurately draw the base load line for 95% of the buildings. The 300 interval points have given higher reliability than using lower numbers of interval points, especially if there are data transmission issues. The 300 intervals assume that there is a good meter, not missing more than 35% of the data points. Anytime we do an analysis, we always do a visual check to see if the base load baseline is kissing most of the bottom edges of the non-office hour's baseline (lower) points. Some ask why we use a year of interval data. The primary reason is to cover all the seasons. A building usually gets a firm baseline across the year. But we want to ensure the baseline holds for summer and winter. If not, then analyze the building to determine the load that changes during those seasons. Before having an automated flow of meter data and the ability to use direct data to calculate the base load with a formula, we would always use the shoulder months (Fall and Spring) to ensure the usage was calculated when AC or heating systems were not required when the OAT was neutral or did not require conditioning in the space. This was how the baseline was calculated for years. With automated systems, we can assess this more quickly and reliably by looking at the system over all seasons and averaging over many interval points.

Let us review the same values from a different type of graph. Figure 10.3 is a scatter plot. It uses the same data as the previous interval graph but gives a different perspective. The vertical axis is the kWh, while the horizontal axis is a cooling degree day (CDD) for that specific hour. A CDD is a temperature where cooling must be applied to a building to maintain the temperature in the space. That is generally calculated as OAT minus 65 °F as long as that stays a positive value. This is because, in general, the space does not require cooling until the OAT exceeds 65 °F. So, we are seeing the usage compared against the CDD generated by the weather. This chart shows how the kWh will increase as the CDD increases. The purple line is the base load or the minimum constant usage. The usage is not variable below this point, meaning the usage or loading on the building (meter) does not change below this mark.

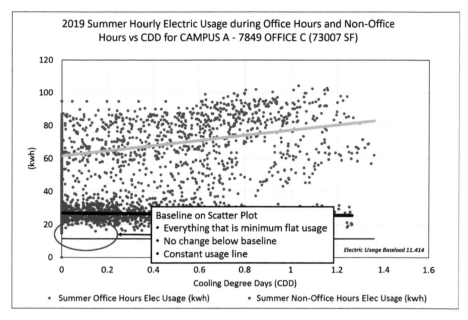

Figure 10.3   Building scatter plot showing base load baseline.

So, we have calculated the base load, but what makes up the base load? Base load is a constant (non-variable) loading on the building. It is composed of flat loads that are broken into two groups. The first is plug load. Plug load, by definition, is all the loading plugged into the receptacles [15]. This can be further broken down into three areas, computers, office equipment, and all other equipment/devices, which are desk equipment, desk lights, coffee pots, etc. The second group is the differential between the plug load and the base load or the equipment that is always left on. We will address those items later in this chapter.

The plug load is discussed in many studies and has different aspects. It is usually discussed about the total load per year in kWh/sf/yr or separately as the maximum instantaneous load. That is exceedingly difficult to address as most studies only focus on one metric or the other. We must know and understand both to successfully benchmark the plug loads. So, to break it down, we must understand the nature of the loading. Breaking it down into the major loads is in Table 10.4.

The plug load has increased in buildings for most of the last 40 years [17]. This has been due to the increase in electronics, particularly individual computers, and monitors assigned to each person. That has reversed somewhat lately due to the transition from CPU towers to laptops. The laptop is 76% [18] more efficient than the CPU tower. That is due to the energy

Table 10.4   Breakdown of major loads by type [16].

Type of load	Percentage of total load
Computers	66%
Office equipment	17%
Other loads	17%

Table 10.5   Comparing desktops vs. laptops in percentage of time on [19].

Mode	Desktop	Laptop
Active mode	30%	10%
Sleep mode	50%	58%
Disconnected	7%	26%

savings mode of the laptop being better for every mode, from active to sleep and to disconnected, as shown in Table 10.5.

So, the plug load is one of two groups of usage that make up the "base load." The second group includes system loads that run constantly. The systems that meet this condition can only fall into one system category during this time period: fans and pumps. Fan/pump systems have a variable load as they ramp up, but the base load is distinct on many systems. Constant volume (CV) air-handling systems (AHS), fan coil units, pumps, exhaust fans, and supply fans will constantly draw on the usage. This usage under the base load that exceeds the plug load indicates that system(s) are overridden (schedule not controlled) within a building. So as seen below in the scatter plot shown in Figure 10.4, the base load is composed of the plug loading, which is a flat load generated by the plug, and the fan/pump system load, which is a flat loading that runs constantly. Figure 10.4 clearly depicts the base load (purple line) broken down between the plug loading and the fan/pump systems left running by an override on the system controls or the building manager. The ratio between these two could vary from 60/40 (plug/fan/pump) to 20/80. If you do not have any orange points above the purple line (base load), the base load probably has minimal fan/pump system load.

So, what should happen with a building where the systems are on a schedule and reading properly? Figure 10.5 shows just the non-office hours. We can determine that proportionally most of the HVAC units are not running during non-office hours. There is some activity slightly above the baseline, which indicates a much smaller system is running all the time, which

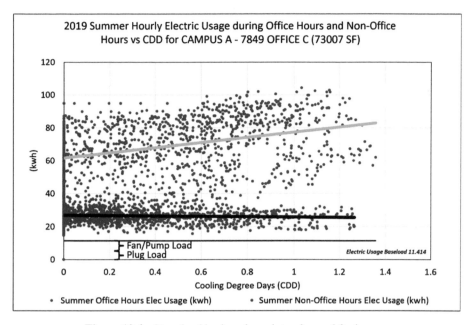

Figure 10.4 Base load broken down into plug and fan/pump.

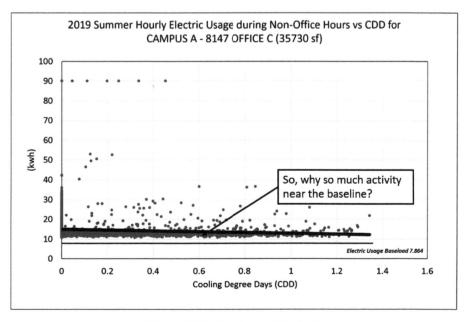

Figure 10.5 Good non-office load.

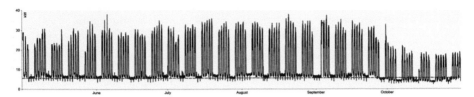

Figure 10.6   Interval plot with changed/reduced base load.

generates the points shown above the baseline. That is generated by a relatively small rooftop unit that does not have a schedule, thereby generating a variable loading. Since it only serves a small space, it does not influence the non-office hour slope to show a correlation to the CDD. The extraneous points above the slope are generally due to personnel coming in early or working late; so it should be blue, indicating a change in office hours, but it was shown as non-office hours due to a fixed schedule.

10.4 Resetting the Base Load

When can the base load vary from an earlier model, and is that a problem? As shown in Figure 10.6, the set baseline (redline) is higher than the real baseline (bottom edge) in a few instances. That is caused when the bottom edge of these lowest points has established a new baseline clearly below the previous line. When this happens, determine if the change is permanent, and then override the computer-calculated baseline value and redraw the line at the real low point or somewhere between that point and where the system seems to base out. In this case, we usually drop it down to the lower point. However, if we know there is a system reason driving a few points and decide to make a slightly higher point that is a more stable baseline, then that should give us a better perspective on where it should be set.

If we made changes to the building system, then that should result in the recalculation of the benchmark depending on the type of system in that building. As shown in Figure 10.6, the campus maintenance personnel made a change to this building that altered the baseline.

The above graph clearly shows a change in the base load. The new baseline is about 1.8 kW less than the previous base load line. As we remember, the base load is a flat usage load that runs continuously; so any change means a piece of equipment or system has been shut down or placed on a schedule, so it is shut down when not required. This reduction of approximately 2 kW is associated with a change in fans or pumps, which will be explained below. These modifications due to a change in the building environment could be

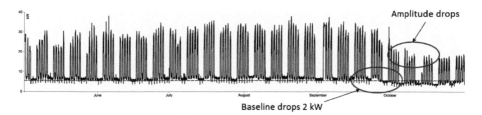

Figure 10.7 Comparing savings changes.

due to a change of mission in the building, the addition or reduction of equipment or the control of the schedule on that equipment, or an energy project. Regardless, the change requires us to determine if it is permanent and adjust the baseline for future analysis.

Figure 10.7 shows two areas in red circles where the maintenance folks changed the system. The first is the drop in the base load of 1.8 kW discussed above. This change is a drop in the flat load, which is generally attributed to bringing a fan or pump under control. So, the start/stop control on the fan/pump is now under control, or the schedule is in place so that the load is no longer flat but responds as a variable load when there is a requirement for that fan or pump. The second area is the amplitude. Note that the amplitude is half the previous month and 60% of the Spring. Since this is October, it should be less than the summer loading for obvious reasons due to lower OAT and solar load. The best time for comparison is the previous shoulder month, at 60% of the Spring loading. This means someone also changed a piece of equipment so that it operates more efficiently.

We reset the base load after changes to the building schedule to establish that line as the new benchmark. Once the facility performance changes, reset the baseline by assessing the numbers at the base of the curves at night and weekends on shoulder months. Then choose a number that kisses the bottom edge of that new curve. That will adjust the base load to the new value. Look at the result shown by the dashed red line in Figure 10.8 and see if it represents the best new baseline fit and reset again if it needs adjusting.

When this performance change is established, reset this as the new baseline for the benchmarking efforts on this building. Measure future progress by this new line.

10.5 Other Building Curves to Benchmark

When we start benchmarking, we must understand how to analyze the diagrams. The interval chart shown in Figure 10.9 indicates how the facility is

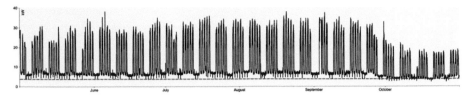

Figure 10.8   Re-baselining after changes.

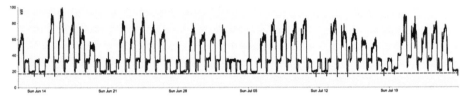

Figure 10.9   Interval showing external lighting load.

used when it is used, what equipment loads impact the usage, and the ratio of those loads to the other loads.

Let us look at how different graphs indicate various issues with a facility. How do we benchmark this facility in Figure 10.9? First, let us state what we know about the building. This is an administrative building. We can see it is a one-shift operation, five days a week. But we see it has a more difficult curve to interpret than those shown previously. It appears to plateau at the beginning and end of each day. It then drops to the baseline but on weekends.

This analysis is easier by showing data during the longest days of the summer. With the longer days, there is a distinct plateau, and then the usage drops back down to the baseline for a brief period of 15 minutes to an hour in the morning, and then it jumps up for the day. Then it drops down at the end of the office day for 30 minutes to an hour and then back up with roughly a 15-kW jump in load. There may be a need to look at a specific point or magnify the area to analyze the specific times better. Many software systems allow us to hover the pointer over a data point where a peak starts and at the end of that peak to get a date/time stamp, and magnitude. Some systems have to enlarge the diagram and superimpose a line that depicts the date/time stamp and the usage. We have enlarged the above interval chart to give us a better look at the times, as shown in Figure 10.10.

In this case, it is easy to see that the plateau load comes on at 8:00 PM and goes off at 6:00 AM. Once we have zoomed in, note that it is a 14-kW load. What might cause this load throughout the night on a one-shift operating building? Since we look at this in the summer, it is easier to determine the

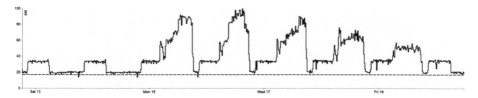

Figure 10.10 One week showing external lighting.

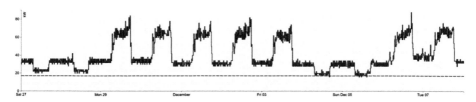

Figure 10.11 Winter plot showing the external lighting.

source because the longer daylight hours allow the kW loading to go down before the building starts up in the morning. At night, the occupants leave before the load begins; so we recognize that it is tied to lighting systems that come on at sunset and turn off at sunrise. These are perimeter and parking lights around the facility. It is easy to see the perimeter lighting load turn off before work starts in summer, making it easier to determine the source vs. analyzing this graph in the winter. In the winter, there is no gap between the lighting load and the normal loading for the facility when people start to work when it is still dark, which makes differentiating the various systems difficult. To visualize this, analyze an interval chart of the same facility in the winter in Figure 10.11. Because of shorter daylight hours, there is no drop in usage from the lights going off and the building coming on, giving us a double-tiered load. We can see the difference on the weekend, with the square-topped peak on Saturday night dropping to base load in the daytime. None of these plateaus affect the baseline, but they certainly make the analysis interesting.

When we scroll in (magnify), we can see a 14-kW load going off at 7:00 AM on the weekend and coming back on at 5:00 PM. That is why the night loads do not go back to baseline. So, the real baseline is only visible on weekends due to the shortness of daylight hours.

Confirm these assumptions in the daily comparison chart shown in Figure 10.12. In the daily comparison chart, MMS overlays the usage by hour for seven days. See the dip when people go home. Then the lights come back on at dusk. Here the lights stay on till people come in for work. This is also evident on weekends when there is an elevated usage all night, and it

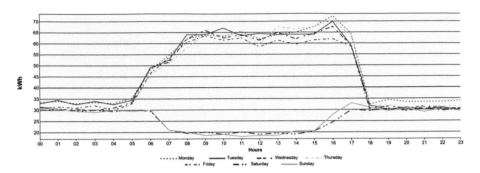

Figure 10.12   Daily usage overlay with external lighting.

drops lower. This chart also helps visualize the usage patterns to determine each system's loading and timing.

Let us review a childcare center as another good example to benchmark. The following graph, Figure 10.13, has several things to learn. First, we can see the symmetric pattern formed for the five weekdays. They then drop down to a weekend and stay close to the baseline. It is important to note here, and if we look back at the previous graphs, that the nights and weekends do not stay at the base load. That is because some equipment is cycling on at night and on weekends. The usual culprit is the AC and fan/pump system(s) left on in the summertime. We will discuss that in Chapter 14, "Understanding and Troubleshooting System Overrides." So, when there is higher OAT at night, a higher weekend temperature, or sufficient solar load, the system will cycle to maintain the set point in the space.

The most important anomaly to understand is the activity around the base load. As shown, it indicates a base load at two different levels. Generally, we would expect a flat or nearly flat base load. Here we see a base load and a secondary base load. This is a clear indicator that two separate schedules affect different equipment pieces. In other words, the main set of equipment is driven by one schedule, while a single piece of equipment is on a different schedule. This generally leads to an expectation of a situation like the perimeter lights discussed previously. This type of usage requires some equipment that follows a different schedule. Our analysis shows that a piece of equipment comes on at night starting at the end of June in Figure 10.13. In May, the base load goes down to the predetermined base load. Then it stops going that low. Something is adding to the base load at night.

When we magnify the usage, as shown in Figure 10.14, there is a distinct ramp down during office hours. It is easier to view on the weekends, where the system goes off at 9:00 AM and comes back on at 9:00 PM. After

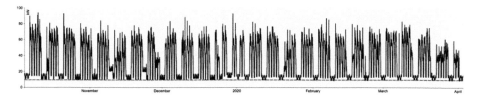

Figure 10.13   Load that is out of the time schedule.

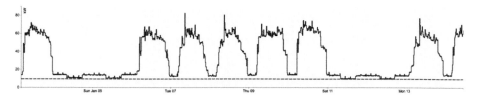

Figure 10.14   Weekly plot of time schedule issues.

the last example, one might think this resembles the perimeter lights example previously but with an odd schedule. Bad schedules happen often; so never assume things are correct until we validate the times. The chart also indicates the size, which is 3–4 kW. Zoom in closer if needed to determine the equipment size. This view was sufficient to determine that it must be the supply fan, as this building had no pumps or other equipment.

Notice the 4-kW drop more clearly on the daily comparison overlay in Figure 10.15, the cycling of a piece of equipment every night and on weekends. See the graph below to get a sense of the synchronization of the equipment. So, what can it be? The only system not on the enterprise management system (EMS) for this building is a supply fan for ventilation. It has a standalone timer. The exhaust fan is smaller and only in the restrooms; therefore, it is not the problem in this case. We surmised this supply fan timer was probably set for PM vs. AM, as we can see it is roughly 12 hours off cycle. Another option may be that any loss of electric power moved the schedule gradually until it is 12 hours off, giving us the pattern shown below. Also, the fan size is clear as it goes from 11.5 up to 14 kW load on the system. The maintenance folks confirmed that the supply fan was 2.5 kW.

Here is another example of what end-use patterns benchmarking will help identify. In Figure 10.16, we identified usage spikes during the day. As shown on the graph, there is a spike that is about 40 kW higher that only occurs in a 15-minute interval. So, the spike comes on and adds 40 kW during a 15-minute interval and then is satisfied. This recurs on many occasions. We checked to see what system on the building has that large of a load and found

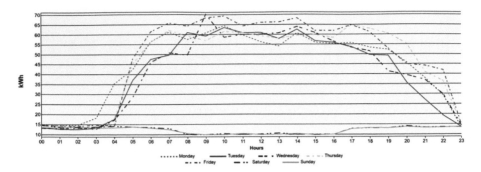

Figure 10.15   Weekly overlay with time schedule issues.

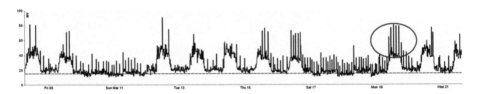

Figure 10.16   AC short cycling.

out that there is not a piece of equipment equal to 40 kW. However, the maintenance crew determined that there were two large AC units – each equaling half (20 kW each) of that calculated load. The investigation found that the AC units were set up to come on at the same return water temperature. This led to both units coming on simultaneously, quickly satisfying the loading requirements and then turning off, thus creating a short cycling of the AC units. This was discovered to be a problem at most buildings across most of the campus. The short cycling will cause an earlier failure in equipment and could impact the bill's demand cost if many units concurrently come on at the same 15-minute time interval around the campus.

10.6 Summary

So, let us review the basics of our analysis on benchmarking:

- The base load is the cornerstone for determining the other loads on the facility.

- When we validate that this is a real baseline of the base load, it shows what energy remains for the other energy systems. Those systems will be broken down and modeled in detail in the next three chapters.

- This chapter covered initial discussions on the base load and introduced the plug load portion.

- In addition to the base load being the main building block, it also gives us a critical point to baseline our system so that we might determine if equipment schedules are working or working properly. As we will show in future chapters, this single issue is the largest impact on energy usage concerning the ROI of any ECM.

- In other words, fixing or adding a schedule to the distribution system is the biggest low-cost/no-cost measure we can implement. This will most likely surpass any other ECM savings and the ROI.

References

[1] Guide to Energy Management eighth edition, B Capehart, W Turner, W. Kennedy, River Publishers, p 710, 2020

[2] Energy Management Handbook, ninth edition, S Roosa, Steve Doty, Wayne Turner, River Publishing, p 352, 2020

[3] Energy Independence and Security Act of 2007, Section 432 (EISA 432)

[4] Zachary Hart, The Benefits of Building Performance, Institute for Market Transformation Dec 2015 p 6,

[5] Energy Information Administration - Wikipedia 2 Aug 2022

[6] Granderson, J, Piette, MA, Rosenblum, B, Hu, L et al. 2011 Energy Information Handbook: Applications for Energy-Efficient Building Operations. Lawrence Berkeley National Laboratory, LBNL-5272E, p 9

[7] Energy Management Handbook, ninth edition, S Roosa, Steve Doty, Wayne Turner, River Publishing, p 28, 2020

[8] Section 432 of the Energy Independence and Security Act of 2007 (EISA 432)

[9] Bynum, J., Claridge, D. E., Ph.D., P.E., Turner, W. D., Ph.D., P.E., Deng, S., P.E., & Wei, G., P.E. (2008, October 20–22). The Cost-Effectiveness of Continuous Commissioning® Over the Past Ten Years. Texas A&M University Libraries. https://oaktrust.library. tamu.edu/bitstream/handle/1969.1/90812/ESL-IC-08-10-44. pdf?sequence=1&isAllowed=y

[10] (n.d.). Commercial Buildings Energy Consumption Survey (CBECS) Table E2. Major fuel consumption intensities (Btu) by end use, 2012. U.S. Energy Information Administration. https://www.eia.gov/ consumption/commercial/data/2012/c&e/cfm/e2.php

[11] (n.d.). Commercial Buildings Energy Consumption Survey (CBECS) Table E6. Electricity consumption intensities (kWh) by end use,

2012. U.S. Energy Information Administration. https://www.eia.gov/consumption/commercial/data/2012/c&e/cfm/e6.php

[12] (n.d.). Commercial Buildings Energy Consumption Survey (CBECS) Table E6. Electricity consumption intensities (kWh) by end use, 2012. U.S. Energy Information Administration. https://www.eia.gov/consumption/commercial/data/2012/c&e/cfm/e6.php

[13] (n.d.). How Many Amps Does A Refrigerator Use? Refrigerator FAQ. https://refrigeratorfaq.com/how-many-amps-does-a-refrigerator-use/

[14] (n.d.). How Often Should A Refrigerator Cycle On And Off? Explained. Go Improve Home. https://goimprovehome.com/how-often-should-a-refrigerator-cycle-on-and-off-explained/

[15] (n.d.). Plug Loads. U.S. General Services Administration. https://www.gsa.gov/governmentwide-initiatives/federal-highperformance-green-buildings/resource-library/energy-water/plug-loads

[16] (2013, May 20). Plug Load Research Review Summary. U.S. General Services Administration. https://www.gsa.gov/system/files/Plug_Load_Research_Review_Summary_PDF.pdf

[17] Desroches, L., Fuchs, H., Greenblatt, J. B., Pratt, S., Willem, H., Claybaugh, E., Beraki, B., Nagaraju, M., Price, S. K., & Young, S. J. (2014, December 1). Computer usage and national energy consumption: Results from a field-metering study. Berkeley Lab. https://eta-publications.lbl.gov/sites/default/files/computers_lbnl_report_v4.pdf

[18] (n.d.). Plug Load Frequently Asked Questions (FAQ). U.S. General Services Administration. https://www.gsa.gov/governmentwide-initiatives/federal-highperformance-green-buildings/resource-library/energy-water/plug-loads/plug-load-faq

[19] (n.d.). Plug Load Frequently Asked Questions (FAQ). U.S. General Services Administration. https://www.gsa.gov/governmentwide-initiatives/federal-highperformance-green-buildings/resource-library/energy-water/plug-loads/plug-load-faq

11

Second-level Benchmarking
(Base Load with Plug Load)

Abstract

This chapter takes benchmarking to the next level, breaking down the base load into plug and other loads and introducing other types of benchmarks. This chapter will detail the amount of loading for the various components of the plug load. It will also discuss the range of the plug load and the various factors that affect that difference. Then we will show that the remaining loading after subtracting the plug load is the fan/pump systems. This will be covered with the overall impact of that loading on savings. Finally, we will transition to introducing other available benchmarking factors to help the user analyze his facility and systems.

11   Second-level Benchmarking

This chapter will continue the concept regarding the importance of breaking down the base load into all its components. We will address the following topics:

- Visualizing potential savings from graphs

- Analyzing the plug load baseline

- Base load minus the plug load (remaining fan/pump systems)

- Comparing differences between base load and non-office hour potential savings

- Introduce a metric to make comparisons in base load

11.1 Visualizing Potential Savings from Graphs

In this chapter, we will continue the analysis of the base load and find out how to use this understanding to determine energy savings associated with

137

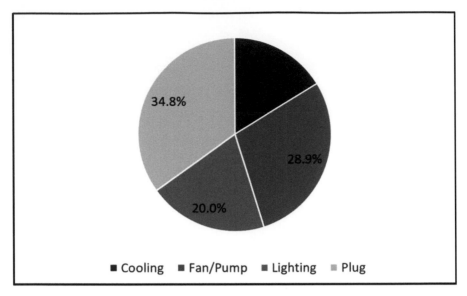

Figure 11.1   Four major components of usage.

the base load and the non-office loading. To help visualize these, we will break down the base load into the plug and other loads and indicate all the components of those two areas and their metrics. As we recall, if everything is balanced, the breakdown of the systems will be close to the percentages shown in Figure 11.1. We will demonstrate how that has evolved over the last 20 years and how it should be adjusted to account for the type of building and the systems included.

As systems get out of balance, the first factor we want to evaluate is the control systems' impact on the energy in these four major systems. The analysis in this chapter will show if there is excess use in either the base load or the non-office hours.

So, let us break this down. There are two areas on the graph where we can understand the savings potential. In Figure 11.2, there is an interval chart that shows the base load and the usage that occurs during non-office hours; so we can identify the two areas with the potential for savings. The first area is the excess usage that is in the base load. The second area is the usage during non-office hours at night and on weekends.

When we look at Figure 11.2, we see there are two areas highlighted. The first on the bottom left is the base load. The base load contains the plug loads, which we will analyze in detail, and the fan/pump systems are left on constantly at all hours. The second set of circled data on the figure indicates

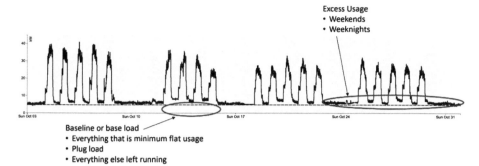

Figure 11.2 Interval kW graph showing two areas of potential savings.

that the usage during nights and weekends oscillating up and down slightly above the baseline is potential savings if we can get the equipment schedule under control. Both areas have a large potential for savings if we can reduce them to the maximum extent possible. Our goal in this chapter is to identify the excess portions attached to the base load and determine what additional non-office hours loading can be reduced.

The graph in Figure 11.3 is a different depiction of the information in Figure 11.2 that indicates the two parts of the usage under the base load. As discussed, this base load comprises a plug and other constant loads.

These "other loads" are the loading that comes from all equipment that runs constantly at night and on weekends when the occupants are not in the building. The nights and weekends equate to 2/3 of the hours for a facility. Understanding the plug and base loading is especially important because of all the time it runs (24 × 7), and any changes will significantly impact the building's usage. The only loading that can run constantly that possibly falls into this category of savings impact would be fan/pump systems during this base load. So, any pump that does not vary their draw is or should be on a start/stop control with a schedule. It could also be any constant volume (CV) fan, such as an exhaust fan, supply fan, or a CV system for space conditioning.

The orange points on the graph emphasize the second target of potential savings, the non-office hour loading. While they are not base load savings, they are variable loadings that are in response to the AC system demand. The systems that will respond during this time are fan/pump systems and AC systems running to satisfy a requirement from OAT or solar loading. It might indicate a few appliance loads that cycle. These will only provide a minor input to these non-office hours loading above the base load, as mentioned in Chapter 10.

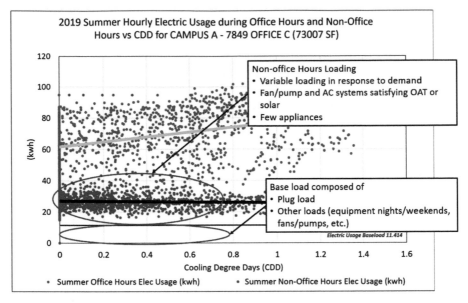

Figure 11.3   Scatter plot graph showing two areas of potential savings.

11.2 Analyzing the Plug Load

Remember from Chapter 10, basic benchmarking (first level) "plug loads" are receptacle loads. The breakdown of the three groups was as follows:

● Computers – 66%

● Office equipment – 17%

● Desk lights, desk equipment, coffee makers, etc. – 17% [1]

Computer loading can break down into several pieces of equipment. The primary ones are desktop computers or central processing unit (CPU) towers, monitors, and laptops. Plug load usage in buildings increased until around 2010. The computer portion, which is the majority, has dropped energy usage by 23% for desktops and 44% for laptops in the last 10 years [2]. Moving to docking stations will further reduce that load and appears to be finally making a difference by reversing the usage trend for the plug load in the other direction. Government energy standards are also leading to reduction by driving down the usage of computers and equipment. Laptops are 94% more effective than desktops based on unit energy consumption (UEC) in the Leidos/Guidehouse study [2]. The reason was discussed in Chapter 10, but we need to realize that this is a major impact, as we will demonstrate later in the overall loading on the building. So, while we are seeing some progress, the long-term projection is for desktop computers to reduce energy consumption by 76%, while laptops will be down by 67% by 2050 over usage in 2012 [2].

The second group is office equipment, including printers, fax machines, copiers, etc. The final group is desk equipment, which includes all the parasitic loads on our desks. Items include clocks, desk lights, appliances, emergency lights, coffee makers, etc.

There have been several studies that break this down. The studies primarily focus on the relationship between the various systems. We will reference these relationships as we address each system over the next few chapters.

A study summary (shown in Table 11.1) that included California surveys and EIA from 20 years ago revealed a range of 2.4–5.9 kWh/sf/yr for miscellaneous loading. The surveys are:

1. CEUS 1997. Commercial End-Use Survey, Pacific Gas & Electric Company (CEUS 2000) [3]

2. CEUS 1999. Commercial End-Use Survey, Pacific Gas & Electric Company. (CEUS (2002) [4]

3. NRNC 1999. Nonresidential New Construction Baseline Study, prepared by RLW Analytics for Southern California Edison (NRNC 1999) [5]

4. Buildings Energy Data Book, 2002. U.S. Department of Energy, Office of Energy Efficiency and Renewable Energy (EIA CBECS 2002) [6]

The overall loading is an average of 15.2 kWh/sf/yr, as shown in Table 11.1, which is much higher than most facilities we analyze today. As we assess all the loads, a major portion may be the miscellaneous load. This will be addressed in more detail as we view other studies and compare these, but we must adjust this plug load lower according to today's real numbers to establish a benchmark.

The Commercial Buildings Energy Consumption Survey (CBECS) is a survey of thousands of buildings run by the Department of Energy to provide information for benchmarking. If we look at the current CBECS from the EIA for 2012 (Table 11.2), we will see that plug loads can range from 2.1 to 3.8 kWh/sf/yr. The most telling difference between all buildings and office buildings is the computer loading. If we add the kitchen equipment (cooking and refrigeration), we have loading that is 4.6 kWh for the office or 34% of the total usage of the building. Note that this report is 10 years later than the previous set of studies, and the total load has been reduced from 15.2 to

Table 11.1   Study summaries of loading.

	CEUS [3]	CEUS [4]	NRNC [5]	CBECS Bldgs. Energy Data Book [6]	Average for All Data Sources	% Of Total Load
	1997	1999	1999	2002	Avg.	
Fans (kWh/ft²/yr)	4	1.5	2.4	1.5	2.4	15.50%
Cooling (kWh/ft²/yr)	3.2	4.5	2.9	2.7	3.3	21.90%
Heating (kWh/ft²/yr)	N/A	N/A	0.4	N/A	0.4	2.60%
Lighting (kWh/ft²/yr)	4.6	3.7	4	8.2	5.1	33.80%
Misc. (kWh/ft²/yr)	2.4	3.1	5.6	5.9	4.3	28.10%
Total Electricity (kWh/ft2/yr)	14.2	12.7	15.3	18.4	15.2	
HVAC % Of Total Electricity	51.00%	47.00%	37.00%	23.00%	39.50%	
Fans % Of HVAC Electricity	56.00%	25.00%	45.00%	36.00%	40.50%	

13.45 kWh/sf/yr, or a reduction of 12%. It is hard to show a correlation over time as each study has different parameters or those parameters changed over time. We have elected to look at averages and, where that is not available, then analyze the total CBECS vs. the office CBECS. The reason is that the CBECS individual numbers do not equal their totals; so there is some interpolation regardless of the factors. So, we found a range of the data in 2002 and a range in 2012 with individual numbers between various categories having some span. We must find a good midpoint to lessen the impact when applying these targets to benchmark any extreme building. To do that, we decided to summarize our buildings' experience to establish a representative set of benchmarks and draw a conclusion from the first two datasets.

We surveyed 7000+ buildings over the last four years and found the usage numbers in Table 11.3. As we can see, the total usage is lower, indicating that some aspects have been gradually falling over the last 20 years,

Table 11.2   CBECS with focus on plug loads [7].

Computing	Plug (Other Loads)	kitchen plug	Plug plus kitchen
1.5	2.1	3.8	5.9
11.20%	15.70%	28.30%	44.00%
3.1	3.8	0.8	4.6
23.00%	28.10%	5.90%	34.00%

Table 11.3   Summary of author surveys.

Two Approaches	kWh/sf/yr
Median for All Campus Buildings that met data cleaning criteria	9.7
Median for all Campus Categories that met data cleaning criteria	10.7

regardless of the data source. Our median for all buildings was 9.7 kWh/sf/yr. Putting all the buildings into groupings by facility usage and then taking a median of the groups gives us a benchmark for categories or facility category types of 10.7 kWh/sf/yr. across all those various categories.

So how do we determine the change in the breakdown of usage shown earlier from 13.4 to 9.7 kWh/sf/yr? Table 11.4 shows the categories that seem to be reduced or eliminated today in the categories we should adjust. This brings the plug down to 1.2 kWh/sf/yr for all buildings and to 1.3 kWh/sf/yr for office buildings. If we concentrate on buildings without the refrigeration load, we have a close pattern of buildings with the major additional load associated with the desktop computers. Note that we have pulled out all the kitchen-related cooking and refrigeration, as we will only add this when evaluating those category types.

Table 11.4   Modified loading calculations with adjusted computer and without kitchen [7].

	Total	Cooling	Ventilation	Water Heating	Lighting	Office Equipment	Computing	New Total	Revised Plug	Revised Total
Plug All Bldgs.	13.4	2.4	2.4	0.2	2.5	0.6	1.5	9.6	1.2	8.7
Usage % All Bldgs.		17.90%	17.90%	1.50%	18.70%	4.50%	11.20%			
Plug Office	13.5	2.2	3.9	0.1	2.7	0.7	3.1	12.7	1.3	10.2
Usage % Office		16.30%	28.90%	0.70%	20.00%	5.20%	23.00%			

Table 11.5   EIA study of desktop intensities [2].

Desktop computers include computer tower units and integrated desktop/monitor units.							
Power draw (w)	2012	2015	2018	2020	2030	2040	2050
High-Active	87	82	74	68	46	31	21
Idle-Short	61	57	52	48	32	22	15
Idle-Long	58	53	48	44	30	20	14
Sleep	3.5	2.2	2.7	2.3	1.1	0.5	0.5
Off	1.6	1	0.3	0.3	0.3	0.3	0.3
	211.1	195.2	177	162.6	109.4	73.8	50.8
Reduction year over year		92.5%	90.7%	91.9%	67.3%	67.5%	68.8%
Reduction 2012 to 2020				77.0%			

This was because we reset the impact of the computer load on the overall loading from the older studies, which brings the overall number into range as the computer load has decreased drastically over the last 20 years, as noted in the EIA Leidos/Guidehouse study [2]. This load will continue to go down per their projections in Table 11.5. We will extrapolate the computer load based on data found in the recent PNNL study details that follow to match the plug load to the totals we are witnessing today. Table 11.5 shows that the desktop draw was reduced by 23% of the load 10 years ago.

EIA also did the same analysis on laptops and noted a 44% reduction in energy in the last 10 years, as per Table 11.6.

The Pacific Northwest National Laboratory (PNNL) did a study that went into detailed measurement of plug loads for five different types of

Table 11.6 EIA study of laptop intensities [2].

COMMERCIAL LAPTOP PCS							
Power draw (w)	2012	2015	2018	2020	2030	2040	2050
High-Active	30	19	18	17	14	11	9.2
Idle-Short	16	9.8	9.4	9	7.2	5.8	4.7
Idle-Long	14	8.5	8	7.6	6.1	4.9	4
Sleep	1	0.8	0.7	0.6	0.5	0.4	0.4
Off	0.5	0.3	0.3	0.3	0.3	0.3	0.3
	61.5	38.4	36.4	34.5	28.1	22.4	18.6
Reduction year over year		62.4%	94.8%	94.8%	81.4%	79.7%	83.0%
Reduction 2012 to 2020				56.1%			

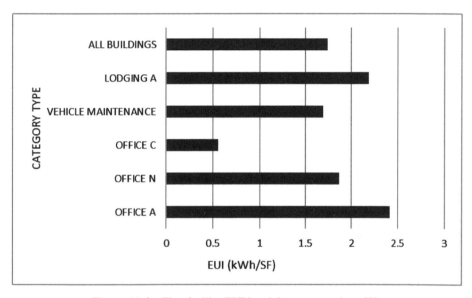

Figure 11.4 Five-facility EUI breakdown comparison [8].

facilities. We can see the different usage breakdowns for each building in Figure 11.4. If we look at their study, the range goes from 0.560 to 2.410 kWh/sf/yr for the plug load. The basic office building (Office A) was higher (around 1 kWh/sf/yr) due to all the personnel's computer equipment being a desktop or tower, with the added disadvantage of that equipment not being programmed to go into sleep or disconnect mode. The lodging building or housing for single members. It will resemble an apartment load from an hours and usage perspective and will be higher than a single-shift administrative space. The main difference for the other spaces primarily hinges on the type of computers or if they have data closets. The Office N building has data center closets of around 0.6 kWh/sf/yr for the computers. The Office C building is around 0.2 kWh/sf/yr for computers. Those are a smaller percentage of the buildings and do not represent a normal single-shift building. The study only focused on the five buildings, and so we must adjust our thoughts based on the issues not present in the normal single-shift buildings. PNNL demonstrated that the average of these five buildings was 1.74 kWh/sf/yr. We recognize that the major variable in the list is the computer. We decided to take the mid-point between the extremes for the computer line item or 0.6 kWh/sf/yr, as this will keep us at the best average for any building, and we can always adjust this factor when benchmarking those facilities that have data closets or many desktops. This brings us to settle on using an overall plug load value of around 1.3 kWh/sf/yr, which has proven to be a good fit in balancing against the other systems where we have data on the other systems.

Earlier, we indicated that the above plug range should be between 0.56 and 1.74 kWh/sf/yr. The upper end of this range is driven mostly by the high usage of desktop computers, and we have seen those drop due to switching to laptops for remote work during COVID. The range of the plug load related to affecting the overall usage ratio will be minor. PNNL also noted that the desktops added a major loading for plug load in their study, plus the policy of leaving them on at night for updates added a tremendous increase over the expected plug.

We center our analysis on this 1.3 kWh/sf/yr median for all buildings as this seems to represent the best approach for each building. The variance from that median for each category type will determine how to adjust the plug load. We will focus our analysis on this median for all buildings from Table 11.4, as supported by our surveys, and include the mix derived from this same table. This represents the best approach for cach building. The plug estimate must be adjusted accordingly, as we have buildings with additional computers and kitchen activities. This can be determined by the base load benchmark discussed in Chapter 17. We will demonstrate the impact of the variance related to all systems as we analyze the other systems and summarize this overall impact in Appendix 3. This will give us a higher degree of confidence in the ability of the scatter plot model to predict the usage in each energy system for every category type. It will enable us to see how much the distinct system types will impact the overall usage numbers and the impact of using an average value.

Table 11.7 Plug load savings measures most pertinent to the general population [8].

	Savings Measure	Savings (%)
1	Implement Sustainable Computer Policy: Power Systems Down Each Night	46%
2	Improve Power Save Settings: Large Copy Print Devices	47%
3	Refrigerators: Replace 20+ Year Old Units with New Energy Star Models	39%
4	Computer Purchase Policy: Purchase Laptop PCs over Desktops + Uninterruptible Power Sources/Supply (UPS)	46%

We will cover a couple of suggestions for energy savings opportunities for plug loads. Many solutions include the installation of sensing strips; the following two types were analyzed in a study that produced the following savings as a percentage of total office plug loads:

- Savings sensor strip average savings is 27.19%.

- Load sensing strip average savings is 27.77% [9].

A recent report published by PNNL identified 10 different savings measures. Of those 10, the savings measures that are the most pertinent to the general population as seen in Table 11.7 above [8].

Plug loads must be understood in terms of the real impact of how much is used for the two time periods. The first time period is the constant plug load, which is the usage when everyone is gone, and that minimum plug load runs 24 hours/day for seven days a week. This is evaluated as watts/sf. This load in watts/sf parameter is required to objectively compare the other loads in the base load. To determine this, we know the office hours have an intensity of over two times based on NREL study graphs ranging from two to six times; so we took a midpoint position on this also, as most seem to be in this range for the non-office hours loading [10]. So, distribute the loading between the constant plug load (included within the base load) and the plug load that increases during office hours. So, adjusting the loading as discussed gives us the breakdown based on the hours used, as indicated in Table 11.8. We estimate the amount it would average during office hours.

So full-time plug load demand is roughly 41% of the office load in watts/sf, calculated from Table 11.8. The combined design total breaks down

Table 11.8   Breakdown of load on plug.

	kWh/sf/yr	Watts/Adjusted sf
Plug 24/7 Loading	0.785	0.0896
Office Additional Loading	0.5067	0.2159
Combined Design	1.2917	0.1475

to 0.785 kWh/sf/yr for plug load base vs. 0.506 kWh/sf/yr for office loading – or an average draw of 0.0896 for plug load base vs. 0.2159 watts/sf for office. It is critical in the breakdown of loading to be as close as possible to the plug, as this load is part of the equation for determining the lighting load. As derived above, this 1.3 kWh/sf/yr for plug loading works well in showing a balance to the equation against lighting that will be covered in Chapter 12, "Third-level Benchmarking (Lighting Systems)."

So, breaking down the load on the plug based on usage over a year in kWh/sf and based on the actual load in the average draw of watts/adjusted sf is indicated in Table 11.8.

Remember, the plug loading will continue to decrease, as noted previously. This is primarily due to the increased efficiency in all phases of the use of computers over the next 30 years.

11.3 Base Load minus the Plug Load (Remaining Fan/Pump Systems)

So, what other items in the base load are not pure plug loads? We discussed that the pure plug load is a constant receptacle load that runs during non-office hours. The remaining portion of the base load can only be a constant load from "other" equipment or systems.

Let us discuss this "other" equipment, which essentially falls into four categories:

- Fan/pump systems that have a schedule for operations but a constant load because the schedule is not working properly. This fan/pump loading type will have a constant load component and may be a variable component.

- Equipment left on that is normally in a traditional start/stop control that does not have a schedule or the schedule has been overridden.

- Equipment that never had a start/stop control.

- Equipment that is constantly running due to problems with maintenance.

What is the impact of this first category? The only loading that can occur during this time that is not variable is a fan/pump system that is constantly running. That limits the systems that can be analyzed as running during this time. The following systems will fall into this category:

- Constant volume (CV) air-handling system (AHS) with an overridden schedule will provide a full fan load within the base load.

- Variable air volume (VAV) systems, where the system is overridden, provide a constant consumption based on minimum box settings.

  - Generally, minimum airflow is designed at 30% for the terminal distribution boxes [11]. Some designers have been discussing going to lower minimums (10%) [12], but this may have been reversed with COVID.

  - The 30% minimum set points in the boxes for flow will require 40%–50% electric energy to maintain that flow, depending on the type of fan [13].

- Rooftops, splits, etc., respond to the space requirements by operating in either an on or off mode so that they will not impact the base load.

The second group is equipment left on that will be grouped into categories such as equipment with no controls and only a start/stop type switch. This includes items such as:

- Wall-mounted fan coils. These are usually push-button panels set by each office at low, medium, or high fan speeds and generally left on 24 × 7. These are difficult to control economically unless we install a control in the breaker – if all the fan coils are on the same circuit. Another option is controls in each office, but validating the economics when it is a retrofit is difficult. Otherwise, we must influence the behavior of the occupants, which is a different set of challenges.

- The start/stop equipment may vary between seasons. This is one case where we may have two different base loads between summer and winter if they run different equipment due to the seasonal requirements. See Figure 11.5, which shows two distinct base loads. We do not see this very often.

- A circulating pump that circulates hot or chilled water throughout the building with air handlers mounted in/on the wall, roof, mechanical room, or ceiling. These may have enterprise control; so if controlled, these need

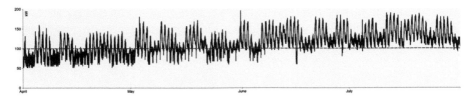

Figure 11.5   Example of a system that has two base loads.

to put the start/stop on schedule. If localized control, then we need to evaluate the economics of an ECM to tie the controller to the EMS.

- Supply air or outdoor air makeup fans will be part of the base load if they do not have a schedule or controller or if they are on an enterprise-level controlled start/stop that is not scheduled, not controlled, or bypassed.

- Exhaust air fans that operate continuously.

- There are several pumping systems that, in many cases, do not have a start/stop schedule:

  ○ Secondary geothermal pumps with a start/stop switch running without a schedule.

  ○ Tertiary pumps from a chiller/high-temperature hot water (HTHW) plant with a start/stop switch or controls without schedules.

  ○ Pumps for chilled water systems where the chiller is in a different building or plant.

As we can see, various loads can be included in the base load. Let us break this down better. The base load would comprise our plug load, the minimum fan loads, and any pump loads. Since the fan and pumps may be on schedules, then the override of that schedule or lack of a schedule creates an elevated or false base load, which is a large potential savings opportunity for us and should be reduced as a no-cost/low-cost energy measure.

We can evaluate the base load in winter and summer to determine if it is similar. Usually, this will not vary, but on rare occasions, we have equipment that only runs during one season, such as a cooling tower, and the pumps or fans may not vary or have a flat portion of their load without a schedule. In those cases, we can validate the real base load against both shoulder periods to ensure we do not have additional loading on the building. A shoulder period is defined as a time in Fall or Spring when heating or cooling is not required

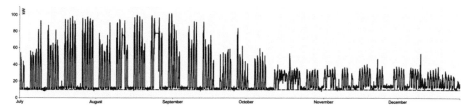

Figure 11.6   Example of a system that has two different amplitudes.

in the space. Generally, this means the system is eligible and can come on but does not engage because there is no driving weather requirement. All of these are contingent on knowing we do not have any system controls over-ridden. Overridden will be defined in detail in Chapter 14, "Understanding and Troubleshooting System Overrides," but for now, it means the system is running when it could – and should – be off.

As we can see from Figure 11.6, the interval graph will demonstrate different usage levels based on the year's various seasons. Spring and Fall of each year will generally have the lowest amplitude. This is because the HVAC units should mostly serve people and solar loads in those shoulder months when the outside air temperature is milder. The peak amplitude is naturally higher if the external loading from OAT and solar loading is much higher than occupant loading.

Based on the OAT and solar loading, we will have higher loading in the summer. If we only have one cooling system, we will see the individual stages of the chiller increase usage as the sun and/or temperature increase during the day. As we add more systems, these stages will tend to smooth out, causing the curve to blend into a smoother sine wave pattern.

We will walk through a series of charts to understand the value of the various inputs. The first is Figure 11.7, where the base load comprises the plug load and everything else is left on constantly. That "everything else" category can only be fan/pump systems to sustain a flat constant load. Only fan/pump systems can provide this type of constant load, identified in this instance as a potential savings opportunity. The opportunity is there if we can economically control those loads during this time by one of several means:

- If the loads are under an enterprise control system, then set up the schedule or set the time correctly.

- If under local control, then add them to the enterprise system.

- If not economical to add, then work out a process with the building manager to control those loads.

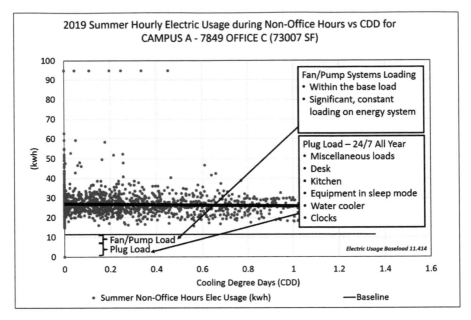

Figure 11.7   Breakdown of the base load.

Figure 11.7 focuses on the fan/pump systems loading within the base load. There is a significant loading there that is a constant loading on the energy system. It is easier to see this energy when we pull out the office hours from the data. Figure 11.8 focuses on the orange points representing the non-office hour's usage. These points signify a potential savings opportunity for the non-office hours loading, including energy usage from fan/pump systems and associated AC systems. These points represent the usage that responds to satisfy the requirements driven by the OAT and solar loading on the facility on nights and weekends. This is a positive slope indicating there is a correlation to OAT rising. This is a clear indicator of a system that is left on, and the AC system is coming on in response to OAT or to a solar load that increases the indoor temperature past the set point.

Figure 11.9 demonstrates the breakdown of that same non-office loading for the winter. In the winter, we must heat the building when the temperature drops below 45°F. This is based on setting the space temperature back to 55°F. Usually, we plan for a differential between the space temperature and the OAT of 10°F before the space temperature drops below 55°F. The line on the chart indicates that point when the energy on the right of the line is less than the 45°F required to sustain the space temperature at 55°F. The energy on the left side of the line can be potentially saved if the control schedule is set properly.

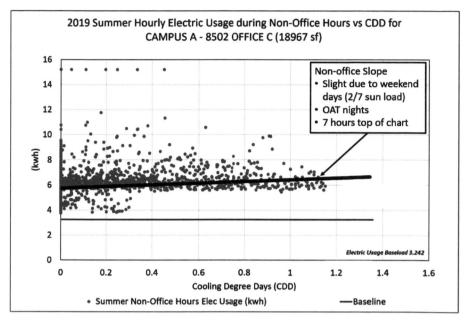

Figure 11.8   Non-office hour variable loading showing correlation to OAT.

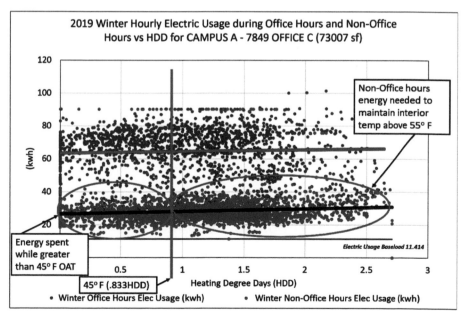

Figure 11.9   Non-office winter hour usage with temperature line for when the system is required to sustain space temperature.

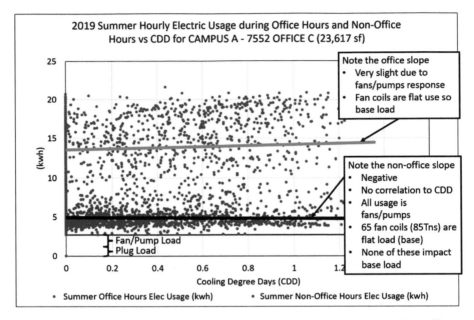

Figure 11.10   Building on chiller plant showing no correlation to temperature but still running during non-office hours.

Figure 11.10 is a different look with a building that relies on a chiller plant (and, therefore, the chiller consumption is not included in the data). So, we notice that the summer load does not respond to the OAT in the slope indicated on the chart, as there is no correlation to the increase in CDD. The blue points for office hours show when the fans are drawing power to satisfy the space temperature and any other variances in office loads. The non-office hours' points above the base load demonstrate some usage that needs to be evaluated to see what can be done to reduce those systems that operate during those non-office hours.

11.4 Comparing Differences Between Base Load and Non-Office Hour Potential Savings

There are two prime targets where we recognize the potential for energy savings. Both groupings must be addressed to get an understanding of savings possibilities. The first target is the additional energy the base load uses above the plug load. This covers the air handling systems and pumps that run constantly. This magnitude is quite large in some cases, but it is the first place to examine where excess energy should be calculated. Some other metrics

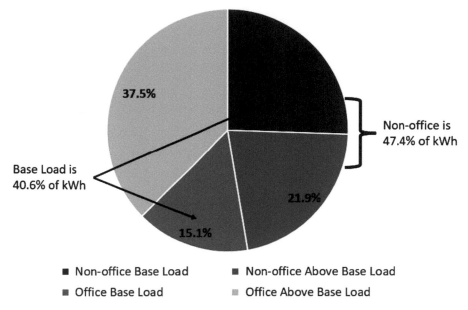

Figure 11.11   Breakdown of base load vs. non-office load.

will identify the exact savings for the excess energy in the base load. Those metrics will be discussed briefly in the next few pages, and then we will get into further details in Chapter 17.

The other potential energy savings opportunity is variable energy usage during non-office hours. The amount of energy spent in non-office time is quite extensive. We can see a comparison of the two in Figure 11.11. As we can see, the base load is slightly over 40% of the usage. We will assume a reasonable 12% target for the plug load. That means that 28% or more of the energy is spent on the fan/pump systems running constantly, which are potential savings. Then the non-office hours depict greater usage than 47%. So, the target plug load plus requirements to cover winter requirements below 45°F leaves a result of 20% energy usage required in non-office hours, leaving 27% of potential savings during non-office hours.

So, what is the difference between the non-office loading over the base load? Let us look at where they come from and how they are calculated. The base load includes all plug loads plus whatever systems are left on otherwise. So, the plug includes some energy usage that is during office hours.

So, the base load includes plug loads and fan/pump systems required for sustaining the facility. This means we can calculate potential energy excesses in two steps. The first is to subtract out the office base load because the system must be on during that time; so it does not matter what the mix is between the plug and the other equipment. So, the best way to calculate this is to take the total base load of 40.6% and subtract the office base load of 15.1%. The remainder is 25.5% of the base load during non-office hours. That is shown as follows:

40.6% total base load − 15.1% for the office hours base load = 25.5% time is the non-office hours base load usage.

That means we now have 25.5% of the energy used during non-office hours, but part of that is the required plug load. We have found that the plug load is 5.25% (from Table 11.9), which must be subtracted from the base load; so 25.5% minus the 5.25% for that required plug load would leave 20.25% of potential savings in the base load.

25.50% non-office baseload − 5.25% of office hours plug energy = 20.25% energy potential savings.

This is the potential savings for systems that are on constantly with their energy calculated in the base load. This does not add the variable loading above the base load line (during the non-office hour), which is generally a large usage component, as discussed below.

Now let us analyze how we calculate the excess usage from the non-office hours. The normal metrics do not as easily calculate the non-office hours, but we can still calculate them in several ways. The first is to calculate it in the scatter plots. The second is to designate two zones on the usage chart: office hours and non-office hours. Then the usage chart can calculate those values. As depicted in Table 11.9, the values demonstrate the non-office usage at 47.4%. The non-office plug load is 5.25%. That brings us down to potential savings of 42.15%. If we remove the usage when the OAT is below 45°F, we must remove 12.4% for zone 5B for this building. That leaves 29.75% of potential electric energy savings potential. So, if we do the math between the savings for non-office hours (29.75%) minus the savings from the base load calculations (20.25%), the difference is 9.5%. The only place that difference can come from is the non-office hour's energy (21.9%) used above the base load and the energy used below 45°F.

Suppose we subtract the 21.9% minus the 12.4% energy used when OAT is below 45°F results in 9.5%. So, the same number comes from two separate calculations for the savings potential. This helps us to see how we can understand and calculate the savings potential using either formula or approach.

This analysis also shows us that the savings potential for this building can be characterized as roughly two-thirds in base load or constant loading,

Table 11.9   Potential savings from non-office hours usage.

		% Of Total Annual kWh Consumed
Total Annual kWh (2019)	**729,796.03**	
Non-Office kWh	345,825.03	47.4%
Winter Non-Office Hour Plug Load	22,222.63	
Summer Non-Office Hour Plug Load	15,915.93	
Total Plug for Year	38,138.56	5.2%
Potential Savings (Non-Office minus Plug Load)	**307,686.47**	**42.2%**
Energy Used to Keep Space Above 45°F	90,263.04	12.4%
Final Potential Savings	**217,423.43**	**29.8%**

with the remaining one-third as the variable load for equipment above the base load. This variable load is all the orange points shown previously that were non-office hours above the base load. This will decrease to zero as we reset the controls to set back to 55°F vs. the current setting in this example of 70°F.

These major savings loads must be addressed before we move to other ECMs. We often see projects as sexy and try to generate projects without addressing these core issues. This is a major shortfall in our understanding and approach to energy management. We must eliminate these ECMs with a high ROI for these no-cost/low-cost projects before going to the longer-term ROI ECMs.

Let us evaluate another building where we can see a clear drop in the non-office hours usage in Figure 11.12. As we can see, the orange hourly usage point pattern mostly runs close to the base load line. So, there is still usage during non-office hours, but it is very limited and not tied to OAT; as we can see, there is no correlation. What is the difference, and where does it show up in the calculation?

Let us break down the various loads from the scatter plot in Figure 11.12. The non-office hours loading is limited in usage compared to previous figures. This shows good schedule control, sprinkling only a few usage hours throughout the non-office hours. There is a concentration of usage near the baseline. That is small compared to the overall load. Upon reviewing the equipment, we find two 40-ton units and one 2-ton unit supporting this facility. The 80 tons have a schedule that works to keep the usage during non-office

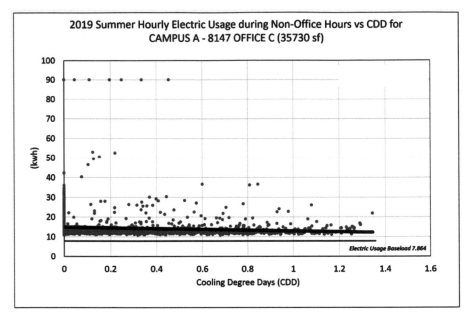

Figure 11.12   Non-office hours usage shows small unit left running.

hours at a minimum. The additional usage near the base load shows that the 2-ton unit is not controlled and running all the time to satisfy the loading from OAT and solar during non-office hours.

Let us go through the same scenario as the previous example to calculate the differences. That means from Figure 11.13 we develop the numbers as follows:

40.1% total base load – 14.8% for the office hours base load =
25.3% time is non-office hours base load loading.

That means we now have 25.3% of our energy used during non-office hours, but part of that is the plug load required during that time. We have determined that the plug load is 7.61%, which must be subtracted from the base load; so 25.3% minus the 7.61% for that required plug load would leave 17.69% of potential savings in the base load:

25.3% non-office load – 7.61% of office hours plug energy =
17.69% energy potential savings.

Now let us analyze how we calculate the excess usage from the non-office hours. The normal metrics do not as easily calculate the non-office hours, but we can still calculate them in several ways. The first is to calculate it in the scatter plots. The second is to designate two zones on the usage chart,

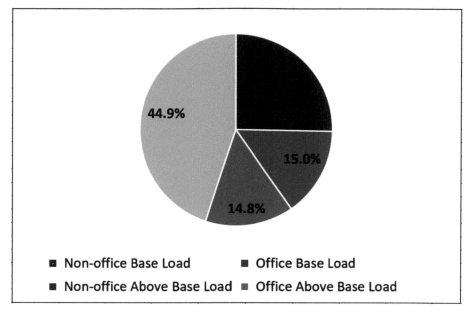

Figure 11.13 Showing a better mix of loading.

an office hours zone, and the non-office hours zone. Then the usage chart can calculate those values. The values demonstrate the non-office usage at 40.17%. The non-office plug load is 7.61%. That brings us down to a potential savings of 32.56%. If we remove the usage when the OAT is below 45°F, we must remove 14.87% for zone 3B for this building. That leaves 17.69% of potential electric energy savings potential. So, if we do the math between the savings for non-office hours (17.69%) minus the savings from the base load calculations (17.69%), the difference is 0%. The management of the system precluded any excess during non-office hours so that we only need to focus our attention on the excesses in the base load from the constant loading. So, this shows that 17.69% should be focused primarily on the constant loading below the base load. We know from Figure 11.12 that some loading on a small system is not controlled. This analysis misses those potential savings due to the ratio based on the magnitude of the other savings.

11.5 Introduce a Metric to Do Comparisons in Base Load

In Chapter 10, we demonstrated how to do benchmarking. The benchmarking was established to give us goals and an approach for monitoring commissioning (MCx) and fixing those overrides. In this section, we will begin the discussion of external benchmarking applications against other buildings. This section will lay out the foundation for those tools and parameters so that we can do that ourselves.

We can easily see how the two approaches in the past sections, base load and non-office hours, help determine what particular issue drives our potential savings. If we only used the base load numbers to calculate the potential savings, we would have left off the difference between the variable load during non-office hours and the office base load. As shown in Section 11.4, the delta between these two can be between 0% and 46%, pointing to a large variable differential, but will always be conservative in relation to actual. The second approach will always be more accurate but requires a scatter plot to develop the numbers.

Are there other ways to develop other metrics that can provide benchmarks that can give us quick checks or provide a different perspective? How can we automate these factors to use the data to perform cross-analysis? One way is to have the MMS automatically calculate our base load for each building and then translate that into a percentage of our total loading.

We will be able to compare the benchmark for a building using the two following metrics:

- Base load in watts/sf

- Base load as a percentage of the total load

Recall from earlier graphs that a line is drawn at the bottom edge of the curves kissing the bottom edge. That is the base load that most software systems can automatically calculate. We want to convert this to a base load in watts/sf to make this more usable. Then it can be compared against any other building. This is a particularly helpful factor of which we will demonstrate the value in several other chapters. For the simplest analysis, we expect that the watts/sf is lower to indicate the building has better control of its systems related to the base load. That means this is an indicator of how much is left on constantly. We can see this in Table 11.10 as an example. We can see the base load in watts/sf compared by climate zone. As we can see, it is very similar regardless of the climate zone. The climate zone theoretically will not affect the base load as the base load is flat, and because it is flat, it does not react or respond to OAT requirements. We can also see the EUI on the right side of Table 11.10. This indicates that EUI does correlate with OAT.

The metric will allow us to compare buildings against the median for any parameter. So, we can compare our building vs. other buildings of the

Table 11.10 Other benchmarks compared against climate zones from our surveys.

Climate Zone	Watts/SF	Baseload as % Consumption	12 Months Extrapolated EUI (Electric)
All	0.329	36.0695	30.258
1	0.374	40.534	29.804
2a	0.302	28.605	31.9095
2b	0.3175	23.165	46.595
3a	0.321	32.933	33.313
3b	0.4	39.24	29.223
4a	0.312	36.536	29.646
5a	0.3325	40.7035	27.262
5b	0.333	42.377	23.766

same category or across a campus. It also makes comparisons across climate zones more useful.

The next factor related to the base load is the percentage of base load compared to the total load. That is an easy factor to put in a table to rank buildings and to determine the simplest and fastest method to calculate the excess usage. As stated above, this will be related to how much plug load is used in the building, with the additional calculated as potential savings. So, in the examples above, the variance here will be between 8% and 12% for plug load, with the remaining being potential savings from the constant loading. That means this will have another 20%–30% of savings available in most examples above.

This is an effective way to understand the magnitude of the savings in a nice tabular form, as depicted below. Note that the variance between the extremes is not very far for the base load in watts/sf. Figure 11.11 gives a breakdown of many common facility types. The base load for administrative is in the middle at 0.33 watts/sf compared to the storage facility at 0.15 watts/ sf. This is understandable as the plug load from desk equipment, computers, and office equipment will be very low. So, it is half probably because it does not have additional equipment running. A medical clinic is 0.559 watts/sf as it will have a lot of equipment with a larger draw at night. Retail stores are high at 1.15 watts/sf due to the additional lights that will show up in plug load and all the equipment that has a draw at night. We do not see a high EUI on any of these except the retail store and the restaurant. This helps us

Table 11.11   Other benchmarks for various types of facilities from our surveys.

Description	Base Load (watts/sf)	% Of Base Load/ Total Load	Extrapolated EUI (kbtu/sf)
All Bldgs.	0.402	40.1%	31.00
Administrative	0.33	35.1%	32.23
Apartments	0.417	31.4%	25.66
Storage Facility	0.15	31.4%	16.57
Resaurant	0.814	29.6%	89.67
Medical Clinic	0.559	41.8%	50.27
Fitness Gym	0.389	31.7%	39.47
Church	0.248	23.5%	41.59
Retail Store	1.15	40.1%	133.55

to differentiate the distribution of loading between base load and total load, which will make us focus on the source when we examine facilities in more detail in future chapters.

References

[1] (2013, May 20). Plug Load Research Review Summary. U.S. General Services Administration. https://www.gsa.gov/system/files/Plug_Load_Research_Review_Summary_PDF.pdf

[2] (2021, April). Analysis and Representation of Miscellaneous Electric Loads in NEMS. U.S. Energy Information Administration. https://www.eia.gov/analysis/studies/demand/miscelectric/pdf/miscelectric.pdf

[3] CEUS 1999. Commercial End-Use Survey, Pacific Gas & Electric Company.

[4] NRNC, 1999. Nonresidential New Construction Baseline Study, prepared by RLW Analytics for Southern California Edison.

[5] Buildings Energy Data Book, 2002. U.S. Department of Energy, Office of Energy Efficiency and Renewable Energy.

[6] (2021, April). Analysis and Representation of Miscellaneous Electric Loads in NEMS. U.S. Energy Information Administration. https://www.eia.gov/analysis/studies/demand/miscelectric/pdf/miscelectric.pdf

[7] (n.d.). Commercial Buildings Energy Consumption Survey (CBECS) Table E6. Electricity consumption intensities (kWh) by end use, 2012. U.S. Energy Information Administration. https://www.eia.gov/consumption/commercial/data/2012/c&e/cfm/e6.php

[8] Dahowski, R. T., Sullivan, G. P., Davila, A. R., & Pennell, B. G. (n.d.). Characterizing Plug Load Energy Use and Savings Potential in Army Buildings. Pacific Northwest National Laboratory. https://www.pnnl. gov/main/publications/external/technical_reports/PNNL-29914.pdf

[9] Acker, B., et al. (2012). Office Building Plug Load Profiles. Boise, ID., University of Idaho: 53.

[10] Torcellini, P., Pless, S., Deru, M., Griffith, B., Long, N., Judkoff, R. (2006). Lessons Learned from Case Studies of Six High-Performance Buildings. Golden, CO: National Renewable Energy Laboratory, Report No. TP-550-37542

[11] (n.d.). Texas Commercial Energy Code 2013. UpCodes. https://up.codes/ viewer/texas/ashrae-90.1-2013

[12] Paliaga, G., P.E., Zhang, H., Ph.D., Hoyt, T., & Arens, E., Ph.D. (n.d.). Eliminating Overcooling Discomfort While Saving Energy. ASHRAE. https://www.ashrae.org/technical-resources/ashrae-journal/ featured-articles/eliminating-overcooling-discomfort-while-saving- energy

[13] Yoon, J., P.E., LEED AP (n.d.). Motors, drives, and HVAC efficiency. Consulting - Specifying Engineer. https://www.csemag.com/articles/ motors-drives-and-hvac-efficiency/#:~:text=Fan%20systems%20 serving%20multiple%20zones%20shall%20be%20VAV,volume%20 and%20one-third%20of%20total%20design%20static%20pressure.

12

Third-level Benchmarking
(Lights and Scatter Plot Modeling)

Abstract

This chapter will specifically show how to benchmark and relate lighting usage to other lighting systems. We will establish metrics for computing a building's lighting benchmarks and learn how to generate a scatter plot to model the loading for a facility.

12 Third-level Benchmarking

This chapter will detail calculating the lighting load and establishing benchmarks. We will address the following topics:

- Focusing on lighting system loading

- How to develop the scatter plot

- Breaking down the system usage via the scatter plot

- Compare the lighting loading metrics

12.1 Focusing on Lighting System Loading

In this set of chapters on benchmarking, we are moving from a broad look at the whole building benchmarking to being able to focus on specific system benchmarks. Therefore, we have focused on the four major systems (plug loading, lighting, fan/pumps, and AC, as shown in Figure 12.1) to define them by the external benchmarks and then against themselves (internal benchmarks). For this chapter, we will concentrate on lighting systems. The lighting and plug load metrics have generally decreased over time, while the AC system loads have increased due to continuous CDD increases over the last 30 years, which will be discussed in Appendix 1.

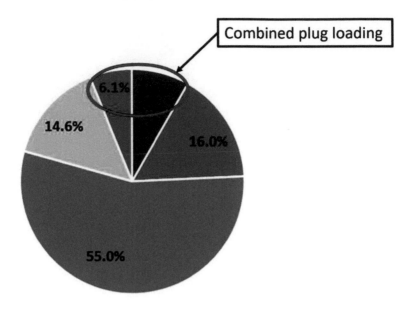

plug ■ lights ■ fan/pump ■ AC ■ office

Figure 12.1   Highlight plug and office plug load from the four major components of usage.

Figure 12.1 shows consumption highly skewed toward fan/pump systems due to overridden system schedules. The two blue areas circled on the figure are the combined plug loading, but we break them down to show the pure plug load (constant load) that runs 24/7 within the base load and the added load on the plug during office hours. We will categorize that additional load as the office load just to help us keep the importance of that portion separated in our minds. The fan/pump systems portion is quite large. It comes in at 55%, which means many systems are overridden, leaving the HVAC systems responding in all seasons to loading during non-office hours. This is a larger load for the fan/pump systems, but we will give the EM some boundaries on some parameters through the examples in this chapter.

This usage can vary a lot for the fan/pump systems. Figure 12.2 shows a different campus located in weather zone 5A, which, like Figure 12.1, has a large fan/pump systems usage rate. This should lead us to conclude that poor management of the fan/pump systems schedule leads to higher fan pump loading across climate zones. Figure 12.3 gives a better loading for fan/pump systems, but it still has room for improvement. This shows a smaller usage for fan/pump systems, but it still has a little room for improvement. The key

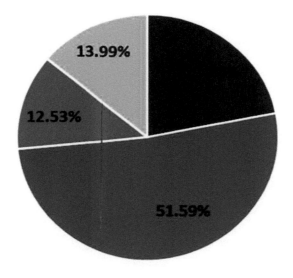

■ lights ■ fan/pump ■ AC ■ office/plug

Figure 12.2   Four major components of usage from another campus building.

takeaway, as emphasized in the last two chapters, is that we have to control those schedules and their associated issues to get the fan/pump systems under control before we embark on other projects.

We will show how we find the lighting load for benchmarking purposes on a normal interval graph. This requires us to isolate the usage when the lighting comes on in the morning or when they go home in the afternoon. The ease of this depends on several things, but it usually takes some time to get it close to the actual kW instantaneous usage. Normally, we start with a time of the year when no multiple usages compete for the same time slot. That generally occurs in a shoulder month. A shoulder month is when a building is not expected to heat or cool the space significantly. We will want to choose a normal shoulder month season (Spring or Fall) that has an OAT that will not require the heating or cooling system to come on; so a temperature in the 50°–65° range. In Figure 12.4, the intervals are shown for a facility. This is the easiest type of graph to evaluate for two reasons. The first is for a facility connected to the central chiller plant. That means we will only have fan/pump systems (beyond lights and office plug) providing the additional loading during office hours. The second reason is that the graph depicts very limited and specific equipment. The responding equipment is on/off and not variable; only a few energy loads are on the building.

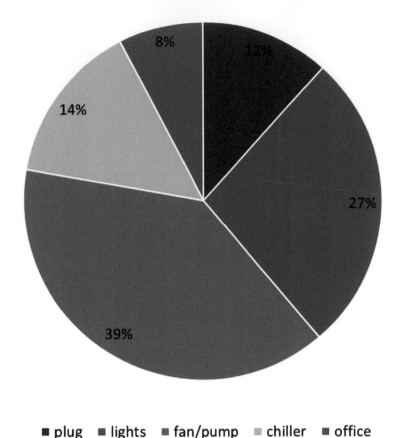

■ plug   ■ lights   ■ fan/pump   ▨ chiller   ■ office

Figure 12.3   Four major components of usage with better fan/pump.

We can see all the separate distinct usages ramp up in increments in Table 12.1. The lights come on at a specific time and stay on. The fan responds to the load at the next increments above the lights in one of the two stages shown here. Those are the final two increments of 12.11 or 16.02 kWh. This first fan stage allows us to calculate the lights at 4.1 kW (12.11 minus 8.01 kW), the subset of energy that includes the lighting and office loads discussed in the last chapter. If we convert that to watts/sf, it gives 0.1742 watts/sf. We will compare that to the lighting load developed in the scatter plot modeling (shown later in this chapter) and determine that it calculated the lights at 0.1437 watts/sf and the office at 0.2159 watts/sf for the duration of the day (0.024 watts/sf/hour if on for 9 hours), which means a total of 0.1677 watts/sf or within 5% of the above. This is the easiest example of calculating the lighting load directly, as the following examples will be

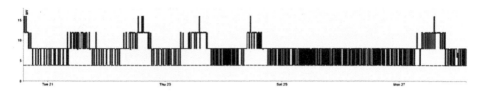

Figure 12.4 Simplest interval graph showing lights.

Table 12.1 Specific tiered load draws for Figure 12.1 (kW).

All readings at the Facility
16.02
12.11
11.91
8.01
7.81
4.01
3.91

more difficult to determine from a time perspective, and the accuracy may decrease. Hopefully, this will lead to an appreciation of using the scatter plot modeling for those situations where it works.

Figure 12.5 is also an easy model to analyze manually. This facility also has a 4.1-kW load for the lights, as these two facilities are almost exactly similar. When we compare this to the scatter plot modeling later in this chapter, we will find that the results are less than 10% apart.

With Figure 12.6, the analysis is getting harder as there are different ramp rates in the morning, appearing to indicate there may be multiple light banks, and they come on in the first hour. If we calculate that over the four intervals and average that across the work week, we get a lighting load within 13% of the scatter plot modeling. As the graph demonstrates, the easier approach may be using the afternoon readings for the analysis. This next facility shows why it is easier to analyze over the afternoon than the morning, as systems are a little more distinct in the shutdown. It still has several intervals but clearer and not as much office load variance in the afternoon. We get to within 7% of the scatter plot modeling as we do that analysis.

Figure 12.7 shows that the lighting loading is getting harder and approaching the normal meter patterns. Like the previous three, this building

Figure 12.5   Interval graph showing lights coming on in similar to the last model.

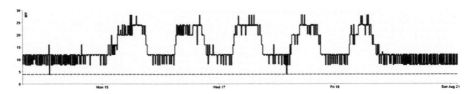

Figure 12.6   Interval graph showing many lighting loads coming on in the facility.

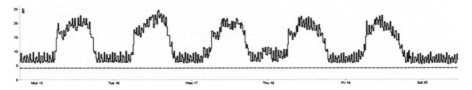

Figure 12.7   Lights coming on in many increments (harder to analyze).

loading is still attached to a chiller plant eliminating the AC system loading. As the example above indicates, there is no clear start and stop portion each day. An EM would have to run the difference over the hour and then average that over a week or more. We accomplished that for the morning and found it was around 19% of the scatter plot modeling value. The analyst must be careful in the afternoons as people generally go home one to two hours early on Friday, which adds a second degree of complexity to our calculations. Sometimes there will be a delay in starting on Monday for an hour and up to two hours late if there is a holiday. The afternoon analysis came within 14% of the scatter plot modeling.

The next few interval graphs show the same approach but with the AC component. That means these buildings are not on a central chiller plant, and the AC system usage is measured on the meter with the other systems. This adds another level of complexity over the last four figures since it includes additional usage tied to the fan/pump systems, which may overlap if we use the interval charts to calculate the lighting loads. We do not have to worry

Figure 12.8 Interval graph showing lights mixed with AC in a facility.

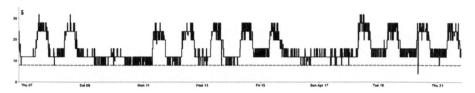

Figure 12.9 Interval graph showing lights in the sections.

about this on the scatter plot modeling as the lighting is in a time period when the energy subset only contains the lighting and office loads.

For Figure 12.8, the morning is staggered so much (and probably mixed with other loads such as exterior lights) that the analysis for lighting is difficult, if not impossible, to establish a reasonable approximation. The afternoon is much clearer, but we have an issue with various height differences from day to day. If we continue through the analysis, we find an average of 18.59 kW (or 0.4491 watts/sf). That is 32% higher than the scatter plot modeling; so it is easy to see that as the complexity increases, the ability to manually calculate the lighting system loading and the fan/pump and AC systems becomes much more difficult.

This next graph in Figure 12.9 is a lot easier to analyze. The equipment has distinct outputs that show increments at approximately 12 different levels. The lights are on when the baseline is at 20 kW. The base load is 8 kW, leaving 12 kW for lighting usage. This analysis brings a value within 17% of the scatter plot modeling. These sectionalized type usages make this an easy way to break down the systems' usage.

Figure 12.10 shows a large building that carries a large loading. One would assume the section that goes up is several banks of lighting. If we ran a quick calculation, we would determine that this value is about twice as large as a load for typical lights. But there is visibly a small plateau halfway up each daily morning rise. It is consistent every day. Using that value would put the manual estimate between 15% and 20% of the scatter plot model. The difference is probably smaller loads that mask the usage of this large building.

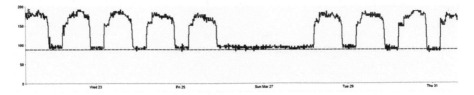

Figure 12.10   Interval graph showing lights embedded in a large section.

12.2 How to Develop the Scatter Plot

We found that the easiest way to determine the system loading for each of the four systems is by breaking the scatter plot into the components. Calculating the various system loads is usually a difficult task that requires either modeling or submetering the individual systems. We will show that it can be accomplished with the scatter plot analysis with almost the same accuracy as modeling. With that, we will break down the scatter plot so that everyone understands it thoroughly and knows how and why we use it to break down the various components. The first question is usually how we generate the scatter plot. The scatter plot is simple in its basic form. We first go and grab the hourly data table for a facility. We use hourly vs. 15-minute intervals because:

1.   Temperature readings from weather stations are only available every hour.

2.   Hourly is more than adequate for the analysis.

Take a year's energy usage data from the hourly table with the accompanying CDD for summer and heating degree days (HDD) for winter. Only count HDD and CDD when the heating and cooling systems are on. We have truncated Table 12.2 to show what the data resembles from the readings.

We will then add a couple of columns to Table 12.2, resulting in Table 12.3, to calculate the cooling degree hours (CDH). CDH is calculated as the difference from above 65°F to 65°F during that hour. These are rolled up and divided by 24 to convert them to CDD. This is considered the time when the OAT drives the space requirements to need air conditioning. CDH is used rarely, much less often than CDD, for analyzing data, but since this table is hourly, it is an hourly impact of cooling requirements. To generate the CDH, subtract 65°F from the hourly temperature. Most EMs do not realize that 65°F is the usually accepted base temperature but not the only option for calculating the CDD. When accomplishing a detailed analysis, we must determine when the building requires cooling to start. It is dependent

Table 12.2   Hourly usage table with temperature.

Commodity	Timestamp	Usage	Units	Temperature °F
Electricity	6/15/2020	79.71	kWh	63
Electricity	6/15/2020	87.64	kWh	71
Electricity	6/15/2020	103.81	kWh	78
Electricity	6/15/2020	103.02	kWh	82
Electricity	6/15/2020	104.54	kWh	84
Electricity	6/15/2020	102.57	kWh	86
Electricity	6/15/2020	101.24	kWh	88
Electricity	6/15/2020	90.20	kWh	90
Electricity	6/15/2020	91.58	kWh	89
Electricity	6/15/2020	94.24	kWh	89
Electricity	6/15/2020	52.74	kWh	89
Electricity	6/15/2020	49.59	kWh	88
Electricity	6/15/2020	47.28	kWh	86
Electricity	6/15/2020	54.89	kWh	80
Electricity	6/15/2020	54.00	kWh	76
Electricity	6/15/2020	53.19	kWh	73
Electricity	6/15/2020	54.16	kWh	70
Electricity	6/16/2020	55.39	kWh	69
Electricity	6/16/2020	53.26	kWh	68
Electricity	6/16/2020	53.19	kWh	67
Electricity	6/16/2020	55.12	kWh	64
Electricity	6/16/2020	53.94	kWh	64

on the design and the construction of a facility. It is also dependent on the climate. Each facility on campus is generally designed and constructed similarly. Since the climate is the same on campus, we can calculate the impact of a different base temperature on the calculations. A detailed analysis of the different base temperatures is included in Appendix 2. For these efforts, we will continue to use 65°F as the base. As we will validate, this is the general default, and we will show in Appendix 2 that the difference between 65°F base temperature and others is insignificant.

So, the three columns from the right of Figure 12.4 are where we convert the CDH to CDD in the second column from the right by dividing it by 24. Then we just arrange the columns with the hourly usage (first column on the right) and the CDD (second column from the right) for easy plotting.

Table 12.3   Hourly usage table with temperature turned into CDH.

Commodity	Timestamp	Usage	Units	Temperature °F	CDH
Electricity	6/15/2020	79.71	kWh	63	0
Electricity	6/15/2020	87.64	kWh	71	6
Electricity	6/15/2020	103.81	kWh	78	13
Electricity	6/15/2020	103.02	kWh	82	17
Electricity	6/15/2020	104.54	kWh	84	19
Electricity	6/15/2020	102.57	kWh	86	21
Electricity	6/15/2020	101.24	kWh	88	23
Electricity	6/15/2020	90.20	kWh	90	25
Electricity	6/15/2020	91.58	kWh	89	24
Electricity	6/15/2020	94.24	kWh	89	24
Electricity	6/15/2020	52.74	kWh	89	24
Electricity	6/15/2020	49.59	kWh	88	23
Electricity	6/15/2020	47.28	kWh	86	21
Electricity	6/15/2020	54.89	kWh	80	15
Electricity	6/15/2020	54.00	kWh	76	11
Electricity	6/15/2020	53.19	kWh	73	8
Electricity	6/15/2020	54.16	kWh	70	5
Electricity	6/16/2020	55.39	kWh	69	4
Electricity	6/16/2020	53.26	kWh	68	3
Electricity	6/16/2020	53.19	kWh	67	2

If we highlight these two columns, go to the "Insert" tab in the Excel program. Click on the Insert Scatter (X, Y) or Bubble Chart in the Charts section. Select "Scatter" from the list of chart types. Since we already highlighted the data above, the Excel function will produce a graph from that data with usage on the vertical axis compared to CDD on the horizontal axis. This is the graph shown on the right side in Table 12.4.

Figure 12.11 depicts the full-size graph from Table 12.4, and we notice a clear break between the top third (roughly speaking) and the bottom two-thirds of the points. They form two separate slopes with a gap in the middle. Because of this, we examined the data and determined that each set of points represents two different usage periods during the day. The top grouping of points represents office hours, while the bottom represents non-office hours. In the last two chapters, we did not get into detail on the scatter plot because we were more interested in conveying the idea of the base load and all that entailed. Now we show how to break it down into the two slopes, office and non-office hours, and analyze the scatter plots. Excel will draw

Table 12.4   Hourly usage table with CDD converted to scatter plot.

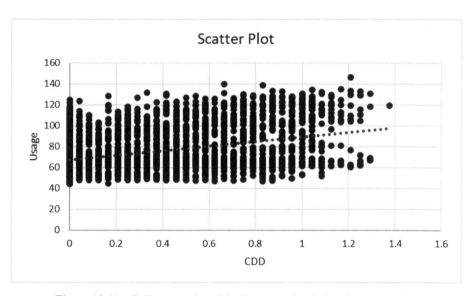

Commodity	Timestamp	Usage	Units	Temperature °F	CDH	CDD	Usage
Electricity	6/15/2020	79.71	kWh	63	0	2.63	57.81
Electricity	6/15/2020	87.64	kWh	71	6	2.96	57.71
Electricity	6/15/2020	103.81	kWh	78	13	3.25	57.36
Electricity	6/15/2020	103.02	kWh	82	17	3.42	56.62
Electricity	6/15/2020	104.54	kWh	84	19	3.50	56.75
Electricity	6/15/2020	102.57	kWh	86	21	3.58	64.97
Electricity	6/15/2020	101.24	kWh	88	23	3.67	87.07
Electricity	6/15/2020	90.20	kWh	90	25	3.75	85.52
Electricity	6/15/2020	91.58	kWh	89	24	3.71	86.76
Electricity	6/15/2020	94.24	kWh	89	24	3.71	88.51
Electricity	6/15/2020	52.74	kWh	89	24	3.71	86.40
Electricity	6/15/2020	49.59	kWh	88	23	3.67	87.99
Electricity	6/15/2020	47.28	kWh	86	21	3.58	91.83
Electricity	6/15/2020	54.89	kWh	80	15	3.33	89.59
Electricity	6/15/2020	54.00	kWh	76	11	3.17	87.57
Electricity	6/15/2020	53.19	kWh	73	8	3.04	86.00
Electricity	6/15/2020	54.16	kWh	70	5	2.92	68.75

Figure 12.11   Full scatter plot with all usage points being the same color.

the best curve fit line over the plots and provide the slope, intercept, and R^2 correlation. Many get carried away with the results by trying to transition to a model where they are predicting usage. We are using the formulae to show a relation of usage to temperature (CDD) and not a direct calculation, as we know other factors are involved. The extent of our interest is to show that it is responding to OAT for office hours, in general, to ensure we are getting the correct relationship. If we have a district cooling plant, we expect this data to be relatively flat as the only correlation will be the fan/pump system reacting to OAT but balanced by the other factors driving the loading. We will use the office and non-office hours intercepts to determine systems (lighting and office plug) represented in that energy subset.

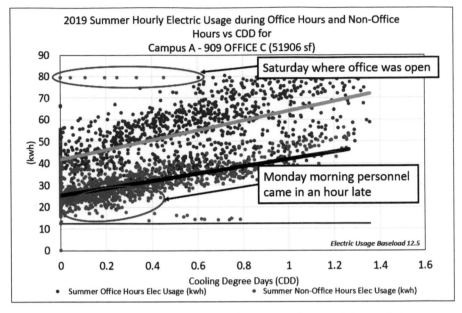

Figure 12.12   Chart showing hours that were not in normal time periods.

The R^2 correlation is only visual to ensure it operates properly based on the system and not to predict where a point of usage would be.

While visually identifying the two distinct slopes, we find that they represent the office hours within the top grouping and the non-office hours in the bottom grouping. We can differentiate these by having the computer color code each time period differently, using orange for non-office hours and blue for office hours. If there is an overlap of the two colors, then it indicates a change in the building schedule directly or indirectly. In other words, office hours changed for that time of day.

For example, in Figure 12.12, notice the orange, non-office hour data points circled at the top of the graph. Upon analysis, we discovered that they were all on a Saturday. Hence, the office was open this Saturday, which is obvious from the orange data points in the higher usage blue (office hours) area. Someone asked how we were able to determine this. Remember how we generated the scatter plot; we pulled the hourly data and graphed it against the temperature. To check these points, we just need to take the energy (kWh) for those points and look them up in the table corresponding to that same temperature. The second series circled in Figure 12.12 occurs on a Monday morning, indicated by the blue points embedded among the orange points. This likely means that personnel came in an hour late on Monday, and based

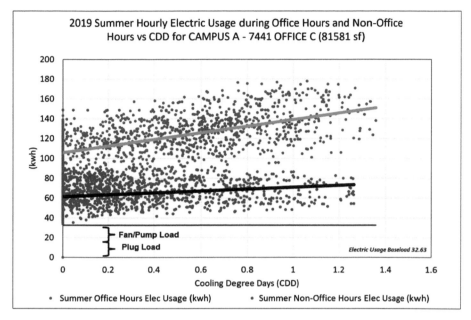

Figure 12.13 First subset of energy includes the plug and fan/pump load.

on our analysis, it appears to be a trend for every Monday. The same goes for Friday as they tend to consistently leave early. On Thursdays, they come in early and leave later, which probably implies they are trying to catch up so that they can leave early on Friday.

12.3 Breaking Down the System Usage via the Scatter Plot

Most analyses utilize daily scatter plots of kWh vs. CDD for normalization. In many instances, these were calculated daily vs. hourly. We use hourly scatter plots to show the impact of usage during office vs. non-office hours. These hourly scatter plots allow us to easily break out the various system loads within their time periods, as shown over the next few pages. Again, the blue dots represent electric usage in kWh during office hours, and the orange dots represent non-office hours. The purple line is the base load. This next example shows the non-office usage breakdown by the system for a one-shift administrative facility in climate zone 3B during the summer of 2019.

As discussed in previous chapters, we use a scatter plot (Figure 12.13) to understand when and where the energy is used. Each hour of energy use is plotted against the temperature as an HDD or CDD. Because of the place it is used and its relationship with the other systems, we can determine which

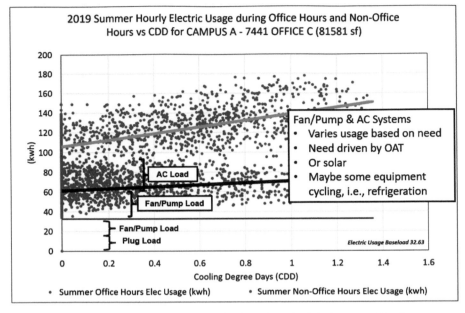

Figure 12.14   Second energy subset is above base load during non-office hours.

system is being used at that time to some degree of accuracy. The degree of accuracy and the variances between components will be addressed in Appendix 3.

We start with the easiest example in Figure 12.14, which includes the plug load we calculated earlier and set aside all that loading to cover the plug load calculation. Since we showed how that is calculated in Chapter 11, "Second-level Benchmarking," it leaves the remainder for the fan/pump systems. That is the first place where fan/pump systems loading is identified in a subset of the scatter plot. We will call this subset the non-office hours base load. As discussed previously, there will be a summer and a winter usage subset for the base load, as both may have a separate baseline but only in rare occurrences. There will also be another usage subset that includes the office hours usage base load. Both subsets contain a plug load that is the same for our calculations. The office hours will also have a winter and summer energy subset; so four energy usage subsets related to the base load can be calculated. It will become easier to visualize these subsets when we get to the waterfall of values that show all the subsets and their components.

Then the next usage breakdown comes with the remaining loading of non-office hours that occurs above the base load usage. All the orange points, which will be above the base load, are the non-office hours in Figure 12.14. The usage during those hours above the base load is a variable loading responding to some requirements on the two systems, fan/pump, and AC systems. In this case, the requirement is generated by the OAT and/or the solar loading on the facility. That drives up the requirements for the AHS and the chiller or whatever AC system is separated from ventilation or distribution. The only load can be a fan/pump or an AC system during this time. As discussed in previous chapters, there may be an occasional stray piece of equipment that cycles, but that is minor compared to this overall usage breakdown.

Figure 12.15 breaks down the loading for the lighting on the scatter plot. The subset of energy usage that identifies the lights is the time period when people come into the office and first turn on the lights. The lights and the office plug load are the two usages that share this energy subset, which occurs in the delta between the intercept of the two slopes. The slopes for the blue office hours indicate the impact for that time period of the energy use in kWh at that zero CDD. The non-office hour usage gives the slope of the energy used during that time period. At the point where both slopes cross zero (0), CDD is where an amount of energy is expended for that subset of energy usage, including those two systems. That is the lighting load and the office plug load.

Let us explain. The office plug load describes the increase in the receptacle load when people come into the office. This includes the computers, coffee pot, office equipment, etc., that are turned on upon arrival in the morning. The constant plug load is still there and counted separately in the base load, but this is the additional plug loading that we quantified in Chapter 11 as being a 2.4:1 ratio of kWh/sf/yr to the plug load in the base load. Calculate the difference between the office hours' intercept and the non-office hours' intercept and then subtract the office plug load. The remainder is the lighting load.

We might ask why there aren't other loads in the data during this temperature and time. Well, the temperature is unique, meaning there should not be any cooling going on at zero CDD. Any cooling required for the building is either handled by optimized start/stop programming or by starting the system before the people arrive. We generally do not have a situation where the temperature is higher in the early morning and drops to zero CDD at the start of work. If there is a surge, it is a small percentage of the time and therefore does not impact the averaging at the intersection. If the morning surge of usage is larger than normal, then the intercept of the graph will become distorted against the non-office hours intercept so that the intercept is higher than it should be. Then the scatter plot analysis will not be proportioned properly to produce legitimate results. This happens about 20% of the time where the data will show a lot of activity at zero CDD. And since it skews the intercept higher, it negates any accurate calculations as the lighting calculation is

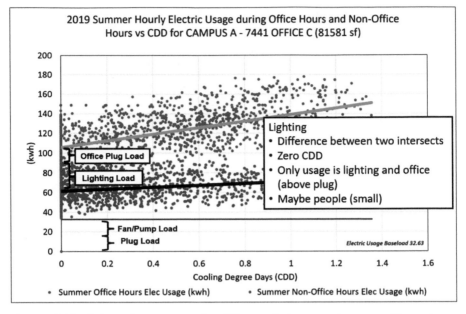

Figure 12.15   Subset of energy covering difference in intercepts between office and non-office hours.

pushed too small or negative. If this happens in the model, those loads are pushed over to the fan/pump system load that resides above the base load. In these instances, the scatter plot modeling tool is not effective.

The other question we encounter involves any occupant and equipment loading on the AC system at zero CDD. The occupant and equipment loading is generally delayed or minor and diluted, leaving the average points remaining primarily distributed between the lighting and the office loading. We do not see any impact on our numbers from the occupant loading or office equipment loading on all our calculations. Between the delay and the temperature differential, the other loads may affect some points but only a small percentage of the points generating this intercept.

Cooling generally has an optimized start/stop program, which has the building up to load when people get to the office. The additional loads' reaction time would have little impact at zero CDD. In many cases, people have difficulty setting the schedule to start earlier than office hours anyway, which means the space temperature has had a chance to stabilize. The percentage of that impact is small; so we will analyze in Appendix 3 to see the significance of these estimated sections. Either way, we have seen the lighting coming in very close to the actual so that we can easily see if they have LED or fluorescent lights in the space.

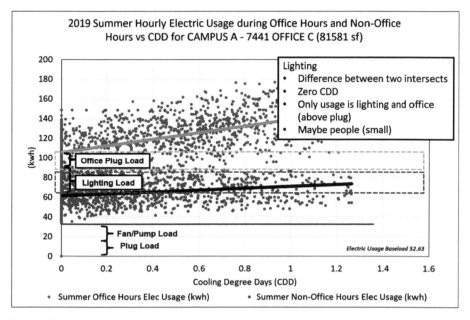

Figure 12.16 Subset of two energy systems between intercepts will be flat usage across the CDD spectrum.

This subset of energy between the previously mentioned intercepts is broken into two groups: the office plug load and the lighting load. Each of those usages will be projected across the entire CDD spectrum. So, draw a box as shown in Figure 12.16; then all the energy in those boxes is used by both the lights during the entire period and the same for the office load. The visual is a little misleading as the individual points are not there. Still, the value is virtually flat for both those groups across the entire CDD spectrum; so the variance in the data points means that there is less energy for the other categories, therefore lowering the level at the time for the office hour usage.

Table 12.5 summarizes four energy end-use studies from 1997 to 2002. The data shows that the lighting energy intensity generally ran between 3.7 and 8.2 kWh/sf/yr with an average of 5.1 kWh/sf/yr. These numbers, from studies around 20 years ago, show a very high lighting power compared to today. This is primarily due to major improvements in lamps and the fixtures themselves.

Lighting usage has gone down in stages, with the 2012 CBECs Table 12.6 showing an average usage for all buildings of 2.5 and 2.7 kWh/sf/yr for office buildings. So, within 10 years, the surveys show half the average from the 1997–2002 usage. That is entirely understandable, as there was a major emphasis over the past 20 years on lighting retrofits.

Table 12.5   The breakdown for lighting from studies 20+ years ago.

	CEUS [1]	CEUS [2]	NRNC [3]	CBECS Bldgs. Energy Data Book [4]	Average for All Data Sources	% Of Total Load
	1997	1999	1999	2002	Avg.	
Fans (kWh/ft²/yr)	4	1.5	2.4	1.5	2.4	15.50%
Cooling (kWh/ft²/yr)	3.2	4.5	2.9	2.7	3.3	21.90%
Heating (kWh/ft²/yr)	N/A	N/A	0.4	N/A	0.4	2.60%
Lighting (kWh/ft²/yr)	4.6	3.7	4	8.2	5.1	33.80%
Misc. (kWh/ft²/yr)	2.4	3.1	5.6	5.9	4.3	28.10%
Total Electricity (kWh/ft2/yr)	14.2	12.7	15.3	18.4	15.2	

Even with that, ASHRAE's target lighting power density (watts/sf) standards for offices 90.1-1999/2001 to 90.1-2004/2007 went from 1.3 to 1.0 watts/sf. To translate this factor into kWh/sf/yr would give values of 3.05 and 2.35 kWh/sf/yr. So, the rapid escalation in the lighting retrofit market eclipses the numbers targeted in the ASHRAE design guides. Our surveys show a range from 0.33 to 2.1 kWh/sf/yr with an average of 1.3 kWh/sf/yr. So, the surveys cannot keep up with the transition as we are already less than half of the 2012 CBECS.

Our experience in the field now sees lighting energy intensity in the range of 0.23–0.38 watts/sf (as validated in Table 12.7 from the Campus P project) or between 0.6 and 0.9 kWh/sf/yr for LED retrofits. So, we would expect the range for lighting to be anywhere from 0.6 kWh/sf/yr to a maximum of 2.5 kWh/sf/yr. If any building runs higher than 0.9 kWh/sf/yr, we can easily calculate the savings for an LED retrofit. As we pass 2.5 kWh/sf/yr for lighting only, we have a great savings ECM or a meter that may have a quality problem with the values. The values generated by the scatter plots will be actual and will be the only place where we can notice any shortcomings in the scatter plot modeling tool. This value for the lighting load will drop to a negative value if office hours cross over with non-office hours to a major extent. Those conditions are the limits for the scatter plot at this point. The target benchmarks have moved so drastically over the past 20 years that the literature cannot keep up with the changes.

Table 12.6 The breakdown for lighting 2012 CBECS [5].

Table E6. Electricity consumption intensities (kWh) by end use, 2012

Electricity energy intensity[1] (kWh/square foot in buildings using electricity for the end use)

	Total	Space heating	Cooling	Ventilation	Water heating	Lighting	Cooking	Refrigeration	Office equipment	Computing	Other
All buildings	14.6	0.5	2.4	2.4	0.2	2.5	1.1	2.7	0.6	1.5	2.7
Principal building activity											
Education	11	0.5	2.5	1.6	0.2	1.9	0.2	1	0.5	1.9	1.6
Food sales	48.7	0.6	1.6	2.8	(*)	3.6	4.3	34.5	0.5	0.6	2.7
Food service	44.9	1.4	5.3	5	1.1	3	15.9	18.3	1.2	0.8	3.4
Office	15.9	0.6	2.2	3.9	0.1	2.7	0.2	0.6	0.7	3.1	2.4
Public assembly	14.5	1	5.2	1.3	(*)	1.9	0.5	1.5	0.4	0.9	3.8

Table 12.7 The target watts/sf for LED installs.

LED	watts	sf	W/sf
high intensity lights	3001	10000	0.30
med	2143	10000	0.21
low	1286	10000	0.13

Table 12.8 Lighting degradation over time.

Year	kWh/sf/yr	% Change
2018	1.2460	NA
2019	1.2648	101.51%
2020	1.2868	101.74%
2021	1.3140	102.11%
2022	1.3470	102.51%

12.4 Compare the Lighting Loading Metrics

The above section details how to generate estimated lighting energy intensity for a building. With the scatter plot analysis, we can benchmark lights against general category types (external benchmark) or against themselves over time (internal benchmark). Let us discuss internal benchmarking first. The EM can run the analysis anytime, but the lights will not degrade that quickly. We would recommend benchmarking them annually against the previous years to track the degradation of the lighting. It is easy to chart that degradation over the years, as shown in Table 12.8.

The second way to benchmark is external, which carries a lot of poten-tial in several ways. The first way to benchmark is based on an increasing

Table 12.9   Lighting usages over sampling of admin/offices (kWh/sf/yr).

Building	Type Usage	Plug	Lights	Fan/ Pump	AC	Office	Total	Climate Zone
1301	office	0.785	0.668	1.382	0.000	0.507	3.342	5B
1002	office	0.785	0.337	2.178	0.000	0.507	3.807	5B
1302	office	0.785	0.868	2.164	0.000	0.507	4.324	5B
1052	office	0.785	0.359	2.119	0.000	0.507	3.769	5B
1102	office	0.785	0.508	3.211	0.000	0.507	5.011	5B
1252	office	0.785	0.624	3.296	0.000	0.507	5.211	5B
1101	office	0.778	0.374	2.958	0.000	0.513	4.624	5B
747	office	0.785	1.472	4.901	1.281	0.507	8.946	5B
3732	office	0.785	1.647	2.997	0.604	0.507	6.540	5B
281	office	0.785	0.738	2.481	0.751	0.507	5.262	5B
4568	office	0.796	0.745	3.029	0.907	0.496	5.972	5B
4737	office	0.778	2.074	6.566	1.324	0.514	11.256	5B
3748	office	0.790	0.504	7.337	2.119	0.502	11.251	5B
1348	office	0.811	0.611	2.216	0.515	0.481	4.634	5B
4767	office	0.775	1.190	1.993	0.658	0.517	5.133	5B
115	office	0.785	1.641	4.424	2.301	0.507	9.657	5A
24	office	0.785	2.052	4.580	1.304	0.507	9.228	5A
1585	office	0.785	2.097	8.150	1.714	0.507	13.253	5A
70	office	0.785	2.044	5.369	1.274	0.507	9.979	5A
1524	office	0.785	1.801	2.604	0.974	0.507	6.670	5A
83	office	0.785	1.724	5.207	1.609	0.507	9.832	5A
251	office	0.785	2.902	4.477	2.157	0.507	10.828	5A
58	office	0.763	0.556	9.893	3.289	0.528	15.029	3A
1741	office	0.808	0.892	4.367	0.972	0.484	7.523	3A
79	office	0.808	0.706	1.608	0.756	0.484	4.362	3A
2677	office	0.808	0.813	5.316	1.719	0.484	9.140	3A
	Average	**0.788**	**1.152**	**4.032**	**1.009**	**0.504**	**7.484**	
	Median	**0.785**	**0.840**	**3.253**	**0.939**	**0.507**	**6.605**	

trajectory over the past few years and to increase efficiency as we go forward. Twenty years ago, we looked at 3.7–8.2 kWh/sf/yr with an average of 5.1 kWh/sf/yr. Ten years ago, we were at 2.5–2.7 kWh/sf/yr. We are running 0.6–2.5 kWh/sf/yr in our surveys, which are dropping over time due in part to the ASHRAE guidelines increasing over time [7].

In Table 12.9, we have shown a sampling of 26 administrative or office buildings. The average runs at 1.1 kWh/sf/yr as a good benchmark. However, the median is 0.84, probably more representative of the current achievable target. Note the variances we are finding in the lighting in these locations. Anything in the range of 0.34–0.86 kWh/sf/yr will be LEDs or with a majority mix of LEDs, and higher than that could be any mix of other types of lighting. This makes it easy to see the savings that can be applied by quickly calculating the kWh/sf and multiplying that by the square footage shown. We know the target; so the savings is a delta to the 0.8 kWh/sf. Then all we have to do is determine if we can install the LEDs within that budget. We will discuss appropriate returns in Chapter 18, "Setting Up for Energy Projects."

References

[1] CEUS 1997. Commercial End-Use Survey, Pacific Gas & Electric Company.
[2] CEUS 1999. Commercial End-Use Survey, Pacific Gas & Electric Company.
[3] NRNC, 1999. Nonresidential New Construction Baseline Study, prepared by RLW Analytics for Southern California Edison.
[4] Buildings Energy Data Book, 2002. U.S. Department of Energy, Office of Energy Efficiency and Renewable Energy.
[5] (n.d.). Commercial Buildings Energy Consumption Survey (CBECS) Table E6. Electricity consumption intensities (kWh) by end use, 2012. U.S. Energy Information Administration. https://www.eia.gov/consumption/commercial/data/2012/c&e/cfm/e6.php

13

Fourth-level Benchmarking (Fan/Pump and AC Systems)

Abstract

In this chapter, we will learn how to generate calculations for determining the fan/pump and AC systems usage directly and from a scatter plot. Then we will demonstrate how the remaining areas of the graph can be easily broken into the loading for the remaining system(s). This section will specifically show how to benchmark the fan/pump and AC systems usage and relate it to other systems. We will also continue to break down the relationship between the fan/pump and the AC systems loading and determine a benchmark for each system and the type of system. We will also develop a method for rating the efficiency of the AC system based on electric usage vs. the traditional based on output.

13   Fourth-level Benchmarking

This chapter will demonstrate calculating the fan/pump and the AC systems load. We will cover the following in this chapter:

- Focus on the last two of the four systems

- Break down the fan/pump and AC system usage via the scatter plot

- Compare the fan/pump system loading metrics

- Compare the AC system loading metrics

- Calculate the AC system efficiency

- Compare the AC system for office hours and non-office hours

- Compare AC systems over various example buildings

- Calculate the waterfall values

13.1 Focus on the Last Two of the Four Systems

This section concludes the discussion of benchmarking the four systems that make up the usage in a facility. We previously discussed plug loads and lighting; in this section, we will introduce the final two systems: fan/pump and AC. As a system, we are benchmarking the entire system(s) included within a facility. A system will comprise everything behind the meter that contributes to the AC loading (AC systems) and the distribution system related to distributing the cooling or heating (fan/pump systems). The distribution system will cover every type of distribution system and also include supply air and exhaust fans. We will concentrate on the cooling as that will cover all the heating distribution systems within that AC distribution range, which will more than cover the electric range during the winter. The AC system would include a chiller, the cooling tower, and the pumps and fans associated with moving and cooling the water associated with the tower or chiller. Suppose there are rooftop units, split systems, and other systems that combine cooling and distribution. In that case, those loads will be determined in this analysis and attributed to the AC system. If a building has a mix of systems, all of those systems will be shown as one combined system in the usage analysis for the fan/pump systems. As discussed in Appendix 1, the increase in CDDs by 56% in the US over the last 70 years, as depicted, will continue to impact the AC system and the fan/pump system loading. The weather-dependent cooling loading will double in 50 years at that rate of increase. In rough calculations, that is a 14%–18% increase in the total loading on the building, depending on the weather zone and construction. This will affect how we design new systems and the replacement sizing.

In Figure 13.1, we see the proportion of the system in the typical ratios found in institutional buildings. As we benchmark this AC system, remember that the mix of systems can be confusing as one system may be operating under control while another has the schedule overridden. Knowing the mix of equipment always helps as we go into the analysis mode with these benchmarks and interpret the interval data. In Figure 13.1, we see the vast majority of the usage in the fan/pump systems; next is the lights with 16%, AC systems at 14.6%, and then, finally, a breakdown of the plug load into two components, the plug load that is constant in the base load and the office load where the plug load increases when people turn on those systems such as computers and office equipment.

Figure 13.1 is representative of institutional facilities. Institutions have trouble controlling HVAC schedules; so systems usually run constantly. That is the primary contributor to the high fan/pump system ratio, as indicated in Figure 13.1.

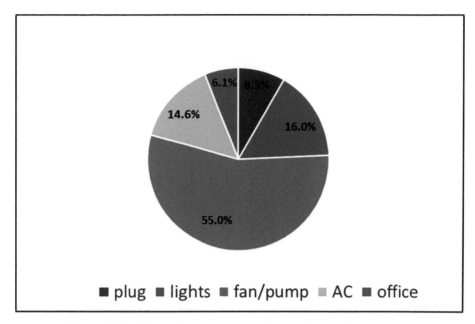

Figure 13.1 Four major components of usage from another campus.

We will show how these loads are broken down on the normal interval chart in several examples. This will give an understanding of how to evaluate a building from the standpoint of breaking down the loads into benchmarks for each system. The breakdown for the base load is easy from these diagrams, as shown in previous chapters. That base load also led to the plug load being broken down during non-office hours and office hours to indicate the increase during office hours from turning equipment on while in the office plug load. Benchmarking other systems requires a lot more work. Some of the systems, such as the lights, were shown in the last chapter. In this chapter, we will continue the discussion of the lighting load benchmark and identify the fans/pumps and AC systems.

In Figure 13.2, the intervals are shown for a facility. We can see the AC and the fan/pump systems coming on at various times. It is obvious in this figure that it includes nights and weekends. At night, notice the system coming on and cycling as required to maintain the space temperature. That will only happen when a schedule is overridden. The space temperature requirements then will drive the system to come on based on OAT driving the requirements to satisfy the inside space set point. These are the only variable loadings at night; so the only systems that will respond during that time are the AC and fan/pump systems. Both respond proportionally to the loading; so they ramp up and down based on that proportion. The average proportion will be

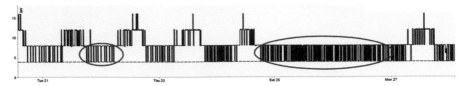

Figure 13.2   AC systems on the interval graph.

analyzed later in this chapter at 48% for the fan/pump system portion of that loading, while 52% is for the AC system side of the usage.

Look at Figure 13.2; the circled section is where the AC/fan/pump systems respond to the nighttime loading requirements. The second circle is for the weekends. As we noticed, there is a requirement on the weekends based on OAT or solar loading. This loading proportionally responds to the requirement to maintain temperature to offset the OAT energy load against the space and the solar loading. The only other loading would be an occasional appliance or piece of office equipment cycling, which is a very small load and infrequent compared to the loading imposed by the overrides of the schedule.

This first example is the simplest diagram where the fan response is distinctly clear for the loading at night and on weekends. Since this building is on a separate chilled water plant, the only data responding to the requirements for cooling will be the fan/pump systems. So, if there is no AC system, the building loading will primarily be fans and pumps that provide most of the inputs with the smaller increments provided by some small requirements from the office loading.

This is clearer when we break down the seven loading increments on this building in Table 13.1. The base load starts at 3.91 kW. There is a small bump up to 4.01 kW; so this load is generated by either the 2-ton package unit or the office load. Since it appears sporadically, it was identified as a 2-ton package unit, but the office load is still possible, depending on the equipment. Then it jumps up, which will be the lights coming on, which adds 3.8 kW to the usage. There is a small increase of 0.2 kW, which would be office loading. The final three tiers (11.91, 12.11, and 16.02 kW) are all loading for the fan/pump systems. The fan/pump system for this building has 21 tons of AC support. There is also a 3-HP hydronic pump in the system. We would surmise that the 3-HP pump is in the base load and runs constantly, and the three loads are broken down by the calling on the 2-ton package unit or the fans responding to the load in increments. In this instance, it is easy to calculate the annual energy usage by the fans. We simply take the reading for that hour

Table 13.1 Interval usages vs. systems impacted.

All Readings at the Facility	Affected Systems
16.02	AC/Fans/Pumps
12.11	AC/Fans/Pumps
11.91	AC/Fans/Pumps
8.01	Office Load
7.81	Lights
4.01	Office Load
3.91	Base load

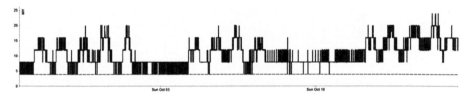

Figure 13.3 AC system on the interval graph.

and subtract the value of 8.01 kW, which is the base load plus the office and lighting load. That difference gives the total used, and we can calculate any value for the fan/pump systems similarly. This is obvious when a chiller plant services the building; we know all values or 95% or more tied into the fans and the 2-ton packaged unit.

Figure 13.3 is very similar to the last figure. Here nine increments respond to the various loads in the facility. The base load and the lighting are coming in at 8.01 kW again. Above that are increments of 3.9, 0.2, 3.71, 0.2, and 3.9 kW. The systems in the building are the same (2-ton air-handling unit and 3-HP pump), and the previous building-size is 24% larger. The difference in the loading is that this facility has a third tier of fan load. This is probably because the previous facility had seven cabinet fan coils, while this one had five cabinets and five duct fan coils. This facility ran 32% higher loading per sf; the only difference was the duct fan coils. So, this is an obvious place to start on the energy analysis.

In Figure 13.4, we add the next level of complexity to the analysis. Still, we are on a central chilled water plant. Here there are 20-plus increments over the base load. There are 54 tons of fan cooling capacity and 10 HP (2 × 5 HP) of hydronic pumps. Automated controls on the fan coil units may cause

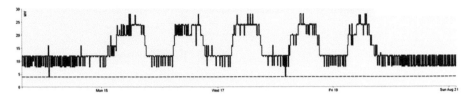

Figure 13.4   Mid-level graph showing fan coil controls impact.

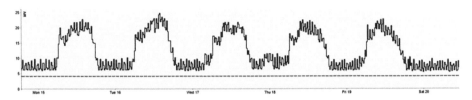

Figure 13.5   AC systems example on the interval graph.

small variations. That would explain the undulations before the lights come on or during non-office hours. During those non-office hours, we see a strong usage pattern, but at various levels, that would suggest fan coils are running 24/7 but do have controls programmed to a set point; otherwise, it would be showing as a larger flat load within the base load.

Figure 13.5 is the next level of detail in analyzing fan/pump systems. This facility has 65 cabinet fan coils and two 3-HP pumps. The data curves flow smoother, indicating the fan coils (or most) have controls and the units respond to space requirements. Otherwise, as stated previously, the usage for those fan coils would show up as a base load. The more the systems and controls, the more the curve blends into a smoother sine wave pattern for usage. This smoother pattern makes manual calculations for benchmarking the lights and fan/pump systems much more difficult.

Figure 13.6 adds the next level of complexity to the graph. This and the following two graphs have added the AC system into the mix (the previous figures were all on a chiller plant). This has multiple configurations based on the number of various AC units in the facility that can come on in several stages. There are also 35,000 cfm of air-handling units and two 5-HP pumps that support the areas. There are 32 plus configurations of the equipment that can be on in different stages, producing the graph during the highest peak of the AC and fan/pump system primary usage. It is hard to identify the lights in this case, which makes it difficult to separate the three systems from this curve. Due to all these usage levels, it is impossible to manually lay these out, or it would take a major effort to determine the many potential configurations

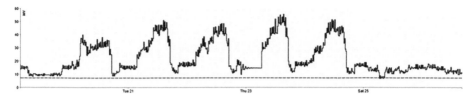

Figure 13.6   AC systems example on the interval graph.

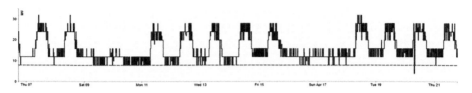

Figure 13.7   AC systems example on the interval graph.

and then assign them values. We could subtract the lights and then add what is above that line, but as shown earlier, getting closer than 30% on the lighting loads is even a difficult task.

In Figure 13.7, it is much easier to assign the AC and fan/pump system loading. So, anything above the lights at 15.5 kWh could be subtracted as the AC/fan/pump system loading plus across the summer. That difference would be their load during the summer, which would be split between the AC and the fan/pump systems, as will be developed later in this chapter.

In this final example in Figure 13.8, notice the jump in the lighting load so that the lighting benchmark is relatively easy to break out. The next load jump would be the AC/fan/pump systems. This one also becomes difficult to allocate the loading manually as there were almost 100,000 sf and many systems and fan/pump systems that could use the load at various stages. This one also has VAV systems that can load at multiple draw levels on the overall loading. Once we have the lighting loading, we must add all the loads each hour above the base, lighting, and office load to get the fan/pump and AC system mix overall. We would also have to subtract the plug from the nights and weekends and add this fan/pump/AC loading to the formula in the previous sentence to get the full extent of the facility's AC/fan/pump system loading. That would require us to subtract the loading during every hour for the summer and winter loading. This gets more complex during winter as we only have to subtract those hours when the temperature is over 45°F. While doable, it requires a lot of manhours, but it may take less manhours than doing a modeling effort.

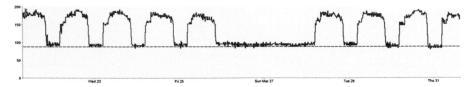

Figure 13.8   AC systems example on the interval graph.

These show the impact of AC systems on energy usage at a point in time. We could calculate every point (hour) and add these, but that is a major effort. The easiest way to calculate that impact is by evaluating it with the scatter plots, as shown in the following section.

13.2 Break Down the Fan/Pump and AC System Usage via the Scatter Plot

So, let us demonstrate how we can simplify the EM's efforts and accuracy by using the scatter plot and distributing the energy use into several energy subsets. We discussed previously how to get the base load. During non-office hours, the remaining loading above the plug load will be split between the AC and fan/pump systems. We will show the details of calculating that ratio, but for now, realize the load is between those two systems. Then the next usage breakdown comes with the remaining loading of non-office hours that occurs above the base load usage. All the orange points are the non-office hours in Figure 13.9. The usage during those hours above the base load is a variable loading responding to some requirements on those two systems (AC and fan/pump systems). In this case, the requirement is generated by the OAT and/or the solar loading on the facility. That drives up the requirements on the AHS and the chiller or any AC system type separated from ventilation or distribution systems. The only load can be a fan/pump or an AC system during this time. As discussed in previous chapters, there may be an occasional stray piece of equipment that cycles, but that is minor compared to this overall usage breakdown.

Figure 13.10 shows the final energy usage subset breakdown covering the fan/pump systems during office hours. All the blue data points above the lighting and office loading subset (discussed in Chapter 12) are the remaining usage values in the office hours loading. The only major loading during this subset of time is the fan/pump and the AC system loading. All the other loads are accounted for, and nothing else responds during this block of variable loading. For example, the office load will vary but generally stay within the energy subset that crosses the spectrum, as shown in Figure 12.10 in

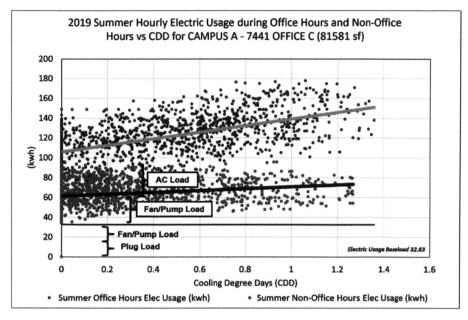

Figure 13.9 Four major components of usage focusing on non-office hours.

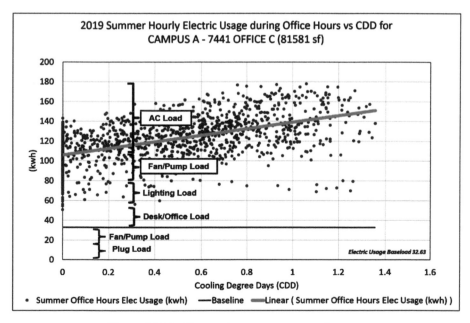

Figure 13.10 Four major energy systems of usage.

Chapter 12. The lighting is more obvious once it is on; it will maintain that same usage regardless of the other subsets of energy use. In Figure 13.10, we show the final data that can be divided between the fan/pump systems loading and the AC system loading.

The next analysis determines the breakdown or ratio between the fan/pump loading and the AC system loading in the variable data. The AC system could be a chiller or a split system, rooftop, etc. The fan/pump systems are the ventilation and/or distribution systems that are distinctly separate from the AC package system. Review the studies we referenced in the previous chapter to see a relationship ratio between fan/pump and AC systems. We have included that table again for reference below (Table 13.2) and high-lighted the value that expresses the ratio of the AC system to the fan/pump system. The table shows a variance for the ratio from the fan/pumps to the AC system of 50/50 overall category and 40/60 for the office loading ratio. This will be broken down in more detail over the next few pages.

Next, we must break down this office hour subset related to the ratio of blue points or usage assigned to the fan/pump vs. the AC system. That percentage depends on the system type for the cooling production and the type of distribution system. Many systems can split the ratio of this usage from 25% to 66% for all the following tables. The oldest studies we analyzed show a range of 25%–56% for the fan/pump systems usage concerning the AC system usage (Table 13.2).

If we move 10 years beyond these studies and review the 2012 CBECS data (Table 13.3), we can see that the ventilation (blue column) is equal (50%) to the cooling (yellow column) for the average across the US. If we review the "Office" category, the ventilation is at 3.9 kWh/sf/yr (blue column) vs. 2.2 kWh/sf/yr for the cooling (yellow column) or 64% of the total of the subset. Suppose we look at just the general average category. In that case, the data has not changed much over the 2012 study vs. the 1997–2002 studies, which is understandable as there have not been major technology changes over those study ranges. Since 2012, chillers have improved from 0.7 to 0.4 kW/ton, and split systems from 21–25 SEER. We are starting to see if we can track that impact on our portfolio.

So, we elected to look at all the systems as laid out in 2012 CBECS, Table 13.4, and add in the studies from previous years to understand the extremes and get an average. The data shows that the various systems run close to 50%. There are two extremes; one is 66% for chiller plants that we eliminate from this analysis because we are not including cooling sources outside the building; so that is not an issue skewing the data. The other is 25% from the abovementioned CEUS 1999 study in Table 13.2. That seems to be an anomaly and may only be a regional issue. We elected to use the ratio

Table 13.2   Summary of surveys from 20 years ago on fan/pump ratios.

	CEUS [2]	CEUS [3]	NRNC [4]	CBECS Bldgs. Energy Data Book [5]	Average for All Data Sources	% Of Total Load
	1997	1999	1999	2002	Avg.	
Fans (kWh/ft^2/yr)	4	1.5	2.4	1.5	2.4	15.50%
Cooling (kWh/ft^2/yr)	3.2	4.5	2.9	2.7	3.3	21.90%
Heating (kWh/ft^2/yr)	N/A	N/A	0.4	N/A	0.4	2.60%
Lighting (kWh/ft^2/yr)	4.6	3.7	4	8.2	5.1	33.80%
Misc. (kWh/ft^2/yr)	2.4	3.1	5.6	5.9	4.3	28.10%
Total Electricity (kWh/ft2/yr)	14.2	12.7	15.3	18.4	15.2	
HVAC % Of Total Electricity	51.00%	47.00%	37.00%	23.00%	39.50%	
Fans % Of HVAC Electricity	56.00%	25.00%	45.00%	36.00%	40.50%	

Table 13.3   Summary of surveys from 10 years ago on fan/pump ratios [6].

Table E6. Electricity consumption intensities (kWh) by end use, 2012

Electricity energy intensity[1] (kWh/square foot in buildings using electricity for the end use)

	Total	Space heating	Cooling	Ventilation	Water heating	Lighting	Cooking	Refrigeration	Office equipment	Computing	Other
All buildings	14.6	0.5	2.4	2.4	0.2	2.5	1.1	2.7	0.6	1.5	2.7
Principal building activity											
Education	11	0.5	2.5	1.6	0.2	1.9	0.2	1	0.5	1.9	1.6
Food sales	48.7	0.6	1.6	2.8	(*)	3.6	4.3	34.5	0.5	0.6	2.7
Food service	44.9	1.4	5.3	5	1.1	3	15.9	18.3	1.2	0.8	3.4
Office	15.9	0.6	2.2	3.9	0.1	2.7	0.2	0.6	0.7	3.1	2.4
Public assembly	14.5	1	5.2	1.3	(*)	1.9	0.5	1.5	0.4	0.9	3.8

from the average developed in Table 13.4 of 48%, and most system types fall within the 5% energy impact of that benchmark percent value of 48%. The overall impact for any variance related to the differences in types of systems related to usage in this subset will be just a shifting of usage between the AC

Table 13.4   Average of every type of application from CBECS and surveys over the past 20 years on fan/pump ratios [6].

Table E6. Electricity consumption intensities (kWh) by end use, 2012					
	Electricity energy intensity[1] (kWh/square foot in buildings using electricity for the end use)				
	Cooling	Ventilation		Total HVAC	Fans % Of HVAC Electricity
Residential-type central air conditioners	1.8	1.5		3.3	45.5%
Heat pumps	2.6	2.2		4.8	45.8%
Individual air conditioners	2.1	1.9		4.0	47.5%
District chilled water	2.2	4.3		6.5	66.2%
Central chillers	3.7	3.6		7.3	49.3%
Packaged air conditioning units	2.5	2.7		5.2	51.9%
Swamp coolers	2.0	2.2		4.2	52.4%
Other	3.5	4.4		7.9	55.7%
Other Surveys					
CEUS [2]	4	3.2		7.2	56.0%
CEUS [3]	1.5	4.5		6	25.0%
NRNC [4]	2.4	2.9		5.3	45.0%
CBECS Bldgs. Energy Data Book [5]	1.5	2.7		4.2	36.0%
Average					48.0%

system usage and the fan/pump system usage. This shift of values, if any, will not impact any decisions on ECMs or at least can be mitigated if a project is close regarding the ROI.

We find an example of good non-office hours in Figure 13.11. Note that this graph is slightly different as we can see the CDD line up along the various temperature points due to the temperature coming in as whole numbers vs. having a decimal place or two. Our recommendation is to use at least one significant digit past the decimal. Notice a negative slope in the scatter plot when comparing kWh to temperature during non-office hours. We do not want energy usage to correlate to the temperature. If a system is not responding to temperature, there is no correlation. This figure shows that there is no correlation to OAT during non-office hours. This means that the system schedule and controls are working correctly and not responding to the outdoor temperature. On the heating side, we would want it to respond to temperature during the winter, but only when the temperature drops below 45°F.

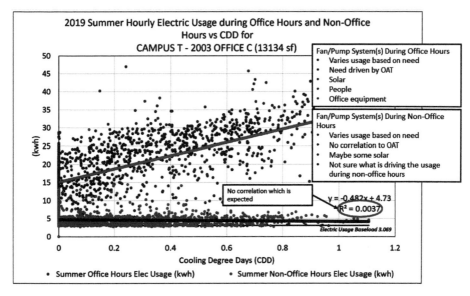

Figure 13.11   Graph showing a good schedule on AC and fan/pump system.

Now, there are two important questions when looking at scatter plots: (1) what is it showing me overall? and (2) why does it respond in this manner?

The small amount of usage shown in Figure 13.11 occurs during non-office hours, indicating a system responding to a small load. That means the largest part of the system does not have a scheduling issue but that certain smaller systems are running without control or schedules. In these cases, there is a much smaller system (usually a package unit) proportionate to the overall load, where the controls are not under a schedule. Hence, the small system runs whenever the OAT or solar loading drives it to respond to the load. Because of its small relative size to the overall AC system, any loading requirements for OAT and solar do not impact the slope of the non-office energy loading.

13.3 Compare the Fan/Pump System Loading Metrics

This section will show ways to benchmark the fan/pump system loads. We will give several examples as they are easily the best way to learn from this benchmark tool. As discussed, the fan/pump systems have not changed much over time. The fan/pump and AC systems have been a very stable energy loading for benchmarking these two systems. There have been limited changes over the last 20 years to the loading in a kWh/sf. Let us review the fan/pump

Table 13.5   Metrics for fan/pump systems from surveys.

Building	Type Usage	Plug	Lights	Fan/ Pump	AC	Office	Total	Climate Zone
747	office	0.785	1.472	4.901	1.281	0.507	8.946	5B
3732	office	0.785	1.647	2.997	0.604	0.507	6.540	5B
281	office	0.785	0.738	2.481	0.751	0.507	5.262	5B
4568	office	0.796	0.745	3.029	0.907	0.496	5.972	5B
4737	office	0.778	2.074	6.566	1.324	0.514	11.256	5B
3748	office	0.790	0.504	7.337	2.119	0.502	11.251	5B
1348	office	0.811	0.611	2.216	0.515	0.481	4.634	5B
4767	office	0.775	1.190	1.993	0.658	0.517	5.133	5B
115	office	0.785	1.641	4.424	2.301	0.507	9.657	5A
24	office	0.785	2.052	4.580	1.304	0.507	9.228	5A
1585	office	0.785	2.097	8.150	1.714	0.507	13.253	5A
70	office	0.785	2.044	5.369	1.274	0.507	9.979	5A
1524	office	0.785	1.801	2.604	0.974	0.507	6.670	5A
83	office	0.785	1.724	5.207	1.609	0.507	9.832	5A
251	office	0.785	2.902	4.477	2.157	0.507	10.828	5A
58	office	0.763	0.556	9.893	3.289	0.528	15.029	3A
1741	office	0.808	0.892	4.367	0.972	0.484	7.523	3A
79	office	0.808	0.706	1.608	0.756	0.484	4.362	3A
2677	office	0.808	0.813	5.316	1.719	0.484	9.140	3A
	Average	0.789	1.379	4.606	1.380	0.503	8.658	
	Median	0.785	1.472	4.477	1.281	0.507	9.140	

system loading and why we categorized them together. We look at these two pieces of equipment (fan/pump) as one category since they are the medium to distribute the chilled/hot water and/or cold or warm air and supply/exhaust air. And while they may vary in loading, they will appear together in the scatter plot analysis. First, let us discuss this from a broad perspective. After removing those on a central plant, we will take approximately 20 buildings (Table 13.5) that were surveyed. Note that the range of the values goes from 2.0 up to 9.9 kWh/sf. The average is 4.6, with the median at 4.5 kWh/sf/yr.

A more appropriate metric might be the percentage of the overall total usage. Table 13.6 shows a much tighter pattern when we look at the fan/pump as a percentage of the overall usage vs. the range of values for the various

Table 13.6 Fan/pump systems percent of total load.

Building	Type Usage	Fan/ Pump	Total	Fan % of Total
747	office	4.901	8.946	54.8%
3732	office	2.997	6.540	45.8%
281	office	2.481	5.262	47.2%
4568	office	3.029	5.972	50.7%
4737	office	6.566	11.256	58.3%
3748	office	7.337	11.251	65.2%
1348	office	2.216	4.634	47.8%
4767	office	1.993	5.133	38.8%
115	office	4.424	9.657	45.8%
24	office	4.580	9.228	49.6%
1585	office	8.150	13.253	61.5%
70	office	5.369	9.979	53.8%
1524	office	2.604	6.670	39.0%
83	office	5.207	9.832	53.0%
251	office	4.477	10.828	41.3%
58	office	9.893	15.029	65.8%
1741	office	4.367	7.523	58.1%
79	office	1.608	4.362	36.9%
2677	office	5.316	9.140	58.2%
	Average	**4.606**	**8.658**	**53.2%**
	Median	**4.477**	**9.140**	**49.0%**

fan/pump examples. The fan will be the largest value in almost every case we surveyed. So, when we review this fan, the data will be within plus or minus 17% of the average fan as a percent of the total load. That still seems large, but maybe we can narrow that down based on the type of system being analyzed.

If we dial into these deeper in Table 13.7, we see the fan/pump system will be slightly higher for the Climate Zone 3A vs. 5A and 5B. This only illustrates a good way to make a comparison, but not entirely conclusive as we do not yet have a statistically relevant grouping.

Note that the fan/pump system benchmarks for a VAV system (Table 13.8) are running a median of 2.6 kWh/sf. This is compared to the 4.7 kWh/sf shown previously. This is a small number of records, as discussed above.

Table 13.7   Metrics for fan/pump systems for climate zones.

Building	Type Usage	Fan/ Pump	Total	Climate Zone	Average for Fan/Pump	Average for Total	Fan % of Total
747	office	4.901	8.946	5B			
3732	office	2.997	6.540	5B			
281	office	2.481	5.262	5B			
4568	office	3.029	5.972	5B			
4737	office	6.566	11.256	5B			
3748	office	7.337	11.251	5B			
1348	office	2.216	4.634	5B			
4767	office	1.993	5.133	5B	3.940	7.374	53.4%
115	office	4.424	9.657	5A			
24	office	4.580	9.228	5A			
1585	office	8.150	13.253	5A			
70	office	5.369	9.979	5A			
1524	office	2.604	6.670	5A			
83	office	5.207	9.832	5A			
251	office	4.477	10.828	5A	4.973	9.921	50.1%
58	office	9.893	15.029	3A			
1741	office	4.367	7.523	3A			
79	office	1.608	4.362	3A			
2677	office	5.316	9.140	3A	5.296	9.014	58.8%
	Average	4.606	8.658				
	Median	4.477	9.140				

In Table 13.9, we will show the comparison across various systems. This is not a direct benchmark but will allow us to correlate the numbers to a high degree. We have checked several aspects of this comparison. For example, the climate zone, as discussed in Appendix 3, is set at 5B. The building being analyzed is an office, generally the simplest type of space, referred to as "Type A." The space has no additional data closets or server towers, and the office equipment is basic copiers, etc. For example, note that the total for the buildings in 2019 and 2021 was very close. We see that 2021 was higher in most cases, probably due to a return from COVID for this particular campus. So, assuming 2021 was a normal year, we have all our package units, split systems, etc., coming in over 20% higher at 5.8 kWh/sf/yr or 1 kWh/sf higher than the base loading. That would all be attributable to the additional energy from the system and maybe from the

Table 13.8 Metrics for fan/pump systems for VAV systems.

Building	Type Usage	Plug	Lights	Fan/ Pump	AC	Office	Total	Climate Zone
3732	office	0.785	1.647	2.997	0.604	0.507	6.540	5B
4737	office	0.778	2.074	6.566	1.324	0.514	11.256	5B
1348	office	0.811	0.611	2.216	0.515	0.481	4.634	5B
4767	office	0.775	1.190	1.993	0.658	0.517	5.133	5B
	Average	0.787	1.380	3.443	0.775	0.505	6.891	
	Median	0.781	1.418	2.607	0.631	0.510	5.836	

Table 13.9 Metrics for fan/pump systems.

	2019 kWh/sf	2021 kWh/sf		
All	4.637	4.727		
Packaged or Splits	5.223	5.792	122.5%	Over Campus Loading
VAV	4.663	4.727	81.6%	Less than Packaged/Splits
Chiller Plant	3.865	3.650	77.2%	Less than Campus

lack of enterprise control over this type of system or at least the smaller units. So, a portion would be assigned to the system, some to the lack of control and some to the AC system itself. This is supported by the next line, which indicates the VAV systems are running the same as the overall numbers. So, we cannot technically consider all of it associated with the fan/pump system loading, and the exact extent would be difficult to establish with just this information.

The previous sections show that the average for lights, plug loads, and office loads runs 1.85–2.56 kWh/sf, leaving between 1 and 1.8 kWh/sf/yr for fan/pump systems in the chiller-plant-cooling scenario. Even though we used this data from the scatter plot results, we can directly calculate both if someone does these calculations frequently in their daily business. That difference ranges from 2.2 to 2.9 kWh/sf/yr in VAV systems for fan/pump systems and AC system loading. For all systems, that range would be 3.2–3.9 kWh/sf/yr for fan/pump systems and AC system loading. Just intuitively, we would surmise that the AC system represents about 1 kWh/sf/yr for this campus and

Table 13.10   Metrics for fan/pump systems for chiller plant.

Building	Type Usage	Plug	Lights	Fan/ Pump	AC	Office	Total	Climate Zone
1301	office	0.785	0.668	1.382	0.000	0.507	3.342	5B
1002	office	0.785	0.337	2.178	0.000	0.507	3.807	5B
1302	office	0.785	0.868	2.164	0.000	0.507	4.324	5B
1052	office	0.785	0.359	2.119	0.000	0.507	3.769	5B
1102	office	0.785	0.508	3.211	0.000	0.507	5.011	5B
1252	office	0.785	0.624	3.296	0.000	0.507	5.211	5B
1101	office	0.778	0.374	2.958	0.000	0.513	4.624	5B
	Average	**0.784**	**0.534**	**2.472**	**0.000**	**0.508**	**4.298**	
	Median	**0.785**	**0.508**	**2.178**	**0.000**	**0.507**	**4.324**	

office building Type A, but that will be discussed further in the next chapter. That leaves the differences related to the fan/pump system loading. This confirms what was shown earlier from the breakdown of the scatter plot numbers if we take them on from a breakdown by the total EUI. This method requires that we lock most of the variables and know all the other parameters, further supporting the advantage in time for scatter plots.

Table 13.10 shows the metrics for fans and pumps for a few buildings on the central plant. They are running a range from 1.4 to 3.2 kWh/sf for the year. Their median is 2.1, while the average is 2.5 kWh/sf/yr. This is low and can be explained easily. This campus has a chiller plant circulating water to each building. These buildings have pumps circulating water to individual fan coils. The power required to circulate water is less than moving air, and the fan coils are usually controlled.

Now we want to analyze the impact of buildings with separate cooling systems. For example, many buildings use chilled water from another source. So, Figure 13.12 depicts four facilities that compare two with separate chilled water plants to two that have chillers at the building. These show the variation of the system loadings. The top two PIE charts show the two facilities that are on the central chilled water plant. The AC system load is zero for each, as the chilled water plant is outside the meter for the facility. The fan varies between 39.9% for one and 50% for the other, showing that the chilled water plant does not drive the number of systems left on. The bottom two PIE charts are facilities that have chilled water systems at the facility itself. Note the variance in the loading is not just between the fan/pump system and the AC system. In the facility at the bottom right corner, both the AC system load and

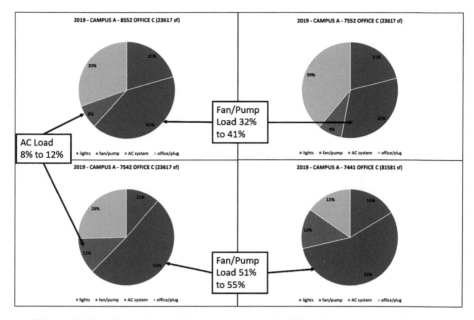

Figure 13.12 Comparing chiller plant usage vs. individual plants at the buildings.

the fan/pump system load are larger than that facility at the bottom left corner. It means we need to focus on where the energy subsets are to determine the "real" usage vs. the perceived usage.

13.4 Compare the AC System Loading Metrics

This section will provide several ways to benchmark the AC system's load. After removing those on a central plant, we will take approximately 20 buildings (Table 13.11) that were surveyed. We notice that the range of the values goes from 0.52 up to 3.3 kWh/sf. The average is 1.38, with the median at 1.28 kWh/sf/yr. We usually like to see the range being within a factor of 2× to be within a reasonable range within the same usage category and at 0.5× for the low end. This particular set of buildings was good overall, with one out-of-range on the top and two on the bottom. Those on the bottom were close enough that they may prove to be very good buildings.

Another metric might be the percent of the overall total usage. As we can see in Table 13.12, this is not as tight a pattern as the fan/pump systems. Over half are within 20%. Two are 40% or higher. This may be related to the type of system or the efficiency of those systems, but now we have two benchmarks or a method to develop a local benchmark.

Table 13.11   Metrics for AC systems on Type A office space (kWh/sf/yr).

Building	Type Usage	Plug	Lights	Fan/ Pump	AC	Office	Total	Climate Zone
747	office	0.785	1.472	4.901	1.281	0.507	8.946	5B
3732	office	0.785	1.647	2.997	0.604	0.507	6.540	5B
281	office	0.785	0.738	2.481	0.751	0.507	5.262	5B
4568	office	0.796	0.745	3.029	0.907	0.496	5.972	5B
4737	office	0.778	2.074	6.566	1.324	0.514	11.256	5B
3748	office	0.790	0.504	7.337	2.119	0.502	11.251	5B
1348	office	0.811	0.611	2.216	0.515	0.481	4.634	5B
4767	office	0.775	1.190	1.993	0.658	0.517	5.133	5B
115	office	0.785	1.641	4.424	2.301	0.507	9.657	5A
24	office	0.785	2.052	4.580	1.304	0.507	9.228	5A
1585	office	0.785	2.097	8.150	1.714	0.507	13.253	5A
70	office	0.785	2.044	5.369	1.274	0.507	9.979	5A
1524	office	0.785	1.801	2.604	0.974	0.507	6.670	5A
83	office	0.785	1.724	5.207	1.609	0.507	9.832	5A
251	office	0.785	2.902	4.477	2.157	0.507	10.828	5A
58	office	0.763	0.556	9.893	3.289	0.528	15.029	3A
1741	office	0.808	0.892	4.367	0.972	0.484	7.523	3A
79	office	0.808	0.706	1.608	0.756	0.484	4.362	3A
2677	office	0.808	0.813	5.316	1.719	0.484	9.140	3A
	Average	0.789	1.379	4.606	1.380	0.503	8.658	
	Median	0.785	1.472	4.477	1.281	0.507	9.140	

It raises the system question since we showed the large degree of variance for the AC systems on similar buildings. That benchmark is provided by CBECS data below in Table 13.13 [7]. As we can see, a central chiller plant has a better value than packaged units. But we must also assess the AC and fan/pump systems' combined value. A district or central plant runs an average savings difference between a combined fan/pump and AC chilled water system of 0.8 kWh/sf/yr over a chiller and distribution system at the building.

If we dial deeper into these comparisons, the climate zone would also be a natural extension of the benchmark. As shown in Table 13.14, the fan/pump will be slightly higher for the Climate Zones 3A and 5A vs. 5B. That goes against our natural thoughts, except we must remember the "A" designation

Table 13.12 Metrics for AC system as percent of the total load (kWh/sf/yr).

Building	Type Usage	AC	Total	AC % of Total
747	office	1.281	8.946	14.3%
3732	office	0.604	6.540	9.2%
281	office	0.751	5.262	14.3%
4568	office	0.907	5.972	15.2%
4737	office	1.324	11.256	11.8%
3748	office	2.119	11.251	18.8%
1348	office	0.515	4.634	11.1%
4767	office	0.658	5.133	12.8%
115	office	2.301	9.657	23.8%
24	office	1.304	9.228	14.1%
1585	office	1.714	13.253	12.9%
70	office	1.274	9.979	12.8%
1524	office	0.974	6.670	14.6%
83	office	1.609	9.832	16.4%
251	office	2.157	10.828	19.9%
58	office	3.289	15.029	21.9%
1741	office	0.972	7.523	12.9%
79	office	0.756	4.362	17.3%
2677	office	1.719	9.140	18.8%
	Average	1.380	8.658	15.4%
	Median	1.281	9.140	14.3%

of the zone has higher humidity. That explains part of the comparison, but one would expect a differentiation between 3A and 5A. We generally want to see 20 or more data points for a good statistical sampling.

Note that the data for the fan/pump system for a VAV system (Table 13.15) is running a median of 0.631 kWh/sf. This is compared to the 1.02 kWh/sf shown in Table 13.14 for Climate Zone 5B, as the VAV systems all come from that campus. This is based on a small number of records, as discussed above, but it is a substantially lower kWh/sf, justifying a serious look at additional data. Suppose these bear out at approximately 40% savings vs. the general population. In that case, it indicates we must look hard at future projects' design standards and retrofits to AHU systems.

Table 13.13   Metrics for fan/pump system for chiller plant (kwh/sf/yr).

Table E6. Electricity consumption intensities				
	Electricity energy intensity[1] (kWh/square foot in buildings using electricity for the end use)			
	Cooling	Ventilation		Total HVAC
Residential-type central air conditioners	1.80	1.50		3.30
Heat pumps	2.60	2.20		4.80
Individual air conditioners	2.10	1.90		4.00
District chilled water	2.20	4.30		6.50
Central chillers	3.70	3.60		7.30
Packaged air conditioning units	2.50	2.70		5.20
Swamp coolers	2.00	2.20		4.20
Other	3.50	4.40		7.90
Average	2.55			

13.5 Calculate the AC System Efficiency

So, how do we determine AC system efficiency? The traditional way is through a coefficient of performance (COP) and energy efficiency ratio (EER) for pieces of equipment. While the traditional COP and EER are interrelated, they use the system's output to determine efficiency.

$$COP = \frac{WattsOut}{WattsIn} = 3.5$$

$$EER = \frac{BTUperHourOut}{WattsIn} = 11.9425$$

$$EER = COP * 3.412.$$

So, if we look at COP vs. EER, it is simple. Let us assume a system has a COP of 3.5 watts. The EER would be 11.942 Btuh/W (COP times 3.412). Since these measure outputs are divided by input, then the higher the number, the higher the efficiency.

We do not have the system output in an MMS, but we do have the usage in energy (kWh) at a set temperature or CDD. When metering a facility, we

Table 13.14 Metrics for AC system for climate zones.

Building	Type Usage	AC	Total	Climate Zone	Average for AC System	Average for Total	AC System % of Total
747	office	1.281	8.946	5B			
3732	office	0.604	6.540	5B			
281	office	0.751	5.262	5B			
4568	office	0.907	5.972	5B			
4737	office	1.324	11.256	5B			
3748	office	2.119	11.251	5B			
1348	office	0.515	4.634	5B			
4767	office	0.658	5.133	5B	1.020	7.374	13.8%
115	office	2.301	9.657	5A			
24	office	1.304	9.228	5A			
1585	office	1.714	13.253	5A			
70	office	1.274	9.979	5A			
1524	office	0.974	6.670	5A			
83	office	1.609	9.832	5A			
251	office	2.157	10.828	5A	1.619	9.921	16.3%
58	office	3.289	15.029	3A			
1741	office	0.972	7.523	3A			
79	office	0.756	4.362	3A			
2677	office	1.719	9.140	3A	1.684	9.014	18.7%
	Average	1.380	8.658				
	Median	1.281	9.140				

Table 13.15 Metrics for AC systems with VAV.

Building	Type Usage	Plug	Lights	Fan/ Pump	AC	Office	Total	Climate Zone
3732	office	0.785	1.647	2.997	0.604	0.507	6.540	5B
4737	office	0.778	2.074	6.566	1.324	0.514	11.256	5B
1348	office	0.811	0.611	2.216	0.515	0.481	4.634	5B
4767	office	0.775	1.190	1.993	0.658	0.517	5.133	5B
	Average	0.787	1.380	3.443	0.775	0.505	6.891	
	Median	0.781	1.418	2.607	0.631	0.510	5.836	

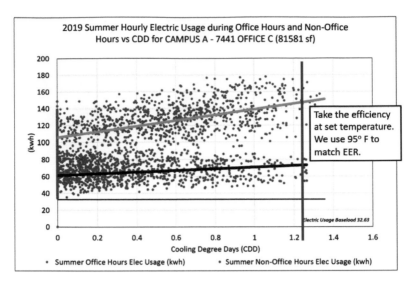

Figure 13.13   Line showing SysE on a scatter plot at 95°F.

only know what energy goes into a facility or a system. Now we have usage (kWh) calculated for every degree of temperature or CDD. So, we create our efficiency benchmark: system efficiency (SysE) in watts/sf required to satisfy the OAT at a specific temperature (i.e.,°F).

$$\text{SysE} = \text{WattsIn@95 °F} = 1.843.$$

This establishes a benchmark for the AC system for the overall building as long as every comparison is at the same temperature. The SysE includes all the AC system's associated components, such as the chiller unit(s), fan, coil, packaged units, all the fan coils, or a combination of all the systems. So, to determine our meter-derived efficiency, we use our formula SysE = watts input at 95°F = 1.843 watts/sf from the graph (see Figure 13.12). It correlates to output, but only the output implied at that temperature and is not divided by input energy. As opposed to COP or EER, in this case, the lower the number, the more efficient the system because it is purely an input kWh or usage to satisfy the load at that temperature.

From Figure 13.13, notice where the line is drawn (95°F), but how do we find the value or reading at that point? The easiest way is to list the hourly energy usage data in one column adjacent to the temperature. Sort the temperature from the highest to the lowest. At the 95°F point, grab the usage data as that SysE value. We would do that each year to make the following comparisons in Section 13.7.

Table 13.16 Comparing office hour vs. non-office hour differences (watts/sf).

	Office	Non-Office
Year	2019	2019
SysE watts/sf at 95 degrees	1.843	0.925
People	0.250	
Plug	0.216	0.090
Sub Total	1.377	0.835
Difference Attributed to Solar	0.542	

13.6 Compare AC System for Office Hours and Non-office Hours?

That set temperature gives us a different SysE for office and non-office hours. That is an important differentiator that will be broken down as follows. It is based on the different usage requirements; so let us look at what each generates. Look at Table 13.16 and note the SysE for office and non-office hours in the green row. We see 0.925 watts/sf in the right column for non-office hours vs. 1.843 watts/sf during office hours in 2019. The difference between office and non-office will have one unknown variable load, solar, and the rest are direct known load calculations – people and office equipment (plug). Those three will be calculated below and are a flat load if we assume them in blocks that will vary at the edges of the block but use the same over an hour. Some ask what happens when the OAT changes? We fix that by setting the reading with the energy output associated with 95°F. OAT is then normalized over time and against other systems because we are comparing it against the same temperature.

So, how do we define the impact of each of these usages? Generally, the rule of thumb for people in the building office space is an equivalent body heat output of 100 watts/person. The type of work they are doing will alter that number, but for this facility and most people in an office in an administrative type of operation, this number is a good standard [8]. So, with 100 watts/person, we calculate the number of people and the square footage for this particular campus, and the average is 400 sf/person for those office spaces. That gives us a total of 0.25 watts/sf. Office equipment is a straight calculation based on the kW, and we just apply that usage directly as a requirement on the AC system load. That gives us 0.0896 watts/sf during non-office hours and 0.216 watts/sf during office hours. Now let us remove the people and plug loads, which results in Table 13.16. That gives us 1.377 watts/sf for office hours and 0.835 watts/sf for non-office hours. If we take the difference between those two, we get 0.542 watts/sf, which will be assigned against the variable of solar loading. This is an average load across the summer office hours based on 2019's usage. This will vary over time based on many factors, such as cloud cover, hours of operations, manning, etc.

13.7 Compare AC Systems over Various Example Buildings

We then do further analysis at the individual building level across several years. Our first example is building 747, which, as we can see in Table 13.17, increased in SysE, signaling better maintenance. Efficiency got better for two consecutive years by almost 5% each year. There is no major change in efficiency; so we would attribute it to gradually improving maintenance. Let us compare that to the usage row over the same period. We observe a large drop from 2017 to 2018. As shown above, we know it was not because of a major efficiency change. For something to drop by 43% would require something major in the usage pattern, such as going from being run 24/7 to getting the system under a schedule. We would agree with these results. It is hard to make those large savings without changing equipment or the running schedule. We know it is not the former based on the SysE numbers; therefore, evaluate the running schedule as the driver. This was when we started the monitoring commissioning (MCx) process (Chapter 15) with this installation. Most likely, they discovered a system being left on at night and fixed the schedule, resulting in a change in annual usage. Those are the kinds of things this type of analysis can tell us and why we demonstrate this procedure.

Our next example, shown in Table 13.18, is building 3478, where we observe SysE going down over the three years (getting better). We see two large jumps, which could be project-related or a significant maintenance fix each year. However, system usage increased greatly from 2017 to 2018, but much larger than the 2018 CDD spike. This most likely indicates system schedules being overridden for a portion of the systems from 2017 to 2018 and an additional system or systems overridden from 2018 to 2019.

And our last example, shown below, is building 3755 in Table 13.19, where we observe consistent efficiency ratings. It also has good annual usage,

Table 13.17 Examining efficiency vs. usage for building 747.

Building 747			
Year	2017	2018	2019
SysE watts/sf at 95 degrees	2.021	1.924	1.843
Efficiency Change		95.2%	95.8%
Usage/yr kwh/sf/yr	2.176	1.246	1.341
Usage Increase		57.3%	107.6%

Table 13.18 Examining efficiency vs. usage for building 3748.

Building 3748			
Year	2017	2018	2019
SysE watts/sf at 95 degrees	3.573	2.826	2.274
Efficiency Change		79.1%	80.5%
Usage/yr kwh/sf/yr	1.073	1.868	2.511
Usage Increase		174.1%	134.4%

Table 13.19 Examining efficiency vs. usage for building 3755.

Building 3755			
Year	2017	2018	2019
SysE watts/sf at 95 degrees	1.527	1.537	1.544
Efficiency Change		100.7%	100.5%
Usage/yr kwh/sf/yr	1.043	1.081	1.572
Usage Increase		103.7%	145.4%

except for the last year. Again, this most likely indicates a system schedule being overridden, and this needs to be investigated.

13.8 Calculate the Waterfall of Values

Shown in Table 13.20 is the waterfall of values for the summertime period. This is broken into four energy subsets. The first energy subset is for the non-office base load waterfall of values. That is composed of the plug load,

Table 13.20   Summer waterfall of values for energy subsets.

Summer

	Non-Office				Office		

Base Load

Subset 1				Subset 3		
Plug	15,915.93	20.48%		Plug	9,465.05	20.27%
Fan/Pump	61,804.79	79.52%		Fan/Pump	37,221.59	79.73%
AC System		0.00%		AC System		0.00%
Subtotal	77,720.72	100.00%		Subtotal	46,686.64	100.00%

Above Base Load

Subset 2				Subset 4		
Fan/Pump	14,636.11	21.12%		Lights	43,061.16	35.95%
AC System	54,675.09	78.88%		Fan/Pump	6,249.88	5.22%
Office		0.00%		AC System	51533.43	43.03%
Subtotal	69,311.20	100.00%		Office	18930.1	15.80%
				Subtotal	119,774.57	100.00%

Non-Office Total	147,031.92

Office Total	166,461.21

All Hours Total	313,493.13

and whatever fan/pump systems load is on comprises the rest of the base load. Those are the only two loads that will show up in that subset. The second energy subset is the non-office hours loading above the base load. Two loads can show up in this subset. Those are the fan/pump systems loading and the AC loading. No other loads will exist in this energy subset except for the incidental load from an appliance or piece of equipment cycling on. That happens once in this period; so the value is insignificant to add to the loading. That completes the energy subsets that are during the non-office time period.

The next are the two subsets that are during office hours. The first (Subset 3), is the base load, which, like the non-office hours, has the same two components: plug load and fan/pump systems load. This is the constant load from the plug and fan/pump systems as covered in Chapters 10 and 11; so these two systems were also included above in the subset non-office hour base load. In the above base load energy subset (Subset 4), we have four systems in play: lights, office plug, fan/pump systems, and the AC system load. The lights and the office plug load are calculated separately as the lights and the office plug load are pulled from the difference between the non-office hour and office hour intercepts. The fan/pump systems and the AC load will respond to all the requirements driving the need to satisfy the space temperature. Those requirements will vary based on OAT, solar, people, equipment, etc.

Table 13.21 is the waterfall of values for the wintertime period. This is broken into four energy subsets, just like the summer table. The first subset is the base load composed of the plug load and whatever fan/pump system load is on that makes up the remainder of the base load. The second energy subset is the non-office hours loading above the base load. In the summer, two loads

Table 13.21   Winter waterfall of values for subsets.

Winter

		Non-Office			Office	
Base Load	**Subset 1**			**Subset 3**		
	Plug	22,222.63	20.48%	Plug	12,947.47	20.27%
	Fan/Pump	86,291.82	79.52%	Fan/Pump	50,916.33	79.73%
	AC System		0.00%	AC System		0.00%
	Subtotal	108,514.45	100.00%	Subtotal	63,863.80	100.00%
Above Base Load	**Subset 2**			**Subset 4**		
	Fan/Pump	90,278.66	100.00%	Lights	73,526.97	47.85%
	AC System		0.00%	Fan/Pump	54,224.07	35.29%
	Office		0.00%	AC System		0.00%
	Subtotal	90,278.66	100.00%	Office	25,894.95	16.85%
				Subtotal	153,645.99	100.00%

Non-Office Total	198,793.11

Office Total	217,509.79

All Hours Total	416,302.90

show up in this subset. In winter, there will only be the fan/pump system loading, assuming there is no electric heat. That closes the energy subsets that are during the non-office time period. The next are the two subsets that are during office hours. The first is the base load, which, like the non-office, has the same two components: plug load and fan/pump system load. In the above base load subset, we have three systems in play: lights, office plug, and fan/pump systems. These are differentiated separately as the lights and the office plug load are pulled from the difference between the non-office and office hour intercepts. The remaining loading in this subset is the fan/pump systems.

Table 13.22 combines the summer and winter values to show the energy in four subsets. Those are the non-office hours base load, the non-office hours above the base load, the office hours base load, and the office hours above the base load. This allows the EM to see where the actual usage is distributed. We have taken each of these subsets and addressed the variance on each subset in Appendix 3, the overall impact each subset has against the other energy loads in that subset, and how much any variations can affect the calculations for a building.

Table 13.23 is a summary of the waterfall values to identify potential savings from non-office hours. We start with the total non-office usage of 345,825.03 kWh to accomplish that task. Then we remove the plug load for the non-office hours from Winter and Summer. We must subtract the plug load as that will be required in most cases, and we are trying to concentrate on the savings related to fan/pump systems and AC system loading that is not required during this time period. That does not preclude us from reducing some of the plug load, but that is for another exercise, and the loading we

Table 13.22   Annual rollup of waterfall of values for energy subsets.

Annual Rollup

	Non-Office			Office		

Base Load

	Subset 1				Subset 3	
Plug	38,138.56	20.48%	Plug	22,412.53	20.27%
Fan/Pump	148,096.61	79.52%	Fan/Pump	88,137.91	79.73%
AC System		0.00%	AC System		0.00%
Subtotal	186,235.17	100.00%	Subtotal	110,550.44	100.00%

Above Base Load

	Subset 2				Subset 4	
Fan/Pump	104,914.77	65.74%	Lights	116,588.13	42.64%
AC System	54,675.09	34.26%	Fan/Pump	60,473.95	22.12%
Office		0.00%	AC System	51,533.43	18.85%
Subtotal	159,589.86	100.00%	Office	44,825.05	16.39%
			Subtotal	273,420.56	100.00%

Non-Office Total	345,825.03		Office Total	383,971.00		All Hours Total	729,796.03

Table 13.23   Using waterfall values to calculate potential savings.

		% Of Total Annual kWh Consumed
Total Annual kWh (2019)	**729,796.03**	
Non-Office kWh	345,825.03	47.4%
Winter Non-Office Hour Plug Load	22,222.63	
Summer Non-Office Hour Plug Load	15,915.93	
Total Plug for Year	38,138.56	5.2%
Potential Savings (Non-Office minus Plug Load)	**307,686.47**	**42.2%**
Energy Used to Keep Space Above 45°F	90,263.04	12.4%
Final Potential Savings	**217,423.43**	**29.8%**

are addressing is large in many cases. Once we have removed that 38,138.56 kWh plug load, all fan/pump systems, and AC system loading remaining are 307,686.47 kWh to assess the potential for savings. This is fine, except where this building is in a climate where the OAT drops below 45°F. A setback to 55°F would require a 10°F differential in OAT before heating is required to maintain 55°F. If we summarize the energy the fan system uses when the OAT is below 45°F, calculate the system usage as 90,263.04 kWh during that time. If we subtract the total usage for those systems minus the system requirements below 45° OAT, then 217,423.43 kWh remains as potential savings available. That is a possible 30% savings on the overall electrical energy usage. This does not include the synergistic savings generated from the gas system in the winter when the electrical distribution system is off.

References

[1] (n.d.). Commercial Buildings Energy Consumption Survey (CBECS) Table E6. Electricity consumption intensities (kWh) by end use, 2012. U.S. Energy Information Administration. https://www.eia.gov/ consumption/commercial/data/2012/c&e/cfm/e6.php

[2] CEUS 1997. Commercial End-Use Survey, Pacific Gas & Electric Company.

[3] CEUS 1999. Commercial End-Use Survey, Pacific Gas & Electric Company.

[4] NRNC, 1999. Nonresidential New Construction Baseline Study, prepared by RLW Analytics for Southern California Edison.

[5] Buildings Energy Data Book, 2002. U.S. Department of Energy, Office of Energy Efficiency and Renewable Energy.

[6] (n.d.). Commercial Buildings Energy Consumption Survey (CBECS) Table E6. Electricity consumption intensities (kWh) by end use, 2012. U.S. Energy Information Administration. https://www.eia.gov/ consumption/commercial/data/2012/c&e/cfm/e6.php

[7] (n.d.). Commercial Buildings Energy Consumption Survey (CBECS) Table E6. Electricity consumption intensities (kWh) by end use, 2012. U.S. Energy Information Administration. https://www.eia.gov/ consumption/commercial/data/2012/c&e/cfm/e6.php

[8] (n.d.). Human Heat Gain: Heat gain from persons in air conditioned spaces - in btu/hr. The Engineering Toolbox. https://www. engineeringtoolbox.com/persons-heat-gain-d_242.html

14

Understanding and Troubleshooting System Overrides

Abstract

This chapter covers the core aspects of potential savings. Potential savings take on many facets, but the majority of the savings will be associated with overriding systems' schedules. This chapter will cover what causes those overrides and the potential savings associated with fixing them.

14 Understanding and Troubleshooting System Overrides

This chapter will detail identifying, understanding, and troubleshooting overrides to system schedules. We will cover the following in this chapter:

- System schedule overrides

- What causes an override?

- How do we fix it?

14.1 System Schedule Overrides

The first thing we need to explain is what an override is. An override for our purposes is when the building, for whatever reason, has deviated from the design intent. The design intent is that the building was intended to operate within certain parameters. For example, an administrative building was planned to be occupied from 7:00 AM to 5:00 PM. It was designed to have a set point of 72°F, be setback to 55°F during winter, and set up to 90°F in summer. Many more detailed parameters go into design intent, but this is, in general, the design intent that we will focus on being overridden. The design intent may change over time based on occupancy or change to the schedule. However, the relevant

219

design intent is required to perform the mission for that space now. Many things prevent that facility from performing to the design intent, and we will address those issues later in this chapter. The main thing to know for now is whatever has stopped that facility from being on schedule or at that temperature is called an override or overridden from a design intent perspective.

Why is the energy manager's job important? We see that an energy manager wears many hats today. They have an administrative function of reporting energy usage in many forms. They have a sustainability function for ensuring their facilities are green and on the path to becoming greener. A project function is to develop projects that save energy but also save maintenance personnel time and provide more reliable equipment. There is a function for carbon and greenhouse gas (GHG) and the reporting associated with GHGs. The primary function of saving money has been relegated to the back burner in many public institutions and private companies. Usually, that results from a lack of time to focus on basics and reporting priorities that have dominated these professionals' time. Suppose we can get them back to the basics in priorities. In that case, it will solve two major problems today: reducing the energy waste in current facilities and the resultant impact that waste has on the production of GHGs. Energy efficiency plays a major role in reducing GHGs with implementation of cost effective efficiency measures delivering 40% of the abatement required for the Paris Agreement [1].

While there is much discussion on the impact of GHGs on climate change, many agencies are taking it very seriously. One of which is in the US military. A study they released in 2019 showed the impact on installations and the potential impact on 79 military bases as the problem continues to increase [2]. One example they used was the impact at the Tyndall Air Force Base (AFB). In October 2018, Hurricane Michael flattened Tyndall AFB in the Florida Panhandle. It was one of only four Category 5 hurricanes to hit the US [3]. As Hurricane Michael headed toward the Florida Panhandle, the warmer waters in the Gulf of Mexico increased the hurricane's intensity well beyond the normal increases. Nearly 700 buildings were destroyed, and 11,000 personnel were forced to relocate [4]. The base's rebuild is projected to cost around $4.9 billion, and they will soon be welcoming more than 70 F-35s, hundreds of airmen, and their families, the first of which will arrive in September 2023 [5]. Several factors conspired to put almost a tenth of the nation's F-22 fleet at risk during this hurricane. The storm appeared and developed swiftly, giving maintenance crews only a few days' warning to get as many jets airworthy as they could. And though the 17 F-22s left behind were put in hangars built to weather tropical storms (Figure 14.1), the buildings were no match for the hurricane, whose winds were clocked at 130

Figure 14.1 Hangar destroyed at Tyndall AFB from 2018 Hurricane Michael [6].

miles an hour before they broke the base's wind gauge [7]. The costs for the 17 F-22s are estimated to add a cost of $2B [8]. Tyndall is not the only base exposed to weather-related threats. Of the 79 installations analyzed in the report, 67% reported that they are currently facing problems from recurrent flooding, and 76% reported that flooding has the potential to create vulnerabilities in the next 20 years [2] . These are a couple of vivid examples of the costs of GHGs and their impact on global warming. The military documented the impact now and their concern for the future in the study mentioned above.

Offutt AFB (Figure 14.2) near Omaha, Nebraska, sustained more than $350 million in damage during severe flooding in March 2019 [4]. Floodwaters covered approximately a third of Offutt AFB.

As energy managers, we are equally concerned by the impact of GHGs but sometimes have trouble putting it into tangible terms. One way to discuss global warming in our terms is by putting it in the context of CDDs and HDDs. EIA has been keeping track of these since the late 1940s. We have plotted out the average for the US over the last 70 years in Appendix A. The appendix shows that HDDs have decreased by 24% over the last 72 years. That was relatively flat for the first 30 years, and most of the reduction occurred over the last 40 years. CDDs have had a bigger jump, 56%, over the last 72 years. All of that came in the last 40 years. It is increasing so that

Figure 14.2   Floodwaters covering Offutt AFB in March 2019 [4].

in another 50 years, it will be between 75% and 100%, with the difference being whether we continue at the same rate of growth or the slope starts growing. That will greatly impact our cooling loads and our design for those increases. It will also start shifting the percentage of impact the cooling has on the overall load of a facility. The CDDs are increasing faster at higher latitudes. Climate Zone 5B has increased by over 110% in the last 70 years. Global warming is melting the permafrost faster in these northern climates, which increases the amount of CO_2 produced. This is causing problems in operations in those areas. So, what we are doing as an energy manager is important. It not only has an impact on saving energy and costs for a campus, but it also has an impact on GHGs and global warming, which helps us battle this huge problem the world currently faces.

We must first evaluate the basic low-cost/no-cost ECMs to address energy systematically. The highest ROI on low-cost/no-cost savings will be in those areas where the schedules have taken the systems out of the design intent. We find that it is rampant in most institutional systems and, many times, in commercial facilities. Schedules are usually correct where buildings have professional building managers. The core approach of this chapter addresses the major savings potential, which is often overlooked. We see a major effort focused on projects and usually miss the easy opportunities for savings. This chapter will address those easy low-cost/no-cost opportunities for savings. These are often dismissed for the sexy renewable projects and construction projects to replace equipment. While these are important, we must systematically prioritize based on an ROI and accomplish these basic projects first and not overstate the other ECMs or equipment project savings. Not only are the ROIs higher on these override projects, but the largest savings are also covered, as these could easily reach 30%–40% of the overall usage, as shown in the benchmarking chapters. Because of this, spending ample time breaking this down for the energy and facilities management audience is imperative. Our experience has found that institutions' campuses without a focused program will have between 70% and 90% of their buildings with one or more of their systems overridden.

We want to emphasize that certified energy manager (CEM) training and other energy management course series emphasize that we do our low-cost/no-cost ECMs first. This is especially important as we are pushed to do projects and sometimes forget the obvious ECMs. If these are not done first, then the measurement & verification (M&V) process is flawed. We need to attack these ECMs in an orderly process with the low-cost/no-cost ECMs to set the stage for the larger projects and the larger-cost ECMs to ensure the analysis is performed correctly.

The highest ROI will always be system schedule overrides. This is the basic building block that an EM starts with, regardless of the system or other enticing ECMs. The monitoring commissioning process (MCx), detailed in Chapter 15, covers the full aspects of the overrides as their basic starting point since the schedule affects 20%–40% of energy. These are usually easy to fix and often can be fixed through the enterprise management system (EMS). The worst case is a system that has localized control. These must be addressed by lock boxes or making the end user a partner in the efforts and training and developing them into energy managers in their building.

As we recall from the benchmarking chapters, the control of systems or the lack thereof generates schedule overrides on fan/pump systems, which has the largest impact on building energy usage. The lack of control of the distribution systems will also impact the AC and heating systems. The plug load and lighting are usually not affected by control schedules. Most buildings in an institutional setting do not have lighting system schedules to worry about. Remember, we showed this wasted usage in previous chapters in two ways. The first is through an interval graph, as shown in Figure 14.3. Notice the weekends when the system is coming on in response to OAT and solar loading. It also shows the sawtooth impact on weeknights as the systems responded to demands due to OAT. The second is a scatter plot (Figure 14.4) showing all the orange points above the purple base load, indicating the system coming on during non-duty hours to satisfy OAT or solar loading.

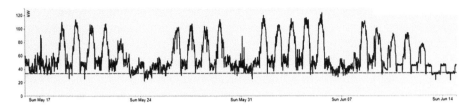

Figure 14.3   Interval kW.

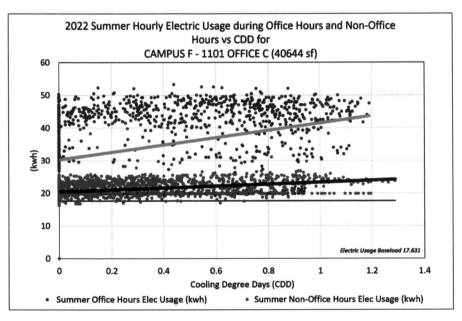

Figure 14.4   Scatter plot showing non-office usage validating overrides.

These figures are clear indicators of the performance of a building. Because of the nature of the interval graph, once we fix the system schedule that was overridden and then flag the new benchmark, we will be notified when the system is overridden again. So that we never receive a false override warning, we set a flag on the usage at the meters at a reasonable percentage above the new baseline. The test flag set point we use is that it must be over 110% of the base at 1:00 AM in the morning. If the system uses 105%, which is less, then it will show it is not overridden, thus a false positive. Our primary concern is that this criterion is large enough to avoid false negatives. We set it up enough to ensure the benchmark is overridden so that we are not responding to those false negatives. We can easily see in Figure 14.3 that every night the system exceeds 10%.

		% Of Total Annual kWh Consumed
Total Annual kWh (2019)	**729,796.03**	
Non-Office kWh	345,825.03	47.4%
Winter Non-Office Hour Plug Load	22,222.63	
Summer Non-Office Hour Plug Load	15,915.93	
Total Plug for Year	38,138.56	5.2%
Potential Savings (Non-Office minus Plug Load)	**307,686.47**	**42.2%**
Energy Used to Keep Space Above 45°F	90,263.04	12.4%
Final Potential Savings	**217,423.43**	**29.8%**

Figure 14.5 Potential savings from getting system schedules fixed.

These issues where the system is overridden on nights or weekends generally will fall into a low-cost/no-cost solution. It can go from a scheduling issue to a lack of control. We will address the various ways scheduling can be addressed later in this chapter. If the system lacks control, it can be handled in one of two ways. The first is to add a control that can add a schedule to or directly schedule that piece of equipment. A cost might be associated with that, determining whether it is economical. The EM can work with the building managers to manage schedules that may be cost-prohibitive or take time to implement. In monthly meetings with the leadership, we have seen campuses rank order buildings by EUI. This competition fostered action on controlling buildings that did not have enterprise controls. As a Lieutenant, I would go around quarterly to ensure the control system schedules and set points were set correctly. It only took a few days to get the systems back to the correct settings, but it was worthwhile from an energy and return perspective. The second approach is for those systems on an enterprise system to set them at the EMS monitor. Either way, we can easily return the controls to the design intent. As shown in the chapters on benchmarking, these overrides of the system cause the usage during non-office hours to be at 49% of the total building load. That is much larger than should be used. As discussed in Chapter 11 and shown in Figure 14.5, there are 29% potential savings here, but it could vary from 20% to 40%. That potential, divided by the low cost, drives the ROI on overrides so large that nothing can touch it. This potential alone requires a concerted effort and will take a weighted priority over any other ECM. So, with a potential average of 30% savings involvement in a systematic evaluation and programmatic response, which we call MCx, one can develop substantial savings across the campus.

So, what do these overrides impact? The benchmarking chapters showed us that the fan/pump system loading takes the brunt of the excess energy, with the AC system a distant second. So how many systems are impacted by a schedule? All HVAC systems and their related electrical equipment are schedule driven.

So, the non-office hour energy subset that contains the consumption for the AC and fans/pumps system can all be impacted directly by the scheduling of the control systems. Since a normal one-shift operation building is only occupied 33% of the time, control schedules can impact usage by leaving things running during those unoccupied times. And, since roughly 90% of institutional buildings are single-shift operations, this has a major impact on the energy usage for an installation.

So how does an energy manager make an impact on this area? It is difficult because it must be a collaborative effort with the maintenance shops. In some cases, there could be several shops involved. Normally we would need to work with the controls shop, but in many cases, that may cross over into the AC systems shop. In some cases, a central plant shop may need to get involved. The goal of this collaboration is to establish a teaming environment. Everyone is a stakeholder, and we establish this relationship to lead into our MCx program.

We have found it easy to work with the shops for short-term goals. It is much harder to incorporate change over the long term. Over the next two chapters, we will try to lay out the process to make those long-term internal dynamics permanent.

14.2 What Causes an Override?

Here is a list of the top 10 reasons a system is overridden from the design intent. Most are schedule related, or they could be equipment related so that they somehow impact the execution of a schedule or a supposed schedule.

1.   Hand off auto (HOA) switch in hand mode

2.   Sub-panel overrides

3.   Main panel overrides

4.   Schedule never programmed

5.   Poor or improper maintenance

Figure 14.6   Siemens HOA selector switch control station.

6.   Broken and failed parts

7.   Linkage disconnected

8.   Equipment incorrectly installed

9.   Incorrect equipment design

10. Incorrect controller program

The first has to do with the HOA switch. As seen in Figure 14.6, this switch accounts for the vast majority (70%–80%) of the overrides observed in inspecting maintenance. These are normally on a fan or pump to allow maintenance. A technician will switch it to hand mode to perform maintenance and then forget to switch it back. When that occurs, the controls are overridden from a schedule perspective. This cannot be viewed by the main monitor in most control systems. So that means once this happens, it can only be caught in a couple of ways. The old way to catch these was a query that would show the system was not performing correctly. This is problematic because we need enough delta T in the OAT for this to occur; so the system may go a month during a shoulder season without the query alarming us of the override. It also requires a lot of disk space to process, and we had to set up a second server just to cover all the queries. This was handled more easily when we installed meters. Before meters, we also had to review the time-consuming queries. Another way is to install "made" switches, which is an easy catch but requires a query to be reviewed. "Made" switches are sail switches in the fan's airstream or amp sensors on the motors. The easiest solution is to flag changes on the meter and email the EM and the shops when it hits a threshold. As discussed in the first two benchmarking chapters, we usually set that at 110% of the base load. An easy way to ensure there aren't any HOA issues in the future is to change the HOAs to on/off switches. The maintenance technician will have to turn the system on before departing since the system will not run until he closes the switch.

The second override is the HOA in the control system panel in the mechanical room. The control technician generally does this and it is rare but occurs when he gets rushed or just forgets to set it back before departing the job site.

The third reason is an override at the front end of the EMS. This happens when a user needs to work in the evening or weekend and asks for a schedule change. These are easy to forget and could linger until a query or flag alerts us to this override.

The fourth reason is an override we never expected to see. It was always a possibility that we had never seen it in practice until a few years ago. It was automatic in our experience when a control company put in controls to ask for a schedule or to set a campus-wide normal schedule for each system installed. On one large campus a few years ago, we found that many controllers never had their schedule established. It was a quick fix, but we were surprised at the oversight.

The fifth reason is related to poor or improper maintenance. There are many examples, but the easiest to envision is a case where maintenance has removed a wire or connected something in reverse; so the controller does not work properly. There are many ways this can occur, but this example gives a general idea of how this can happen.

The sixth reason is similar to the fifth, in that something has broken, preventing the controller from working properly. It could be the controller, a relay, or a power source that would override the control schedule.

The seventh is having the linkage disconnected. This is when maintenance is called out on a hot/cold call. They are trying to resolve the situation to keep the occupant happy. They cannot find the root cause, or it has taken too long; so they resolve it by disconnecting a linkage to a box or duct. They bypass the system to solve the immediate problem but never return to fix the underlying issue. In our early days, this happened a lot with outdoor air dampers. We saw many disconnected dampers, and the position was set based on a position drawn on the duct based on the time of year. We even saw many calibrated 2 × 4s with the two positions labeled in slots on the board. Hopefully, we are beyond those control issues today.

The eighth through the tenth are problems associated with poor or inadequate commissioning (Cx). These last three items are similar in that they occur during design and construction. They should be caught during Cx, but as we know, the quality of commissioning varies greatly, and if a building is over 10 years old, then the likelihood that it was commissioned properly is small. An example for eight is equipment installed backward, such as a linkage or motor set up backward. These are basic things that used to be prevalent before Cx. Cx has gotten much better over the past 5–10 years. The focus on Cx was better on more complex buildings but has been expanded to all buildings lately. Design and construction must still be managed properly to achieve the required results.

Equipment design should be caught if the Cx agent's scope includes the design phase. Many are used only during construction, which may cause us to miss critical design issues. This can usually be seen in equipment mismatches. There are several ways to catch this, but be aware of the situation.

The final is an incorrect controller program. This can take the form of an incorrect set point, an incorrect schedule, and many other basic issues that are relatively simple to fix. The more costly programming issues are related to more complex systems containing a preheat coil and insufficient length between the fan and the outdoor air intake. In one case, this situation caused the maintenance shop to set the preheat coil to a higher temperature, which caused simultaneous heating and cooling. There was a simple programming solution, but the tension between the energy manager and the shops was so contentious that they could not resolve the problem, thus costing them millions of dollars a year in overheating at the preheat coils and overcooling at the main cooling coil.

An energy manager needs to know of all these things to properly understand why their system is overridden from the design intent. Understanding is one thing, but correcting it is another matter dealt with in Chapter 15. The energy manager must also realize that one control override, such as a schedule or a fan, may wipe out all other control sequence savings. Once these overrides occur, they will stay until the energy manager takes action or until the maintenance shop changes foremen and the processes change in the shop. Without a proactive program by the shop, the systems will all degrade to override over time.

14.3 How Do We Fix It?

While it is more difficult to effect permanent change, we must change the current operating norm. We should be incentivizing the changes and their corresponding results. We need a systematic and all-encompassing process dependent on interaction with our operations & maintenance (O&M) shops. We must establish a good working relationship with these shops and make them stakeholders. Sometimes the EMs and shops do not work together daily or even weekly. For the program to work, there must be a good dialog and a process where each party agrees to the goals and process and why it is important. Unfortunately, this is the most difficult aspect of the process. This step has to be built on a good communication process, and a good history will help make this successful. If there has been a contentious relationship in the past, it can make working through this step more challenging. Even if the relationship has been cordial or good, we must find common ground to get this process moving. And, since we are engineers, it is sometimes difficult to communicate effectively.

The Handbook of Energy Engineering indicates that the most likely and greatest initial rate of return is due to establishing a good maintenance management program. Normally, unscheduled calls should be around 20% of the labor hours. When we have overrides and other maintenance-related issues, the unscheduled calls can increase to 50% of maintenance labor time, according to one study done accomplished by the author in 1985-1986 for the Air Force across 12 installations . A good balance and a systematic approach will save those maintenance hours for other work orders. In a recent Association of Energy Engineers webinar, "Monitoring-based Commissioning and the Continuous Improvement Cycle," Marie Curatolo, Senior Project Manager for Energy+Eco, Environmental System Design, Inc., noted that the process directly impacts O&M costs. She said that they had seen a 40% reduction in HVAC-related complaints, which has extended the equipment's useful life due to a less frequent need for servicing. She also stated that they had seen a 50% improvement in HVAC-related O&M hours, with a 30% average decrease in the duration of HVAC-related problems. They have also recorded a 10% reduction in asset breakdown rates [9].

So, in summary, we have shared the importance of system overrides and their impact on energy usage and savings. We must establish a systematic energy management strategy and implement a systematic monitoring approach at each campus. Also required is coordination with O&M shops to develop a mutually agreed upon approach to work energy-related issues. This includes re-establishing the building schedule to "current" design conditions and validating the savings via an M&V program. We will expand on this in the next chapter on MCx.

References

[1] (n.d.). Emissions savings. International Energy Agency. https://www.iea.org/reports/multiple-benefits-of-energy-efficiency/emissions-savings

[2] (2019, January). Report on Effects of a Changing Climate to the Department of Defense. Wordpress.com. https://climateandsecurity.files.wordpress.com/2019/01/sec_335_ndaa-report_effects_of_a_changing_climate_to_dod.pdf

[3] Thompson, L. (2022, September 24). After destruction, Florida Air Force base rebuilds to face effects of climate change. NBC News. https://www.nbcnews.com/science/environment/destruction-florida-air-force-base-rebuilds-face-effects-climate-chang-rcna43091

[4] Wesner Childs, J. (2019, May 1). Rebuilding of Tyndall, Offutt Air Force Bases After Storms Stalled Due to Lack of Funds. The Weather Channel. https://weather.com/news/news/2019-05-01-tyndall-offutt-hurricane-flood-rebuilding-stalled

[5] Williams, N. (2021, May 2). Tyndall Air Force Base on its way to becoming the "base of the future". News Channel 7 WJHG. https://www.wjhg.com/2021/05/03/tyndall-air-force-base-on-its-way-to-becoming-the-base-of-the-future/

[6] Associated Press. (2018, October 12). Tyndall Air Force Base sustained 'catastrophic' damage during Hurricane Michael. NBC News. REUTERS/Terray Sylvester. https://www.nbcnews.com/news/us-news/tyndall-air-force-base-sustained-catastrophic-damage-during-hurricane-michael-n919611

[7] Philipps, D. (2018, October 17). Exposed by Michael: Climate Threat to Warplanes at Coastal Bases. The New York Times. https://www.nytimes.com/2018/10/17/us/tyndall-afb-damage-hurricane-michael.html

[8] Panda, A. (2018, October 15). Nearly 10 Percent of the US F-22 Inventory Was Damaged or Destroyed in Hurricane Michael. The Diplomat. https://thediplomat.com/2018/10/nearly-10-percent-of-the-us-f-22-inventory-was-damaged-or-destroyed-in-hurricane-michael/#:~:text=A%20

significant%20proportion%20of%20the%20total%20F-22%20
Raptor,been%20significantly%20damaged%20or%20destroyed%20
in%20the%20hurricane

[9] Curatolo, M. (2020, April 9). Monitoring-based Commissioning and the Continuous Improvement Cycle [Webinar]. Association of Energy Engineers.

15

Monitoring Commissioning (MCx) Process

Abstract

This chapter covers the monitoring commissioning (MCx) approach to energy management, the MCx phases, the interaction with building operations and support (BOS) contract(s), how to implement change management, understanding the override degradation curve, and how these have been applied to other campuses.

15 Monitoring Commissioning (MCx) Process

This chapter will go into detail on the monitoring commissioning process covering the following topics:

*   Introduction

*   What is MCx?

*   Total building commissioning (Cx)

*   Degradation curve

*   Summary

15.1 Introduction

This chapter focuses on identifying specific areas of operational improvements at several campuses and the coordination efforts that are required for the phases of the energy management monitoring commissioning (MCx) process. Reviewing the buildings over our career, we found consistent issues that crossed all campuses. Further analysis found that most single-shift operation controls and/or schedules were overridden for institutions. If these overrides can be corrected as anticipated by the installation, the savings will be between 20% and 40%, as demonstrated in the chapters (11 and 14).

It is easy to get confused with all the various types of commissioning. We talk about various commissioning types so much that it can get confusing. A summary of a few types is:

1. Commissioning (Cx): Total building commissioning is applied to an entire building when it is initially commissioned. The building undergoes an intensive quality assurance process that begins during design and continues through construction.

2. Recommissioning or commissioning a building that was already commissioned: Recommissioning is another type of commissioning that occurs when an event such as building performance, change in use, or change of ownership occurs.

3. Retro-commissioning is commissioning a building to design intent that was never commissioned. Retro-commissioning is a process that seeks to improve how building equipment and systems function together [1].

4. Monitoring-based commissioning (MBCx): MBCx is a process that maintains and continuously improves building performance over time. MBCx is defined as implementing an ongoing commissioning process focusing on continuously monitoring and analyzing large amounts of data and validating with field measurements [2].

5. We will focus on a subset called monitoring commissioning (MCx), which means we focus on elements that can be flagged in the FDD process from our desktop. It is a subset of MBCx but covers 85% of savings potential without all the fieldwork.

Let us simplify the commissioning process to ensure the system or systems function properly to the design intent.

15.2 What is MCx?

Monitoring commissioning (MCx) is the continuous monitoring and ongoing commissioning – active energy management as in real-time energy monitoring – process to reduce energy use and increase cost savings in buildings at every site/installation.According to the US Department of Energy, energy savings from maintenance usually have the quickest paybacks because the investment is minimal (Industrial Assessment Center Database 1980–2018). However, the maintenance budgets are often the first to get reduced when times get tight. In addition, all these technologies and energy management systems do not ensure high-performing buildings or energy efficiency. This is where training comes in. We must train our energy managers (EMs) and resource efficiency managers (REMs) to utilize the technologies and systems to maximize functionality and get the best results. This is why MCx is so important!

15.2.1 Phases of MCx

There are several phases of MCx. Each of the first few phases is similar in number and type of steps. Each phase includes six steps supporting a specific set of similar control sequences. We will see those as follows (note: the control sequences are shown in Section 15.2.2).

Phase 1: Benchmarking and correcting basic schedule-related control sequences.

1. Determine baseline on benchmark for energy systems (control sequences 1–6).

2. Establish priority of potential savings options for the various systems and which systems can be resolved.

3. Evaluate the organization's internal dynamics and establish internal processes to solve the problem.

4. Resolve overrides.

5. Reset baseline to the "design intent," which is the intent that the current building occupants require.

6. Perform M&V at each level to validate the savings.

Phase 2: Benchmarking and correcting control sequences continued with additional sequences.

The same six steps, except the first step, go to a second set of control sequences, say sequences 7–10 (user's choice based on easiest to benchmark).

Phase 3: Benchmarking and correcting control sequences continued with additional sequences.

The same six steps, except the first step, go to a second set of control sequences, say sequences 11–14 (user's choice based on easiest to benchmark).

Phase 4: Benchmarking and correcting control sequences continued with additional sequences.

> The same six steps, except the first step, go to a second set of control sequences, say sequences 15–20 (user's choice based on easiest to benchmark).

> If the EM decides to benchmark fewer control sequences in a phase, that would just extend the number of phases.

Phase 5: The last phase includes detailed analytics of the other factors we can benchmark. Those steps are:

1. To prioritize requirements, use extrapolated EUI, base load, or percentage of base load vs. total load.

2. Determine what building systems from a project development report meet economic criteria to be upgraded.

3. Develop projects for low-cost and high-payback systems.

4. Implement low-cost projects.

5. Develop larger project economics based on the project development report.

6. Develop major project programs in project or building groups.

7. Implement major projects.

8. Perform M&V at each level to validate the savings.

We describe this process as peeling back the layers of an onion. Technically, we will have more steps, but the steps are redundant by the third and fourth phases, and one step is shown for the grouping. The first step is to lay out the benchmark for the overrides. We are benchmarking a group of control sequences contributing to the overrides. The first group of controls is any controls with a schedule or start/stop that can be overridden so that the control remains running. We have a basic set of controls listed in Section 15.2.2, but there can be 20 or more control sequences.

15.2.2 Control sequences

The 20 control sequences below are just a few that can be analyzed or evaluated to establish a benchmark. Some may have to be evaluated in sets due to the energy subset where they impact the meter usage. So, these line items for control sequences are an example set that can have many variations. These are, for example, teaching purposes and are not intended to cover all possibilities [3].

1.   Air-handler schedule

2.   Chilled water pump start/stop

3.   Hot water pump start/stop

4.   Supply fan schedule

5.   Exhaust fans start/stop

6.   Water tower fans/pumps schedule

7.   OAT reset chilled water

8.   OAT reset of hot water

9.   Economizer cycle (many variants)

10. Reset terminal boxes

11. Optimized start/stop (many variants)

12. Night setback max/min temp

13. Minimum OA strategies

14. VAV return fan capacity control

15. Mixed air low-limit control

16. Sequenced heating and cooling

17. Chilled water load determination and sequencing

18. Chiller staging

19. Hot water load determination

20. Variable frequency drive programming sequence

15.2.3 Putting it all together

The MCx phases and control sequences just give us a basis for the application. The first group will make the majority of the savings approaching 80% if the schedules are overridden. So, for example, in this case, we will target the first three control sequences. There might be more start/stop or schedules related to controls in other cases, but for this example, we will assume that these are the only three of the six for this building however, the phase will benchmark against the six control sequences due to the nature of their energy use. So, in this first phase, we will benchmark the overrides of these six control sequences as they appear as one override in the graphs. In this first step, we baseline those overrides to determine the savings potential in step 2 and prioritize the actions. In step 3, we establish a team to determine the best approach to resolve the overrides and actions to get that resolved. The maintenance shop, energy manager, or building manager takes action to resolve the overrides (step 4). At that point, we will validate the results to ensure that all the overrides were resolved. Once confirmed, we reset the baseline (step 5) to the new value and flag this revised baseline so that whenever some action overrides the baseline, the EM will be notified to check and quickly resolve the situation. Then, perform M&V (step 6) to validate the savings against the potential savings identified in step 2. This first phase of control sequences is easy to plan and manage and does not take much time or effort.

The next phase of control sequences will attack whichever set of sequences is the biggest problem for the organization. We must have the first phase completely under control to go into this phase, as the vast usage in the first phase will taint any other analysis. Some think the best control sequence to check in this phase is the boxes drifting out of calibration; others may want to deal with OAT resets. Either of these or other issues will follow the same six steps as the first phase except with different control sequences. Now each control sequence has to be benchmarked differently. Some are easier than others. For example, at an installation that has issues with economizer cycles, we can benchmark the usage but still need support from EMS to determine the mixed air temperatures to calculate if the economizer cycle is working properly. Once that is established, we can benchmark the usage for that building and determine the potential savings if this is controlled properly. The maintenance shops can fix the outdoor air damper so that it is adjusting appropriately to the OAT. Once we have established that parameter correctly, then we can benchmark so that we can watch to see when they go out and if it forces a rise in the kW or the usage (kWh). Once benchmarked in the MMS, we can go to the next step of establishing the potential savings, going through the resolution with the shops, resetting the baseline, and doing an M&V to determine if savings met the projections and why.

The next phase would be to take another control sequence and go through the next phase of those six steps. Our previous phasing shows one phase for each set of control sequences that can be benchmarked together but realizes that each phase represents the six-step process. We can stop after the first phase, which will generate the most potential savings. However, we have found plenty of savings in other phases, including simultaneous heating and cooling, OAT resets, etc. Once we establish each benchmark reset, we monitor the benchmarks periodically or have the MMS notify the interested parties when it flags a change.

The rest of MCx adds the fundamental energy management steps with a metering system. Having the information, we can do all aspects of analysis and comparison. So, step 13 shows that we have a set of benchmarks that we can use for buildings, which ranks them by the energy use intensity (EUI), the base load in watts/sf, and the percentage of the base load to the overall consumption. After we do the earlier steps, this will be the next step to determine how buildings by the usage category compare to their counterparts. This enables us to rank those for priority based on usage. This gets superseded by the next report (step 14), which ranks buildings by savings, giving us a better picture of costs and returns vs. just a path to prioritize for audits. Step 13 is useful if we plan a team to do energy audits. We can also use step 14 for prioritizing audits, depending on the overall approach. Step 14 is an easy way to sort out which system needs to be replaced and the economics of that decision. This step allows the EM to determine a good grouping of "like" system projects in the office. We have two chapters on steps 13 and 14 (Chapters 17 and 18, respectively). Steps 15 and 16 are basic management steps to develop and implement low-cost/no-cost projects. Steps 17, 18, and 19 are to evaluate larger projects, develop them, and finally implement them. While they do not have as much to do with the monitoring, we did not want to just cut off the identification of issues at the end of the process. We do not need to discuss these in detail for this textbook. Finally, whatever we do project-wise can and should be monitored for M&V. M&V will be hard with only building meters. Still, the EM can see if combining steps produces the anticipated results. The EM can easily break down the systems through other reports we produce to see if the impact was in the appropriate system.

15.3 Total Building Commissioning (Cx)

To adequately address commissioning, we must define it and address the process it represents. If we look at several agencies that certify commissioning agents, we see they all teach the same processes and have the same definitions. Let us take the United States Army Corps of Engineers' [4] definition for building commissioning: "Building Commissioning (Cx) is a systematic process of ensuring, using appropriate verification and documentation, during the period beginning on the initial day of the design phase of the facility and ending not earlier than one year after the date of completion of the facility, that all facility systems perform interactively in accordance with the design documentation and intent of the facility" [4]. If we study all the other commissioning agencies, we find their definitions are very close but agree on the following core statements. The first is that all commissioning is described as a systematic process. A documented checklist of procedures is followed to ensure the testing and verification are followed and completed. The second consistent factor is that those processes require procedures to be documented and validated against the design. The final core statement is that the purpose is for systems to work interactively or together to meet design intent. As defined previously, design intent is how the facility should work in its current configuration. So, the commissioning is to ensure that the building and/or systems are working together to meet the schedule and set points for the current occupant.

The various systems in a building that are surveyed during full building commissioning are:

- Heating, ventilating, and air conditioning (HVAC) systems and associated controls

- Interior and exterior lighting and day-lighting controls

- Domestic hot water systems

- Renewable energy systems (wind, solar, etc.)

- Electrical sub-metering systems

- Building envelope (building air tightness test)

- Other common systems that could be included are protective (fire suppression, lightning protection, etc.); plumbing (water distribution, sanitary, storm water, etc.); communications systems (telecommunications sound, video, etc.); alarm systems (fault detection, security, leak detection, etc.) [5].

When focusing on MCx, we will focus purely on energy use, specifically controls and their associated HVAC equipment. First, we must differentiate MCx from monitoring-based commissioning (MBCx).

Lawrence Berkeley National Laboratories (LBNL) defined MBCx as "a process which maintains and continuously improves building performance over time. MBCx is defined as implementing an ongoing commissioning process focusing on continuously monitoring and analyzing large amounts of data" [6]. Let us read through LBNL's MBCx template. They are very good at breaking down the process for documentation of equipment, incorporating the EMS and its controls into the analysis, calibration, and validation of equipment, tracking and documenting the progress on each piece of equipment. This is a great process and certainly gets into a full commissioning mode of the equipment, controls, and EMS. All other MBCx are very similar in this approach, which is very close to Continuous Commissioning® from Texas A&M Energy System Lab. They developed a guidebook for Continuous Commissioning® for the Department of Energy in 2002 that outlines a similar process [7]. Both programs define a detailed process that measures and validates the energy use at the equipment and controls.

We explain MCx as a result of benchmarking the various systems based on their usage. Some might confuse it with automated fault detection and diagnostics (AFDD); however, the MCx is the process that generates the parameters for AFDD. We are only concerned with the usage and if that is overridden from the design intent. One might call MCx an MBCx-lite because it does not require all the equipment data or the control systems information. We are merely taking care of the most critical analysis phase: the energy systems and their controls are on schedule or operating under the correct control parameters. This impacts 20%–40% of institutional customers energy usage and should be reviewed first for all commercial customers. Once this is dialed in, we might consider expanding into a full MBCx program. This is also a way to ease in without committing full resources to MBCx. LBNL estimated that 5%–30% of energy use in commercial buildings is wasted due to faults and errors in operations. FDD technologies can address this waste by identifying (detecting) deviations from normal operations (faults) and resolving (diagnosing) the type of problem or its location, minimizing the need for complex manual analysis of operational data. Although underutilized, AFDD is a powerful approach to ensuring efficient building operations. AFDD offers the potential to greatly improve performance and to do so cost-effectively [8].

The best way to do this is to give one example. In Figure 15.1, we can evaluate a building benchmarked for the base load. A couple of red flags indicate that the design intent was overridden. The first is a base load higher than the medians for that usage category. That is substantiated by analyzing two benchmarks, base load in watts/sf, and base load as percentage of the total consumption. These two benchmarks will be addressed in detail in Chapter 17. The second indicator is the visual indication from Figure 15.1, showing the systems are coming on at night and on weekends. The noise or sawtooth effect at night and weekends demonstrates the AC systems are responding to OAT at night and solar and OAT loading on weekends.

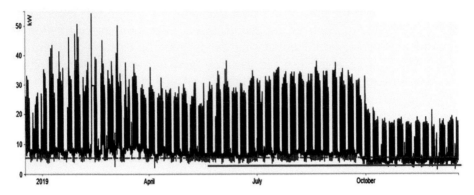

Figure 15.1   Simple system with kWh responding over time.

After a call with the shops and the energy manager, they resolved two issues when they visited the building. The first issue was a pump that did not have the schedule programmed for the start–stop controller. Therefore, it ran 24/7; so its energy shows up in the base load causing the base load to be higher as indicated by the revised base load benchmark. Putting a schedule on the start/stop for that pump solved that issue. The second issue relates to something the maintenance shop found in the field. The amplitude of the curve dropped as compared to a similar season. Their adjustment to the AC system resulted in a significant drop in the amplitude resulting in additional savings. Now we notice that they were not able to resolve all the system overrides. We can still see some systems not on enterprise control schedules since they run at night and on weekends. That will require one of several options. Resolving the override by one of many options is covered in Chapter 14. In most cases, these will resolve the issues shown in the diagram. If the system does not have controls, we must determine the cost–benefit by adding controls. Controls tying to the enterprise control system are generally an easy payback. Our experience is that in 85% of the situations, it is resolved by the override checks stated in Chapter 14. At that point, we have completed the MCx as a low-cost/no-cost ECM. At most, the EM might want to work with the maintenance shops to ensure processes for training or follow-up. For this situation, with the two implemented changes, the EM now re-baselines to ensure those fixes stay implemented. When the system goes off schedule again, we have a flag to notify us of system changes, prompting us to coordinate with the shops to resolve the issue. The solid red line in Figure 15.1 is the new baseline. We can set a flag on it now so that when it is overridden, the EM can alert the maintenance folks. The amplitude can also be flagged so that when it is overridden, the EM can alert maintenance shops to fix it at their convenience. We then performed M&V to track the savings from this change.

Over our careers, we have found that a healthy relationship between the EMs and the maintenance shop is critical to success. We always form a team where the team determines the best solution and success, which is a success for the team. We have witnessed an adversarial relationship with blame assigned, leading to a difficult work environment. Most overrides are inadvertent, either due to inattention or haste. Realize that is a given and set the flags to ensure it is caught when it happens. Over time, the maintenance personnel will develop a habit of checking the HOAs, when they leave the mechanical room, helping to prevent that issue in the future. After going back to check something, it reinforces a checklist mindset. Our most successful situations were when we had checklists for the maintenance technician and the EM monitoring the EMS. They could then troubleshoot together, and the strength of that teaming increased the troubleshooting exponentially.

15.4 Degradation Curve

When discussing system schedule overrides and getting buildings' schedules back to operating at current design conditions, we see the conditions degrade – or deteriorate in level or standard of performance – gradually over time when not continuously monitored. As shown in Chapter 14, overrides generally happen when maintenance is performed. That quarterly maintenance can impact; therefore, degradation will continue over time. The maintenance staff generally do not find the overrides in the normal process of maintenance action items. For that reason, the number of overrides will increase over time if not abated.

Our experience has shown that:

- Commercial facilities degrade to a base level (highest level) of overrides between 48 and 60 months.

- Institutions degrade to a base level of overrides between 18 and 24 months.

We always follow that generic rule, but others have a more diagnostic approach. One commissioning group seems to have a good approach, and an article on their website lays out the following points related to their experiences in recommissioning (RCx). Even one operator override could wreak havoc on the control sequences intended to operate systems efficiently. As those overrides stack up, the likelihood of systems operating inefficiently increases. They leaned toward a three-year RCx check-up; however, it is not a hard and fast rule depending on the level of maintenance. Some buildings needed RCx immediately after construction since the original design and commissioning were done improperly. Some buildings operate optimally for 5+ years because they have a good ongoing commissioning program. They have implemented successful RCx projects in buildings smaller than 50,000 square feet, but as a general rule, they find it difficult to achieve cost-effective results in buildings of this size. Larger buildings typically yield more cost-effective results because there are costs associated with the RCx process (mobilization, data processing, reporting, etc.) that do not scale linearly based on the building size.

Based on an LBNL study, the industry average cost for RCx ranges from $0.05 to $0.50 per square foot (sf). That is a huge range attributed to many factors, not the least of which is the building size. RCx costs for a small building will likely be closer to $0.50 per sf, and the savings potential in those smaller buildings is lower due to lower overall energy consumption compared to larger buildings. Higher cost per sf and lower savings potential means getting a reasonable payback on a smaller building is much harder [9].

So, the point is to maximize the savings potential that MCx can accomplish before turning to the more expensive MBCx or RCx. In those cases, complete the higher payback fixes from MCx, at least for the first set of control sequences. Then build up information for the next set of control sequences for the maintenance shop or let the items build up until we can do a surgical RCx for specific systems on the entire campus, reducing cost exposure and increasing savings.

If we look at the LBL study mentioned above, we read that they found average annual non-energy commissioning benefits of $0.26 per square foot for existing buildings. The median estimated total energy savings for our sample was 3.2 kbtu/sf/yr (0.55 kWh/sf/yr for electricity, 0.1 watts/sf for peak electrical demand, and 2.2 kbtu/sf/yr for natural gas). Unless all recommendations are implemented "on the spot" by the commissioning provider, any time lapse may decrease the probability of success as to what degree of anticipated energy savings are, in fact, captured. In this way, there is a potential found by their study that ECMs recommended for the potential savings were not implemented (58% of the existing buildings projects partially or fully verified their measures to have been implemented), or the clarity that ECMs were accomplished but not reported [10]. We find that the longer an ECM goes beyond the study, the likelihood of implementation goes down exponentially.

We are seeing an evolution in maintenance towards energy-centered maintenance, which started in 2012 and is now being incorporated into a computerized maintenance management system (CMMS) [11]. CMMS is an automated maintenance management system that picks certain parameters to perform maintenance. Those could be running hours or, in this case, energy usage. MCx can even be integrated into the front end to simplify the issues for maintenance shops. It will save them the lag time that is so critical to effectively managing their time.

As discussed above, there is a degradation curve associated with over-rides, but it is very distinct between commercial and institutional buildings. Commercial facilities degrade to a base level of overrides on average between 48 and 60 months. That is why RCx was generally performed every three years after occupancy to hit the height of the degradation curve for return on investment for the RCx. This can be modified based on the size of the building and overall energy use to hit the right timing for the ROI. Institutions degrade to a base level of overrides between 18 and 24 months. This is because maintenance is generally based on a "fix it when broke" strategy and response-type maintenance vs. an emphasis on preventive or predictive maintenance. This happens when the emphasis focuses on how responsive the maintenance shop is to calls rather than proactively preventing the call in the first place. Federal and state institutions fall into this category as we have inspected more than 70 campuses directly and over 100 indirectly, with this being the main driver. This leads to faster degradation of the overrides in the routine and unscheduled maintenance visits. The unscheduled calls were core to Buster's master's thesis, which found that the lag time on unscheduled calls dominated 30% of the overall hours limiting the maintenance hours. So, we can see how the lack of time impacted the scheduled routine maintenance. This caused a vicious cycle of one impacting the other until unscheduled calls approached 50% of the manhours.

If we approach the overrides with a purpose, they decrease after a few months of effort. Here is one example (Figure 15.2) of an institution's campus where the EM was one of the best observed. Still, he had over 60% overrides (which is much better than most institutional campuses). After three months, he dropped that value to 20% through MCx. He had challenges because it was an Air Force installation, and the shop was in constant turnover; so we were in constant training mode to keep it down to 20%. The numbers crept up every time the EM was on vacation for a week or more.

While it is rather obvious over the past 20 years of doing MCx, to drive home the point, we started "Buster's law," which is:

"Without a smart, continuous, and aggressive program to maintain automatic control, the control system applications will quickly migrate toward manual (override) positions."

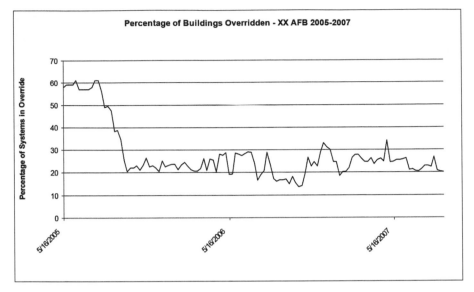

Figure 15.2   Degradation of overrides at one campus.

The corollary to that law relates directly to energy savings associated with MCx:

> "Without a continuous diagnostics approach, energy usage will be 20-40% higher than required to provide a comfortable and healthful indoor environment."

As shown in Figure 15.3, energy savings are possible from one of two groups. The first is the constant energy use, which is fans/pump system(s) that are on constantly. The lower purple arrow shows where this energy usage appears in the scatter plot. The second is the variable energy that comes from the system running during non-office hours to satisfy the temperature in the space as the OAT changes or as the solar load adds a requirement for cooling.

15.5 Summary

What is the value of doing MCx?

- A large portion of the institutional buildings have one or more overrides. Our experience has shown that 70%–90% have at least one system overridden. The potential savings from fixing overrides alone is

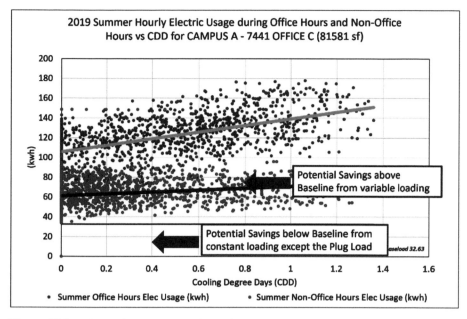

Figure 15.3 Visual of energy waste from the constant loading or variable loading during non-office hours that MCx will identify.

20%–40% of the energy for the facility. A continuous MCx program will maximize those savings.

- With a campus electric cost of $10M per year, that would mean $2–4M potential savings. This alone justifies the first priority in resources.

- In summary, we have tried to do the following with our MCx process:

- Establish a systematic energy management strategy: We have shown the importance of approaching energy systematically. Otherwise, an EM gets oriented on projects and forgets to do the basics, which taints project results.

- Roll out a systematic monitoring approach with the metering system: We have systematically laid out a process with MMS by automating various functions that give us reports, as well as milestones to review and metrics to help manage the energy program.

- Coordinate with operations and maintenance shops to develop an agreed approach to work energy-related issues.

- Re-establish building systems to "current" design conditions.

- Benchmark energy usage groups at the new condition.

- Monitor and validate the savings via a measurement and verification (M&V) program.

- Continue to perform MCx to ensure it stays set or to fix it when it is changed.

- Go to the next level of MCx.

References

[1] (n.d.). Building Commissioning A Golden Opportunity for Reducing Energy Costs and Greenhouse-Gas Emissions. Berkeley Lab Energy Technologies Area. https://cx.lbl.gov/definition.html

[2] Kramer, H., Crowe, E., & Granderson, J. (2017, June). Monitoring-Based Commissioning (MBCx) Plan Template. Lawrence Berkeley National Laboratory. https://buildings.lbl.gov/sites/default/files/MBCx%20Plan %20Template_June%202017_Final.pdf

[3] (n.d.). AUDS August 2018 Cover. American University. https://www. american.edu/finance/facilities/upload/auds-division-25-integrated-automation.pdf

[4] (n.d.). Engineering and Design Total Building Commissioning Procedures. Department of the Army. https://www.publications.usace. army.mil/Portals/76/Publications/EngineerRegulations/ER_1110-345-723.pdf

[5] (2020, December 1). Unified Facilities Criteria (Ufc) High Performance And Sustainable Building Requirements. Whole Building Design Guide. https://wbdg.org/FFC/DOD/UFC/ufc_1_200_02_2020_c2.pdf

[6] Kramer, H., Crowe, E., & Granderson, J. (2017, June). Monitoring-Based Commissioning (MBCx) Plan Template. Lawrence Berkeley National Laboratory. https://buildings.lbl.gov/sites/default/files/MBCx%20Plan %20Template_June%202017_Final.pdf

[7] Liu, M., Ph.D., P.E., Claridge, D. E., Ph.D., P.E., & Turner, W. D., Ph.D., P.E. (2002, October). Continuous Commissioning[SM] Guidebook Maximizing Building Energy Efficiency and Comfort. CiteSeerX Penn State University. https://citeseerx.ist.psu.edu/document?repid=rep1&-type=pdf&doi=0f9e4342c56a453f9597aca690b3ed894d517aa0

[8] Granderson, J., Lin, G., Singla, R., Mayhorn, E., Ehrlich, P., & Vrabie, D. (2018, August 1). Commercial Fault Detection and Diagnostics Tools: What They Offer, How They Differ, and What's Still Needed.

Lawrence Berkeley National Laboratory. https://eta-publications.lbl.
gov/sites/default/files/commercial_fault_detection_and_diagnostics_-_
granderson.pdf

[9] (n.d.). Does your building need retro-commissioning (RCx)? Our top 5
signs your building is ready. KW Engineering. https://kw-engineering.
com/signs-building-ready-needs-retro-commissioning-rcx-tune-up-
energy-savings/

[10] Mills, E., Friedman, H., Powell, T., Bourassa, N., Claridge, D., Haasl, T.,
& Piette, M.A. (2004, December 15). The Cost-Effectiveness of
Commercial Buildings Commissioning. Lawrence Berkeley National
Laboratory. Portland Energy Conservation Inc. Energy Systems
Laboratory, Texas A&M University.

[11] Alshakhshir, F., Howell, M. T. (2021, May). Data Driven Energy
Centered Maintenance. River Publishers.

16

Evaluating the Energy Use Intensity (EUI) Value to the Energy Manager

Abstract

This chapter shows all the ways to use EUIs to prioritize buildings to approach auditing and quickly determine the buildings with the highest energy usage.

16   Evaluating the Energy Use Intensity (EUI) Value to the Energy Manager

This chapter will go into detail on evaluating the energy use intensity (EUI) report and its value to an energy manager. This chapter will cover the following topics:

- General EUI background

- EIA compared to federal facilities

- Value of EUI charts

- EUI compared by total, electric, and gas

- Summary

16.1 General EUI Background

EUI stands for energy use intensity or energy usage per unit of floor area. There are several ways an EM can develop an EUI. The most common way is to convert all annual energy consumption to thousand Btu (kBtu) and divide it by the square footage (sf) of a building. The comparison of kBtu/sf was used for many years as the standard for benchmarking. EIA established these per sf comparisons as benchmarks in 13 categories since 1979 and went to 18 categories by 2018 [1]. Technically, we can use any energy comparison/sf as, in many instances, we use kWh/sf as a benchmark today since it is an easier term to compare in most of our minds. We can compare the energy to other standards, which will be discussed later. There are many versions of EUI in the DOE and EPA metrics that we will explain in the following paragraphs:

- Site EUI (kBtu/ft²)

- Source EUI (kBtu/ft²)

- Site EUI – adjusted to current year (kBtu/ft²)

- Source EUI – adjusted to current year (kBtu/ft²)

- National median site EUI (kBtu/ft²)

- National median source EUI (kBtu/ft²)

- Weather normalized site EUI (kBtu/ft²)

- Weather normalized source EUI (kBtu/ft²)

These EUIs listed above are the various EUIs used in the standard by the Energy Information Administration. The US Energy Information Administration (EIA) collects, analyzes, and disseminates independent and impartial energy information to promote sound policymaking, efficient markets, and public understanding of energy and its interaction with the economy and the environment. The same EIA Standard also has a selection of tables that depict the national median by source for an EUI. The first is the site EUI, which is how we normally track most benchmarks (EIA).

"Site energy" is the kBtu/sf measured at the building meter. EPA has determined that source energy (depicted in Figure 16.1) is the most equitable unit of evaluation for comparing different buildings to each other.

"Source energy" represents the total raw fuel required to generate the electricity a building uses (from the source, i.e., the utility generation plant) and other fuels combusted at the building. It incorporates all transmission, delivery, and production losses. Considering all energy use, the score provides a complete assessment of the overall energy impact of a building.

Most buildings use the site energy metric, the amount of heat and electricity consumed by a building as reflected in the utility bills or the building meter. So, when we see an EUI, it will default to site energy unless someone specifies otherwise. Looking at site energy can help us understand how the

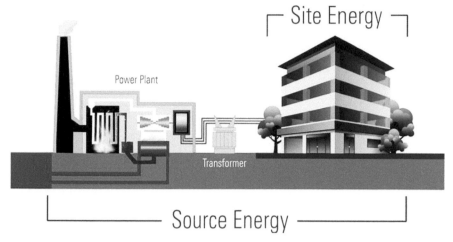

Figure 16.1 U.S. Environmental Protection Agency, Energy Star® figure that breaks down site vs. source energy [2].

energy use for an individual building has changed over time and compare it against other buildings' usage by an EUI [2].

Site energy can be subcategorized into primary or secondary energy. Primary energy is the raw fuel burned to create heat and electricity, such as natural gas or fuel oil used in onsite generation. Secondary energy is the energy (hot water, steam, or electricity) created away from a building but transmitted to the building via a distribution system. A unit of primary and a unit of secondary energy consumed at the site are not directly comparable because one represents a value on site. In contrast, the other represents a value that has to be larger to account for transmission and distribution losses. Therefore, to assess the relative efficiencies of buildings with varying proportions of primary and secondary energy consumption, it is necessary to convert these two types of energy into equivalent units of energy. EPA calls this accounting a calculation for source energy [2].

EIA uses this data from Commercial Buildings Energy Consumption Survey (CBECS) to track our progress and determine if we are doing the correct things to stay on track for reducing energy consumption. CBECS is a DOE program that tracks usage, with the latest being in 2018, for an estimated 5.9 million US commercial buildings that consumed 6.8 quadrillion BTUs. Figure 16.2 shows how they track this in five major sectors. As we can see in the commercial sector, they predicted a slight increase after COVID but are tracking to reduce by 13% in the commercial sector over the next 30 years [3].

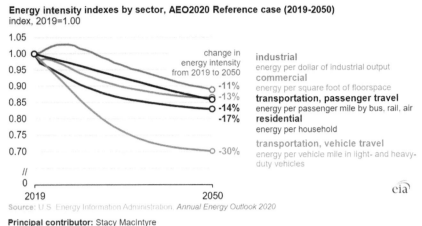

Figure 16.2   EIA figure that predicts energy usage [3].

16.1.1 Weather normalized energy

Weather-normalized energy is the energy a building would have used under average conditions (also called climate normals). The weather in a given year may be much hotter or colder than a building's normal climate; weather-normalized energy accounts for this difference. Note that the adjustment is for weather only, but not climate. The metric evaluates a building over time but does not account for differences between that particular building and other locations with different average (normal) climates. Climate refers to regional variations in average weather conditions. For example, Florida has a warmer climate than Maine. Weather refers to annual variations at a single location over time. For example, this year we had a very hot summer [4].

A ratio is used in the EPA's Portfolio Manager to convert to source energy. They use national average ratios for the conversion to source energy to ensure that no specific building will be credited (or penalized) for the relative efficiency of its energy provider(s). All Portfolio Manager energy meter types for the US will have a source to site ratio for electricity (grid purchase) at a 2.80 multiplier [5].

16.1.2 Adjusted to current year

"Adjusted to current year" allows us to compare a previous year's energy use (set baseline year for a campus) with the current year's energy use by adjusting for weather and property operations (number of workers, number of computers, etc.). This allows for an "apples to apples" comparison. For example,

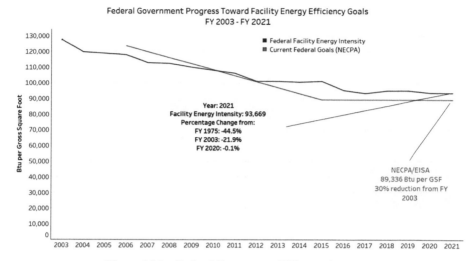

Figure 16.3   Federal Government EUI over time [6].

say we want to compare 2020 with 2010 when we initiated a major energy efficiency upgrade. But 2010 had a really cold winter, and the staffing for that building was 20% larger, which caused increased energy use. The "adjusted to current year" metrics will convert the energy use from a baseline year into the current year's terms for an accurate comparison to the current year. To translate that into the energy comparison, we are adjusting the energy use of 2010 to the current year's weather and operating characteristics. Hence, we have a fair comparison of the baseline year (2010) to the current year (2020) [7]. The EPA's Portfolio Manager is probably the best source that uses "adjusted to current year." The adjusted metrics are only available for properties with a score in the EPA portfolio manager.

16.2 Value of EUI charts

The US total energy average for all buildings is 82 kBtu/sf, as discussed in the benchmarking chapters. We have mentioned that institutional buildings have more challenges and will run higher. The Federal Government has an average of 93.7 kBtu/sf [7]. Figure 16.3 shows how well the Government has dropped over the last 18 years, but it is still behind commercial standards. That is 14.3% higher than the US average and was discussed in previous chapters.

The EUI charts were the only way to manage benchmarks before metering systems and MCx. We would generate an EUI figure like the one shown

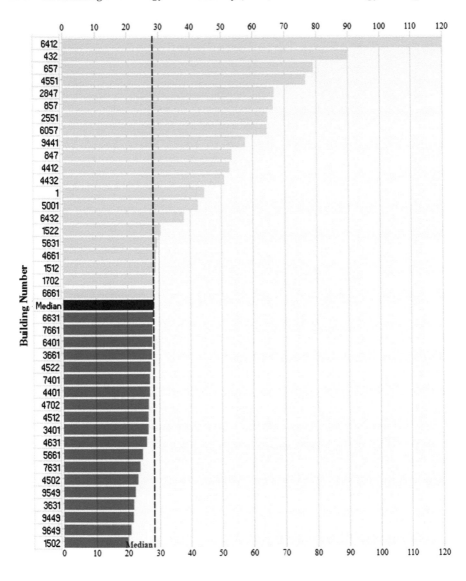

EUI (kbtu/sqft)
Commodity: Electric, Gas

Figure 16.4   EUI for electric and gas for all dormitories on campus.

in Figure 16.4. This allowed us to determine the highest probability of success for performing an audit. These charts can be used, but the more practical solution is a report prioritizing the EUIs. We use figures like Figure 16.4 to show a visual relationship, which is very effective in presentations. So, in this figure, there is a comparison of dormitories on campus. The ones on top in yellow are those that are above the median. As we will learn later, any values greater than two times the median have an 85% probability that the meter data quality is not good enough to use for analysis. So, in the figure below, we observe eight buildings where the value is over 2× the median. In those cases, the EM should check the individual commodities meters to determine, whether there is a high probability that the meter is not operating properly and should not be used by the energy manager for analysis/comparison. The remaining yellow buildings should be examined for why they are higher than the other dormitories. The green buildings are those that are better than the median. This chart includes electric and gas. Our preference is to analyze each utility separately. That allows us to focus on the fuel that is most critical from the perspective of potential savings.

When we break this down into an electric EUI (Figure 16.5), we notice the differences are much closer to the median. This is expected in dormitories as most are designed the same on campus. As we can see, no electric meters are out of range in this example. However, on the lower end, there is one building where the meter is less than half of the median. We have found that, statistically, being less than half the median gives us a high probability (85%) that the meter is bad. Generally, it is a multiplier that is misapplied.

Figure 16.6 shows the gas EUI for the same dormitories. As we can see, there are two buildings (6412 and 432) with meters greater than 2× the median. The remaining buildings fall in line here as in the electric figure above. That means that the combination of commodities skewed the total commodities and only three buildings (versus the eight in the total) may have bad meters, and only two of those were high, which were the gas meters. This is why we prefer to break down the commodities before reaching any conclusion.

Figure 16.7 is Category Office Type C facilities. We notice a similar grouping surrounding the good median, and the extremes on each end must be evaluated. These buildings are consistent in people usage and design, which provides a basic requirement for including specific lights, AC systems, and fans to distribute the AC and heating energy. The plug load does not vary much from facility to facility. In Figure 16.7, the top two buildings (715 and 57) are more than 2× the median; so we need to see the breakdown by type meter (electric and gas). Several buildings at the bottom of the charts are below 50% of the median; so we also need to check on the individual utility meters to determine which meters may need evaluation. The rest can be ranked for follow-up audits or having a team go with a mini-audit to determine the best actions.

The following electric meters in Figure 16.8 show a lot of clarity on the building's usage and the meters that may require evaluation. Two buildings

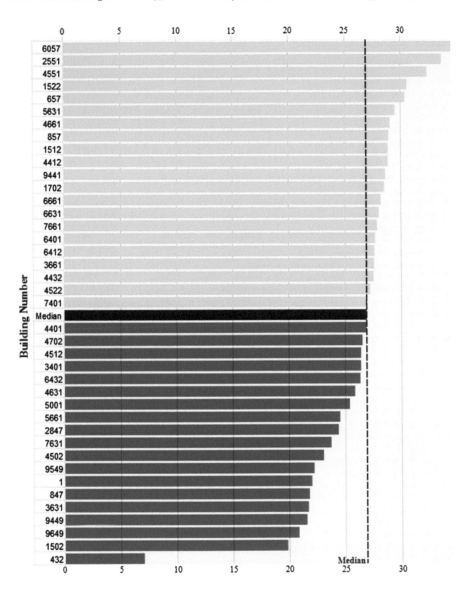

EUI (kbtu/sqft)

Commodity: Electric only

Figure 16.5 EUI for electricity for all dormitories on campus.

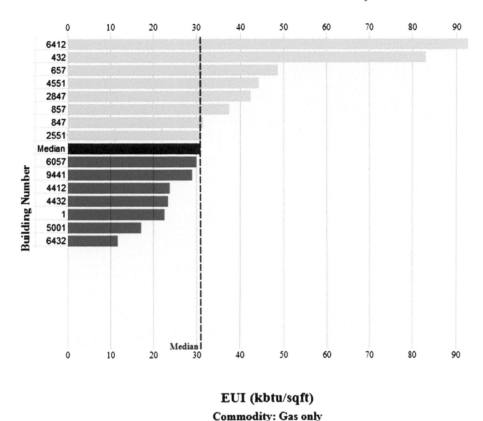

EUI (kbtu/sqft)

Commodity: Gas only

Figure 16.6 EUI for gas for all dormitories on campus.

(715 and 7572) need to be evaluated since the usage outliers indicated from these meters are above the normal limits of the median for this category type. One building, 8702, must be evaluated at the bottom end of the figure to ensure the meter is operating properly. Two other buildings, 457 and 9401, do not show any usage, indicating the meter is off line. As discussed before, an EM wants to make sure they spend their time effectively so that we do not evaluate data that may be wrong. With the exception of these outliers that are beyond normal limits and are probably a bad meter from a data quality perspective, we do have buildings that use more energy than normal and deserve the EM's attention.

Figure 16.9 covers the gas for facilities that are Category Office Type C space. One meter (building 57) must be checked at the top end and four at the bottom of this list. Otherwise, 13 buildings use more than 10% additional gas compared to the median. This is a nice start for auditing.

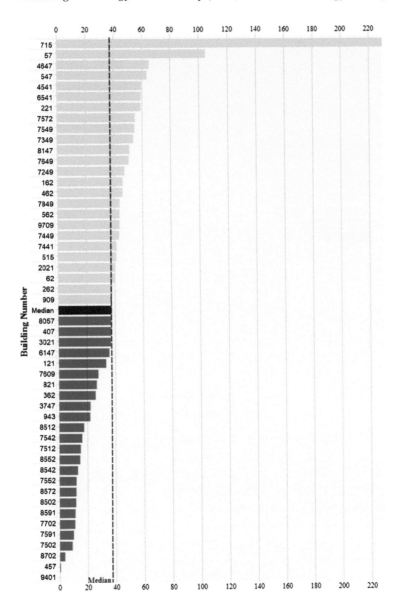

EUI (kbtu/sqft)
Commodity: Electric, Gas and/or Steam

Figure 16.7   EUI for Category Office Type C space.

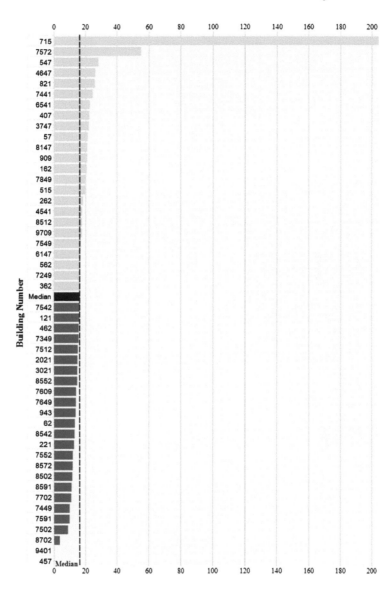

EUI (kbtu/sqft)
Commodity: Electric only

Figure 16.8   EUI for electricity for Category Office Type C space.

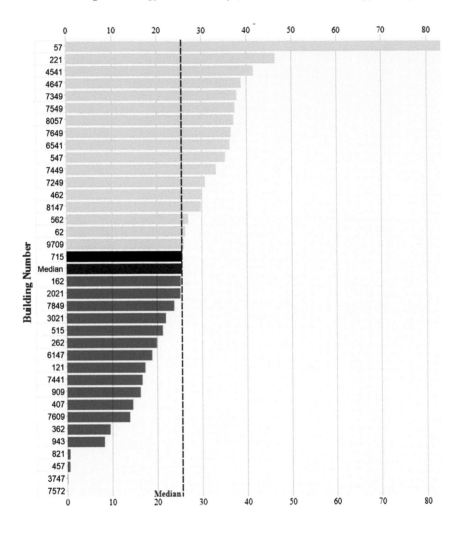

EUI (kbtu/sqft)

Commodity: Gas only

Figure 16.9   EUI for gas for Category Office Type C space.

One of the best ways to check the data is to look at the monthly data to see if it has a pattern. The monthly pattern will differ from the building interval or even hourly patterns. We are looking to see if there is an active season and an off-season. As we show in Figure 16.10, there are two seasons. Because this building is in climate zone 5B, it will have two seasons for electricity: winter, and summer. The summer is associated with the AC and fan/

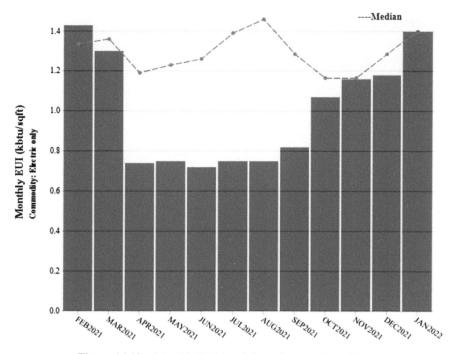

Figure 16.10 Monthly EUI breakdown for a single building.

pump systems responding to CDDs. Winter in these climate zones requires a high fan/pump system loading in response to the HDDs. We have to visualize the winter season in two parts as it is split in half in the figure. December and January are the two columns on the right, while February and March are the first two columns on the left side of the figure.

To give an example of a problem graph, we have Figure 16.11. This indicates that there were some months where the meter was not reporting correctly. Note that May through September are much lower than the normal monthly production rates for the same usage periods in shoulder months or the winter. Now a solution that will make this slightly more reasonable is extrapolating the values. We have found that the EM can easily extrapolate the values if there are small periods. The lack of data may skew the results if the missing period exceeds 40% of the values. It depends on how long the gaps of data run. It also depends on what season we are interpolating. If it is in the shoulder months, we will probably have an overstated EUI because the winter and summer are much larger in this climate zone. However, if the extrapolation is in a summer or winter season, then the EUI will be slightly understated.

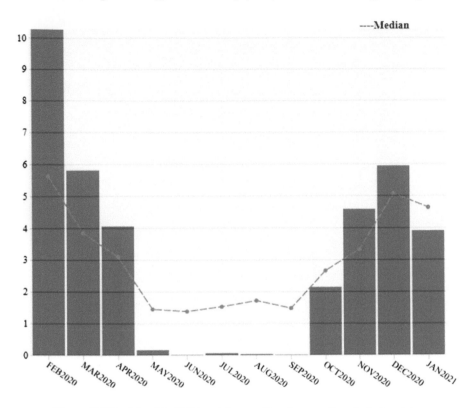

Figure 16.11   Monthly EUI breakdown with a few months of missing data.

16.3 EUI Compared by Total, Electric, and Gas

Another way to use EUI is to set up categories of "like" buildings and then compare the subset in that category to each other. For example, Table 16.1 shows 20+ categories on a campus. Each of those categories has one or more buildings within each category. Thus, we can set a median EUI and the top 25th and the bottom 25th percentile. This is very helpful in determining where this building stands against its peers and if it truly is a "like" building. In this Table 16.1, we compare Office C at 15.62 vs. Office D at 45.24 and Office A at 25.78. This is a large difference, so an EM needs to evaluate the use differences for these categories.

We can take the EUI analysis one step further by examining a specific type of system. Let us take a campus that has some buildings with geothermal systems and break those out. First, we will look at the total energy, electricity, and gas used at these seven facilities in Figure 16.12. One would expect the geothermal to be relatively close to each other as part of the system is outside the meter. So, the largest variable will be the fan/pump systems. Here those

Table 16.1   Category type metrics for installation/campus.

Category Type Performance Metrics

Organization: Campus
Commodity: Electric

Category Type	Building Count	Bottom 25th Percentile EUI	Top 25th Percentile EUI	Median EUI
OFFICE C	43	13.949	18.657	15.622
REPAIR SERVICES	37	17.095	27.847	23.938
LODGING A	36	21.709	28.358	25.242
OFFICE N	16	22.833	31.991	27.350
OFFICE D	7	29.766	58.342	45.244
OFFICE A	6	20.416	33.828	25.798
OFFICE U	5	45.120	65.278	63.120
OFFICE M	4	14.243	24.939	22.997
LODGING F	4	21.414	88.795	23.977
FOOD SALES	4	39.175	110.471	76.884
PHYS FIT CENTER	3	19.582	29.928	19.890
OFFICE W	2	28.261	34.441	31.351
MAINTENANCE	2	18.928	20.899	19.914
TRAINING A	2	12.118	13.071	12.595
FIRE STATION	2	34.613	66.855	50.734
SCHOOL	2	46.445	-1.000	47.032
FOOD SERVICES	2	17.548	32.314	24.931
TRAINING B	1	27.487	27.487	27.487
SUPPORT SERVICES	1	34.892	34.892	34.892
OFFICE OTHER	1	192.791	192.791	192.791
CONTROL SERVICES	1	42.103	42.103	42.103

vary by 30%–40% around the median, which surprises us; so we will look at the breakdown.

Let us separate the EUIs by commodity. We notice that the gas in Figure 16.13 varies a lot, and the first one is out of range from the others. There is no reason for it; so the gas meter is probably not working properly. The others are close in range to some extent, but primarily because they are small numbers. Most likely, there is no need to worry that some are twice the size of others.

The more important factor for this system would be the electric commodity usage. Figure 16.14 shows the electric median at almost 27 kBtu/sf. This is higher than the average office buildings on this campus. A geothermal system should be less than the average for the other office buildings. So, this alone makes us concerned about what causes these sites' excess usage. We would check the top three as they are proportionally higher than the median for the geothermal systems. Also, they are proportionally higher than normal office buildings on this campus. Two strong reasons for a full study on

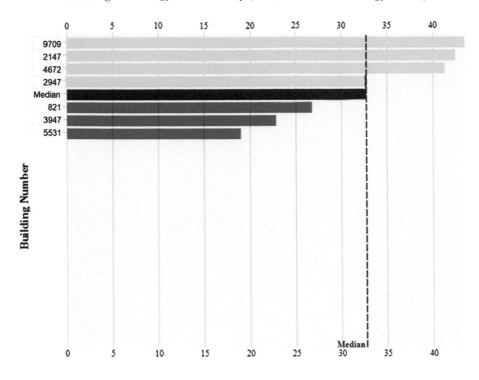

EUI (kbtu/sqft)
Commodity: Electric, Gas and/or Steam

Figure 16.12   Geothermal total energy EUI.

the excess usage of these three buildings since they are appreciably higher than office buildings on this campus. We would expect these buildings to be 15%–20% below the comparable office building of this type, which is not the case. It may be caused by having extra equipment in this building, but that is doubtful for the entire category.

16.4 Summary

The EUI has been used extensively since 1979 by the US Government to assess building performance. This was common sense and used by EMs for campuses, but the US Government decided to facilitate this process for everyone and set up a national set of medians for an EM to use. While EUI is used, it is limited because it only has 18 categories in CBECS. However, any

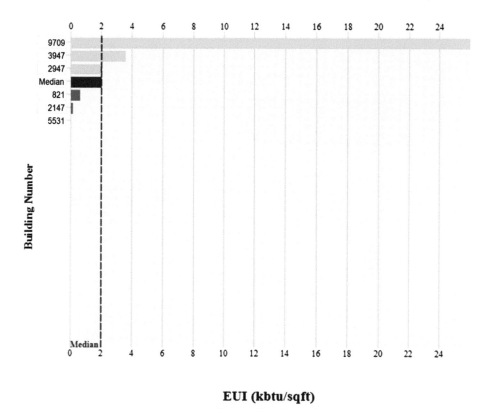

EUI (kbtu/sqft)
Commodity: Gas only

Figure 16.13 Geothermal gas energy.

good campus environment can generate its standards across its portfolio and generate a better benchmark.

The most useful product of EUIs is to establish a portfolio of buildings that are out of range; so we can schedule audits. It is a quick review process that generates the priorities for this approach. It also helps identify any buildings where the meters may need to be inspected for maintenance. The previous section that shows that a table for each category type of facilities is helpful as it will show the medians and the top 25th and the bottom 25th percentiles. This gives us a good indication of where a targeted building falls in the spectrum of similar buildings.

While this chapter has some good basic information, we will build on the lessons learned in this section to develop tools that are much more effective and provide more information in future chapters.

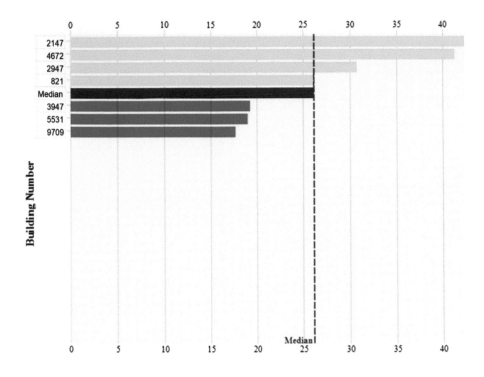

EUI (kbtu/sqft)

Commodity: Electric only

Figure 16.14   Geothermal electric energy.

References

[1] (n.d.). About the Commercial Buildings Energy Consumption Survey. U.S. Energy Information Administration. https://www.eia.gov/ consumption/commercial/about.php#:~:-text=The%20energy%20 data%20are%20collected%20using%20a%20

[2] (n.d.). The Difference Between Source and Site Energy. Energy Star. https://www.energystar.gov/buildings/benchmark/understand_metrics/ source_site_difference

[3] (n.d.). EIA projects U.S. Energy intensity to continue declining, but at a slower rate. U.S. Energy Information Administration. https://www.eia. gov/todayinenergy/detail.php?id=42895

[4] (n.d.). Portfolio Manager Technical Reference: Climate and Weather. Energy Star. https://www.energystar.gov/buildings/tools-and-resources/ portfolio-manager-technical-reference-climate-and-weather

[5] (n.d.). Benchmark Your Building Using Energy Star® Portfolio Manager®. Energy Star. https://portfoliomanager.energystar.gov/pdf/reference/Source%20Energy.pdf

[6] (n.d.). FY 2021 Government-wide Performance Findings. U.S. Department of Energy. https://www.energy.gov/sites/default/files/2022-06/fy2021-performance-findings.pdf

[7] (n.d.). What does "Adjusted to Current Year" mean? Energy Star. https://energystar-mesa.force.com/PortfolioManager/s/article/What-does-Adjusted-to-Current-Year-mean-1600088550817

17

Comparing EUI to Other Metrics

Abstract

This chapter brings in two other benchmarks – base load in watts/sf and base load as a percentage of the total energy consumption – combined with EUI to give a broader picture of a building and where it stands in relation to other buildings. This section also develops the value of the two new benchmarks not used elsewhere. These two benchmarks give us a new perspective and allow additional analytics and a combined synergy with all three benchmarks.

17   Comparing EUI to Other Metrics

This chapter will go into detail, comparing the EUI report to other metrics. The following topics will be covered:

- What are the relevant parameters?

- Top 30 category types.

- Other ways to compare benchmark metrics.

17.1 What are the Relevant Parameters?

Three factors will be covered in this chapter. They are:

1.   Base load (translated into watts/sf)

2.   Base load as a percent of the total consumption

3.   EUI (extrapolated to cover any missing data)

The first is the base load. The concept was covered in both the basic and second-level benchmarking chapters. As discussed in those chapters, a line is drawn under the usage that kisses the bottom of the usage curve for an interval chart. This depicts the usage that is flat or on constantly. We also showed the same energy subset in the scatter plots in most of the benchmarking chapters. The baseline for the base load was the purple line, the minimum usage representing the maximum constant value year-round. So, when no more points were below the lowest orange point (non-office hours usage), we identified the base load. Again, this shows that we do not have any variable loading in the base load section. That is important as it indicates the load used constantly in the building. As discussed, this includes the plug load and any continuous loads left on. That base load kW was divided by square footage to give the watts per sf for that base load. Now we find that the usage of that number, watts/sf, should not vary much on a category type. If it does vary, then we have extra equipment in that building. We can check this benchmark with only a few months of data as it does not require a full year's worth of data like an EUI requires to be effective.

The second factor is the percentage of base load divided by the total consumption. This gives us an indication of how much potential savings are available. As we will find out later in this chapter, theoretically, we only have a minimum base load usage requirement, which is approximately 15% or the maximum plug load. The maximum we can theoretically leave on in a building is 75%. That means everything is left on around the clock. The load of 75% would be everything (lights, office equipment, etc.) left running 24/7, leaving the last 25% for the variable loads related to the AC and fan/pump systems cycling in response to OAT or solar load. Recalling from the PIE charts on the distribution, this would require fans and pumps to be almost completely in a constant volume mode to equal these numbers. The only type of facility that exceeds these criteria are buildings with mostly flat loads like a pumping station, communications facility, data center, etc. In essence, a building that is pure equipment or a building that is 24/7 with an exceptionally high equipment load. As most institutional buildings are one-shift operations and have some office-type function, any percent above 15% is excess usage that should be examined.

The final factor is extrapolated EUI. This was discussed somewhat in Chapter 16, but it means that we have a complete year's worth of data; so we are comparing apples to apples. Most EUIs only use the data available, and we do not know if the EM provided a full year's worth of data to establish the EUI for benchmarking against the other buildings. For this reason alone, we can see why a full year's data is required; otherwise, we have a lingering uncertainty in benchmarking values as to whether they are accurate.

Table 17.1   Portion of Energy Star US energy use intensity by property type [1].

Broad Category	Primary Function	Further Breakdown (where needed)	Source EUI (kBtu/ft²)	Site EUI (kBtu/ft²)	Reference Data Source - Peer Group Comparison
Healthcare	Ambulatory Surgical Center		138.3	62.0	CBECS - Outpatient Healthcare
	Hospital	Hospital (General Medical & Surgical)*	426.9	234.3	Industry Survey
		Other/Specialty Hospital	433.9	206.7	CBECS - Inpatient Healthcare
	Medical Office*		121.7	51.2	CBECS - Medical Office
	Outpatient Rehabilitation/Physical Therapy		138.3	62.0	CBECS - Outpatient Healthcare
	Residential Care Facility		213.2	99.0	Industry Survey
	Senior Care Community*		213.2	99.0	Industry Survey
	Urgent Care/Clinic/Other Outpatient		145.8	64.5	CBECS - Clinic/Outpatient
Lodging/Residential	Barracks*		107.5	57.9	CBECS - Dormitory
	Hotel*		146.7	63.0	CBECS - Hotel & Motel/Inn
	Multifamily Housing*		118.1	59.6	Fannie Mae Industry Survey
	Prison/Incarceration		156.4	68.9	CBECS - Public Order and Safety
	Residence Hall/Dormitory*		107.5	57.9	CBECS - Dormitory
	Residential Care Facility		213.2	99.0	Industry Survey
	Senior Care Community*		213.2	99.0	Industry Survey
	Single Family Home		N/A	N/A	None Available
	Other - Lodging/Residential		143.6	63.6	CBECS - Lodging
Manufacturing/Industrial	Manufacturing/Industrial Plant		N/A	N/A	None Available
Mixed Use	Mixed Use Property		89.3	40.1	CBECS - Other
Office	Medical Office*		121.7	51.2	CBECS - Medical Office
	Office*		116.4	52.9	CBECS - Office & Bank/Financial
	Veterinary Office		145.8	64.5	CBECS - Clinic/Outpatient
Parking	Parking		N/A	N/A	None Available

We discuss internal and external benchmarks in Chapters 10 and 11. These three benchmarks can be used similarly as we have an internal component to track progress for each factor over time against a specific facility. We also can compare a building externally against a campus, an entire portfolio, a category type, or a climate zone. There are many ways to do an external benchmark, and we can combine several of the above, which is what we normally do to get the best understanding during analysis. We can even do a hybrid between internal and external as we compare the variance over time to the median variance against the category type.

One external source we did not mention in EUI bears a discussion. We discussed the EIA CBECS database and those benchmarks. EPA also publishes one that is shown below in Table 17.1. This Energy Star figure is similar to CBECS, except that it has a larger amount (49) of category types than CBECs (18). Even though these benchmark databases are extensive and have a lot of metadata, the lack of breakdown in the office category prevents this from being helpful, especially if we have a large portfolio. The office category for CBECS has one category for office. In contrast, Energy Star has three categories, whereas the Federal Government may have more than 50 office-type categories, and the same applies to most institutional campuses. It certainly applies to a large commercial portfolio. The benefit of CBECs and Energy Star is when our portfolio is only a few buildings; it helps establish a general basis for where a building should stand in a benchmark [1].

Table 17.2   EUI for Category Type Office C.

| | | | | Median | 0.28 | | | 39.6 | 24.70 | | |
Campus	Building Number	Square Footage	Category Type	Base Load (KW)	Watts/SF	12 Months Consumption (kWh)	Baseload as % Consumption	12 Months EUI (Electric)	12 Months Extrapolated EUI (Electric)	% of Data Availabl e	Climate Zone
Campus S	100	34,215	Office C	55.1	1.61	2,803,428	11.9	279.58	404.94	69	3A
Campus O	6814	4,149	Office C	21.0	5.07	416,014	44.3	342.13	342.13	100	3A
Campus P	3912	16,120	Office C	37.8	2.34	80,079	45.3	16.95	154.67	11	3A
Campus H	43028	6,976	Office C	5.3	0.76	306,228	15.1	149.78	149.78	100	2A
Campus E	D1713	1,584	Office C	2.0	1.26	50,515	34.5	108.82	109.12	100	3A
Campus L	249L	26,002	Office C	31.4	1.21	813,341	33.9	106.73	106.73	100	4A
Campus C	2933	10,761	Office C	19.2	1.78	319,557	52.6	101.33	101.33	100	3A
Campus E	2884	6,335	Office C	12.3	1.93	180,026	59.6	96.97	96.97	100	3A
Campus H	9413	8,095	Office C	6.1	0.75	220,825	24.1	93.09	93.09	100	2A
Campus H	43030	5,939	Office C	11.5	1.94	161,065	62.6	92.54	92.54	100	2A
Campus O	5911	27,660	Office C	34.3	1.24	749,479	40.0	92.46	92.46	100	3A
Campus E	A2565	40,219	Office C	32.5	0.81	1,081,657	26.3	91.77	91.77	100	3A
Campus A	106	2,261	Office C	4.0	1.76	49,073	58.8	74.06	89.51	83	3A
Campus A	103	33,580	Office C	4.0	0.12	793,783	4.4	80.66	80.66	100	3A
Campus N	810	15,152	Office C	2.1	0.14	353,872	5.1	79.69	79.69	100	4A
Campus M	3665	27,134	Office C	20.3	0.75	604,176	29.4	75.98	75.98	100	3A
Campus P	3913	25,032	Office C	3.7	0.15	58,820	6.0	8.02	73.16	11	3A
Campus Q	1531	13,595	Office C	31.4	2.31	104,326	94.6	26.18	72.96	36	2A
Campus E	33327	36,000	Office C	35.6	0.99	761,405	40.8	72.17	72.37	100	3A
Campus N	812	23,559	Office C	3.1	0.13	490,522	5.5	71.04	71.04	100	4A
Campus C	2932	6,824	Office C	14.0	2.05	141,731	86.5	70.87	70.87	100	3A
Campus P	3911	25,394	Office C	3.8	0.15	59,075	6.4	7.94	70.67	11	3A
Campus S	232	7,286	Office C	4.0	0.55	103,371	23.3	48.41	70.12	69	3A
Campus E	A2547	41,925	Office C	56.8	1.35	847,485	58.7	68.97	68.97	100	3A
Campus E	32633	4,322	Office C	4.0	0.92	86,902	39.8	68.61	68.80	100	3A

17.2 Top 30 Category Types

Let us review the EUI first since it was covered in the last chapter. We can have the MMS process the data; so it comes out in the tabular form. Any good meter management system (MMS) can process these and extrapolate the EUI. A good example (Table 17.2) is included below that has all three benchmark factors and the following additional fields:

- Campus

- Building number

- 12 months of consumption

- Square footage

- Category type

- Percentage of data available

- Climate zone

The EUI can be sorted by category type to get a good evaluation of the overall EUI. Here we have used a Category Type of Office C. There are enough of these types around the US to build a statistically significant comparison. So,

Table 17.3   EUI for Category Type Office C in Climate Zone 3A.

			Median	0.40			38.6		32.99		
Campus	Building Number	Square Footage	Category Type	Base Load (KW)	Watts/SF	12 Months Consumption (kWh)	Baseload as % Consumption	12 Months EUI (Electric)	12 Months Extrapolated EUI (Electric)	% of Data Available	Climate Zone
Campus S	100	34,215	Office C	55.1	1.61	2,803,428	11.9	279.58	404.94	69	3A
Campus O	6814	4,149	Office C	21.0	5.07	416,014	44.3	342.13	342.13	100	3A
Campus P	3912	16,120	Office C	37.8	2.34	80,079	45.3	16.95	154.67	11	3A
Campus E	D1713	1,584	Office C	2.0	1.26	50,515	34.5	108.82	109.12	100	3A
Campus C	2933	10,761	Office C	19.2	1.78	319,557	52.6	101.33	101.33	100	3A
Campus C	2884	6,335	Office C	12.3	1.93	180,026	59.6	96.97	96.97	100	3A
Campus O	5911	27,660	Office C	34.3	1.24	749,479	40.0	92.46	92.46	100	3A
Campus E	A2565	40,219	Office C	32.5	0.81	1,081,657	26.3	91.77	91.77	100	3A
Campus A	106	2,261	Office C	4.0	1.76	49,073	58.8	74.06	89.51	83	3A
Campus A	103	33,580	Office C	4.0	0.12	793,783	4.4	80.66	80.66	100	3A
Campus M	3665	27,134	Office C	20.3	0.75	604,176	29.4	75.98	75.98	100	3A
Campus P	3913	25,032	Office C	3.7	0.15	58,820	6.0	8.02	73.16	11	3A
Campus E	33327	36,000	Office C	35.6	0.99	761,405	40.8	72.17	72.37	100	3A
Campus C	2932	6,824	Office C	14.0	2.05	141,731	86.5	70.87	70.87	100	3A
Campus P	3911	25,394	Office C	3.8	0.15	59,075	6.4	7.94	70.67	11	3A
Campus S	232	7,286	Office C	4.0	0.55	103,371	23.3	48.41	70.12	69	3A
Campus E	A2547	41,925	Office C	56.8	1.35	847,485	58.7	68.97	68.97	100	3A
Campus E	32633	4,322	Office C	4.0	0.92	86,902	39.8	68.61	68.80	100	3A
Campus E	A3265	40,219	Office C	23.1	0.58	790,658	25.6	67.08	67.08	100	3A
Campus E	A6057	1,821	Office C	2.0	1.08	35,216	48.6	65.99	66.17	100	3A
Campus E	OX201	37,715	Office C	18.5	0.49	718,339	22.5	64.99	64.99	100	3A
Campus A	160	3,976	Office C	0.6	0.14	75,373	6.5	64.68	64.68	100	3A
Campus E	A4251	41,925	Office C	54.4	1.30	752,804	63.3	61.27	61.27	100	3A
Campus E	56110	2,304	Office C	2.0	0.87	40,185	43.5	59.51	59.68	100	3A
Campus C	9026	3,867	Office C	0.0	0.01	66,770	0.5	58.92	58.92	100	3A

in this case, we find the median for the electric EUI is 24.70. We can then rank a building against this median to see how far a building is out of range. To make this easier, we generate medians, the top 25th percentile, and the bottom 25th percentile for these three benchmark factors for all our category types. This makes it easier to know where a building stands from a relative perspective, but we can also see if that building is in the top 25th percentile, meaning a facility is in the worst grouping and needs attention. If we are in the bottom 25th percentile, the building is in the top 25% of a category and should be recognized as such, which in the Federal Government is equivalent to getting an Energy Star plaque.

The next level of benchmarking would be to take the EUI for that Category Type of Office C and sort it out by climate zone. In Table 17.3, we have shown Climate Zone 3A. That climate zone is the Southeastern Central US with normal humidity, so hot and humid compared to most of the US. This EUI comes out with a median of 32.99. That is higher than the median for the US for that category by 34%.

We all recognize that the EUI for Climate Zone 3A should be higher than the median overall for that category. But to show how this works across the climate zone, we have to take all the medians and plot them for this category type. Once we accomplish this, it generates a graph, as shown in Figure 17.1.

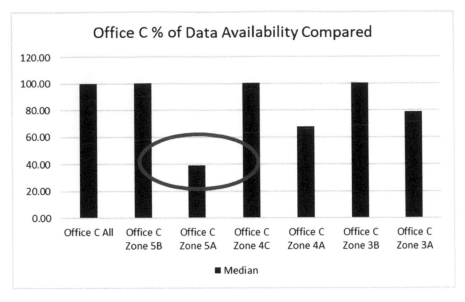

Figure 17.1   Data availability for Category Type Office C.

We will demonstrate in Figure 17.1 that we have broken down the availability percentage for the data by each Climate Zone. The reason is to highlight any value for EUI that may be problematic due to the quality of that data. Figure 17.2 shows an overall median and each median EUI for each Climate Zone for the Category Type Office C. As we show, there is one median for Climate Zone 5A, where the availability is down around 40%. We have found that anything below 60% availability must be analyzed further to validate if it can be used. If we draw a line across the zones, we see an increase in EUI as the weather zones progress toward the hotter climates, except Climate Zone 5A is off, as we thought it might be due to the data issues.

The base load is the next benchmark, and it will be measured in watts/sf and can be sorted by category type to evaluate the overall base load. Again, we will use the Category Type Office C; in this case, the median for the watts/sf is 0.276, as shown in Table 17.4. We can then rank this building against a median to see how far it is out of range. To make this easier, we provide medians across our portfolio and the top 25th and bottom 25th percentile for these benchmarks as for EUI. This makes it easier to know where a building stands from a relative perspective, but we can also see if a building is in the top 25th percentile, meaning a facility is in the worst grouping and needs

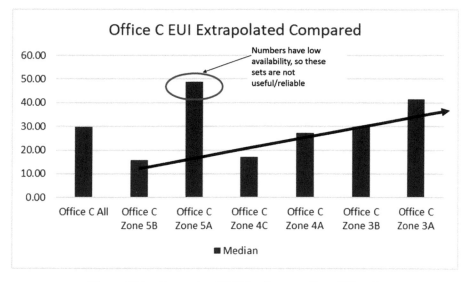

Figure 17.2 Extrapolated EUI for Category Type Office C.

Table 17.4 Base load in watts/sf for Category Type Office C.

							Baseload	12	12		
				Base		12 Months	as %	Months	Months	% of	
Campus	Building Number	Square Footage	Category Type	Load (KW)	Watts/SF	Consumption (kWh)	Consumption	EUI (Electric)	Extrapolated EUI (Electric)	Data Availab le	Climate Zone
Median				0.28			39.6		24.70		
Campus S	100	34,215	Office C	55.1	1.61	2,803,428	11.9	279.58	404.94	69	3A
Campus O	6814	4,149	Office C	21.0	5.07	416,014	44.3	342.13	342.13	100	3A
Campus P	3912	16,120	Office C	37.8	2.34	80,079	45.3	16.95	154.67	11	3A
Campus H	43028	6,976	Office C	5.3	0.76	306,228	15.1	149.78	149.78	100	2A
Campus E	D1713	1,584	Office C	2.0	1.26	50,515	34.5	108.82	109.12	100	3A
Campus L	249L	26,002	Office C	31.4	1.21	813,341	33.9	106.73	106.73	100	4A
Campus C	2933	10,761	Office C	19.2	1.78	319,557	52.6	101.33	101.33	100	3A
Campus C	2884	6,335	Office C	12.3	1.93	180,026	59.6	96.97	96.97	100	3A
Campus H	9413	8,095	Office C	6.1	0.75	220,825	24.1	93.09	93.09	100	2A
Campus H	43030	5,939	Office C	11.5	1.94	161,065	62.6	92.54	92.54	100	2A
Campus O	5911	27,660	Office C	34.3	1.24	749,479	40.0	92.46	92.46	100	3A
Campus E	A2565	40,219	Office C	32.5	0.81	1,081,657	26.3	91.77	91.77	100	3A
Campus A	106	2,261	Office C	4.0	1.76	49,073	58.8	74.06	89.51	83	3A
Campus A	103	33,580	Office C	4.0	0.12	793,783	4.4	80.66	80.66	100	3A
Campus N	810	15,152	Office C	2.1	0.14	353,872	5.1	79.69	79.69	100	4A
Campus M	3665	27,134	Office C	20.3	0.75	604,176	29.4	75.98	75.98	100	3A
Campus P	3913	25,032	Office C	3.7	0.15	58,820	6.0	8.02	73.16	11	3A
Campus Q	1531	13,595	Office C	31.4	2.31	104,326	94.6	26.18	72.96	36	2A
Campus E	33327	36,000	Office C	35.6	0.99	761,405	40.8	72.17	72.37	100	3A
Campus N	812	23,559	Office C	3.1	0.13	490,522	5.5	71.04	71.04	100	4A
Campus C	2932	6,824	Office C	14.0	2.05	141,731	86.5	70.87	70.87	100	3A
Campus P	3911	25,394	Office C	3.8	0.15	59,075	6.4	7.94	70.67	11	3A
Campus S	232	7,286	Office C	4.0	0.55	103,371	23.3	48.41	70.12	69	3A
Campus E	A2547	41,925	Office C	56.8	1.35	847,485	58.7	68.97	68.97	100	3A
Campus E	32633	4,322	Office C	4.0	0.92	86,902	39.8	68.61	68.80	100	3A

Table 17.5   Watts/sf for Category Type Office C in Climate Zone 3A.

									12	
									Months	% of
				Base		12 Months	Baseload	12	Extrapola	Data
	Building	Square	Category	Load		Consumption	as %	Months	ted EUI	Availabl	Climate
Campus	Number	Footage	Type	(KW)	Watts/SF	(kWh)	Consump tion	EUI (Electric)	(Electric)	e	Zone
						Median 0.40		38.6	32.99		
Campus S	100	34,215	Office C	55.1	1.61	2,803,428	11.9	279.58	404.94	69	3A
Campus O	6814	4,149	Office C	21.0	5.07	416,014	44.3	342.13	342.13	100	3A
Campus P	3912	16,120	Office C	37.8	2.34	80,079	45.3	16.95	154.67	11	3A
Campus E	D1713	1,584	Office C	2.0	1.26	50,515	34.5	108.82	109.12	100	3A
Campus C	2933	10,761	Office C	19.2	1.78	319,557	52.6	101.33	101.33	100	3A
Campus C	2884	6,335	Office C	12.3	1.93	180,026	59.6	96.97	96.97	100	3A
Campus O	5911	27,660	Office C	34.3	1.24	749,479	40.0	92.46	92.46	100	3A
Campus E	A2565	40,219	Office C	32.5	0.81	1,081,657	26.3	91.77	91.77	100	3A
Campus A	106	2,261	Office C	4.0	1.76	49,073	58.8	74.06	89.51	83	3A
Campus A	103	33,580	Office C	4.0	0.12	793,783	4.4	80.66	80.66	100	3A
Campus M	3665	27,134	Office C	20.3	0.75	604,176	29.4	75.98	75.98	100	3A
Campus P	3913	25,032	Office C	3.7	0.15	58,820	6.0	8.02	73.16	11	3A
Campus E	33327	36,000	Office C	35.6	0.99	761,405	40.8	72.17	72.37	100	3A
Campus C	2932	6,824	Office C	14.0	2.05	141,731	86.5	70.87	70.87	100	3A
Campus P	3911	25,394	Office C	3.8	0.15	59,075	6.4	7.94	70.67	11	3A
Campus S	232	7,286	Office C	4.0	0.55	103,371	23.3	48.41	70.12	69	3A
Campus E	A2547	41,925	Office C	56.8	1.35	847,485	58.7	68.97	68.97	100	3A
Campus E	32633	4,322	Office C	4.0	0.92	86,902	39.8	68.61	68.80	100	3A
Campus E	A3265	40,219	Office C	23.1	0.58	790,658	25.6	67.08	67.08	100	3A
Campus E	A6057	1,821	Office C	2.0	1.08	35,216	48.6	65.99	66.17	100	3A
Campus E	OX201	37,715	Office C	18.5	0.49	718,339	22.5	64.99	64.99	100	3A
Campus A	160	3,976	Office C	0.6	0.14	75,373	6.5	64.68	64.68	100	3A
Campus E	A4251	41,925	Office C	54.4	1.30	752,804	63.3	61.27	61.27	100	3A
Campus E	56110	2,304	Office C	2.0	0.87	40,185	43.5	59.51	59.68	100	3A
Campus C	9026	3,867	Office C	0.0	0.01	66,770	0.5	58.92	58.92	100	3A

attention. If a building is in the bottom 25th percentile, it is in the top 25% of the category, as discussed previously.

The next level of benchmarking would be to take the watts/sf for that Category Type Office C and sort it out by climate zone. In Table 17.5, we have shown Climate Zone 3A. This watts/sf comes out with a median of 0.395. That is higher than the median for the US for that category by 43%. We generally do not see much variance with the base load, as the weather should not affect it. This does show up in the variance around the midpoint line across weather zones depicted in Figure 17.4.

To prove the above assumption, we will study how the watts/sf reacts across the climate zones; so, to understand this, we have taken all the medians and plotted them for this category type. Once we accomplish this, it produces a graph, as shown in Figure 17.3. We will see in Figure 17.3 that we have broken down the availability percentage for the data by each climate zone as in the previous set of figures. The reason is to highlight any value for watts/sf that may be problematic due to availability, affecting that data's quality. Figure 17.4 shows an overall median and each median watts/sf for each climate zone for the Category Type Office C. As we notice, there is one median for Climate Zone 5A, where the availability is down around 40%. Climate

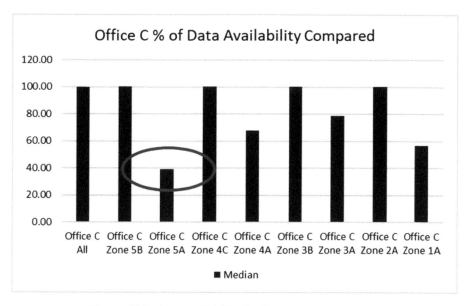

Figure 17.3 Data availability for Category Type Office C.

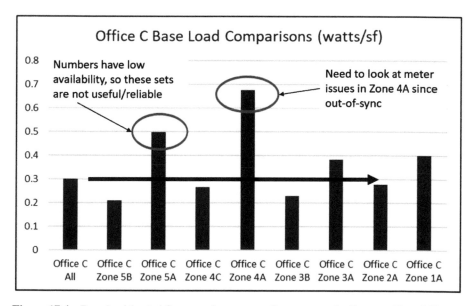

Figure 17.4 Base load (watts/sf) comparison across climate zones for Category Type Office C.

Zone 4A is slightly above 60%, and the value falls outside the average across the zones. If we draw a line across the zones, we show that the watts/sf is relatively flat across all the climate zones with a slight variance from zone to zone. So, this is important as we found a benchmark that can be generated with only a few weeks of data; therefore, it does not require a year's worth of data (a few months is preferred) and is relatively consistent across all weather zones. If a facility has two benchmarks, use the lower benchmark, generally in winter. This will be a good tool for us to use as a benchmark since it is generated quickly and is not dependent on the weather zone. A campus is generally very close in values due to the same design in general and mainte- nance force. One can and should lower these, but they will go down together as both MCx and maintenance improve.

The base load percentage of the total annual consumption is an import- ant benchmark of the equipment left on in a facility as a constant load. As discussed above, the target rate would be the plug load, for which the max- imum will be around 15%, but it could be as low as 8%, depending on the plug load. We generally set the threshold at 15%, covering a normal facility's maximum plug load. Any base load percentage above that includes equip- ment that is left on that maintains a constant loading. We cover that type of equipment in our basic and first-level benchmarking chapters, i.e., Chapters 10 and 11. So in Table 17.6, we have a median of 39.6%, which is 24.6% above the basic plug load maximum expected loading. So this indicates that a lot of equipment is on constantly. For those over the median, the impact is much larger. But on average, if we can control these issues, we can greatly impact savings for these category facilities. Theoretically the maximum the base load percentage can be is 75%, which means everything that can sustain a constant draw will be left on. That is added as follows from the systems as indicated below. The loads that can be left on easily to make a constant load are:

1. Plug   12%

2. Lights   27%

3. Fan/pumps   33% of 39% for VAV   13%

This is 52% if the load of the normal stuff is left running. If it is a constant volume fan, the total is 78%. The fans usually draw more, and the lights less; so the maximum load is approximately 75% at a constant rate. The other loads, like office, AC systems, and a portion of the fan/pump systems, are all variable for the remaining 25%. There are exceptions for buildings with a single piece of equipment that runs constantly, etc.

Table 17.6   Base load percentage of total usage for Category Type Office C.

		Median		0.28			39.6		24.70		
									12		
				Base		12 Months	Baseload as %	12 Months	Months Extrapola	% of Data	
	Building	Square	Category	Load		Consumption	Consump	EUI	ted EUI	Availabl	Climate
Campus	Number	Footage	Type	(KW)	Watts/SF	(kWh)	tion	(Electric)	(Electric)	e	Zone
Campus S	100	34,215	Office C	55.1	1.61	2,803,428	11.9	279.58	404.94	69	3A
Campus O	6814	4,149	Office C	21.0	5.07	416,014	44.3	342.13	342.13	100	3A
Campus P	3912	16,120	Office C	37.8	2.34	80,079	45.3	16.95	154.67	11	3A
Campus H	43028	6,976	Office C	5.3	0.76	306,228	15.1	149.78	149.78	100	2A
Campus E	D1713	1,584	Office C	2.0	1.26	50,515	34.5	108.82	109.12	100	3A
Campus L	249L	26,002	Office C	31.4	1.21	813,341	33.9	106.73	106.73	100	4A
Campus C	2933	10,761	Office C	19.2	1.78	319,557	52.6	101.33	101.33	100	3A
Campus C	2884	6,335	Office C	12.3	1.93	180,026	59.6	96.97	96.97	100	3A
Campus H	9413	8,095	Office C	6.1	0.75	220,825	24.1	93.09	93.09	100	2A
Campus H	43030	5,939	Office C	11.5	1.94	161,065	62.6	92.54	92.54	100	2A
Campus O	5911	27,660	Office C	34.3	1.24	749,479	40.0	92.46	92.46	100	3A
Campus E	A2565	40,219	Office C	32.5	0.81	1,081,657	26.3	91.77	91.77	100	3A
Campus A	106	2,261	Office C	4.0	1.76	49,073	58.8	74.06	89.51	83	3A
Campus A	103	33,580	Office C	4.0	0.12	793,783	4.4	80.66	80.66	100	3A
Campus N	810	15,152	Office C	2.1	0.14	353,872	5.1	79.69	79.69	100	4A
Campus M	3665	27,134	Office C	20.3	0.75	604,176	29.4	75.98	75.98	100	3A
Campus P	3913	25,032	Office C	3.7	0.15	58,820	6.0	8.02	73.16	11	3A
Campus Q	1531	13,595	Office C	31.4	2.31	104,326	94.6	26.18	72.96	36	2A
Campus E	33327	36,000	Office C	35.6	0.99	761,405	40.8	72.17	72.37	100	3A
Campus N	812	23,559	Office C	3.1	0.13	490,522	5.5	71.04	71.04	100	4A
Campus C	2932	6,824	Office C	14.0	2.05	141,731	86.5	70.87	70.87	100	3A
Campus P	3911	25,394	Office C	3.8	0.15	59,075	6.4	7.94	70.67	11	3A
Campus S	232	7,286	Office C	4.0	0.55	103,371	23.3	48.41	70.12	69	3A
Campus E	A2547	41,925	Office C	56.8	1.35	847,485	58.7	68.97	68.97	100	3A
Campus E	32633	4,322	Office C	4.0	0.92	86,902	39.8	68.61	68.80	100	3A

In Table 17.7, we will look at Category Type Office A. This is the most generic office type of our portfolio. So, in this case, we find the median for the EUI is 30.97. We can then rank a building against this median to see how far it is out of range. Note that the upper end of the range goes to over 7000 kbtu/sf. These are out of range from the median by much greater than 2×, meaning those meters must be evaluated to determine if they work properly.

The next level of benchmarking would be to take the EUI for Category Type Office A and sort it out by climate zone. In Table 17.8, we have shown Climate Zone 3A. This EUI comes out with a median of 35.82. That is higher than the median for the US for that category by 15.6%, which logically should be slightly above.

We all recognize that the EUI for Climate Zone 3A should be higher than the median overall. But just as we demonstrated with Category Type Office C, we will pull the climate zone medians and plot them for this category type. Once we accomplish this, it gives a chart, as shown in Figure 17.5. We will notice in Figure 17.5 that we have broken down the availability percentage for the data by each climate zone. In contrast to the availability noted for Category Type Office C, this category type has good data availability for all these climate zones. Figure 17.6 shows an overall median and each median EUI for each climate zone for the Category Type Office A. If we

Table 17.7   EUI for Category Type Office A.

			Median	0.31		36.1		30.97	
Campus	Building Number	Square Footage	Category Type	Base Load (KW)	Watts/SF	12 Months Consumption (kWh)	Baseload as % Consumption	12 Months EUI (Electric)	12 Months Extrapolated EUI (Electric)	% of Data Available Climate
Campus Z1	3334	2,100	Office A	92.5	44.04	1,625,192	18.4	2,640.66	7,139.56	37 3A
Campus I	123	1,664	Office A	0.1	0.08	2,359,987	0.0	4,839.31	5,791.30	84 4A
Campus Y	20	3,236	Office A	0.4	0.13	3,321,610	0.1	3,502.41	3,994.94	88 5A
Campus H1	26145	6,250	Office A	4.0	0.64	2,338,741	1.3	1,276.82	1,451.83	88 3B
Campus I	839	5,618	Office A	1.9	0.34	1,494,936	0.9	907.96	1,101.02	82 4A
Campus D	1099	13,803	Office A	6.1	0.44	1,705,450	3.1	421.59	421.59	100 4A
Campus G	31637	672	Office A	2.0	2.97	57,644	30.3	292.69	293.50	100 3A
Campus A	1049	1,169	Office A	6.3	5.41	85,757	64.5	250.31	250.31	100 3A
Campus T	746	7,140	Office A	29.8	4.17	264,828	50.0	126.56	249.70	51 3A
Campus D	319	9,896	Office A	51.3	5.19	626,222	71.8	215.91	215.91	100 4A
Campus E	1796	2,350	Office A	5.3	2.27	132,587	35.3	192.51	192.51	100 3A
Campus E	2670	5,844	Office A	19.9	3.40	315,988	55.1	184.50	184.50	100 3A
Campus D	245	113,150	Office A	0.0	0.00	3,626,715	0.0	109.37	180.63	61 4A
Campus V	140	3,833	Office A	14.6	3.80	153,062	73.1	136.26	155.42	88 5B
Campus E	9187	6,000	Office A	5.2	0.86	271,619	16.6	154.47	154.47	100 3A
Campus D	358	23,667	Office A	96.0	4.06	1,064,147	79.0	153.42	153.42	100 4A
Campus F1	3304	38,278	Office A	89.4	2.34	1,713,871	45.7	152.78	152.78	100 5A
Campus D	3245	65,000	Office A	0.0	0.00	1,185,128	0.0	62.21	143.72	43 4A
Campus E	6000	11,208	Office A	0.3	0.03	469,405	0.6	142.91	142.91	100 3A
Campus D	386	40,365	Office A	147.3	3.65	1,098,627	76.6	92.87	142.43	65 4A
Campus Z1	3651	15,980	Office A	0.1	0.00	614,210	0.1	131.15	131.15	100 3A
Campus D	612	10,861	Office A	13.3	1.23	249,338	28.3	78.33	129.37	61 4A
Campus F	11339	87,565	Office A	262.8	3.00	3,266,620	70.5	127.29	127.29	100 3B
Campus A	247	1,587	Office A	5.1	3.21	53,676	83.1	115.41	115.41	100 3A
Campus D	1839	47,461	Office A	126.3	2.66	1,561,748	70.8	112.28	112.28	100 4A
Campus D	3165	15,459	Office A	36.0	2.33	506,250	62.3	111.74	111.74	100 4A

Table 17.8   EUI for Category Type Office A in Climate Zone 3A.

			Median	0.33		33.2		35.82	
Campus	Building Number	Square Footage	Category Type	Base Load (KW)	Watts/SF	12 Months Consumption (kWh)	Baseload as % Consumption	12 Months EUI (Electric)	12 Months Extrapolated EUI (Electric)	% of Data Available Climate
Campus Z1	3334	2,100	Office A	92.5	44.04	1,625,192	18.4	2,640.66	7,139.56	37 3A
Campus G	31637	672	Office A	2.0	2.97	57,644	30.3	292.69	293.50	100 3A
Campus A	1049	1,169	Office A	6.3	5.41	85,757	64.5	250.31	250.31	100 3A
Campus T	746	7,140	Office A	29.8	4.17	264,828	50.0	126.56	249.70	51 3A
Campus E	1796	2,350	Office A	5.3	2.27	132,587	35.3	192.51	192.51	100 3A
Campus E	2670	5,844	Office A	19.9	3.40	315,988	55.1	184.50	184.50	100 3A
Campus E	9187	6,000	Office A	5.2	0.86	271,619	16.6	154.47	154.47	100 3A
Campus E	6000	11,208	Office A	0.3	0.03	469,405	0.6	142.91	142.91	100 3A
Campus Z1	3651	15,980	Office A	0.1	0.00	614,210	0.1	131.15	131.15	100 3A
Campus A	247	1,587	Office A	5.1	3.21	53,676	83.1	115.41	115.41	100 3A
Campus A	420	4,186	Office A	6.7	1.61	129,966	45.4	105.94	105.94	100 3A
Campus T	3668	3,501	Office A	1.1	0.32	9,470	10.5	9.23	91.05	10 3A
Campus T	455	52,699	Office A	64.2	1.22	408,400	42.6	26.44	85.41	31 3A
Campus G	31137	4,000	Office A	2.0	0.50	92,436	18.9	78.85	79.07	100 3A
Campus E	130	30,698	Office A	0.0	0.00	711,196	0.0	79.05	79.05	100 3A
Campus G	31632	3,168	Office A	2.0	0.63	71,335	24.5	76.83	77.04	100 3A
Campus E	2506	1,983	Office A	0.6	0.31	44,674	12.0	76.87	76.87	100 3A
Campus G	M2621	37,875	Office A	56.8	1.50	850,561	58.4	76.63	78.84	100 3A
Campus X	290	39,033	Office A	24.7	0.63	602,308	24.8	52.65	76.26	69 3A
Campus E	71	6,083	Office A	8.2	1.35	134,437	53.7	75.41	75.41	100 3A
Campus E	4631	4,896	Office A	2.1	0.43	107,032	17.2	74.59	74.59	100 3A
Campus W	336	4,247	Office A	3.9	0.92	14,606	37.8	11.74	72.60	16 3A
Campus G	Y7603	1,344	Office A	2.0	1.49	28,282	61.7	71.80	72.00	100 3A
Campus Z1	7442	29,206	Office A	58.0	1.99	259,963	82.5	30.37	71.98	42 3A

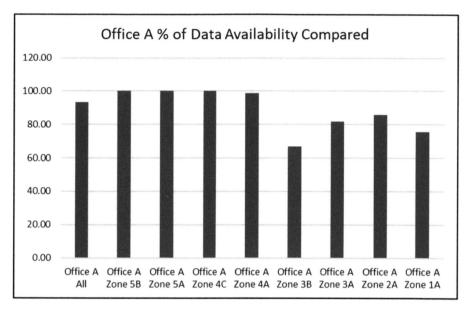

Figure 17.5 Extrapolated EUI for Category Type Office A.

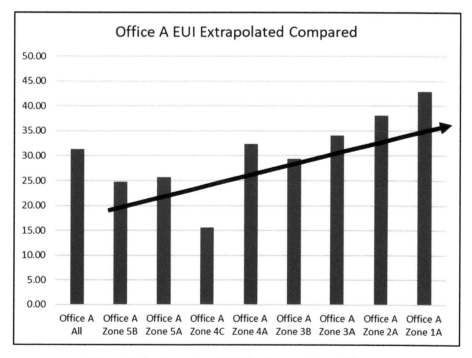

Figure 17.6 Extrapolated EUI for Category Type Office A.

Table 17.9   Base load in watts/sf for Category Type Office A.

| | | | | | | | Median (0.31) | 36.1 | 30.97 | | |

Campus	Building Number	Square Footage	Category Type	Base Load (KW)	Watts/SF	12 Months Consumption (kWh)	Baseload as % Consumption	12 Months EUI (Electric)	12 Months Extrapolated EUI (Electric)	% of Data Available	Climate
Campus Z1	3334	2,100	Office A	92.5	44.04	1,625,192	18.4	2,640.66	7,139.56	37	3A
Campus I	123	1,664	Office A	0.1	0.08	2,359,987	0.0	4,839.31	5,791.30	84	4A
Campus Y	20	3,236	Office A	0.4	0.13	3,321,610	0.1	3,502.41	3,994.94	88	5A
Campus H1	26145	6,250	Office A	4.0	0.64	2,338,741	1.3	1,276.82	1,451.83	88	3B
Campus I	839	5,618	Office A	1.9	0.34	1,494,936	0.9	907.96	1,101.02	82	4A
Campus D	1099	13,803	Office A	6.1	0.44	1,705,450	3.1	421.59	421.59	100	4A
Campus G	31637	672	Office A	2.0	2.97	57,644	30.3	292.69	293.50	100	3A
Campus A	1049	1,169	Office A	6.3	5.41	85,757	64.5	250.31	250.31	100	3A
Campus T	746	7,140	Office A	29.8	4.17	264,828	50.0	126.56	249.70	51	3A
Campus D	319	9,896	Office A	51.3	5.19	626,222	71.8	215.91	215.91	100	4A
Campus E	1796	2,350	Office A	5.3	2.27	132,587	35.3	192.51	192.51	100	3A
Campus E	2670	5,844	Office A	19.9	3.40	315,988	55.1	184.50	184.50	100	3A
Campus D	245	113,150	Office A	0.0	0.00	3,626,715	0.0	109.37	180.63	61	4A
Campus V	140	3,833	Office A	14.6	3.80	153,062	73.1	136.26	155.42	88	5B
Campus E	9187	6,000	Office A	5.2	0.86	271,619	16.6	154.47	154.47	100	3A
Campus D	358	23,667	Office A	96.0	4.06	1,064,147	79.0	153.42	153.42	100	4A
Campus F1	3304	38,278	Office A	89.4	2.34	1,713,871	45.7	152.78	152.78	100	5A
Campus D	3245	65,000	Office A	0.0	0.00	1,185,128	0.0	62.21	143.72	43	4A
Campus E	6000	11,208	Office A	0.3	0.03	469,405	0.6	142.91	142.91	100	3A
Campus D	386	40,365	Office A	147.3	3.65	1,098,627	76.6	92.87	142.43	65	4A
Campus Z1	3651	15,980	Office A	0.1	0.00	614,210	0.1	131.15	131.15	100	3A
Campus D	612	10,861	Office A	13.3	1.23	249,338	28.3	78.33	129.37	61	4A
Campus F	11339	87,565	Office A	262.8	3.00	3,266,620	70.5	127.29	127.29	100	3B
Campus A	247	1,587	Office A	5.1	3.21	53,676	83.1	115.41	115.41	100	3A
Campus D	1839	47,461	Office A	126.3	2.66	1,561,748	70.8	112.28	112.28	100	4A
Campus D	3165	15,459	Office A	36.0	2.33	506,250	62.3	111.74	111.74	100	4A

draw a line across the zones, we see an increase in EUI as the weather zones progress toward the hotter climates as anticipated. One zone, 4C, is a little out of bounds which may be related to the low number of buildings in that climate zone.

The base load is the next benchmark, and it will be measured in watts/sf and can be sorted by category type to evaluate the overall base load. Again, we will use the Category Type Office A. So, in this case, the median for the watts/sf is 0.31, as shown in Table 17.9. We then can rank a building against this median benchmark to see how far it is out of range.

The next level of benchmarking would be to take the watts/sf for Category Type Office A and sort it out by climate zone. In Table 17.10, we have shown Climate Zone 3A. This base load comes out with a median of 0.33. That is slightly higher than the US median shown in Table 17.9 of 0.31. In most cases, we would determine that the warmer climate zones have a slightly higher median to the EUI but minimal change to the base load.

17.3 Other Ways to Compare Benchmark Metrics

Let us give a three-year comparison of the two category types mentioned above. That is the core of an internal benchmark. While it is not what is

Table 17.10   Base load in watts/sf for Category Type Office A in Climate Zone 3A.

Campus	Building Number	Square Footage	Category Type	Base Load (KW)	Watts/SF	12 Months Consumption (kWh)	Baseload as % Consumption	12 Months EUI (Electric)	12 Months Extrapolated EUI (Electric)	% of Data Available	Climate
			Median		0.33		33.2		35.82		
Campus Z1	3334	2,100	Office A	92.5	44.04	1,625,192	18.4	2,640.66	7,139.56	37	3A
Campus G	31637	672	Office A	2.0	2.97	57,644	30.3	292.69	293.50	100	3A
Campus A	1049	1,169	Office A	6.3	5.41	85,757	64.5	250.31	250.31	100	3A
Campus T	746	7,140	Office A	29.8	4.17	264,828	50.0	126.56	249.70	51	3A
Campus E	1796	2,350	Office A	5.3	2.27	132,587	35.3	192.51	192.51	100	3A
Campus E	2670	5,844	Office A	19.9	3.40	315,988	55.1	184.50	184.50	100	3A
Campus E	9187	6,000	Office A	5.2	0.86	271,619	16.6	154.47	154.47	100	3A
Campus E	6000	11,208	Office A	0.3	0.03	469,405	0.6	142.91	142.91	100	3A
Campus Z1	3651	15,980	Office A	0.1	0.00	614,210	0.1	131.15	131.15	100	3A
Campus A	247	1,587	Office A	5.1	3.21	53,676	83.1	115.41	115.41	100	3A
Campus A	420	4,186	Office A	6.7	1.61	129,966	45.4	105.94	105.94	100	3A
Campus T	3668	3,501	Office A	1.1	0.32	9,470	10.5	9.23	91.05	10	3A
Campus T	455	52,699	Office A	64.2	1.22	408,400	42.6	26.44	85.41	31	3A
Campus G	31137	4,000	Office A	2.0	0.50	92,436	18.9	78.85	79.07	100	3A
Campus E	130	30,698	Office A	0.0	0.00	711,196	0.0	79.05	79.05	100	3A
Campus G	31632	3,168	Office A	2.0	0.63	71,335	24.5	76.83	77.04	100	3A
Campus E	2506	1,983	Office A	0.6	0.31	44,674	12.0	76.87	76.87	100	3A
Campus G	M2621	37,875	Office A	56.8	1.50	850,561	58.4	76.63	76.84	100	3A
Campus X	290	39,033	Office A	24.7	0.63	602,308	24.8	52.65	76.26	69	3A
Campus E	71	6,083	Office A	8.2	1.35	134,437	53.7	75.41	75.41	100	3A
Campus E	4631	4,896	Office A	2.1	0.43	107,032	17.2	74.59	74.59	100	3A
Campus W	336	4,247	Office A	3.9	0.92	14,606	37.8	11.74	72.60	16	3A
Campus G	Y7603	1,344	Office A	2.0	1.49	28,282	61.7	71.80	72.00	100	3A
Campus Z1	7442	29,206	Office A	58.0	1.99	259,963	82.5	30.37	71.98	42	3A
Campus Z1	3687	5,004	Office A	0.0	0.00	105,447	0.1	71.90	71.90	100	3A
Campus Q	1562	25,168	Office A	30.2	1.20	517,338	51.1	70.14	70.14	100	3A

normally considered an internal benchmark, it is in the sense that it compares a like benchmark against previous years. That does not follow under the external benchmarks as we are not comparing them against other facilities. One might say it is a hybrid, but we do not get that wrapped up in categorizing these to that extent. The three-year comparison covers the median for the benchmark for each of these over the last three years. We can then see how the median has changed over those years for the base load (watts/sf). We can also show the last three years for the base load divided by the total loading. Finally, we can list the last three years for the EUI (extrapolated) and show that result. The three years compare as shown in Table 17.11. We will demonstrate how these two benchmarks vary over three years.

Next, we will take the same category types and compare them across climate zones. We can see those compared in Figures 17.7 and 17.8. Figure 17.7 compares the base load across six climate zones for Category Office Type A. We do not see any real progress between the years 2020 and 2022. We do see the base load increase as the climate zones grow colder. That makes us wonder what drives the increase in the base load. In Figure 17.8, we notice the EUI for Category Office Type A. As we can see, the EUI progresses upward as the climate zones grow warmer (from 5 to 1). This is an easier answer than the base load above. The increased temperature or CDD for each climate zone drives the EUI up as we go to warmer climate zones.

Table 17.11   Three-year comparison example against base load and extrapolated EUI.

Category		Base Load (W/sf)	EUI (kBtu/sf)
Office Type C	2020	0.272	28.44
	2021	0.271	24.42
	2022	0.268	23.21
Office Type A	2020	0.353	33.56
	2021	0.293	29.86
	2022	0.315	32.30

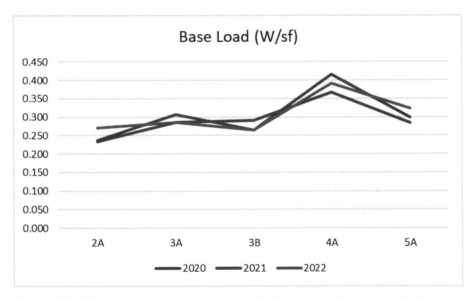

Figure 17.7   Three-year comparison against base load against the climate zones for Category Office Type A.

We discussed data quality in Chapter 7. We decided to show that the medians in these two primary benchmarks, base load (watts/sf) and extrapolated EUI, do not vary much regardless of whether it is all datasets or only quality datasets. We show the base load benchmark compared in Figure 17.9.

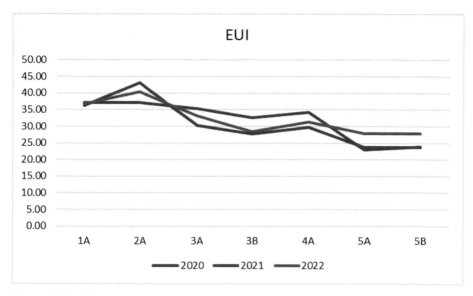

Figure 17.8 Three-year comparison against extrapolated EUI against the climate zones for Category Office Type A.

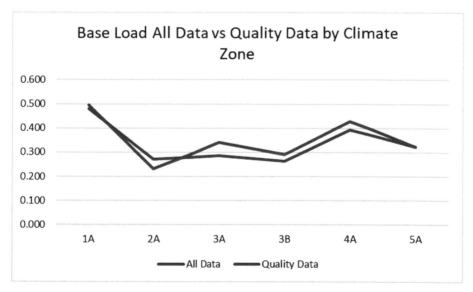

Figure 17.9 Base load (watts/sf) comparing all datasets vs. just quality datasets for Category Type Office A.

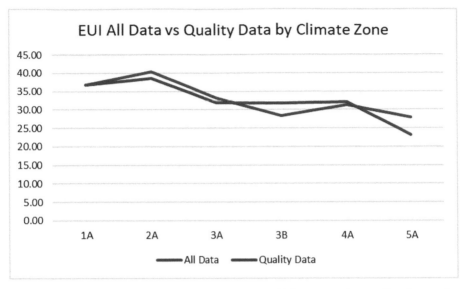

Figure 17.10   Extrapolated EUI (kbtu/sf) comparing all datasets vs. just quality datasets for Category Type Office A.

As we can see, the full dataset is relatively close to the quality-only dataset in several weather zones. This does not seem to vary in relation to the size of the datasets. This is also shown in Figure 17.10 for extrapolated EUI. Those points across each weather zone do not vary much from the total dataset to the quality dataset.

These are the traditional metrics. Other metrics have been pursued for various situations where kbtu/sf may not be appropriate. Sometimes the number of people may be the biggest driver. Calculating people/sf is important when there are a lot of people. This is applicable in auditoriums or other highly populated dense facilities. Sometimes this is applied for dormitories or hotels, but generally, that is calculated by occupied rooms. Another metric that is different from kbtu/sf is for industrial facilities. They usually use units of production. So, a plant that makes doors would count kbtu/door, etc.

For this comparison, we can take a snapshot of a portfolio. The snapshot of this portfolio will cover 30 category types. Table 17.12 will give the medians for the three metrics across the portfolio. The only thing that might make this a little better benchmarking would be taking the EUI (extrapolated)

Table 17.12 Three medians by the top category types for portfolio.

Category Type	Building Count	Bottom 25th Percentile Watts/SF	Top 25th Percentile Watts/SF	Median Watts/SF	Bottom 25th Percentile EUI	Top 25th Percentile EUI	Median EUI	Bottom 25th Percentile Baseload as % of Consumption	Top 25th Percentile Baseload as % of Consumption	Median Baseload as % of Consumption
			Median	0.31			31.07			36.22
LODGING A	519	0.21	0.52	0.39	19.31	31.57	25.95	31.8	57.9	45.2
OFFICE A	424	0.17	0.57	0.32	18.66	46.98	30.65	21.5	53.4	37.0
OFFICE C	391	0.17	0.44	0.27	15.96	36.46	23.80	27.4	48.7	38.4
REPAIR SERVICES	307	0.17	0.45	0.31	17.75	38.49	27.29	24.7	46.4	35.6
OFFICE N	182	0.23	0.58	0.36	25.13	44.58	34.32	23.4	48.0	36.9
EDUCATION	110	0.15	0.56	0.29	21.61	51.52	34.44	16.0	44.2	31.2
WAREHOUSE B	97	0.05	0.33	0.15	6.94	32.01	15.93	15.8	52.8	37.0
OFFICE M	89	0.06	0.52	0.24	11.29	34.99	23.00	24.1	45.1	35.3
OFFICE D	80	0.24	0.87	0.44	25.42	57.08	41.93	29.5	52.3	39.3
FOOD SALES	77	0.47	1.36	0.84	57.04	110.38	83.16	20.6	41.6	28.2
PHYS FIT CENTER	66	0.16	0.53	0.33	24.95	58.10	35.04	18.9	42.1	28.2
HEALTH CLINIC	65	0.27	1.11	0.56	34.67	71.19	45.02	25.3	54.3	42.9
LODGING E	63	0.00	0.28	0.01	22.54	37.02	29.07	0.4	33.5	0.8
WAREHOUSE C	62	0.04	0.27	0.11	5.87	30.41	14.90	16.0	45.5	31.3
OFFICE U	58	0.24	0.78	0.51	43.62	74.49	60.76	17.7	37.8	23.8
LODGING B	54	0.24	0.44	0.37	19.93	42.60	28.25	21.1	45.1	34.6
OFFICE H	50	0.13	0.49	0.25	12.22	34.88	20.45	21.9	61.4	42.1
OFFICE T	50	0.17	1.71	0.65	32.01	127.62	56.84	19.1	53.4	36.9
OFFICE R	46	0.08	0.43	0.35	15.31	52.69	37.41	13.1	44.6	26.2
LODGING C	44	0.21	0.35	0.27	14.03	32.19	22.73	24.0	55.4	38.3
MERCANTILE	41	0.44	2.59	0.95	42.63	182.74	120.21	30.6	55.0	41.9
RECREATION	39	0.08	0.39	0.16	11.97	80.41	29.25	7.5	43.1	16.7
MAINTENANCE	37	0.10	0.42	0.16	12.69	35.26	19.95	16.7	41.1	32.5
CHAPEL	37	0.09	0.50	0.23	28.26	50.71	34.32	10.2	32.8	23.7
LODGING	36	0.17	0.59	0.33	19.25	39.28	31.49	27.7	40.8	32.0
TRAINING	33	0.06	0.43	0.08	3.47	24.95	8.14	23.1	72.8	43.9
FIRE STATION	33	0.35	1.00	0.69	31.02	61.17	41.69	34.6	60.0	46.6
COLLEGE	31	0.07	0.60	0.22	25.08	45.64	32.73	8.6	49.5	28.7
DORMITORY	31	0.04	0.41	0.14	7.86	39.42	25.68	7.1	47.4	37.7
ENERGY/POWER	31	0.24	6.52	1.96	78.32	648.82	207.90	12.8	56.8	38.8

and setting the benchmark for each climate zone. As discussed in previous chapters, the EUI is directly impacted by climate zone; so a better benchmark would be by climate zone for each category type.

References

[1] (n.d.). What is Energy Use Intensity (EUI)? Energy Star. https://www.energystar.gov/buildings/benchmark/understand_metrics/what_eui

18

Setting Up for Energy Projects

Abstract

We will examine how to use data analytics to establish projects. This chapter will review the various tools and their usefulness in identifying buildings to audit. This chapter will focus on a quick audit type of tool to generate potential projects and savings without the detailed EM time involvement. This tool can help focus the EM on which buildings and which system to prioritize for each project. We will go over the applications of this tool when it is best to use, and examples to show the breakdown and potential savings.

18　Setting Up for Energy Projects

This chapter will go into detail on setting up the information required for energy projects. The following topics will be covered:

- Introduction

- Energy use intensity (EUI)

- Extrapolated EUI

- Category type performance metrics

- Individual buildings data quick audit tool

18.1 Introduction

This chapter covers different approaches for identifying areas of potential savings, such as EUI, base load comparison report with extrapolated EUI, block approach from the category type performance metrics report, and, finally, dissecting individual buildings' usage into energy systems and various potential projects by the system. Each method covers energy impact, with the first method starting at the general overall approach to establish

291

worst-case buildings. Each additional method gets more granular until we get to the individual building system method. These methods cover the magnitude of savings and its effectiveness for the particular situation and even give examples to show the breakdown for potential savings. We will discuss each of these methods or approaches below.

- EUI

- Extrapolated EUI

- Category type performance metrics

- Individual buildings data quick audit tool

The EUI is the oldest method used and was all an EM originally could use that would prioritize their buildings short of doing an audit or modeling. Modeling 50 years ago was tedious and very limited in flexibility but required the EM to be knowledgeable on the software program's idiosyncrasies to model the building successfully. This required a lot of knowledge of how the modeling program worked and how to input data vs. energy analytics, and the input process was laborious. The EMs had to send off the results to be run at a special computer facility. This was time-consuming. Today, we can model more easily, but it still takes time and should be preceded by some form of vetting to ensure we use our time wisely and only model buildings with some degree of possibility of success. The only way to get a general idea of the energy impact 50 years ago was from the EUI benchmark and by applying a cost against each commodity. That just gives us an idea of which buildings to attack first, which might be the most economical from a 30,000-foot view. That is still true today, but a few other tools can help us focus more accurately or be used in conjunction with the EUI. As discussed previously, the simplest improvement to the EUI approach is by pulling an extrapolated EUI. That gives a better answer than the EUI but is still a 30,000-foot view.

The more focused tools use similar benchmarks but in a more defined role, such as the category types and climate zones. This provides a much better comparison and allows us to understand the specific building type in this situation. Other metrics applied in this situation can show how a building rates against several metrics.

The final method for determining energy savings potential is a quick audit tool. This is based on a few known parameters that allow us to break down the energy systems based on normal usage analysis across the campus. Those parameters allow us to break down the total energy consumption for the year into the four-energy systems usage and a usage for the overrides.

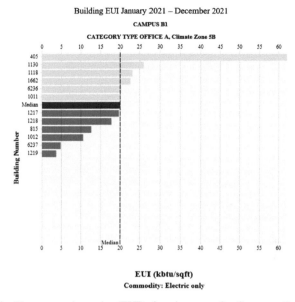

Figure 18.1 Energy use intensity (EUI) electric report for Category Type Office A.

That energy consumption is then monetized and applied against several saving scenarios to give the EM a feel for anticipated savings and construction costs so that the EM can turn this into a reliable tool to determine which projects and buildings to pursue in detail.

18.2 Energy Use Intensity (EUI)

This graph (Figure 18.1), which can be exported into Excel, is the first method of analysis that we used 40–50 years ago. This shows the worst-performing buildings for the selected report options at the top in yellow, compared to a median EUI (the dotted gray line) of the buildings in that weather region across a portfolio. We need to validate that the monthly increments are running correctly to ensure the EMs are getting readings for the entire year, as discussed in Chapter 16, to double-check if the meter is reporting accurately. Now that the EM has these, they can determine the magnitude of the savings potential by comparing it against the median.

So, in this case, we want to subtract the difference in EUI of those higher buildings (in yellow or at the top of the list) from the median. This is easier to do inside a table (Table 18.1). The EM can take each building above the median and subtract that difference in value. As shown in Table 18.1, the delta in savings potential is shown in kbtu. We can multiply that difference by the

Table 18.1   Energy use intensity (EUI) electric report for Category Type Office A.

Building Number	Building SqFt	Category Type	Year Built	EUI	EUI Delta	Potential Savings (kbtu)	Estimated Savings
405	2,448	Office A	2012	62.08	42.10	103,061	$ 2,566
1130	9,840	Office A	1966	26.08	6.10	60,024	$ 1,495
1118	55,319	Office A	1958	23.21	3.23	178,680	$ 4,449
1662	8,734	Office A	1967	22.69	2.71	23,669	$ 589
6236	19,988	Office A	1942	20.27	0.29	5,797	$ 144
1011	40,644	Office A	1956	19.98	0.00	-	$ -
Median	-			19.98			
1217	51,867	Office A	1958	19.67			
1218	51,867	Office A	1958	17.77			
815	5,756	Office A	1959	12.66			
1012	40,644	Office A	1956	10.61			
6237	20,648	Office A	1942	4.83			
1219	51,867	Office A	1958	3.70			

blended electric rate or use another adjusted rate to come up with a rough estimate of the savings against the median. In this case, we have added a column
on the far right that indicates the dollar savings for each building. Figure 18.1
is the graph showing the relationship of each meter to the median. Table 18.2 is
the conversion of that graph into a table where we can subtract those buildings
that are above the median. Here we can see a few savings for this Category
Type Office A. The difficulty in this method is that we only know that there is
a difference. We do not know what system or systems are causing the differential; so this method was used primarily to rank buildings for audits or modeling.

We have completed the same process for the gas savings, as shown in
Figure 18.2. Figure 18.2 shows five buildings that are above the median.

We translated the graph to an Excel file and determined the delta between
each building's gas EUI and the median. That is shown in Table 18.2. That
difference is multiplied by the gas rate to show the potential savings. Those
are included in the last column of Table 18.2. This shows a value but does not
tell us if it was caused by the overrides or by an inefficient boiler. Again, we
must do a model or audit to understand the requirements and costs.

The second thing to look at is how these numbers trend in Table 18.3.
We can do that by checking for three consecutive years. This is called an
internal benchmark, as discussed in previous chapters. In this case, we can
see the variance from 2019 through 2021. Usage is decreasing each year;
so our maintenance is improving, and the overall energy use is reducing for
these buildings.

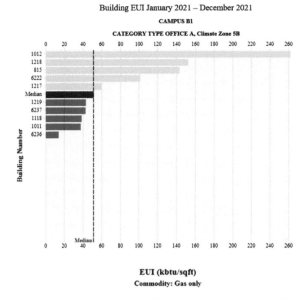

Figure 18.2 Energy use intensity (EUI) gas report for Category Type Office A.

Table 18.2 Energy use intensity (EUI) gas report for Category Type Office A.

Building Number	Building SqFt	Category Type	Year Built	EUI	EUI Delta	Potential Savings (kbtu)	Estimated Savings
1012	40,644	Office A	1956	261.91	210.58	8,558,610	$ 213,109
1218	51,867	Office A	1958	152.48	101.15	5,246,088	$ 130,628
815	5,756	Office A	1959	143.12	91.79	528,314	$ 13,155
6222	19,225	Office A	1942	101.60	50.27	966,345	$ 24,062
1217	51,867	Office A	1958	59.50	8.17	423,494	$ 10,545
Median	-			51.34			
1219	51,867	Office A	1958	43.17			
6237	20,648	Office A	1942	42.81			
1118	55,319	Office A	1958	38.61			
1011	40,644	Office A	1956	37.58			
6236	19,988	Office A	1942	13.82			

18.3 Extrapolated EUI

This report is similar to the EUI report, but it fills in for the deficiency of the EUI report. When an EM views an EUI report, they do not know if it has been reporting all year or for a portion thereof. This is a dilemma, as most systems do not show how much is missing. This causes an EM to compare apples to oranges. It is easy to extrapolate or interpolate the gaps. We interpolate the internal gaps

Table 18.3 Energy use intensity (EUI) electric comparison report for three years for Category Type Office A.

2019

Building Number	Building SqFt	Category Type	Year Built	EUI
405	2,448	Office A	2012	108.70
1118	55,319	Office A	1958	33.09
815	5,756	Office A	1959	31.26
1662	8,734	Office A	1967	27.63
1130	9,840	Office A	1966	27.26
1219	51,867	Office A	1958	27.06
Median	-			27.06
6236	19,988	Office A	1942	27.04
1217	51,867	Office A	1958	22.12
1218	51,867	Office A	1958	21.34
1012	40,644	Office A	1956	13.42
1011	40,644	Office A	1956	11.34

2020

Building Number	Building SqFt	Category Type	Year Built	EUI
405	2,448	Office A	2012	48.83
1130	9,840	Office A	1966	27.01
6236	19,988	Office A	1942	25.51
1118	55,319	Office A	1958	23.87
1011	40,644	Office A	1956	23.77
Median	-			23.77
1662	8,734	Office A	1967	21.60
1218	51,867	Office A	1958	19.08
1012	40,644	Office A	1956	11.67
1217	51,867	Office A	1958	11.00
815	5,756	Office A	1959	8.27
1219	51,867	Office A	1958	7.43

2021

Building Number	Building SqFt	Category Type	Year Built	EUI
405	2,448	Office A	2012	62.08
1130	9,840	Office A	1966	26.08
1118	55,319	Office A	1958	23.21
1662	8,734	Office A	1967	22.69
6236	19,988	Office A	1942	20.27
1011	40,644	Office A	1956	19.98
Median	-			19.98
1217	51,867	Office A	1958	19.67
1218	51,867	Office A	1958	17.77
815	5,756	Office A	1959	12.66
1012	40,644	Office A	1956	10.61
6237	20,648	Office A	1942	4.83
1219	51,867	Office A	1958	3.70

with all smoothing programs. The deficiency occurs at either end if a meter was installed after the year started or if it went off before the end of the year. This extrapolation ensures that we are always comparing a year's worth of data. This is the only way to compare EUIs from an analytic perspective. As a side note, we would identify how much was extrapolated based on a percentage so that the EM can decide if the extrapolation is reasonably close. We have found that any percentage above 60% of the data available seems to provide a reasonable answer to compare. We have not accomplished a statistical analysis of the percentage below 60% to determine if and when it may be viable.

Like the last, this method is designed to focus on audit candidates; so it does not directly provide costs/savings potential per system. Table 18.4 shows an example of a campus' Category Type Office C buildings extrapolated and filtered (highlighted in yellow) in descending order for potential audit candidates. This method gives us a more reliable comparison than the previous method, which has data missing for various reasons.

Let us convert this to a value of potential savings. We have expanded Table 18.4 with a value in Table 18.5. Here we have the EUI for each of the buildings that are above the median. We then subtract the median from each EUI and multiply that by the square footage. That gives potential savings in kbtu. Then we multiply that by the cost of a kbtu of electricity. As discussed above, this savings does not address the system or systems that cause the situation, therefore an audit or modeling will be required to determine which system is impacted. This method just highlights where we should focus our efforts on a more detailed study.

18.4 Category Type Performance Metrics

This approach is just a simple refinement of the EUI to focus on different aspects of the application. First, we can benchmark it against the extrapolated

Table 18.4   Extrapolated EUI for Category Type Office C.

Building Number	Square Footage	Category Type	12 Months Consumption (kWh)	12 Months Extrapolated EUI (Electric)	Climate Zone
2757	24,000	Office C	380,936	54.16	5B
1447	81,581	Office C	609,347	25.49	5B
7450	27,613	Office C	203,543	25.15	5B
1456	16,107	Office C	109,811	23.26	5B
704	32,341	Office C	219,944	23.21	5B
1280	46,608	Office C	308,368	22.58	5B
7464	19,972	Office C	131,442	22.46	5B
9090	51,906	Office C	330,347	21.72	5B
9427	46,613	Office C	276,137	20.21	5B
515	41,401	Office C	245,270	20.21	5B
7418	35,730	Office C	195,226	18.64	5B
750	10,107	Office C	54,887	18.53	5B
7473	65,939	Office C	357,381	18.49	5B
1454	10,048	Office C	54,027	18.35	5B
9457	52,297	Office C	278,631	18.18	5B

Table 18.5   Potential savings for Category Type Office C.

Building Number	Square Footage	Category Type	12 Months Consumption (kWh)	12 Months Extrapolated EUI (Electric)	Climate Zone	EUI Delta	Potential Savings (kbtu)	Estimated Savings
2757	24,000	Office C	380,936	54.16	5B	39.14	939,240	$ 23,387
1447	81,581	Office C	609,347	25.49	5B	10.46	853,500	$ 21,252
7450	27,613	Office C	203,543	25.15	5B	10.13	279,664	$ 6,964
1456	16,107	Office C	109,811	23.26	5B	8.24	132,706	$ 3,304
704	32,341	Office C	219,944	23.21	5B	8.18	264,582	$ 6,588
1280	46,608	Office C	308,368	22.58	5B	7.55	351,937	$ 8,763
7464	19,972	Office C	131,442	22.46	5B	7.43	148,432	$ 3,696
9090	51,906	Office C	330,347	21.72	5B	6.69	347,355	$ 8,649
9427	46,613	Office C	276,137	20.21	5B	5.19	241,921	$ 6,024
515	41,401	Office C	245,270	20.21	5B	5.19	214,871	$ 5,350
7418	35,730	Office C	195,226	18.64	5B	3.62	129,343	$ 3,221
750	10,107	Office C	54,887	18.53	5B	3.51	35,435	$ 882
7473	65,939	Office C	357,381	18.49	5B	3.47	228,742	$ 5,696
1454	10,048	Office C	54,027	18.35	5B	3.32	33,390	$ 831
9457	52,297	Office C	278,631	18.18	5B	3.16	164,997	$ 4,108
2457	23,617	Office C	125,419	18.12	5B	3.10	73,118	$ 1,821
9487	73,007	Office C	364,800	17.05	5B	2.03	147,912	$ 3,683
2650	49,140	Office C	242,652	16.85	5B	1.83	89,681	$ 2,233
9437	46,611	Office C	229,301	16.79	5B	1.76	82,129	$ 2,045
2558	23,617	Office C	113,445	16.39	5B	1.37	32,261	$ 803
2610	66,673	Office C	317,291	16.24	5B	1.21	80,941	$ 2,015
1210	78,946	Office C	367,038	15.86	5B	0.84	66,315	$ 1,651
1203	13,908	Office C	63,391	15.55	5B	0.53	7,343	$ 183
2630	87,254	Office C	384,177	15.02	5B			

EUI, against a base load, and against a base load percentage of the total load. This gives us three types of benchmarks for a particular building and many ways to apply those benchmarks. The added benefit is many ways to apply those three benchmark types. How can we apply a benchmark differently? When we have a portfolio, there are many ways we can benchmark against that portfolio. The first is on the campus itself, and then by category type on the campus. The next way is against all buildings in a climate zone, and then against the category type in that climate zone. The final is against all buildings in a portfolio, and then against the category type in the portfolio. We can do this for each type of benchmarks.

The category type charts indicate several good milestones for the EM, including the median, the highest 25th percentile, and the lowest 25th percentile, giving us a relative position for any building for each category type in an EM's portfolio. We can take each category type and benchmark against any level from portfolio down to campus. That is especially important for facilities with fewer buildings in a category type; so we expand the field in those cases.

Let us address these three types of benchmarks and just show examples of how they can be applied. The first is extrapolated EUI. Our recommendation on the best application here is to apply against a category type. The EUI is sensitive to the climate zone. So, the best benchmark for EUI would be against the same climate zone if feasible. Feasibility depends on having enough buildings for a statistical sampling in that climate zone. A sampling size generally is made of 30, but in these cases, we set it at 20 buildings.

We generally just subtract the electric EUI from the median to determine the potential savings, much like the first two project identification approaches mentioned earlier. This benchmark guide by category type can also give us a sense of ranking. This focuses on the highest potential saving candidates and helps provide a general sense of savings. In Table 18.6, we can see the results for Category Type Office C for EUI.

Using this type of report, we have a few strategic points: the median, the top 25th, and the bottom 25th percentile. Anything above the top 25th percentile is either a bad meter or an excessive energy user. Anything between the median and the top 25th percentile uses more energy than most and must be evaluated to see if we can save energy economically. Anything below the bottom 25th percentile is doing exceptionally well, or the meter is not reporting accurately. For the lower 25th percentile, we would recommend that the EM check the building as to the accuracy of the meter first, and if it is good, then determine why this building is doing so well. Use it as a good example for others.

Table 18.6   Focus on Category Type Office C against a building.

Category Type	Building Count	Bottom 25th Percentile Watts/SF	Top 25th Percentile Watts/SF	Median Watts/SF	Bottom 25th Percentile EUI	Top 25th Percentile EUI	Median EUI	Bottom 25th Percentile Baseload as % of Consumption	Top 25th Percentile Baseload as % of Consumption	Median Baseload as % of Consumption
OFFICE A	401	0.144	0.623	0.308	17.89	47.07	29.64	14.60	56.17	38.89
OFFICE C	331	0.172	0.482	0.287	16.32	35.58	25.32	18.53	51.22	39.91
REPAIR SERVICES	251	0.183	0.472	0.308	18.90	35.51	26.84	16.52	48.92	34.91
OFFICE N	159	0.261	0.645	0.435	25.53	45.98	33.58	21.07	59.05	40.39
EDUCATION	101	0.134	0.721	0.334	22.91	53.28	35.53	8.77	54.85	35.25
WAREHOUSE B	91	0.033	0.328	0.140	3.38	34.34	14.20	8.18	59.08	35.32
OFFICE D	75	0.313	0.914	0.524	29.35	57.18	42.10	23.07	57.31	42.49
FOOD SALES	71	0.510	1.634	0.849	51.26	119.68	84.53	20.46	50.88	34.32
OFFICE M	69	0.074	0.458	0.275	13.09	30.76	22.87	18.79	51.33	39.53
HEALTH CLINIC	60	0.192	0.999	0.551	31.23	66.65	49.92	14.04	58.78	40.56
PHYS FIT CENTER	58	0.157	0.615	0.363	23.35	49.66	35.81	14.05	49.60	30.77
OFFICE U	51	0.265	0.953	0.514	46.41	74.85	58.62	8.82	48.25	26.92
OFFICE H	51	0.098	0.457	0.227	14.11	34.76	19.17	13.93	50.16	31.27
WAREHOUSE C	45	0.037	0.261	0.107	5.93	30.26	11.63	5.40	63.46	30.68
Portfolio Medians		0.118	0.615	0.335	21.02	53.28	34.12	12.76	51.33	35.06

In this case, we will measure a building in the bottom 25th percentile against the median for the Category Type Office C building. If we take a building from that same climate zone and that category type, we see a median of 25.316 kbtu/sf while the top 25th percentile is 35.579. So, if a building comes out at that value, the difference is 10.263 kbtu/sf. When we take that value at 10,000 sf, the energy savings is 102,630 kbtu. At 0.0219 $/kbtu, we have a $2,247/10,000 sf of savings. If we have a 60,000-sf building, that would be $13,485/year. The full span would be from the upper 25th to the bottom 25th percentile. If we do that math, the range of possibilities is $25,306 in savings. This is the maximum range of savings. An EM would use the EUI for that building to perform that same math. This would result in savings by subtracting down to the median, but the goal would be the bottom 25th percentile.

The next way to look at this, Table 18.7, is against the base load on a watts/sf basis. That benchmark is good at showing what the constant (flat) load excess energy usage is. While the previous analysis will give a combined total excess usage, this analysis will concentrate on the constant load. This will help the EM identify the impact of fan/pump systems loading that can be resolved by scheduling or adding schedules to the start/stop controls. So, the delta from the top 25th percentile to the median is 0.195 watts/sf. That is 17,082 kWh/every 10,000 sf or $1537 per 10,000 sf. The range to the bottom or bottom 25th percentile gives a dollar value of $2444 per 10,000 sf. At 60,000 sf, that value is $14,664 range. While we do not anticipate any project achieving the entire range as that is just the maximum extent, it gives us the maximum dollar value achievable if all conditions are perfect. Viewing each building and using the building numbers and taking them against the bottom 25th percentile is a good approach for target savings.

The third benchmark, Table 18.8, we developed is the percentage of base load that the base load (watts/sf) represents. This is represented as a

Table 18.7 Focus on Category Type Office C against a building.

Category Type	Building Count	Bottom 25th Percentile Watts/SF	Top 25th Percentile Watts/SF	Median Watts/SF	Bottom 25th Percentile EUI	Top 25th Percentile EUI	Median EUI	Bottom 25th Percentile Baseload as % of Consumption	Top 25th Percentile Baseload as % of Consumption	Median Baseload as % of Consumption
OFFICE A	401	0.144	0.623	0.308	17.89	47.07	29.64	14.60	56.17	38.89
OFFICE C	331	0.172	0.482	0.287	16.32	35.58	25.32	18.53	51.22	39.91
REPAIR SERVICES	251	0.183	0.472	0.308	18.90	35.51	26.84	16.52	48.92	34.91
OFFICE N	159	0.261	0.645	0.435	25.53	45.98	33.58	21.07	59.05	40.39
EDUCATION	101	0.134	0.721	0.334	22.91	53.28	35.53	8.77	54.85	35.25
WAREHOUSE B	91	0.033	0.328	0.140	3.38	34.34	14.20	8.18	59.08	35.32
OFFICE D	75	0.313	0.914	0.524	29.35	57.18	42.10	23.07	57.31	42.49
FOOD SALES	71	0.510	1.634	0.849	51.26	119.68	84.53	20.46	50.88	34.32
OFFICE M	69	0.074	0.458	0.275	13.09	30.76	22.87	18.79	51.33	39.53
HEALTH CLINIC	60	0.192	0.999	0.551	31.23	66.65	49.92	14.04	58.78	40.56
PHYS FIT CENTER	58	0.157	0.615	0.363	23.35	49.66	35.81	14.05	49.60	30.77
OFFICE U	51	0.265	0.953	0.514	46.41	74.85	58.62	8.82	48.25	26.92
OFFICE H	51	0.098	0.457	0.227	14.11	34.76	19.17	13.93	50.16	31.27
WAREHOUSE C	45	0.037	0.261	0.107	5.93	30.26	11.63	5.40	63.46	30.68
Portfolio Medians		0.118	0.615	0.335	21.02	53.28	34.12	12.76	51.33	35.06

Table 18.8 Focus on Category Type Office C against a building.

Category Type	Building Count	Bottom 25th Percentile Watts/SF	Top 25th Percentile Watts/SF	Median Watts/SF	Bottom 25th Percentile EUI	Top 25th Percentile EUI	Median EUI	Bottom 25th Percentile Baseload as % of Consumption	Top 25th Percentile Baseload as % of Consumption	Median Baseload as % of Consumption
OFFICE A	401	0.144	0.623	0.308	17.89	47.07	29.64	14.60	56.17	38.89
OFFICE C	331	0.172	0.482	0.287	16.32	35.58	25.32	18.53	51.22	39.91
REPAIR SERVICES	251	0.183	0.472	0.308	18.90	35.51	26.84	16.52	48.92	34.91
OFFICE N	159	0.261	0.645	0.435	25.53	45.98	33.58	21.07	59.05	40.39
EDUCATION	101	0.134	0.721	0.334	22.91	53.28	35.53	8.77	54.85	35.25
WAREHOUSE B	91	0.033	0.328	0.140	3.38	34.34	14.20	8.18	59.08	35.32
OFFICE D	75	0.313	0.914	0.524	29.35	57.18	42.10	23.07	57.31	42.49
FOOD SALES	71	0.510	1.634	0.849	51.26	119.68	84.53	20.46	50.88	34.32
OFFICE M	69	0.074	0.458	0.275	13.09	30.76	22.87	18.79	51.33	39.53
HEALTH CLINIC	60	0.192	0.999	0.551	31.23	66.65	49.92	14.04	58.78	40.56
PHYS FIT CENTER	58	0.157	0.615	0.363	23.35	49.66	35.81	14.05	49.60	30.77
OFFICE U	51	0.265	0.953	0.514	46.41	74.85	58.62	8.82	48.25	26.92
OFFICE H	51	0.098	0.457	0.227	14.11	34.76	19.17	13.93	50.16	31.27
WAREHOUSE C	45	0.037	0.261	0.107	5.93	30.26	11.63	5.40	63.46	30.68
Portfolio Medians		0.118	0.615	0.335	21.02	53.28	34.12	12.76	51.33	35.06

percent, and the percentiles, while informative of the universe of the portfolio, do not help understand the value of the savings as those in the first two benchmarks. In this benchmark, we know the building would go down to 10%, and we know what the Category Type ranges from top to bottom. So, the top 25th percentile accounts for some of the worst buildings at 51%. In this case, that has to go down to 10%, which means a savings of 41% is possible. If we go down from the median to the lowest percentile, which gives us a potential of 39% down to 18% or a potential savings of 21% for the best practice, but we still know we can theoretically go down to 10%, so that the total potential would be 29%. These savings are also a constant value, indicating fan/pump systems that are constantly running.

In this next example, Table 18.9, we will take another Category, Type Office D, which is in the top 25th percentile, and measure the EUI against the median for that Category Type. We are using this example as there is a larger variance from the median to the top and bottom 25th percentile. If we take a

Table 18.9 Focus on Category Type Office D against a building.

Category Type	Building Count	Bottom 25th Percentile Watts/SF	Top 25th Percentile Watts/SF	Median Watts/SF	Bottom 25th Percentile EUI	Top 25th Percentile EUI	Median EUI	Bottom 25th Percentile Baseload as % of Consumption	Top 25th Percentile Baseload as % of Consumption	Median Baseload as % of Consumption
OFFICE A	401	0.144	0.623	0.308	17.89	47.07	29.64	14.60	56.17	38.89
OFFICE C	331	0.172	0.482	0.287	16.32	35.58	25.32	18.53	51.22	39.91
REPAIR SERVICES	251	0.183	0.472	0.308	18.90	35.51	26.84	16.52	48.92	34.91
OFFICE N	159	0.261	0.645	0.435	25.53	45.98	33.58	21.07	59.05	40.39
EDUCATION	101	0.134	0.721	0.334	22.91	53.28	35.53	8.77	54.85	35.25
WAREHOUSE B	91	0.033	0.328	0.140	3.38	34.34	14.20	8.18	59.08	35.32
OFFICE D	75	0.313	0.914	0.524	29.35	57.18	42.10	23.07	57.31	42.49
FOOD SALES	71	0.510	1.634	0.849	51.26	119.68	84.53	20.46	50.88	34.32
OFFICE M	69	0.074	0.458	0.275	13.09	30.76	22.87	18.79	51.33	39.53
HEALTH CLINIC	60	0.192	0.999	0.551	31.23	66.65	49.92	14.04	58.78	40.56
PHYS FIT CENTER	58	0.157	0.615	0.363	23.35	49.66	35.81	14.05	49.60	30.77
OFFICE U	51	0.265	0.953	0.514	46.41	74.85	58.62	8.82	48.25	26.92
OFFICE H	51	0.098	0.457	0.227	14.11	34.76	19.17	13.93	50.16	31.27
WAREHOUSE C	45	0.037	0.261	0.107	5.93	30.26	11.63	5.40	63.46	30.68
Portfolio Medians		0.118	0.615	0.335	21.02	53.28	34.12	12.76	51.33	35.06

building from that category type, we see a median of 42.103 kbtu/sf, while the top 25th percentile is 57.183. So, hypothetically, if a building comes out at that value, the difference is 15.080 kbtu/sf. When we take that value at 10,000 sf, the energy savings is 150,800 kbtu. At 0.0219 $/kbtu, we have a $3302/10,000 sf savings. That is 50% higher than the previous example. Now the full span would be from that upper 25th percentile to the bottom 25th percentile, and the range of possibilities is $36,579 in savings. An EM would use the EUI for that building to perform the same math. This would result in savings to the difference from the median, but the ultimate goal would be the bottom 25th percentile.

We will also look at a benchmark, base load, Table 18.10, on a watts/sf basis. As discussed previously, this metric will affect fan/pump systems loading, which can be resolved by scheduling or adding schedules to the start/stop controls. At 60,000 sf, for example, that value is in the $28,429 range. Viewing each building and using the building numbers and taking them against the bottom 25th percentile is a good approach for target savings.

Again, with Category Type Office D, we will address the third benchmark in Table 18.11. In this benchmark, we know the building would go down to 10%, and we know what the Category Type ranges from top to bottom. So, the top 25th percentile accounts for some of the worst buildings at 57%. That should be able to theoretically reach 10%, which means a savings of 47% is possible. If we go down from the median to the lowest percentile, which gives us a potential of 42% down to 23% or a potential savings of 19% for the best building, there is a high potential in savings for the worst buildings. We know that, ultimately, we can go down to 10%; so the total potential would be 32%, just to the median. These savings are also a constant value, indicating fan/pump systems that are constantly running.

Table 18.10   Focus on Category Type Office D against a building.

Category Type	Building Count	Bottom 25th Percentile Watts/SF	Top 25th Percentile Watts/SF	Median Watts/SF	Bottom 25th Percentile EUI	Top 25th Percentile EUI	Median EUI	Bottom 25th Percentile Baseload as % of Consumption	Top 25th Percentile Baseload as % of Consumption	Median Baseload as % of Consumption
OFFICE A	401	0.144	0.623	0.308	17.89	47.07	29.64	14.60	56.17	38.89
OFFICE C	331	0.172	0.482	0.287	16.32	35.58	25.32	18.53	51.22	39.91
REPAIR SERVICES	251	0.183	0.472	0.308	18.90	35.51	26.84	16.52	48.92	34.91
OFFICE N	159	0.261	0.645	0.435	25.53	45.98	33.58	21.07	59.05	40.39
EDUCATION	101	0.134	0.721	0.334	22.91	53.28	35.53	8.77	54.85	35.25
WAREHOUSE B	91	0.033	0.328	0.140	3.38	34.34	14.20	8.18	59.08	35.32
OFFICE D	75	0.313	0.914	0.524	29.35	57.18	42.10	23.07	57.31	42.49
FOOD SALES	71	0.510	1.634	0.849	51.26	119.68	84.53	20.46	50.88	34.32
OFFICE M	69	0.074	0.458	0.275	13.09	30.76	22.87	18.79	51.33	39.53
HEALTH CLINIC	60	0.192	0.999	0.551	31.23	66.65	49.92	14.04	58.78	40.56
PHYS FIT CENTER	58	0.157	0.615	0.363	23.35	49.66	35.81	14.05	49.60	30.77
OFFICE U	51	0.265	0.953	0.514	46.41	74.85	58.62	8.82	48.25	26.92
OFFICE H	51	0.098	0.457	0.227	14.11	34.76	19.17	13.93	50.16	31.27
WAREHOUSE C	45	0.037	0.261	0.107	5.93	30.26	11.63	5.40	63.46	30.68
Portfolio Medians		0.118	0.615	0.335	21.02	53.28	34.12	12.76	51.33	35.06

Table 18.11   Focus on Category Type Office D against a building.

Category Type	Building Count	Bottom 25th Percentile Watts/SF	Top 25th Percentile Watts/SF	Median Watts/SF	Bottom 25th Percentile EUI	Top 25th Percentile EUI	Median EUI	Bottom 25th Percentile Baseload as % of Consumption	Top 25th Percentile Baseload as % of Consumption	Median Baseload as % of Consumption
OFFICE A	401	0.144	0.623	0.308	17.89	47.07	29.64	14.60	56.17	38.89
OFFICE C	331	0.172	0.482	0.287	16.32	35.58	25.32	18.53	51.22	39.91
REPAIR SERVICES	251	0.183	0.472	0.308	18.90	35.51	26.84	16.52	48.92	34.91
OFFICE N	159	0.261	0.645	0.435	25.53	45.98	33.58	21.07	59.05	40.39
EDUCATION	101	0.134	0.721	0.334	22.91	53.28	35.53	8.77	54.85	35.25
WAREHOUSE B	91	0.033	0.328	0.140	3.38	34.34	14.20	8.18	59.08	35.32
OFFICE D	75	0.313	0.914	0.524	29.35	57.18	42.10	23.07	57.31	42.49
FOOD SALES	71	0.510	1.634	0.849	51.26	119.68	84.53	20.46	50.88	34.32
OFFICE M	69	0.074	0.458	0.275	13.09	30.76	22.87	18.79	51.33	39.53
HEALTH CLINIC	60	0.192	0.999	0.551	31.23	66.65	49.92	14.04	58.78	40.56
PHYS FIT CENTER	58	0.157	0.615	0.363	23.35	49.66	35.81	14.05	49.60	30.77
OFFICE U	51	0.265	0.953	0.514	46.41	74.85	58.62	8.82	48.25	26.92
OFFICE H	51	0.098	0.457	0.227	14.11	34.76	19.17	13.93	50.16	31.27
WAREHOUSE C	45	0.037	0.261	0.107	5.93	30.26	11.63	5.40	63.46	30.68
Portfolio Medians		0.118	0.615	0.335	21.02	53.28	34.12	12.76	51.33	35.06

18.5 Individual Buildings Data Quick Audit Tool

This is a unique way to do a shortcut for auditing buildings from the EM's desk. It is not foolproof, but it will generally get us within 10%. This calculation tool is based on using the base load, which will be a safe estimate and under the total usage based on it being a smaller subset of the wasted energy. It is used in this case because it is easier to determine than the total non-office hours energy. That difference is usually a minimum of 7%, and we can view that comparison in the benchmarking chapter on the difference between the base load and the non-office hour loading. For comparison, we calculated the base load, shown as the 40.6% value in Figure 18.3. The non-office hours are 47.4% from Figure 18.3, but they must be developed from the scatter plot, which is a more complex analysis and sensitive to working properly. This tool shows that the difference between the two methods is 7% and can vary from 5% to 30%. Using the base load, we can estimate the loading quickly

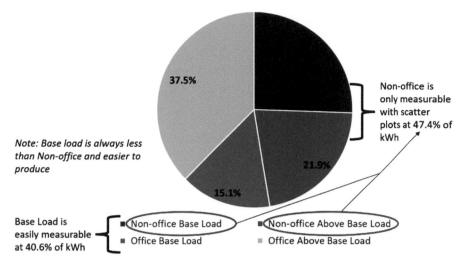

Non-office is only measurable with scatter plots at 47.4% of kWh

Note: Base load is always less than Non-office and easier to produce

Base Load is easily measurable at 40.6% of kWh

- Non-office Base Load
- Office Base Load
- Non-office Above Base Load
- Office Above Base Load

37.5%   15.1%   21.9%

Figure 18.3 Comparison of base load vs. non-office hour loading.

and easily and always be conservative by 5%–30% less than the more rigorous scatter plot analysis.

So, with this tool, we can be very successful in our audit with readily available data and produce a conservative savings projection. If the buildings have a consistent composition across campus and operate similarly, then we can easily do the audit with those same assumptions within an hour. Finishing a campus will take longer if we need to vary the parameters. Once we set the parameters, we can check the buildings periodically against the updated usage. The best benefit is that this tool allows an EM to remove buildings that are not economical to audit; so we can concentrate on those that may produce economically viable projects.

The premise of this tool is that we can take the total electrical energy consumption for each building and break it down into the four systems outlined in the benchmarking chapters:

1. Plug

2. Lights

3. Fan/pump systems

4. AC systems

The tool allocates the energy based on the ratios developed in the waterfall chart from the scatter plots. Those ratios will generally stay consistent across the campus with similar building types, system types, and construction. Most campuses are usually consistent with those criteria. So, we can run a few scatter plots, and if they come out with the same ratios, we can use those ratios across a campus. If they vary, then run a scatter plot for each type of building construction and use those ratios for each building in the project identification or audit tool. As stated above, campus construction is so similar that the ratio between systems is close. With this method, we allocate the overall energy that the four energy systems use for each building. We then calculate the cost for each system by multiplying that usage by the average cost of electricity for the installation. This project development tool is easy when we have the variable data already established in the database; so the usage data rolls in to populate this tool whenever we desire to check our buildings. With these, we can quickly check the system usage for each building. Once we get the energy distribution, we analyze the potential savings based on a discussion with the facility maintenance shops. We must decide what ECM they can do and roughly the costs to finalize each system's potential savings impact for that solution set. This method allows the EM to work the project analysis backward by determining which buildings have enough potential savings to justify the capital costs. This eliminates a lot of unnecessary audit time by determining which buildings have the potential for a project to be successful based on the potentially available cost savings. Once we determine the buildings with the headroom to justify a project, we can do an audit or work with a utility energy services contract (UESC) or an energy savings performance contract (ESPC). We will show how this tool breaks down the savings by each system and the cost associated with producing those savings. Then between the EM and the facility maintenance group, we can get a rough idea of what needs to be fixed on a system and the savings associated with the repair. That may only be a rough estimate, but it gives us an idea of how much cost is associated with a specific percentage of savings.

Let us first walk through the general parameters of the development. We arc only approaching the electric in this model as that drives the medium for savings for heating and cooling and generally impacts 85%–90% of the facility costs. This does not account for the additional synergistic savings from managing electric usage to the gas savings for some ECMs. Still, an EM must realize that thermal energy will not be used if the distribution medium shuts down. If we examine Table 18.12, we can see the variables that can be adjusted for this quick audit tool with the first two default values being the cost/kWh, a blended rate, and the number of office hours. The cost/kWh is basic and will be adjusted later for each project type based on its impact on demand. The office hours are how the system allocates the non-office vs. the office energy. The next value is the percentage related to the plug and

Table 18.12 Variables for the quick audit.

Campus	B1
Cost per kWh	0.0526
Office Hours	2607
% (Plug Load + Weather Load)	18.00
AC System % of Load	15.00
Fan/Pump System % of Load	55.00
Lighting System % of Load	16.00
Plug Load % of Load	14.00
% of Maximum Savings	30.00
% Demand Impact on Cost for Overrides	65.00
% Demand Impact on Cost for AC System	80.00
% Demand Impact on Cost for Fan/Pump System	85.00
% Demand Impact on Cost for Lighting System	95.00

weather. That will be broken down later in this chapter. Then we get into the four values, which are the percentage of the program's load to the four energy systems in a building. The relationship between the four systems for institutions will be heavy on the fan/pump systems as they generally stay on a lot. So, fans/pumps on institutional buildings generally run from 40% to 55%. The other three systems, lighting, AC systems, and plug loads, will be close to the same or around 15% each. The next variable is the EM's ability to vary the maximum percentage loading applied for the potential of energy savings. The maximum defaults to 30%, but that value can be modified here if we have a project such as VFDs that might save 50%. The next few variables relate to how much of the cost/kWh is applied to the specific system ECM savings. For example, the US's standard cost/kWh (blended rate) is broken into three parts. We have the base rate, the demand rate, and the additional flat charges. The majority of the bill is that base rate which averages 65% of the total blended rate in the US. That means any ECM that does not impact peak energy usage during demand hours will only impact 65% of the blended rate. This 65% is applied to overrides that will impact night and weekend hours, which are generally not during the demand period of rate structures across most of the US. So, we multiply that ECM by 65% of the blended rate to get the real cost for that ECM covering overridden controls. We can change this if we have a different base vs. blended rate mix or if the demand comes at

Table 18.13   Example building potential savings calculations.

		% Of Total Annual kWh Consumed
Total Annual kWh (2019)	**729,796.03**	
Non-Office kWh	345,825.03	47.4%
Winter Non-Office Hour Plug Load	22,222.63	
Summer Non-Office Hour Plug Load	15,915.93	
Total Plug for Year	38,138.56	5.2%
Potential Savings (Non-Office minus Plug Load)	**307,686.47**	**42.2%**
Energy Used to Keep Space Above 45°F	90,263.04	12.4%
Final Potential Savings	**217,423.43**	**29.8%**

night during non-office hours. The second demand cost adjustment is related to the AC system ECM. It says 80% of the blended rate will apply if we do an AC system ECM. This assumes the demand period occurs between 200 and 400 PM. If the campus is in California and the demand charge occurs after 600 PM, then we would have to go back to probably a 65% adjustment, which means the AC system does not impact the demand charge. The third is the adjustment for fans and pump systems. We have given them a heavier weight for impacting the demand; so we assigned them 85% since they are a flatter load than the AC system, but that is a value we have to determine based on the campus. The final system impact is the lights, and that would be a pure impact on demand in areas except California or anywhere the demand charge period is after office hours. Since lights are a flat load, we have assigned 95% of the blended rate as there will always be some charges that are additional flat charges to a bill and are not impacted by kWh reductions.

The item labeled "% (plug load + weather load)" in Table 18.12 is the minimum energy requirement to operate during non-office hours. The two values required to be on or the minimum usage during non-office hours are the plug load and the energy required to keep the building from freezing. We calculate that value by adding the non-duty plug load for summer and winter. That is shown in Table 18.13 as 38,138.56 kWh. We calculate the energy required to run the system to prevent freezing when the OAT is below 45°F. We can adjust this, but normally we would see a setback temperature of 55°F in winter for the interior space. To maintain an internal temperature of 55°F would normally require an OAT to be no more than 10°F below, depending

Table 18.14 Individual buildings' base load comparison.

Building	Square Footage	12 Months Consumption (kWh)	Baseload as % Consumption	12 Months Extrapolated EUI (Electric)	Electric Cost Annually	Overrides of Schedule	Air Conditioning Loading 15.0%	Fan/Pump 55.0%	Lights 16.0%	Plug 14.0%
4782	103,742	2,588,563	49.60	85.14	$ 107,483	$ 26,968	$ 8,111	$ 24,080	$ 19,581	$ 18,359
229	206,000	3,087,259	38.69	51.14	$ 128,189	$ 23,075	$ 11,313	$ 38,027	$ 21,841	$ 20,352
5125	185,500	2,207,729	43.26	40.61	$ 91,670	$ 19,223	$ 7,601	$ 24,455	$ 16,029	$ 14,973
103	195,045	1,859,180	48.19	32.53	$ 77,197	$ 18,663	$ 5,954	$ 18,039	$ 13,928	$ 13,048
1142	74,780	1,113,840	63.23	50.82	$ 46,249	$ 15,702	$ 2,729	$ 5,757	$ 9,457	$ 8,953
71	195,533	1,232,307	53.58	21.50	$ 51,168	$ 14,161	$ 3,619	$ 10,042	$ 9,599	$ 9,023
6271	23,221	825,864	61.93	121.35	$ 34,292	$ 11,352	$ 2,078	$ 4,617	$ 6,921	$ 6,545
113	26,590	817,044	57.99	104.85	$ 33,925	$ 10,362	$ 2,219	$ 5,575	$ 6,600	$ 6,223
429	40,268	1,017,738	48.56	86.24	$ 42,259	$ 10,316	$ 3,241	$ 9,770	$ 7,643	$ 7,162
9003	51,548	1,349,658	36.46	89.34	$ 56,041	$ 9,273	$ 5,091	$ 17,430	$ 9,437	$ 8,784
6782	25,008	640,352	59.04	87.37	$ 26,589	$ 8,303	$ 1,705	$ 4,162	$ 5,222	$ 4,927
203	110,000	829,988	47.29	25.75	$ 34,463	$ 8,128	$ 2,695	$ 8,266	$ 6,180	$ 5,787
833	19,323	558,204	61.82	98.57	$ 23,178	$ 7,656	$ 1,408	$ 3,140	$ 4,672	$ 4,418
43	49,696	746,524	48.60	51.26	$ 30,997	$ 7,576	$ 2,376	$ 7,157	$ 5,608	$ 5,255
9014	12,173	570,617	59.09	159.95	$ 23,693	$ 7,406	$ 1,518	$ 3,700	$ 4,655	$ 4,393
8033	30,022	536,351	61.81	60.96	$ 22,270	$ 7,355	$ 1,353	$ 3,018	$ 4,489	$ 4,245

on the building construction. We will assume that 10°F is the calculation point to determine the kWh usage for this building when the OAT was below 45°F giving us 90,263.04 kWh, as shown in Table 18.13. This is technically more energy than required because this building did not have a setback to 55°F (and we find this same problem in most institutions); so the real usage to maintain at 55°F would be somewhat less, but we will use that value for this example. That generates a 12.4% minimum requirement for usage to ensure the building does not freeze. So, adding the 12.4% with the non-office plug results in 17.6%, which we usually round to 18% for the energy used during the project calculation. This is in Climate Zone 5B; so we see this is very conservative. As we already stated, the usage indicated in Table 18.13 is higher because the building currently sustains an indoor temperature of 70°F vs. 55°F, and the weather zone is one of the coldest. So, 18% for this value means we will likely have better real-life savings than estimated here with this tool. We will assume this is probably the worst-case scenario for this discussion. The number overall will range from 6% to 22%, primarily due to the variance across climate zones. We might see 6% in Climate Zone 2 and 22% if we are in Climate Zone 7. Those in Climate Zone 5 and above will have a higher number due to the OAT being lower as the climate zone number rises.

The next breakdown we will cover is the distribution of those four system values, and the proportion that is distributed to the overrides is split across the total consumption. Table 18.14 will break down those four systems, as discussed before. Each percentage is highlighted and shown as AC systems 15%, fan/pump systems 55%, lights 14%, and plug 14%. Each building load is proportioned from the total energy cost in the column below that title. The cost of each of the energy systems is weighted in several ways. The first is that the system override impact is pulled out proportionately based on the base load impact in that building. The second is based on the demand impact on each energy system. As we look down the list, we can see that this energy is allocated based on the percentage shown against each minus the amount taken out for overrides and for the demand impact on that system. As discussed previously, these demand numbers are weighted based on the average for the US but can be modified based on the local utility. So, if we add up the four energy systems and the override cost, it would be less than the total building energy cost. Each system column tells us about how much energy cost is distributed to that system for the year. We will take away from those values the impact of the overrides but will discuss that later in this chapter as we can see the values of each system in dollars of use. As discussed before, we can only affect the systems based on the impact that ECM has on demand, which means we cannot take full credit for the blended rate. These values are the maximum usages based on using base load as the quick calculation method; so they will be under the actual detailed calculations by between 15% to 30%, as can be produced by the scatter plots. Scatter plots are harder to generate and are not always accurate for every building; so this is a good tool for establishing a start to an audit.

Let us review each of these systems individually. The first and most important savings will be attributable to the overrides. The override load is calculated as discussed above according to Figure 18.3. That figure showed a base load of 40.6%. We calculate the difference between a minimum theoretical base load percentage that can be achieved as the target baseline for savings minus that base load calculated from the data for each building, with the remainder contributed to overrides. These are constant values or usages by the equipment represented in these overrides. Therefore, as discussed before, they are conservative numbers because the total non-office hours kWh will be 7%–8% more than those discussed earlier. While this will be less, it is very conservative and helps us focus on savings while realizing that 7% would be a 15% increase over the savings projected based on the normal ratio of values.

The freeze limit protection adds about 12.4% to the base load, as shown above, and the plug load adds another 5.2%. These together set the lower limit for minimum energy required for the building as 18%. So, if the base load is 40.6% and the real base should be 18%, we have a minimum potential savings of 22.6%. We know from Figure 18.3 that up to another 7% could be added with the excess usage in non-office hours that are not considered here in base load modeling. Each building could have savings of roughly 25% for the overridden constant and variable loading. We will accomplish those first

Table 18.15 Override dollars impact by building.

Building	Square Footage	Watts/SF	12 Months Consumption (kWh)	Baseload as % Consumption	12 Months Extrapolated EUI (Electric)	Electric Cost Annually	Overrides of Schedule ($)
5341	136,200	1.094	1,900,49⬭	68.67	47.61	$ 99,966	$ 32,922
9302	82,827	1.806	2,107,829	62.18	86.83	$ 110,872	$ 31,839
2312	140,007	0.558	1,336,017	51.19	32.56	$ 70,274	$ 15,162
249	137,633	0.524	1,238,509	51.05	30.71	$ 65,146	$ 13,995
9591	55,300	1.019	950,885	51.92	58.67	$ 50,017	$ 11,026
622	39,688	1.134	539,697	73.04	46.40	$ 28,388	$ 10,156
308	203,000	0.277	1,124,40⬭	43.88	18.90	$ 59,144	$ 9,948
7669	116,650	0.361	720,337	51.18	21.07	$ 37,890	$ 8,172
5362	51,617	0.696	461,245	68.20	30.49	$ 24,261	$ 7,917
3369	72,083	0.419	514,337	51.47	24.35	$ 27,054	$ 5,886
248	62,488	0.493	566,568	47.67	30.94	$ 29,801	$ 5,747
5262	51,617	0.493	347,283	64.22	22.96	$ 18,267	$ 5,488
5562	34,571	0.675	322,696	63.31	31.85	$ 16,974	$ 4,998
2418	45,200	0.501	299,828	66.21	22.63	$ 15,771	$ 4,942

since these ECMs will be low-cost/no-cost. This override percentage only impacts the fan/pump systems and the AC system; therefore, this energy is now pulled from the fan/pump systems percentage and the AC system percentage. Those two systems are the only ones impacted by the overrides. We have found the impact is generally around 80% applied against the fan/pump systems and 20% to the AC systems. This is because the driver for this differential is the base load, which is a flat or a constant load. As discussed in the benchmarking chapters, that only impacts the fan/pump systems in most situations. A few exceptions exist, but the split between fan/pump and AC systems in the variable energy subsets averages a 45/55% ratio. We know that there will be little impact from AC systems in the constant mode; so our calculations show the ratio around 83% for fan/pump systems vs. 17% for AC systems.

The right column in Table 18.15 shows the total value of the overrides on a building. Remember, this is about 7% under this tool but under the non-office hours' number it will have about 15% impact on the savings numbers. The numbers in this tool will always be understated; so we know we are always safe in our estimates. These will be low-cost/no-cost changes to get the overrides back on track, and this is the highest payback, and thus the highest priority of ECMs to resolve immediately. As discussed in the previous chapters, the impact comes from the base load as a percentage of the overall consumption. From the building in the first row, we can see that the circled value shows a 68% base load percentage, which is 50% above the maximum projected. That leaves a lot of energy on the system that is running constantly. For that same building, we can see the cost for the overridden system is above $30K. An EM can easily find a solution that may even support the cost of installing a control system for that magnitude of savings. In the second example, the base load is at 43%. That still leaves 25% as projected savings based on the average numbers. This particular building can support savings of almost $10K per year. Much work can be done on controls for less than $10K in construction costs.

The AC system is the first energy system that we will evaluate. Evaluating the AC system requires us to break down the four systems within the total consumption. The AC system usage is broken out in Table 18.16. That value is summed up in the middle column under the heading "Air Conditioning Loading." This is then broken down under the next three columns, with the cost of savings broken into three categories. We have savings in descending order for all the usage values in dollars for AC systems. The projected savings are set up in bracketed values where we might approximate or at least get a close estimate for the savings ECMs we may employ for that building. We do this by working with the facilities staff to see if they have any ideas on what upgrades are needed for the AC system in those respective buildings. The specified percent, 30%, can be changed in the variables table in case we want to be more precise or increase the number. The maintenance shops give us a rough cost and collectively determine what savings that might generate. This can be modified if an ECM needs additional definition or a more detailed savings analysis. We do this to look at these in buckets so that we can evaluate them quickly to determine if there are ECMs that can make the economics work. So, we might look at an AC system and determine that replacing the chiller would produce a savings of 30%. Remember that, as discussed before, we can change the 30% number up or down to one appropriate for the solutions set. We can change the 30% savings to another savings, say 34%, on the variables page if we need to come in with a more detailed analysis. We look at that value of savings to determine if those savings can justify the construction costs. So, this tool backs into the viability of the ECM by calculating a construction cost that is supportable at that percentage of savings. So, the matching construction costs are justified by those percent savings, 10%, 20%, 30%, as indicated on the last three columns. This is just a simple calculation that assumes we want to meet a 10% internal rate of return (IRR) as a financed project; so it will list the total development and construction costs we must be below to meet that IRR. So, the first example in the red circles below shows that the AC system costs $13,649/year. If the maintenance shop says, they can replace the evaporator and save 20% of the energy. This model then says that 20% savings will support a financed construction project cost of up to $27,297. Therefore, if we and the maintenance shop think we can get

Table 18.16 Various savings options for an AC system.

Building	Square Footage	12 Months Consumption (kWh)	Electric Cost Annually	% Off Duty Base Load - Plug Load	Air Conditioning Loading	Projected savings for ECM - 10%	Projected savings for ECM - 20%	Projected savings for ECM - 30%	Construction Costs supportable for 20 years contract for 10% savings	Construction Costs supportable for 20 years contract for 20% savings	Construction Costs supportable for 20 years contract for 30% savings
329	221,301	5,264,419	$218,590	49.4%	13,649	$1,365	$2,730	$4,095	$13,649	$27,297	$40,946
2682	84,000	2,700,380	$112,125	0.0%	$13,455	$1,346	$2,691	$4,037	$13,455	$26,910	$40,365
5423	286,066	2,640,058	$109,621	0.0%	$13,154	$1,315	$2,631	$3,946	$13,154	$26,309	$39,463
5243	286,211	2,542,229	$105,559	0.0%	$12,667	$1,267	$2,533	$3,800	$12,667	$25,334	$38,001
229	206,000	3,087,259	$128,189	27.7%	$11,313	$1,131	$2,263	$3,394	$11,313	$22,626	$33,938
123	287,716	2,099,045	$87,157	0.0%	10,459	$1,046	$2,092	$3,138	10,459	$20,918	$31,376
5731	98,047	1,727,590	$71,733	0.0%	8,608	$861	$1,722	$2,582	8,608	$17,216	$25,824
5043	245,656	1,715,847	$71,246	0.0%	8,549	$855	$1,710	$2,565	8,549	$17,099	$25,648
4782	103,742	2,588,563	$107,483	38.6%	8,111	$811	$1,622	$2,433	8,111	$16,221	$24,332
5323	51,549	1,528,496	$63,466	0.0%	7,616	$762	$1,523	$2,285	7,616	$15,232	$22,848
5125	185,500	2,207,729	$91,670	32.3%	7,601	$760	$1,520	$2,280	7,601	$15,203	$22,804
5025	197,888	1,583,933	$65,768	14.2%	6,826	$683	$1,365	$2,048	6,826	$13,652	$20,478
5033	243,481	1,751,715	$72,735	26.9%	6,484	$648	$1,297	$1,945	6,484	$12,968	$19,452
169	66,934	1,258,191	$52,243	0.0%	6,269	$627	$1,254	$1,881	6,269	$12,538	$18,807
103	195,045	1,859,180	$77,197	37.2%	5,954	$595	$1,191	$1,786	5,954	$11,907	$17,861
5103	179,631	1,808,779	$75,104	37.5%	5,766	$577	$1,153	$1,730	5,766	$11,533	$17,299
53	54,521	1,103,349	$45,813	0.0%	5,498	$550	$1,100	$1,649	5,498	$10,995	$16,493
9003	51,548	1,349,658	$56,041	25.5%	5,091	$509	$1,018	$1,527	5,091	$10,182	$15,273
234	54,521	1,016,665	$42,214	0.0%	5,066	$507	$1,013	$1,520	5,066	$10,131	$15,197
192	84,314	1,005,489	$41,750	0.0%	5,010	$501	$1,002	$1,503	5,010	$10,020	$15,030

a project to replace the evaporator for under that cost, then this project may be supportable in a group of AC system ECMs in a financed project. This simply says that the project should be taken to the next level if we can replace that AC system for under $27,000 for the first building on the list. This is an easy way to do a clearing house of possible projects based on our collective best engineering estimate of savings and cost. Being able to treat these as a group of projects and assuming the solution is similar for each may make a financed project easier as we can have one vendor focused on the same ECM or at least the same energy system at multiple buildings, which allows the cost to be lower for construction. This one report will save the EM countless hours evaluating buildings that will never meet the payback standards for ECMs. It allows us to dismiss buildings below the economic cutoff once we apply this tool against the override spreadsheet and the four systems and determine that finding a project at the anticipated savings would be impossible.

So, in Table 18.16, let us use the second example of 30% highlighted based on implementing a VFD on the cooling tower. If we take that building, we have $2.582 per year savings. That will support a construction financing project of $25,824. Again, if we collectively, with the facilities team, determine that the cost to implement that ECM is less than that amount, then taking a project to the next level is advisable. We go down the entire list stopping when the savings no longer support the construction costs. All those buildings above the line would be bundled together in a project. This becomes an easy project to work with the utility or ESCO or through self-financing with a contractor. We generally look at AC system usage costs down to $5K just to see where the point of diminishing returns resides. It will become clear very quickly where that line of economic viability exists; so those below that line will not require a more detailed audit, or at least for this energy system.

The next energy system to evaluate in this audit tool is the fan/pump system(s). This follows the same process as the AC system breakdown. The fan/pump system usage is calculated based on the relationship established for the ratios developed by the detailed scatter plot breakdowns for a campus. The result is a dollar value assigned to the usage that is based on those previously discussed ratios and the impact of the fan/pump system on the demand portion of the costs. These were discussed earlier in the chapter; so we do not need to cover the details of that breakdown or how to modify it for a particular campus. The fan/pump systems' usage dollar value is included in one of the middle columns, labeled "Fan/Pump," in Table 18.17. This is then ranked in descending order for all the fan/pump systems costs. As we can see, there is a group of buildings whose usage costs for this campus are above $25,000 per building. Again, we will treat these as a group of projects, and assuming the solution is similar for each, then we will attempt to develop a financed project. This is an easier approach as we can have one vendor focused on the same ECM at multiple buildings, which lowers the cost of design and construction. This one report will save the EM countless hours evaluating buildings that will never meet the payback standards for ECMs. It also allows us to discount buildings once we go through the override tab and the four systems and determine the feasibility of finding a project at that savings amount. So, in Table 18.17, let us use the 50% example circled on the table. We have determined that these fans do not have VFDs and that VFDs will have savings of around 50%. If we take building 2682, we have savings of $26,209. That will support a construction financing project of $262,093. That is probably an easy ECM to bring in below that construction cost. If we, collectively with the facilities team, determine that these all require VFDs and the design and construction cost is less than those costs shown, then consolidating and taking a project to the next level is advisable. We go down the entire list until the savings no longer support the construction, and we can bundle this project together. Then we can easily combine the buildings with a utility, ESCO, or self-financing to develop this into a combined project.

The next system to evaluate is the lighting system. The lighting system usage for each building is broken out in Table 18.18. That value is summed up in the middle column labeled "Lights." This is then ranked in descending order for lighting systems' usage. Several buildings may fit the economic criteria for lighting upgrades. We have broken it down by projected savings

Table 18.17 kWh usage cost for fan/pump systems.

Building	Square Footage	12 Months Consumption (kWh)	Electric Cost Annually	Fan/Pump	Projected savings for ECM - 10%	Projected savings for ECM - 20%	Projected savings for ECM - 50%	Construction Costs supportable for 20 years contract for 10% savings	Construction Costs supportable for 20 years contract for 20% savings	Construction Costs supportable for 20 years contract for 50% savings
529	819,130	14,237,731	$ 591,180	$276,377	$27,638	$55,275	$138,188	$276,377	$552,754	$1,381,884
761	457,465	5,110,920	$ 212,216	$99,211	$9,921	$19,842	$49,606	$99,211	$198,422	$496,055
5014	160,802	3,411,512	$ 141,653	$66,223	$6,622	$13,245	$33,111	$66,223	$132,446	$331,114
423	277,324	2,789,430	$ 115,823	$54,147	$5,415	$10,829	$27,074	$54,147	$108,294	$270,736
2682	84,000	2,700,380	$ 112,125	$52,419	$5,242	$10,484	$26,209	$52,419	$104,837	$262,093
5423	286,066	2,640,058	$ 109,621	$51,248	$5,125	$10,250	$25,624	$51,248	$102,495	$256,238
5243	286,211	2,542,229	$ 105,559	$49,349	$4,935	$9,870	$24,674	$49,349	$98,697	$246,743
123	287,716	2,099,045	$ 87,157	$40,746	$4,075	$8,149	$20,373	$40,746	$81,492	$203,729
229	206,000	3,087,259	$ 128,189	$38,027	$3,803	$7,605	$19,014	$38,027	$76,054	$190,136
5731	98,047	1,727,590	$ 71,733	$33,535	$3,354	$6,707	$16,768	$33,535	$67,070	$167,676
5043	245,656	1,715,847	$ 71,246	$33,307	$3,331	$6,661	$16,654	$33,307	$66,615	$166,536
329	221,301	5,264,419	$ 218,590	$31,922	$3,192	$6,384	$15,961	$31,922	$63,843	$159,608
5323	51,549	1,528,496	$ 63,466	$29,671	$2,967	$5,934	$14,835	$29,671	$59,341	$148,353
893	6,013	1,357,026	$ 56,347	$26,342	$2,634	$5,268	$13,171	$26,342	$52,684	$131,710

blocks of 10%, 20%, and 50%, similarly to how we did it for the fan/pump systems. The 50% column represents converting T8s to LEDs. The EM must know this directly from visits or discussions with the maintenance shops. This can be gleaned from the scatter plots also. Remember, the projected savings are set up in bracketed values where we might approximate or at least get a close estimate for the savings ECM we may employ for that building. Again, this can be modified if an ECM needs additional definition or a more detailed savings analysis. So, we might look at some lighting systems and determine that an LED retrofit would save 50%. As stated above, we then use this tool to determine what construction costs would support that specified percentage of savings. As we did with the last example, we assume we want to meet a 10% IRR as a financed project; so it will list the total development, design, and construction costs below to meet that IRR. In this example, shown in red circles, we see a 50% savings generates $5723 annually. That will support design and construction costs of $57,229. This is probably feasible and should be pursued to the next level. The next building has over 250,000 sf; so the construction cost may be higher than that value. For this type of ECM, we would add a column at a cost/sf, giving the EM a quick guide to what is feasible from a construction cost perspective. If we have a group of buildings that could use LEDs, we could easily see which buildings fall within the limits of meeting the economic criteria. We need to determine which buildings can support those construction estimates, bundle those together for an ECM, and find a contractor to check the numbers. This, again, is used as a clearing house of possible projects based on the best engineering estimate of savings and cost.

So, in summary, these methods are good indicators for ranking projects for detailed analysis. In general, for determining where to audit, use the EUI,

Table 18.18   Various savings options for a lighting system.

Building	Square Footage	12 Months Consumption (kWh)	Electric Cost Annually	Lights	Projected savings for ECM - 10%	Projected savings for ECM - 20%	Projected savings for ECM - 50%	Construction Costs supportable for 20 years contract for 10% savings	Construction Costs supportable for 20 years contract for 20% savings	Construction Costs supportable for 20 years contract for 50% savings
9302	82,827	2,107,829	$ 110,872	$21,065	$2,106	$4,213	$10,532	$21,065	$42,129	$105,323
5341	136,200	1,900,491	$ 99,966	$20,123	$2,012	$4,025	$10,061	$20,123	$40,246	$100,615
2312	140,007	1,336,017	$ 70,274	$12,358	$1,236	$2,472	$6,179	$12,358	$24,716	$61,789
4412	152,684	1,277,054	$ 67,173	$12,251	$1,225	$2,450	$6,125	$12,251	$24,502	$61,254
249	137,633	1,238,509	$ 65,146	$11,446	$1,145	$2,289	$5,723	$11,446	$22,892	$57,229
8	254,000	1,378,624	$ 72,516	$11,403	$1,140	$2,281	$5,701	$11,403	$22,805	$57,013
2551	123,860	1,178,112	$ 61,969	$10,622	$1,062	$2,124	$5,311	$10,622	$21,244	$53,111
6412	152,684	1,082,346	$ 56,931	$10,582	$1,058	$2,116	$5,291	$10,582	$21,164	$52,911
308	203,000	1,124,408	$ 59,144	$9,981	$998	$1,996	$4,991	$9,981	$19,962	$49,905
4432	152,684	1,029,456	$ 54,149	$9,905	$990	$1,981	$4,952	$9,905	$19,809	$49,523
6432	152,684	974,904	$ 51,280	$9,373	$937	$1,875	$4,687	$9,373	$18,747	$46,866
9591	55,300	950,885	$ 50,017	$8,835	$883	$1,767	$4,417	$8,835	$17,669	$44,173
1569	1,680	1,004,971	$ 52,861	$8,233	$823	$1,647	$4,116	$8,233	$16,466	$41,165
657	95,858	896,117	$ 47,136	$8,169	$817	$1,634	$4,084	$8,169	$16,338	$40,844
332	26,500	949,733	$ 49,956	$8,045	$804	$1,609	$4,022	$8,045	$16,090	$40,224
9449	124,346	759,736	$ 39,962	$7,873	$787	$1,575	$3,937	$7,873	$15,746	$39,366
9549	124,346	752,748	$ 39,595	$7,680	$768	$1,536	$3,840	$7,680	$15,361	$38,401
9649	122,066	690,409	$ 36,316	$6,903	$690	$1,381	$3,452	$6,903	$13,806	$34,516

extrapolated EUI charts, or category type performance metrics. For determining a quick analysis based on distributed loading and the ability to finance, use the quick audit tool as a quick energy audit to determine if it is feasible and is in the ballpark range. We have grown so accustomed to this audit tool that we use it as the first step in most cases. This still requires some level of validation by the contractor. However, these methods get us in range and avoid wasting our valuable time on buildings that would never pass economic criteria.

19

Comparing Campus Consumption to Individual Building Statistics

Abstract

This chapter compares campus billing statistics and analytics to individual MMS building analytics. Campus billing is a macro look but allows EMs to compare against other organizations' campuses. This can be done by comparing the portfolio based on EUI. This provides a comparison across the portfolio to see where management requires emphasis. It also allows the EM to compare against the individual buildings as a sanity check for a meter or usage in general. We use this method when reviewing new meters to ensure the values are in range. This is very important as users can use it on a macro scale or even down to the building level in comparing how the individual buildings compare against the campus median. This helps users understand if they have any meter issues or if a building uses too much energy compared to the campus standard.

19 Comparing Campus Consumption to Individual Building Statistics

This chapter will compare campus consumption to individual building metering statistics. The following topics will be covered in this chapter:

* Introduction
* Value added with campus wide statistics
* Square foot analytics
* Electricity analytics
* Thermal and water analytics
* Assess the meter situation
* Summary

19.1 Introduction

Too often, we look at the meters or the buildings on campus, but we do not have the context of the overall utility bill for the entire campus. That will provide many insights into the use of energy overall. The use of energy on campus is broken into two or more components. This helps put analysis and overall strategy into focus. The energy is converted into EUIs to enable a portfolio manager to compare the health of each campus and where to focus manpower and money on the most urgent requirements.

The macro view of the campus also provides an opportunity to check the validity of certain building readings. New meters should always be checked against the campus kbtu/sf or other appropriate metrics to ensure the readings are in range. We can always dial into more appropriate metrics by category type, but the campus metrics are a good sanity check. This chapter will cover many examples that allow us to see the value in these quick checks. It will also make it easy to see in what direction to go for the next steps in analytics.

19.2 Value Added with Campus-wide Statistics

Let us look at a few campuses in a portfolio. Figure 19.1 shows that the 15 campuses in this portfolio consumed $461M in energy costs. The cost of electricity was slightly over 67%, with thermal being 32%. This ratio is common for most campuses. Electricity will drive most costs, forcing the decision on which systems to target easily. We find a different emphasis as we look at some of the campuses. For example, in the first row, the H1 campus runs 95% of its costs in electricity. The warmer climate zone drives all the energy costs. In another example, in row 3 for Campus B, the ratio of electric costs is 82%. The focus on electrical usage is easier in most cases as analytics for electricity support the analysis of the distribution systems, and distribution systems drive the preponderance of the costs, as shown in Chapter 9. Conversely, for Campus R1, the electricity is 17%. This is straightforward also, as it is driven by central plants that support manufacturing processes. We usually track these from year to year to determine if these ratios shift and then analyze the reason.

The next thing we want to understand is the ratio of energy. The electric energy shown in the second column is 44% of the overall energy. This shows that electric energy costs more proportionally than thermal energy. This is a common ratio in most of the US, but we must check the usage to validate those results. We would want to concentrate on usage if we were trying to

Campus	Electricity Consumption (MMBTU)	Electricity Cost	Thermal Consumption (MMBTU)	Thermal Cost	Total Energy Consumption (MMBTU)	Total Energy Cost
Campus H	730,649	$ 50,819,976	82,086	$ 2,528,331	812,735	$ 53,348,307
Campus R	395,284	$ 18,253,377	853,583	$ 26,017,252	1,248,867	$ 44,270,629
Campus B	2,055,955	$ 35,726,195	1,239,604	$ 7,553,930	3,295,559	$ 43,280,125
Campus H1	1,045,099	$ 28,792,331	599,233	$ 12,809,266	1,644,332	$ 41,601,597
Campus B1	482,433	$ 21,523,306	1,098,464	$ 19,643,983	1,580,897	$ 41,167,289
Campus A	1,048,951	$ 21,740,355	1,793,431	$ 12,443,474	2,842,382	$ 34,183,829
Campus B2	885,179	$ 25,942,976	649,251	$ 6,253,515	1,534,430	$ 32,196,491
Campus L	681,578	$ 17,345,931	819,668	$ 9,324,363	1,501,246	$ 26,670,294
Campus S	266,378	$ 13,512,217	280,396	$ 10,279,746	546,774	$ 23,791,963
Campus R1	218,235	$ 4,164,362	2,707,367	$ 19,374,322	2,925,602	$ 23,538,684
Campus Z	295,510	$ 14,930,323	357,047	$ 6,637,711	652,557	$ 21,568,034
Campus C	836,186	$ 18,279,573	782,716	$ 3,135,497	1,618,901	$ 21,415,070
Campus W	262,243	$ 12,732,817	192,096	$ 5,633,048	454,339	$ 18,365,865
Campus H2	499,940	$ 16,449,899	817,946	$ 1,799,303	1,317,886	$ 18,249,202
Campus J	880,726	$ 12,120,996	1,153,849	$ 6,106,343	2,034,575	$ 18,227,339
Total	10,584,346	$ 312,334,634	13,426,737	$ 149,540,084	24,011,082	$ 461,874,718
	44.1%	67.6%	55.9%	32.4%		

Figure 19.1   Select campus statistics in a portfolio for macro view.

meet a goal related to saving BTUs or just a percentage of the energy. Most users let economics drive their decisions vs. usage.

19.3 Square Foot Analytics

The next aspect of analytics will focus on the amount of square footage (sf) covered. This gives us an idea of how much is covered by the meters and how much is not covered, thereby knowing the extent of the analytics capability of the meters. So, from Figure 19.2, we can see that each campus has a percentage of its overall meters covered. Let us look at several examples and what that means. The first row is Campus D. The percent of sf of buildings metered is 107%. That is impossible; so let us discuss what could cause that discrepancy. Generally, there is a disconnect between the records for the campus and the buildings. That would occur if the campus sf records were not updated with building changes. We have found that there is a lag in updating records. More impressive is the percentage of electricity measured by the MMS program vs. utility billing. Campus D comes in at 98%, which is great, considering the meters successfully measure usage across the spectrum. If we look at the second Campus F, we see the meters cover 75% of the sf on the campus. The ratio for electric energy usage is 83%, which is reasonable as we generally meter the most energy-intensive buildings; so the usage would be slightly larger than the sf metered. The third example is Campus K, where the sf metered is 66%, but the usage is 111%. That is excessive and is probably the result of a meter or set of meters that are

Campus	MMS/Utility Billing Electricity (%)	MMS Real Property (SF)	MMS/ Utility Billing SF (%)
Campus D	97.8	22,302,805	107.1
Campus F	83.0	11,391,418	74.5
Campus K	111.3	15,035,432	65.6
Campus N	112.7	7,635,596	72.1

Figure 19.2   Select campus statistics in a portfolio for macro view.

over-reporting. This needs to be investigated. The same can be determined from the fourth example, Campus N. Obviously, some meter issues must be resolved. We would try to isolate which meters were out of range and analyze the situation this comparison identified. Another thing to consider is that the MMS total accumulated comparison will probably be about 10% less than the utility bill for a campus. In most campus situations, owning the substation and buying the power at high voltage rates is more economical. That means we will have a delta that includes the transformer losses from the high voltage to a medium voltage and then the transformer losses from medium to low voltage at the building. There will be minimal losses to streetlights, signs, parks, etc., and they are usually not metered. That total will be between 8% and 10%; so make sure we realize that we must account for those losses.

In Figure 19.3, the examples tell us a few other things we must understand. In the two cases below, they each have a much larger meter sf ratio than the ratio of the actual meter electricity usage. This can be explained in a couple of scenarios. First, we installed the meters later in the year; therefore, their usage was for only a partial year. The second but similar option is that the connectivity was bad, and we only recorded a portion of the year. Either of these would account for the situation in the two examples below. The first, Campus M, is a factor of 3.5 off from the meter, and it would probably be greater than 4× since the initial meters generally use more energy proportionally as the highest intensity buildings are used first by best practices. The second is a factor of 2.5× off, which is less than the first campus but is still a lot. We generally find that the cause of this difference is related to a multiplier being off for many, if not all, building meters in this situation. While we usually do not think about a factor of 2.5× being very large, it is a large magnitude of error in metering. We showed in Chapter 14 that a factor greater than 2× the median has an 85% probability that the meter is off in calibration,

Campus	MMS/Utility Billing Electricity (%)	MMS Real Property (SF)	MMS/ Utility Billing SF (%)
Campus M	6.9	1,176,587	26.9
Campus J2	29.0	971,733	77.9

Figure 19.3 Select campus statistics in a portfolio for macro view.

Campus	MMS/ Utility Billing Gas (%)	MMS/ Utility Billing Water (gal/SF)(%)	Gas MMS/ Utility Billing SF (%)	Water MMS/ Utility Billing SF (%)
Campus E	3.7	2.6	20.9	48.5
Campus I	14.3	16.1	47.2	45.9
Campus G	37.0	16.3	48.0	50.2
Campus Q	84.7	0.0	74.7	0.0

Figure 19.4 Select campus statistics for gas and water comparison.

connectivity, or multiplier. These are off by much greater than that; so they should be evaluated accordingly.

Let us look at water and gas to see how they compare in Figure 19.4. They are very similar, as we can see from Campus E. The sf metered for gas and water is much higher for both commodities than the percentage of gas and water used. Note that we included a comparison of water in gal/sf. The ratio is the same for a gal as for gal/sf. The second line, Campus I, is also off by a sizeable amount. We would examine whether the meters reported all year on this and the previous campus. The third example, Campus G, is much closer to the reporting we would expect but still needs a little evaluation by the meter. The water is off and needs analysis to see what is causing the problem. The last example is Campus Q, which is reasonably close since the measured may be a higher intensity output than those not metered yet. Since we are always cautious, comparing by building to check the individual meters would be good.

19.4 Electricity Analytics

Another way to evaluate the usage is by using the kWh/sf to indicate any issues with the meters at the building level. The first way is to look at a building meter and determine if it is in a reasonable range with the utility meter.

Campus	Utility Billing Electricity (Kwh/SF)	MMS Electricity (Kwh/SF)
Campus T	20.1	7.3
Campus O	18.4	15.5
Campus P	12.6	10.5

Figure 19.5   Electric kWh/sf comparison.

In Figure 19.5, we can see three campuses that have a utility billing kWh/sf. If we have a specific meter we want to evaluate, then we compare it to that specific benchmark. It should be within a reasonable range, say 40% of that number. Once it is outside of 2× or less than half, we have a high probability that it is a problem with the meter. The next way to check the meters or the usage is by comparing the MMS kWh/sf to the utility kWh/sf. As shown in the first example, Campus T, the utility ratio is almost three times that of a metering system. This indicates one of several issues. The first is that the multiplier is off on some of the meters, and that skews the overall numbers. The second is that the meters are not reporting correctly. If they have lost connectivity or were broken, they would also under-report. For this kind of scale, we would have two-thirds that have not reported all year. That is a lot of meters down for any reason. The second example, Campus O, is within 20%, which means a few meters are out or have not had good connectivity. The same is true for Campus P.

19.5 Gas Analytics

The gas has a similar analysis for meters. In Figure 19.6, we can see a few campuses and have added a comparison percentage to enable a quick visual of how they stand. They are ranked by the percent of the MMS meter numbers vs. the utility meters in an MMBTU/sf. The first example, Campus Q, has a percentage above 113%. That means the MMS meters report higher by 13%. This could be because of minor discrepancies in the meters or because one or more of the meters are over-reporting. The second example, Campus U, is also very close, but the meter output is under by 5%. This can be from a meter(s) being out of service to problems with connectivity. The last example, Campus Y, is under by 20%; so many meters are not reporting fully.

Campus	Utility Billing Thermal (KBTU/SF)	MMS Gas (KBTU/SF)	MMS/Utility Billing Gas (KBTU/SF)(%)
Campus Q	29.8	33.8	113.4
Campus U	28.9	27.6	95.4
Campus Y	39.0	31.4	80.5

Figure 19.6 Gas kbtu/sf comparison.

Campus	Utility Billing Water (gal/SF)	MMS Water (gal/SF)	MMS/ Utility Billing Water (gal/SF)(%)
Campus AG	15.2	20.6	135.3
Campus V	38.7	23.2	59.8
Campus X	58.0	30.0	51.8
Portfolio	30.9	11.6	37.7

Figure 19.7 Water gal/sf comparison.

19.6 Water Analytics

Water meters are similar to gas meters in many ways. In Figure 19.7, we can see a few campuses and added a comparison percentage to visualize how they stand. They are ranked by the percent of the MMS meter vs. the utility meters in a gal/sf. The equalizer is the gal/sf or kbtu/sf ratio in the energy meters. Since we are comparing the MMS vs. the utility, the numbers larger than 100% are because of over-reporting, such as that shown in our first example, campus AG, which is 135%. In this case, we will also note the portfolio average of 30.87 gal/sf. Campus AG is less than half the utility compared to the average for the portfolio (bottom line). That would also bear looking into why there is such a disparity from the average. Most of these are admin-type activities. The second example, Campus V, is under-reporting by 40%. This can be from a meter(s) being out of service to problems with connectivity. The last example, Campus X, is under by 48%; so many meters are not reporting fully. Campus X is also used because it is twice the portfolio's rate. That is noteworthy, and the EM should look at each meter on the same gal/sf basis to determine where the problem resides, as this could indicate a leak.

Campus	Utility Billing Electricity (Kwh/SF)	MMS Electricity (Kwh/SF)	MMS/ Utility Billing Electricity Kwh/SF (%)	Multiplier Average Off
Campus AD	15.9	0.0	0.2%	564.0
Campus N1	14.3	0.1	1.0%	104.4
Campus G1	6.8	0.2	3.1%	31.9

Figure 19.8   Electric kWh/sf comparison.

19.7 Is the Multiplier Off on an Electric Meter?

This section addresses an issue that tends to be pervasive across a campus whenever it occurs. That is a misprograming of the multipliers on the electric meters. The multiplier is the factor that is programmed into a meter based on the meter specifications. Figure 19.8 identifies several campuses with an issue between the MMS kWh usage and the utility usage. As we can see, the first Campus AD, the MMS kWh/sf, was a small percentage of the utilities. The average is off by a factor of 564. That indicates a large multiplier difference on many, if not all, the meters. The solution here would be to check the individual meters against the EUIs or base load benchmarks. The second campus, Campus N1, was off by a factor of greater than 100×. In this case, we would look at the individual meters to determine which, if not all, meters need adjustments. The final example, Campus G1, is off by a multiplier of around 32. We use the campus list to see if we have a systemic problem with multipliers. As we start getting smaller than 30, determining the number gets harder in this general 30,000-ft analysis. In those cases, we must look at the information in detailed analytics of the building meters.

19.8 Are We Adjusting Consumption for Double-counting or for Generation Assets?

The last adjustment is an accounting issue that does not get handled correctly. Two things can cause this behavior by the meters. Figure 19.9, the first example, covers the situation where the EM double-counts the meter redundancy. For example, if we have meters on each building, the EM can easily double-count certain usage if they are not meticulous with their summary data. The comparison to utility vs. the MMS meters depends on measuring apples to apples to ensure we are not double-counting. Substations, main campus meters, etc., can cause this problem. The usage reported above the

Campus	Utility Billing Electricity (Kwh/SF)	MMS/ Utility Billing Electricity (%)	MMS Electricity (Kwh/SF)	MMS/ Utility Billing Electricity Kwh/SF (%)
Campus AB	16.4	115.8	36.1	219.8
Campus HH	14.7	104.2	34.8	237.8
Campus Q1	11.9	103.7	16.8	141.0
Campus K	7.0	99.2	10.6	152.5
Total	10.4	51.3	10.3	99.4

Figure 19.9   Electric kWh/sf comparison.

building level should not be rolled up into the total usage, as this is counted against the total for the MMS system. We must exclude the substations and master meters for the campus from accumulating in the consumption to keep consumption from being excessive. The best way to check is to use the portfolio benchmark as a guide. Here the utility portfolio is 10.35 kWh/sf, which matches the MMS system numbers. Anything appreciably above that in the MMS system would draw our attention. Assuming we have a reasonable amount of space metered on campus, say 25% or more, then the kWh/ sf for the MMS values should be within 20% unless there are mitigating factors such as extreme climate zone or space use. So those three examples shown are suspects, and we would question the reporting. We would first validate that there was no double-counting with substations, etc. Then we would check to see if there was generation on site included in the campus usage. Too many times, we see that renewables, cogeneration plants, and generation plants are in the campus energy and are not added to the usage that they offset. This could cause the problem in Figure 19.9, or it could be a batch of over-reporting meters that requires us to check the individual meter data.

Figure 19.10 shows several campuses with generation assets. The first example is a generation plant that is not removed from the total MMS usage. The second example, Campus X1, also has a generation plant. That plant is large in proportion; as we can see, the SF metered is 12%. The generation is overcompensating for the small footprint of the meters. Finally, we see Campus A3, where the usage is around 25% above the SF ratio. That was caused by a solar field that was included in the total MMS numbers erroneously.

Campus	MMS/Utility Billing Electricity (%)	MMS Real Property (SF)	MMS/ Utility Billing SF (%)
Campus R2	162.0	6,864,319	85.8
Campus X1	158.2	932,943	12.2
Campus A3	104.6	2,789,533	83.4

Figure 19.10   Electric kWh/sf comparison.

19.9 Summary

The utility input comparison against the MMS inputs is valuable for checking several validation points. First, it indicates how much we use and if we are metering the utilities that can influence the finances first. The second analysis is good for understanding if the meters are working properly. That means comparing the MMS meters and the utility meters. Either can be wrong, and we want to ensure we pay correctly. The third validation is for the meter usage to be counted correctly. Do we have a multiplier issue, or are we double-counting or erroneously adding in renewables? We generally use this as a sanity check to show us where to focus our efforts before looking at all the individual meter data.

20

Cross-referencing Three Metrics for Evaluating Buildings

Abstract

This chapter combines a series of three metrics into a stop-light chart. Each chart is tied to a category type for the 30 largest category types in the portfolio. Then the charts are color-coded for each of the three metrics to show where they fall compared to their peers. Each category has an if–then logic to tell us if the meter is bad and how it stands against other buildings, i.e., the top 25% or bottom 25%, etc.

20 Cross-referencing Three Metrics for Evaluating Buildings

This chapter will discuss combining the three metrics into a stop-light chart. In this chapter, we will cover the following topics:

- Introduction
- Summary

20.1 Introduction

The color-coded stop-light chart combines a series of three metrics and is tied to a category type for the 30 largest category types in the portfolio. The chart is color-coded for each of the three metrics to show where each building falls compared to its peers. Each category has an if–then logic to tell us if the meter is bad, where we stand against other buildings, i.e., top 25% or bottom 25%, etc.

What are the three factors to compare?

- Base load
  - Not affected by weather
  - Minimum point of usage that establishes the base for flat non-variable usage
  - Very good factor for telling us certain things
  - Includes plug plus whatever systems were left on
  - Calculated in watts per square foot (watts/sf)
- Percentage base load of consumption
  - Not affected by weather
  - Divided by the total consumption
  - Theoretically, 10%–18% is the bottom boundary
  - The top boundary is set at 75%
  - Sets the base for energy savings potential
- Extrapolated EUI
  - Dependent on the weather zone
  - Usage based on the unit of size for easy comparison
  - Very good metric for a portfolio

Let us look at one example, Table 20.1, showing our base load comparison, where we have got all three factors for Category Type Office C. The yellow highlighted column shows the watts/sf, the green column is the base load as the percentage of consumption, and the blue column is the extrapolated EUI for 12 months. This is a very quick and easy way to make this comparison.

Then, we break this comparison down further using the stop-light charts. While we will analyze and clarify specific examples in this chapter, the legend below in Table 20.2 shows the classifications of the color coding in each of the three metrics analyzed.

The first example we will look at is the category watts/sf for the top range of the report results, shown in Table 20.3. We ran the report for training campuses' entire portfolio, filtered the exported report on the Category Type Office C, and then sorted the watts/sf column in descending order, outlined

Table 20.1 Base load comparison for Category Type Office C.

Campus	Building Number	Square Footage	Category Type	Base Load (KW)	Watts/SF	12 Months Consumption (kWh)	Baseload as % Consumption	12 Months EUI (Electric)	12 Months Extrapolated EUI (Electric)	% of Data Available	Climate Zone
					Median 0.28		39.6	12	24.70		
Campus S	100	34,215	Office C	55.1	1.61	2,803,428	11.9	279.58	404.94	69	3A
Campus O	6814	4,149	Office C	21.0	5.07	416,014	44.3	342.13	342.13	100	3A
Campus P	3912	16,120	Office C	37.8	2.34	80,079	45.3	16.95	154.67	11	3A
Campus H	43028	6,976	Office C	5.3	0.76	306,228	15.1	149.78	149.78	100	2A
Campus E	D1713	1,584	Office C	2.0	1.26	50,515	34.5	108.82	109.12	100	3A
Campus L	249L	26,002	Office C	31.4	1.21	813,341	33.9	106.73	106.73	100	4A
Campus C	2933	10,761	Office C	19.2	1.78	319,557	52.6	101.33	101.33	100	3A
Campus C	2884	6,335	Office C	12.3	1.93	180,026	59.6	96.97	96.97	100	3A
Campus H	9413	8,095	Office C	6.1	0.75	220,825	24.1	93.09	93.09	100	2A
Campus H	43030	5,939	Office C	11.5	1.94	161,065	62.6	92.54	92.54	100	2A
Campus O	5911	27,660	Office C	34.3	1.24	749,479	40.0	92.46	92.46	100	3A
Campus E	A2565	40,219	Office C	32.5	0.81	1,081,657	26.3	91.77	91.77	100	3A
Campus A	106	2,261	Office C	4.0	1.76	49,073	58.8	74.06	89.51	83	3A
Campus A	103	33,580	Office C	4.0	0.12	793,783	4.4	80.66	80.66	100	3A
Campus N	810	15,152	Office C	2.1	0.14	353,872	5.1	79.69	79.69	100	4A
Campus M	3665	27,134	Office C	20.3	0.75	604,176	29.4	75.98	75.98	100	3A
Campus P	3913	25,032	Office C	3.7	0.15	58,820	6.0	8.02	73.16	11	3A
Campus Q	1531	13,595	Office C	31.4	2.31	104,326	94.6	26.18	72.96	36	2A
Campus E	33327	36,000	Office C	35.6	0.99	761,405	40.8	72.17	72.37	100	3A
Campus N	812	23,559	Office C	3.1	0.13	490,522	5.5	71.04	71.04	100	4A
Campus C	2932	6,824	Office C	14.0	2.05	141,731	86.5	70.87	70.87	100	3A
Campus P	3911	25,394	Office C	3.8	0.15	59,075	6.4	7.94	70.67	11	3A
Campus S	232	7,286	Office C	4.0	0.55	103,371	23.3	48.41	70.12	69	3A
Campus E	A2547	41,925	Office C	56.8	1.35	847,485	58.7	68.97	68.97	100	3A
Campus E	32633	4,322	Office C	4.0	0.92	86,902	39.8	68.61	68.80	100	3A
Campus E	A3265	40,219	Office C	23.1	0.58	790,658	25.6	67.08	67.08	100	3A

Table 20.2 Stop-light chart legend.

Legend		
Watts/SF	**Baseload as % Consumption**	**Extrapolated EUI**
Bad Meters	Bad Meters	Bad Meters
Needs Help	Needs Help	Needs Help
OK	Good	OK
Median		Median
Good		Good
Great		Great
N/A*		N/A*

*No other buildings in Category Type for reliable comparison data.

with the purple box. The median is 0.292 for the ~330 buildings for Category Type Office C. Notice the color-coded cells based on their values against the median and other entries within that column. The red cells are greater than two times the median, which is the point where we find that the probability of being a bad meter is above 85%. These indicate bad meters or a base load that was not set properly. We apply the color-coding on the other two columns, the base load as percentage of consumption and the extrapolated EUI, and one thing to note here in this example is that we have a row in the middle

Table 20.3 Top range watts/sf for Category Type Office C.

								12			
			Base		12 Months	Baseload	Months	12 Months		
	Building	Square	Category	Load		Consumption	as %	EUI	Extrapolated	% of Data	Climate
Campus	Number	Footage	Type	(KW)	Watts/S	(kWh)	Consumptic	(Electr	EUI (Electric	Availab	Zone
Campus Q	8401	46507	Office C	601.977	12.944	298,754.352	1,175.123	21.919	32.924	66.575	2A
Campus Q	8416	61231	Office C	702.719	11.477	322,107.248	1,272.326	17.950	26.961	66.575	2A
Campus Q	8422	73951	Office C	800.969	10.831	697,125.706	670.073	32.166	48.315	66.575	2A
Campus Q	8427	73951	Office C	666.719	9.016	688,837.086	564.474	31.783	47.740	66.575	2A
Campus E	C4626	39873	Office C	285.250	7.154	247,266.028	1,007.796	21.160	21.218	99.726	3A
Campus O	6814	4149	Office C	21.032	5.069	404,676.113	45.529	332.806	332.806	100.000	3A
Campus F	517	16710	Office C	39.249	2.349	68,070.814	505.097	13.900	13.900	100.000	5B
Campus P	3912	Workbook last saved: Just now	750	2.342	243,863.384	60.558	51.619	115.588	44.658	3A
Campus C	2932	6824	Office C	13.993	2.051	124,636.395	98.351	62.321	62.321	100.000	3A
Campus C	2884	6334.5	Office C	12.251	1.934	176,942.972	60.652	95.312	95.312	100.000	3A
Campus C	2933	10761	Office C	19.195	1.784	323,108.627	52.040	102.453	102.453	100.000	3A
Campus E	26118	23998	Office C	42.078	1.753	31,018.129	156.274	4.410	33.537	13.151	3A
Campus K	840	12155	Office C	16.650	1.370	225,508.926	64.678	63.305	63.305	100.000	4A
Campus E	A2547	41925	Office C	56.752	1.354	824,594.345	60.290	67.111	67.111	100.000	3A
Campus R	12931	16317	Office C	21.744	1.333	234,418.768	81.254	49.021	49.021	100.000	4C
Campus F	2757	24000	Office C	32.000	1.333	382,967.132	73.197	54.447	54.447	100.000	5B
Campus E	A4251	41925	Office C	54.425	1.298	80,210.652	594.395	6.528	6.528	100.000	3A
Campus E	D1713	1584	Office C	1.997	1.281	49,015.679	35.598	105.586	105.870	99.726	3A
Campus L	249	26002	Office C	31.432	1.209	664,962.175	41.408	87.260	87.260	100.000	4A
Campus C	259	16432	Office C	17.606	1.071	229,440.875	67.218	47.644	47.644	100.000	3A

(8,829,980 — 0.292 median — 25.683 median)

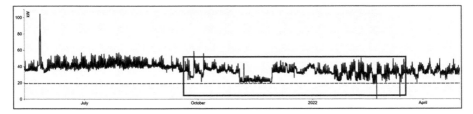

Figure 20.1 Example of inconsistent meter over time.

where all three of our factors are red. This indicates a very high likelihood that this is a bad meter.

We then dive into several buildings in the red range utilizing the MMS benchmarking tool.

As we can see from the example at Campus C in Figure 20.1, the meter has been inconsistent over time. It started in last July with the symmetry we expected but went bad around October. It never recovered; so this meter is bad or not reporting properly.

As we drill in further on the timeframe in the left purple box, shown in Figure 20.2, note that in our first purple box, we see the weekends going up to a start point at 1700 that mirrors that of a weekday and then peak bottoms around 0200. The pattern shown in the right purple box indicates that the workforce is going home between 2300 and 0400, which is not likely, and the symmetry of the pattern is somewhat symmetrical but not consistent. Therefore, this is not a normal symmetry, as shown in Figure 20.3, after enlarging the screen.

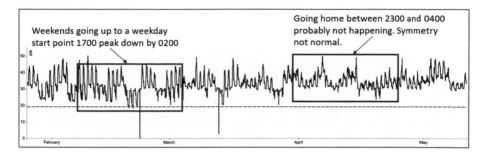

Figure 20.2 Inconsistent meter over time drilled in further.

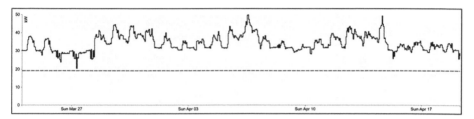

Figure 20.3 Inconsistent meter over time drilled in even further.

Next, we look at the bottom range for the category watts/sf column, as shown in Table 20.4, which shows values down to the mid-point – or our median in the blue cell – down to the bottom. Yellow means it may or may not be a bad meter, but it has excessive energy use. The beige highlighted cells above the median may have some savings, but those savings could be hard to find or justify economically since these are just slightly above the median. The green highlighted cells indicated good energy management, as they are in the top 50%–75% of the overall category type. The light blue cells indicate exceptional energy use, probably in the top 75th percentile for good energy management. However, there is a slight chance that the meter could be bad as it is on the boundary of small values. The red highlighted cells indicate that, most likely, the meter is bad, which in general indicates a wrong meter multiplier or meter connectivity issue – as the meter is not successfully reporting to the MMS enough to produce a good baseline.

The following examples analyze one of these buildings in the red range utilizing the MMS benchmarking tool. In Figure 20.4, the building's pattern looks okay but is sporadic and inconsistent. Note also that the base load is set too low – 2.24 kW or watts/sf – which triggers the base load number being out-of-range on the low side. The baseload baseline should kiss the bottom edge of the daily curves.

In Figure 20.5, shown below, we have reset the baseline to 9.63 based on the benchmarking tool's guide for the last 30 days, which calculates to

Table 20.4   Bottom range watts/sf for Category Type Office C.

Campus	Building Number	Square Footage	Category Type	Base Load (KW)	Watts/S	12 Months Consumption (kWh)	Baseload Consumptic as %	12 Months EUI (Electr)	12 Months Extrapolated EUI (Electric)	% of Data Availab	Climate Zone
Campus C	5115	14864	Office C	9.005	0.606	168,661.142	46.789	38.717	38.717	100.000	3A
Campus M	2268	24720	Office C	14.731	0.596	229,152.096	56.314	31.630	31.630	100.000	3A
Campus E	C1936	9988	Office C	5.845	0.586	78,854.626	64.930	26.939	26.939	100.000	3A
Campus E	A3265	40219	Office C	23.107	0.575	791,265.901	25.582	67.130	67.130	100.000	3A
Campus H	39020	25168	Office C	13.864	0.551	216,830.910	56.012	29.397	29.397	100.000	2A
Campus Y	296	7814	Office C	3.887	0.497	8,299.841	58.450	3.624	25.440	14.247	3B
Campus E	A3467	9843	Office C	4.835	0.491	147,338.766	28.666	51.076	51.216	99.726	3A
Campus H	34001	16006	Office C	7.788	0.487	149,962.629	45.492	31.969	31.969	100.000	2A
Campus C	9151	19333	Office C	9.327	0.482	201,685.895	40.511	35.596	35.596	100.000	3A
Campus E	H5240	20258	Office C	6.713	0.331	210,536.994	27.856	35.462	35.559	99.726	3A
Campus D	21135	63463	Office C	18.758	0.296	165,176.984	53.693	8.881	16.454	53.973	3B
Campus K	841	12155	Office C	3.572	0.294	67,932.914	42.405	19.070	20.716	92.055	4A
Campus C	9155	13260	Office C	3.901	0.294	97,195.226	35.156	25.011	25.011	100.000	3A
Campus H	39042	24200	Office C	7.094	0.293	105,257.494	59.043	14.841	14.841	100.000	2A
Campus C	9154	13260	Office C	3.843	0.292	117,591.263	28.628	30.259	30.259	100.000	3A
Campus E	A5145	15665	Office C	4.171	0.266	91,567.423	39.792	19.945	20.000	99.726	3A
Campus R	3384	41480	Office C	10.996	0.265	168,515.267	57.159	13.862	13.862	100.000	4C
Campus E	A5445	18592	Office C	3.270	0.176	118,431.492	24.123	21.735	21.795	99.726	3A
Campus F	2600	66673	Office C	11.733	0.176	242,145.873	42.447	12.392	12.392	100.000	5B
Campus C	4966	2000	Office C	0.344	0.172	26,157.428	11.530	44.626	44.626	100.000	3A
Campus H	18027	5945	Office C	1.013	0.170	21,601.374	41.076	12.398	12.398	100.000	2A
Campus F	2758	22895	Office C	3.452	0.151	76,694.628	39.434	11.430	11.430	100.000	5B
Campus P	3913	25032	Office C	3.678	0.147	177,054.152	8.125	24.134	54.043	44.658	3A
Campus F	750	10107	Office C	1.490	0.147	55,573.854	23.493	18.762	18.762	100.000	5B
Campus F	2640	54621	Office C	8.000	0.146	186,006.281	37.676	11.620	11.620	100.000	5B
Campus E	X4817	22420	Office C	1.997	0.089	107,285.139	16.308	16.328	16.328	100.000	3A
Campus E	X5017	24510	Office C	2.000	0.082	104,328.238	16.747	14.524	14.564	99.726	3A
Campus H	56022	14879	Office C	1.035	0.070	19,324.820	13.234	4.432	15.705	28.219	2A
Campus M	2255	29767	Office C	1.846	0.062	344,163.610	4.078	39.451	39.451	100.000	3A
Campus W	472	2342	Office C	0.109	0.047	4,479.853	21.334	6.527	6.527	100.000	1A
Campus P	1604	8331	Office C	0.283	0.034	19,037.746	11.817	7.797	8.598	90.685	3A

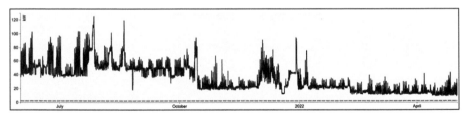

Figure 20.4   Sporadic and inconsistent building interval pattern.

0.323 watts/sf. This is in a good range, which will also reset the percentage of base load calculations.

We then repeat these same analysis steps on the top, mid, and bottom ranges for both the percentage base load of consumption and the extrapolated EUI factors.

The next step is to perform an integrated analysis of the three factors. Looking at the top range, as we stated in our first example if there are three red highlighted cells across all three metrics, then there is a high probability that we have a bad meter. If there are two red cells (in baseload and % baseload), it is most likely an improperly set base load. Run the MMS benchmarking tool for the building and see if the baseline kisses the bottom edge of the curve and that the curve is symmetrical. If these are set correctly, then we probably have a bad meter.

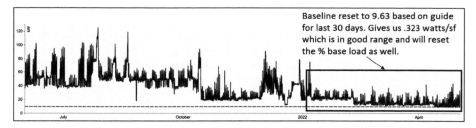

Figure 20.5   Reset baseline.

Yellow highlighted cells for two or three metrics indicate the building needs to be looked at for excessive energy use or the slight possibility of a meter issue. The beige highlighted cells above the median may have some savings, but these are probably the last buildings to evaluate as the savings potential is low.

Analyzing the bottom range, green cells in two or three metrics indicate good energy management. If we have two or three metrics in the light blue cells, it confirms this building has exceptional energy use – top 25%. If we have 2–3 metrics in the red cells at the bottom of the scale, then it indicates a bad meter, with the likelihood of a wrong meter multiplier or a meter connectivity issue – as in the meter is not consistently reporting to the MMS enough to produce a good baseline.

20.2 Summary

In summary, we can use the stop light chart breakdown to help us do an analysis. We have a chart for each of the top 30 category types based on the number of buildings. We can use these charts to get a general feel for where our buildings stand within the portfolio's category types. The rule of thumb is that anything above two times the median value indicates a bad meter and needs attention, whereas anything 1–1.35 times above the median is probably okay. On the lower end, below 0.5 times, the median value indicates a bad meter, whereas 0.75–0.5 times below the median is great, and 0.75–1 times below the median is good.

Appendix 1

The Transition of HDD and CDD Over the Last 70 Years

Abstract

This appendix shows the impact of HDD decline and CDD increase over the last 70 years and its importance to an energy manager's (EM) motivation to save energy. This will show the impact of global warming and greenhouse gases in a pragmatic approach that EMs work with every day. This will also show the importance of the EM's job in facing this challenge and how their work is vital to helping solve this situation.

A1 Introduction

This chapter will introduce the EM to the source for finding annual HDDs and CDDs for the US. It will show how HDDs have decreased over the last 70 years and, conversely, how CDDs have increased. There will be graphs to show the impact of the change over time and how the impact of global warming has increased over the last 30–40 years. The impact will affect our design of systems and the usage of the facilities. The Energy Information Agency (EIA) collects extensive useful data and information for an EM. We have discussed many of those in the previous chapters. The HDDs and CDDs are important as they can show how the climate is changing and give us a sense of urgency on the importance of our energy management performance. We will cover these through many graphics to give a picture of the situation's urgency to energize us to do our job with renewed purpose. In this appendix, we will learn:

- US average HDDs over the last 70 years and the projection forward.

- Breakdown of the HDDs by decade.

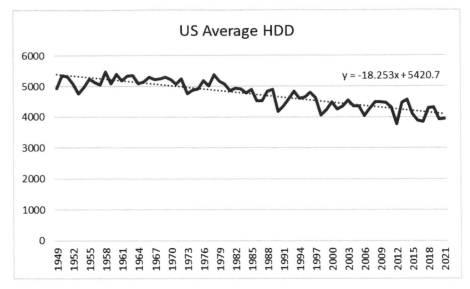

Figure A1.1   US average HDD over 70 years.

- Breakdown for the next 30 years of HDDs based on the trend line from the 1990s until the present.

- US average CDDs over the last 70 years and the projection forward.

- Breakdown of the CDDs by decade.

- Breakdown for the next 30 years of CDDs based on the trend line from the 1990s until present.

- Summary.

A1.1 US Average HDDs Over the Last 70 Years and the Projection Forward

These first datasets (Figure A1.1) are the US average HDDs across the last 70+ years. As we can see, the annual HDDs have decreased over the last 70 years. The overall slope on that curve is −18, which is a good decline, especially when the slope was relatively flat for the first 30 years. The slope shows an intercept of 5420 HDDs; if we calculate the formula for 2021, we have 4106 HDDs. That is a drop of 24.3% over the 70+ years.

If we continue that projection for 30 more years, we will have Figure A1.2, as shown below. That gives us a projection of 3558 HDDs for 2051, or 34.3% lower than in 1949.

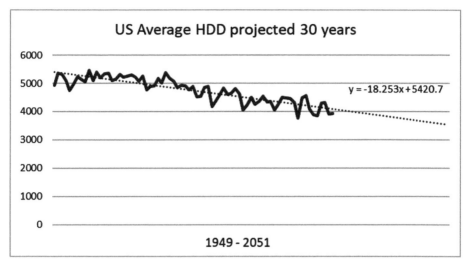

Figure A1.2 US average HDD over 70 years projected out for 30 more years.

A1.2 Breakdown of the HDDs by Decade

We generally look at HDDs or CDDs per decade to see a trend, as the weather will vary around the trend line. Therefore, we will show each decade over the last seven to show the trend over time. As we can see in Figure A1.3, there was a slight cooling trend in the 1950s.

The trend in Figure A1.4 for the 1960s shows that the decade had a decrease in HDDs or trends a little warmer. There is a slight slope down of −7.7 over that decade.

This reverses a little in the 1970s, as shown in Figure A1.5. But as witnessed over the first 30 years, HDDs have been relatively flat.

This changed drastically in the 1980s, as seen in Figure A1.6. The slope is −60 showing a major decrease in HDDs.

The 1990s continued that major trend in the reduction of HDDs. The 1980s and 1990s define a major drop in HDDs, which makes us wonder what happened in that period or slightly before that caused the major drop in HDDs over these two decades.

In the 2000s (Figure A1.8), we show a decade of relative flat usage. After the last two decades, one would wonder what changed to slow or put on hold the global warming that was so pervasive in the previous two decades.

In the 2010s (Figure A1.9), we return to a strong global warming trend. So, over the last 40 years, a consistent drop in HDDs shows the largest impact of global warming effects on those four decades.

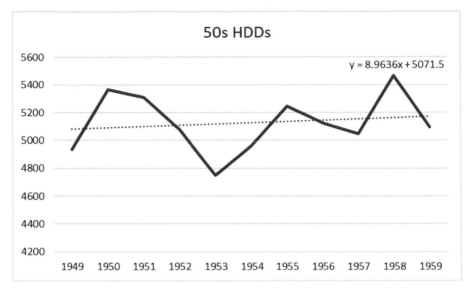

Figure A1.3   US average HDD for the decade of the 1950s.

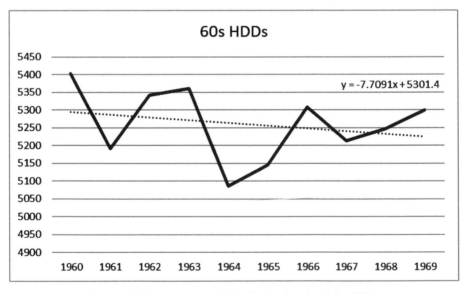

Figure A1.4   US average HDD for the decade of the 1960s.

A1.3 Breakdown for the Next 30 Years of HDDs Based on the Trend Line from the 1990s Until Present

With the last section showing that global warming accelerated or was prevalent over the past 40 years, we decided to examine the projection for the next

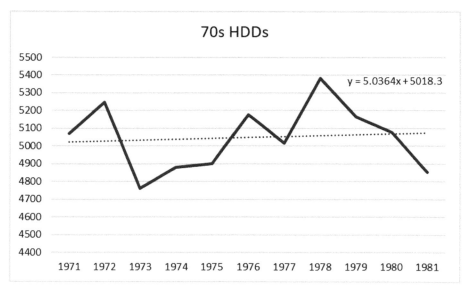

Figure A1.5   US average HDD for the decade of the 1970s.

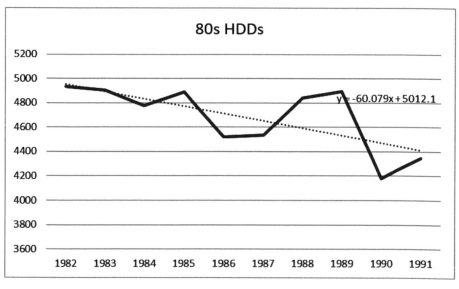

Figure A1.6   US average HDD for the decade of the 1980s.

30 years. The previous 30-year look ahead was based on the past 70 years. Let us look at this projection based on the past 30 years to see what that impact will be. In Figure A1.10, we see a negative slope of −20.6.

Figure A1.11 shows a 30-year projection forward based on the past 30 years. If we calculate that endpoint, it would be 3455 HDDs. That is a 25.7% drop from

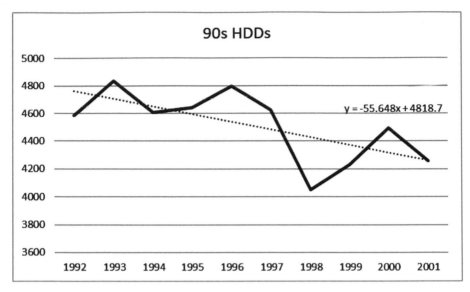

Figure A1.7   US average HDD for the decade of the 1990s.

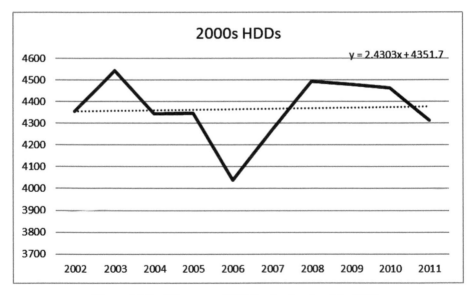

Figure A1.8   US average HDD for the decade of the 2000s.

the intersect of 4648 HDDs for 1991. Does this vary much from the projection based on the 70 years of data? From the first section, the formula gave us a projection of 3558 HDDs, a difference of approximately 3%. That difference is small for HDDs. It indicates that the ramp rate appears to increase over time, as we would have expected. This gives us a sense of urgency on how we do our jobs as EMs.

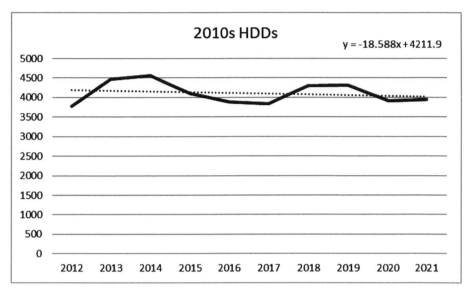

Figure A1.9   US average HDD for the decade of the 2010s.

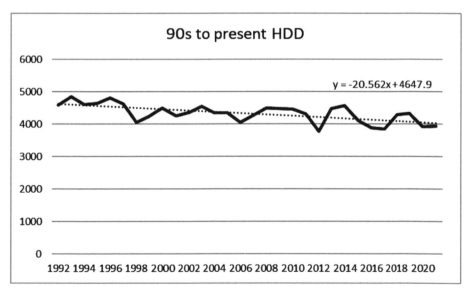

Figure A1.10   US average HDD over the past 30 years.

A1.4 US Average CDDs Over the Last 70 Years and the Projection Forward

These first datasets (Figure A1.12) are the US average CDD across the last 70+ years. As we can see, the annual CDDs have increased over the last

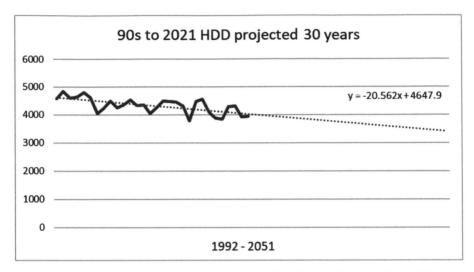

Figure A1.11   US average HDD projections forward for 30 years based on the past 30 years.

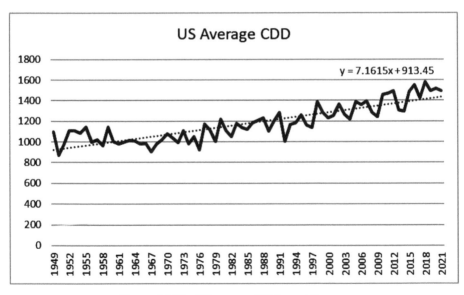

Figure A1.12   US average CDD over 70 years.

70 years. The overall slope on that curve is 7.2, which is a good increase, especially when we notice that the slope only slightly increased in the first 20 or even 30 years. The slope shows an intercept of 913 CDDs; if we calculate the formula for 2021, we have 1429 CDDs. That is an increase of

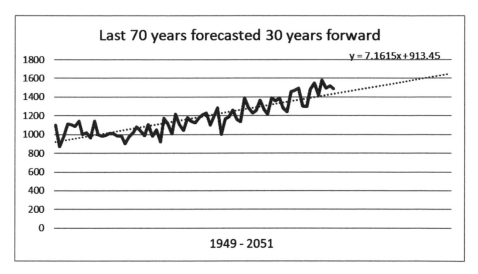

Figure A1.13 US average CDD over 70 years.

56.4% over the 70+ years. This is a much larger increase than the 24.2% decrease shown in HDDs. We have not seen a study, but the best conclusion we draw is that the increase in degree days is not across the board but happens in a greater proportion at a pivot point somewhere around 45–50 °F. A pivot point in that range would account for a 2 to 1 increase in CDDs vs. HDDs. We would welcome anyone who has studied this to send us a copy.

If we project the CDDs out for another 30 years, we get a result, as shown in Figure A1.13. That gives us a projected CDD from the formula of 1644 for 2051. So, from an intercept in 1949 of 913, we have an 80% increase in CDDs.

A1.5 Breakdown of the CDDs by Decade

As discussed above, we generally look at CDD per decade to see a trend, as the weather will vary around the trend line. Therefore, we will show each decade over the last seven to show the trend in CDDs over time. As we can see in Figure A1.14, there was a slight warming trend in the 1950s.

In the next decade (1960s), Figure A1.15 shows a slight warming but nothing significant.

In the 1970s, Figure A1.16 shows the warming trend with a jump to a slope of 12 to 1, where we see the start of global warming from a CDD perspective that never falters after this point.

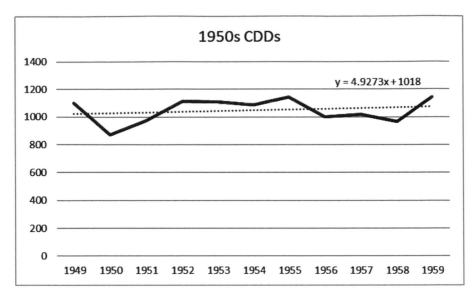

Figure A1.14   US average CDD for the decade of the 1950s.

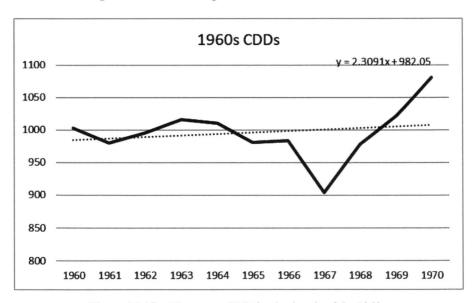

Figure A1.15   US average CDD for the decade of the 1960s.

In the 1980s, Figure A1.17 shows an increase in global warming, with the slope increasing to 14.7 to 1.

In the 1990s, Figure A1.18 shows a jump in CDDs, with the slope increasing to 21.7 to 1. This is the largest jump for a decade over the last 70 years.

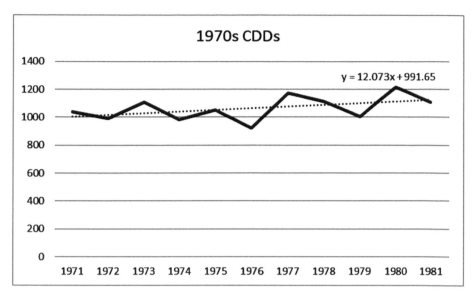

Figure A1.16   US average CDD for the decade of the 1970s.

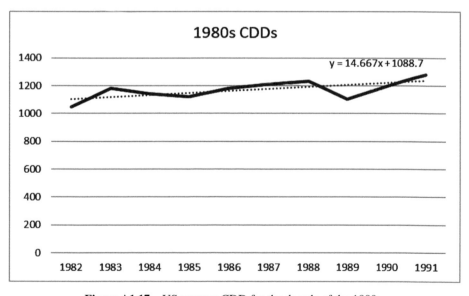

Figure A1.17   US average CDD for the decade of the 1980s.

In the 2000s, Figure A1.19 shows that the rate of increase slowed some-what to 12.7 to 1.

In the 2010s, Figure A1.20 shows the rate of increase back to a slope that appears to be close to the normal for the last 30 years at around 15 to 1. The normal rate of increase for the last 30 years will be around 13 to 1, as shown in the next section.

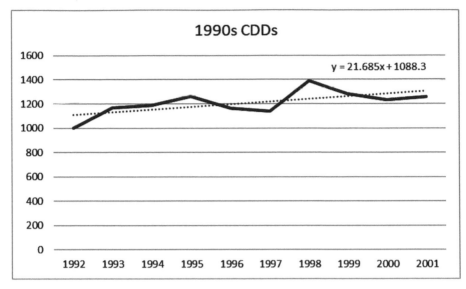

Figure A1.18   US average CDD for the decade of the 1990s.

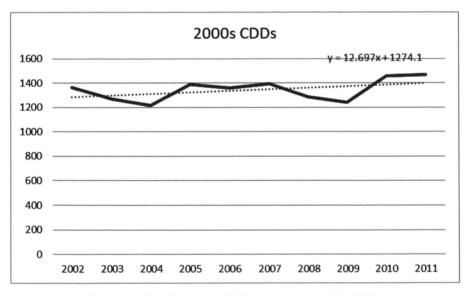

Figure A1.19   US average CDD for the decade of the 2000s.

A1.6 Breakdown for the Next 30 Years of CDDs Based on the Trend Line from the 1990s Until Present

Section 1.5 showed that global warming accelerated from the 1970s. So, we decided to analyze the projection for the next 30 years. The previous 30-year

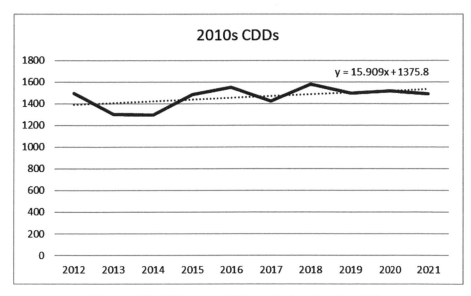

Figure A1.20   US average CDD for the decade of the 2010s.

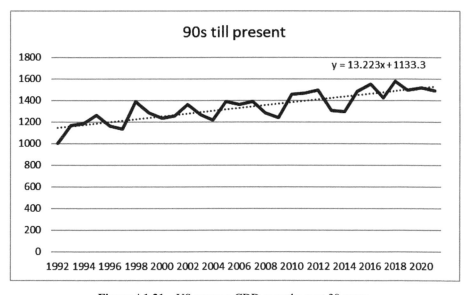

Figure A1.21   US average CDD over the past 30 years.

look ahead in Section 1.4 was based on the past 70 years. Let us look at this projection based on the past 30 years to see the impact of the near-term (last 30 years) escalation. In Figure A1.21, we see a slope of −13.2 to 1.

Figure A1.22 shows that projection forward based on the past 30 years. If we calculate that endpoint, it would be 1927 CDDs. That is a 70% increase

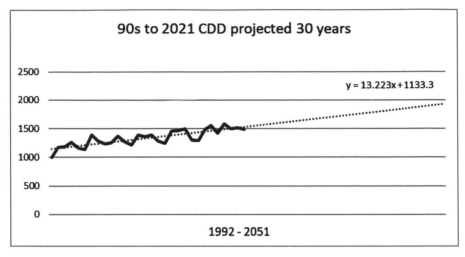

Figure A1.22   US average CDD projections forward for 30 years based on the past 30 years.

from the intersecting point of 1133 CDDs for 1991. How does this vary against the projection based on the 70 years of data in Section 1.4? From Section 1.4, the formula gave us a projection of 1644 CDDs, a difference of approximately 17%. These differences were only 3% for the 70-year vs. the 30-year base against a 2051 HDD projection. It strongly indicates that the ramp rate for CDDs is increasing more over time than for the HDDs. This also supports our previous discussion that the pivot point may shift to a higher temperature over time.

A1.7 Summary

In summary, this is an interesting topic, but how does it impact the EM when he performs his job every day? Our purpose in this appendix was to show the major impact of a decrease in HDDs and an increase in CDDs impacting our systems. That increase is directly related to global warming and greenhouse gas emissions. If we reduce our consumption through energy-saving best practices and better maintenance, then this reduces the usage in two ways. The first is the direct usage from reducing the energy at the building. The second is by reducing the source usage for the generation itself. That double benefit will reduce the impact of each saved BTU on global warming by times 2. An EM has to work with CDDs and HDDs every day. These are

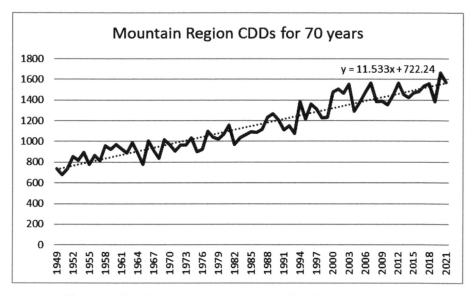

Figure A1.23 US mountain region average CDD for the last 70 years.

easier to understand than discussing a 0.1° rise over the planet and rising sea level. Those terms are not relatable to the EM's tasks every day. Seeing the drastic rise (35%) in CDDs over the last 30 years is eye-opening as to how we design and deal with the demand on our HVAC systems. This will also impact how we plan for energy savings projects as the loading ratio between the energy subsets shifts over time.

We gave the numbers in this appendix based on the average across the US. Many studies show global warming increases as we go toward the Arctic. To demonstrate this, we will show the data for the Rocky Mountain region in Figure A1.23. As we can see, the intercept in 1949 was 722 CDDs and is 1553 CDDs in the formula for 2021. That is a 215% increase. The US average was 156% for the same time period. We also see that the increase has been consistent for the last seven decades vs. the increase in the US average started in the 1970s.

This awareness also helps us, as EMs, to know that everything we do is important. Seeing the CDD increase should give us a sense of urgency to find and maintain savings. Savings from avoidance or efficiency are worth much more than the BTU or kW saved. For a kW, it reduces the source energy, which is between 2.5 and 3 times the energy on-site. Thermal depends on the source, but we still have a significant multiplier.

References

[1] (n.d.). Units and calculators explained Degree days. U.S. Energy Information Administration. https://www.eia.gov/energyexplained/units-and-calculators/degree-days.php

Appendix 2

Determine the Impact of Variance on Calculating Various Degree Day Base Temperatures

Abstract

This appendix shows the impact of the base temperature on calculating CDDs and HDDs. We will review several examples to show the impact of using temperatures other than 65°F as the base temperature when calculating CDDs and HDDs. We will give the variance on actual for those examples and discuss the degree of error introduced by using 65°F as the base for all calculations.

A2 Determine the Impact of Variance on Calculating Various Degree Day Base Temperatures

This chapter will discuss the impact of the base temperature on the degree day temperature formula. The base temperature is the temperature where the OAT (translated into degree days) causes the space to respond to the rising temperature by cooling the space. We will test several examples of base temperature at two climate zones and for CDD and HDD variance from a known value. Through this analysis, we will show the level of error introduced by using one base temperature over another.

- Example of CDD from Climate Zone 5B

- Example of HDD from Climate Zone 5B

- Example of CDD from Climate Zone 3A

- Example of HDD from Climate Zone 3A

Table A2.1   Calculation of CDD as base 63.5°F.

Hourly Usage Report
Campus F, Building 7849 (73007 sf)
Commodity: Electric

Timestamp	Usage	Units	Temp °F	Base Temp Cooling	Degree Hours	Degree days	Calculated Usage
2019-05-16 00:00	23.75	kWh	66	63.5	2.5	0.104	23.75
2019-05-16 01:00	23.75	kWh	63	63.5	0	0.000	23.75
2019-05-16 02:00	22.75	kWh	62	63.5	0	0.000	22.75
2019-05-16 03:00	23.00	kWh	60	63.5	0	0.000	23.00
2019-05-16 04:00	23.50	kWh	59	63.5	0	0.000	23.50
2019-05-16 05:00	23.00	kWh	58	63.5	0	0.000	23.00
2019-05-16 06:00	47.50	kWh	56	63.5	0	0.000	47.50
2019-05-16 07:00	64.50	kWh	61	63.5	0	0.000	64.50
2019-05-16 08:00	60.50	kWh	66	63.5	2.5	0.104	60.50
2019-05-16 09:00	50.50	kWh	69	63.5	5.5	0.229	50.50
2019-05-16 10:00	59.75	kWh	70	63.5	6.5	0.271	59.75
2019-05-16 11:00	62.50	kWh	71	63.5	7.5	0.313	62.50
2019-05-16 12:00	62.25	kWh	74	63.5	10.5	0.438	62.25
2019-05-16 13:00	61.75	kWh	75	63.5	11.5	0.479	61.75
2019-05-16 14:00	61.00	kWh	76	63.5	12.5	0.521	61.00
2019-05-16 15:00	58.00	kWh	76	63.5	12.5	0.521	58.00
2019-05-16 16:00	51.00	kWh	77	63.5	13.5	0.563	51.00
2019-05-16 17:00	39.00	kWh	79	63.5	15.5	0.646	39.00
2019-05-16 18:00	31.25	kWh	79	63.5	15.5	0.646	31.25
2019-05-16 19:00	30.25	kWh	77	63.5	13.5	0.563	30.25

A2.1 Example of CDD from Climate Zone 5B

This first example will take the temperature for a year and develop a scatter plot to determine the formula for the degree days at a specific base temperature. We will then compare the revised usage based on the new base temperature CDDs. This will show the impact of the base temperature for the CDDs on calculating the usage. We will develop this for several base temperatures above and below the 65° base temperature normally used. Those values will be calculated into the new usage for that base temperature and summed for the year. The calculated formula values at each base temperature test case are compared to the actual usage. The comparison across the various base temperatures will show the error involved.

The first table (Table A2.1) will show how we calculate the Climate Zone 5B campus formula. This is a truncated table for ease of viewing. The base degree of 63.5°F is subtracted from the hourly temperature. That

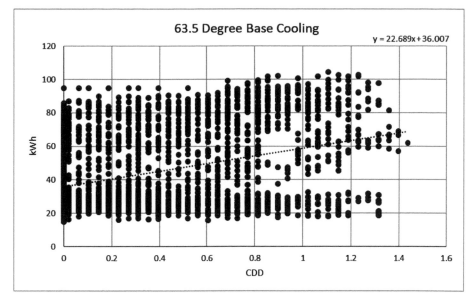

Figure A2.1   Scatter plot using 63.5°F for base on formula.

becomes a degree hour converted into a degree day by dividing by 24. These are the degree days recalculated at the new base temperature of 63.5°F. We add the column of usage adjacent to that column of degree days to make plotting easier. The scatter plot is shown in Figure A2.1 with the formula for the trend line. To calculate the new usage, we use the trend line formula to calculate the usage at each of those degree days. This generates a calculated usage based on that degree base.

In Table A2.2, we can see those various base temperatures compared. We looked at this table in half-degree increments to see how sensitive the calculations would be at those increments. As we can see from the table, there was almost no significant variance as we continued this same analysis for each temperature increment up to 67°F.

If we look at each of these, we will find the level of error introduced by the different base temperatures. It was an insignificant variance in this particular climate zone; therefore, the error was so small that it would not be a factor in any calculation performed on the data.

We plotted the differences in Figure A2.2, and we noticed that the crossing point where the error is closest to zero is around 65.6°F. While that may give us a point to use, it is so insignificant in error from using the traditional 65°F that we chose to stick with 65°F in this case.

This test case is applied to a particular building as the reaction to OAT or degree days depends on a few things. A building reacts to weather based

Table A2.2 Comparing the impact of the base degree day against the actual.

Base Temp Cooling °F	Cooling Degree Hours	Cooling Degree Days	Actual Usage	Calculated Usage by Formulae	Base Temp Variance vs Actual	% Difference
63.5	25,959	1,082	143,796	143,796	99.9995%	-0.0005%
64	24,876	1,037	143,796	143,795	99.9992%	-0.0008%
64.5	23,852	994	143,796	143,795	99.9993%	-0.0007%
65	22,827	951	143,796	143,795	99.9991%	-0.0009%
65.5	21,864	911	143,796	143,796	99.9998%	-0.0002%
66	20,900	871	143,796	143,797	100.0005%	0.0005%
67	19,078	795	143,796	143,797	100.0005%	0.0005%

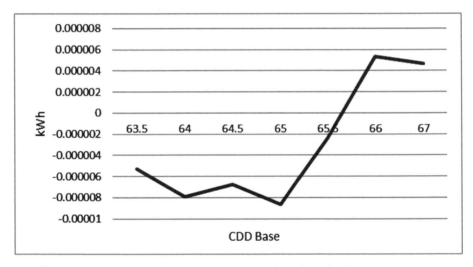

Figure A2.2 Plot of various base degrees showing where the data has zero errors.

on several factors, construction, orientation, usage, equipment, fenestration, etc. Most campuses have very similar factors in most buildings, as construction is generally standardized, and usage and equipment are similar. This will lead us to assume that most buildings on site will be closely related to the same degree of base temperature. The small variance introduced makes this assumption moot.

A2.2 Example of HDD from Climate Zone 5B

The second example will take the same building and calculate this for the heating season. This example will follow the same process as the previous,

Table A2.3 Calculation of HDD as base 62°F.

Hourly Usage Report
Campus F, Building 7849 (73007 sf)
Commodity: Electric

Timestamp	Usage	Units	Temp °F	Base Temp Heating	Degree Hours	Degree days	Calculated Usage
2019-01-01 00:00	26.75	kWh	6	62	56	2.333	26.75
2019-01-01 01:00	30.75	kWh	6	62	56	2.333	30.75
2019-01-01 02:00	38.25	kWh	6	62	56	2.333	38.25
2019-01-01 03:00	39.75	kWh	6	62	56	2.333	39.75
2019-01-01 04:00	40.75	kWh	5	62	57	2.375	40.75
2019-01-01 05:00	41.25	kWh	5	62	57	2.375	41.25
2019-01-01 06:00	52.5	kWh	4	62	58	2.417	52.50
2019-01-01 07:00	41.25	kWh	3	62	59	2.458	41.25
2019-01-01 08:00	45.5	kWh	2	62	60	2.500	45.50
2019-01-01 09:00	38.125	kWh	4	62	58	2.417	38.13
2019-01-01 10:00	38.094	kWh	5	62	57	2.375	38.09
2019-01-01 11:00	38.75	kWh	7	62	55	2.292	38.75
2019-01-01 12:00	37.75	kWh	9	62	53	2.208	37.75
2019-01-01 13:00	38.75	kWh	9	62	53	2.208	38.75
2019-01-01 14:00	37.5	kWh	11	62	51	2.125	37.50
2019-01-01 15:00	37.75	kWh	10	62	52	2.167	37.75
2019-01-01 16:00	42.5	kWh	10	62	52	2.167	42.50
2019-01-01 17:00	41	kWh	7	62	55	2.292	41.00

except that we take the temperature for the heating season and develop a scatter plot to determine the formula for the degree days at a specific base temperature. We will then compare the revised usage based on the new base temperature HDDs. This will show the variance of actual usage vs. the usage based on a set base temperature for the HDDs. We will develop this for several base temperatures above and below the 65° base temperature normally used as the base temperature for the calculation. Those values will be calculated into the new usage for that base temperature and summed for the season. The calculated formula values at each base temperature test case are compared to the actual usage. The comparison across the various base temperatures will show the error involved at each base temperature.

Table A2.3 will show how we calculate the formula for the heating season for Climate Zone 5B campus. This is a truncated table for ease of viewing. The base degree of 62°F is subtracted from the hourly temperature to become degree hours, which is converted into a degree day by dividing by 24. This is the degree days recalculated at the new base temperature of 62°F. We added the column of calculated usage adjacent to the column of degree

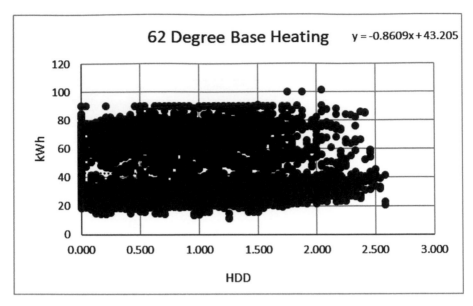

Figure A2.3   Scatter plot using 62°F for base formula.

days to simplify the plotting process. The scatter plot is shown in Figure A2.3 with the formula for the HDD trendline. To calculate the new usage, we use the trend line formula to calculate the usage based on the revised HDDs. This generates a calculated usage based on that degree base. The pattern shown for all the usage points in this figure's plots is all over the spectrum. Remember, this is plotting electric usage and comparing that to HDDs. The only electric load supporting the heating system or responding to the change in HDDs will be the fan/pump systems if there is no electric heat. So, this particular graph in Figure A2.3 appears broken into two distinct patterns. The lower pattern will cover those items that are minor electric loads and not associated with heating. The upper pattern is the usage associated with the fan and pump system.

In Table A2.4, we can see those various base temperatures compared for the heating season. We approached the heating season analysis in degree increments to see how the calculations would respond to those increments. As shown in the table, there was almost no significant variance as we analyzed each temperature increment up to 67°F.

If we look at each of these, we will find the level of error introduced by the different base temperatures. In this particular climate zone, there was an insignificant variance. Therefore, the error was so small that it would not be a factor in any calculation performed on the data.

Table A2.4 Comparing the impact of the base degree days against the actual.

Base Temp Heating °F	Heating Degree Hours	Heating Degree Days	Actual Usage	Calculated Usage by Formulae	Base Temp Variance vs Actual	% Difference
62	123,957	5,165	229,899	229,897	99.9993%	-0.0007%
63	128,938	5,372	229,899	229,902	100.0011%	0.0011%
64	133,964	5,582	229,899	229,900	100.0005%	0.0005%
65	139,036	5,793	229,899	229,898	99.9994%	-0.0006%
66	144,158	6,007	229,899	229,900	100.0005%	0.0005%

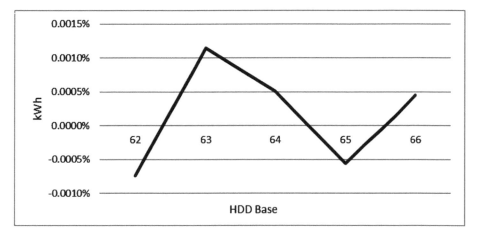

Figure A2.4 Plot of various base degrees showing where the data has zero errors.

We plotted the differences in Figure A2.4 and noted there was more than one crossing point where the error is closest to zero projected across the range of base degrees. The figure shows that the crossing point where the value is zero errors occur in three places; so there is not one point where the usage matches the base temperature for calculating the HDD. The amount of error varies back and forth, with the maximum in this range being 1.1 ten thousandths of a percent. The difference between any two points across the range conveys little difference as one can see that the difference between each point introduces little or no error regardless of the base temperature. Therefore, in this case, we will stick with the standard 65°F for convenience and to maintain a consistent process.

As discussed previously, each test case is applied to a particular building as the reaction to OAT or degree days is dependent on a few things. In the heating season, this does not change. A building reacts to colder weather, similar to summer, based on several factors, construction, orientation, usage, equipment, fenestration, etc. In cold weather, the transition times are harder to be disciplined in keeping the building tight and avoiding leakage. After the temperature remains colder, the occupants self-discipline increases; so we do not waste as much energy once we have reached that stable cold environment as opposed to those transitional times. Most campuses have very similar results for people's behavior and construction, where it is generally standardized, and usage and equipment are similar in most cases. This will lead us to assume that most buildings on site will be closely related to the same degree of base temperature. While all the above assumptions and observations are probably true, the small variance introduced makes this assumption moot.

A2.3 Example of CDD from Climate Zone 3A

This next example will address a cooling season in Climate Zone 3A. This cooling season is longer than that for Climate Zone 5B for obvious reasons. As previously stated, we take the temperature for the cooling season and develop a scatter plot to determine the formula for the degree days at that specified base temperature. We will then apply the formula to generate the revised usage based on the new base temperature CDDs. As shown previously, the CDDs change by around 7% for each degree change. This alone is a little disorienting as we generally consider CDDs set in stone. The change is based on how we determine what OAT is required to impact the usage. So far, the delta in OAT does not have much of an impact as we must realize the AC equipment and the fan/pump system to distribute in response to the OAT are a small percentage of the total electricity usage for a building. Factors other than OAT drive the overall usage more in this climate zone. This case study will show the impact of the base temperature for the CDDs on calculating the usage. We developed these examples for several base temperatures above and below the 65° base temperature normally used. Those values will be calculated into the new usage for that base temperature and summed for the year, similar to that accomplished in the first example. The calculated formula values at each base temperature test case are compared to the actual usage. The comparison across the various base temperatures will show the error involved.

The first table (Table A2.5) will show how we laid out the Climate Zone 3A campus formula. As discussed previously, this is a truncated table as we only need to see a sampling of the line items. The base degree of 62°F is subtracted from the hourly temperature. That becomes a degree hour, which is converted into a degree day by dividing by 24. This is the degree days

Table A2.5   Calculation of CDD as base 62°F.

Hourly Usage Report
Campus C, Building 6882 (19752 sf)
Commodity: Electric

Timestamp	Usage	Units	Temp °F	Base Temp Cooling	Degree Hours	Degree days	Calculated Usage
2022-04-15 00:00	20.28	kWh	62	62	0	0.000	20.28
2022-04-15 01:00	20.28	kWh	60	62	0	0.000	20.28
2022-04-15 02:00	19.08	kWh	58	62	0	0.000	19.08
2022-04-15 03:00	17.52	kWh	56	62	0	0.000	17.52
2022-04-15 04:00	16.32	kWh	54	62	0	0.000	16.32
2022-04-15 05:00	18.48	kWh	52	62	0	0.000	18.48
2022-04-15 06:00	15.36	kWh	51	62	0	0.000	15.36
2022-04-15 07:00	15.72	kWh	48	62	0	0.000	15.72
2022-04-15 08:00	14.76	kWh	48	62	0	0.000	14.76
2022-04-15 09:00	15.12	kWh	54	62	0	0.000	15.12
2022-04-15 10:00	16.56	kWh	62	62	0	0.000	16.56
2022-04-15 11:00	16.68	kWh	68	62	6	0.250	16.68
2022-04-15 12:00	19.20	kWh	73	62	11	0.458	19.20
2022-04-15 13:00	19.68	kWh	75	62	13	0.542	19.68

recalculated at the new base temperature of 62°F. We add the column of usage adjacent to that column of degree days to make plotting easier. The scatter plot is shown in Figure A2.5 with the formula for the trend line. To calculate the new usage, we use the trend line formula to calculate the usage at each of those degree days. This generates a calculated usage based on that 62°F degree base. The other examples will follow suit as we increase the base temperature by 1° in each example.

In Table A2.6, we indicate those various base temperatures compared. These instances are very similar to those shown in the first example. We looked at this table in degree increments to evaluate how the formula reacted across the range as before. As we can see from the table, there was almost no significant variance as we continued this same analysis for each temperature increment up to 67°F.

If we look at each of these, we will find the level of error introduced by the different base temperatures. So, it appears neither the climate zone nor the CDDs or even HDDs introduce an error of any magnitude that impacts the decision regarding the base temperature.

We plotted the differences in Figure A2.6, and we can see that the crossing point where the error is closest to zero is in two places, the first

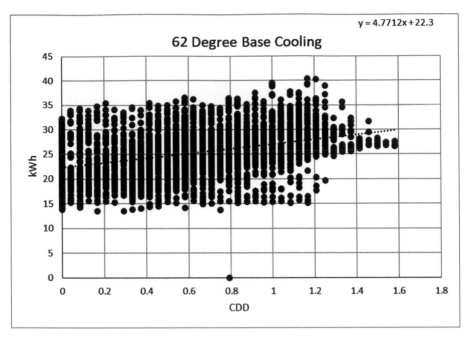

Figure A2.5   Scatter plot using 62°F for base on formula.

Table A2.6   Comparing the impact of the base degree day against the actual.

Base Temp Cooling °F	Cooling Degree Hours	Cooling Degree Days	Actual Usage	Calculated Usage by Formulae	Base Temp Variance vs Actual	% Difference
62	63,490	2,645	111,097	111,099	100.0016%	0.0016%
63	59,477	2,478	111,097	111,097	100.0005%	0.0005%
64	55,513	2,313	111,097	111,095	99.9985%	-0.0015%
65	51,624	2,151	111,097	111,098	100.0007%	0.0007%
66	47,802	1,992	111,097	111,098	100.0010%	0.0010%
66	20,900	871	143,796	143,797	100.0005%	0.0005%
67	19,078	795	143,796	143,797	100.0005%	0.0005%

around 63.4°F and the second around 64.6°F. This is around 1.5 thousand of a percent, as stated above. While that may give us a point, it is so insignificant in error from using the traditional 65°F that we stick with 65°F in this case.

This test case furthers our previous thought that all buildings on site will be closely related to the same degree of base temperature. The small variance in the multiple examples with no major differences in the calculations or the

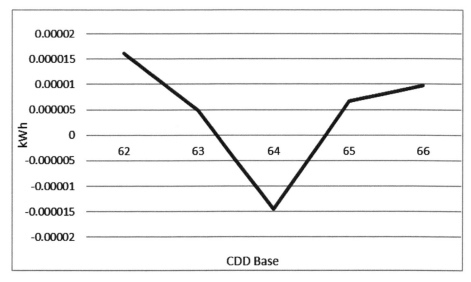

Figure A2.6 Plot of various base degrees showing where the data has zero errors.

variance further supports our conclusion that the cooling needs no further study, and error arguments are moot.

A2.4 Example of HDD from Climate Zone 3A

This last example will take the same building from Climate Zone 3A and calculate this for the heating season. This example will follow the same process as the previous, except that it will take the temperature for the heating season and develop a scatter plot to determine the formula for the degree days at a specific base temperature. We will then compare the revised usage based on the new base temperature HDDs. This will show the variance of actual usage vs. the usage based on a set base temperature for the HDDs. We will develop this for several base temperatures above and below the 65° base temperature normally used as the base temperature for the calculation. Those values will be calculated into the new usage for that base temperature and summed for the season. The calculated formula values at each base temperature test case are compared to the actual usage. The comparison across the various base temperatures will show the error involved at each base temperature.

Table A2.7 will show how we calculate the formula for the heating season for the Climate Zone 3A campus. This is a truncated table for ease of viewing. The base degree of 62°F is subtracted from the hourly temperature

Table A2.7   Calculation of HDD as base 62°F.

Hourly Usage Report
Campus C, Building 6882 (19752 sf)
Commodity: Electric

Timestamp	Usage	Units	Temp °F	Base Temp Heating	Degree Hours	Degree days	Calculated Usage
2022-01-01 00:00	24.24	kWh	70	62	0	0.000	24.24
2022-01-01 01:00	24.60	kWh	70	62	0	0.000	24.60
2022-01-01 02:00	24.36	kWh	70	62	0	0.000	24.36
2022-01-01 03:00	23.16	kWh	70	62	0	0.000	23.16
2022-01-01 04:00	24.36	kWh	70	62	0	0.000	24.36
2022-01-01 05:00	24.36	kWh	70	62	0	0.000	24.36
2022-01-01 06:00	24.48	kWh	69	62	0	0.000	24.48
2022-01-01 07:00	23.16	kWh	70	62	0	0.000	23.16
2022-01-01 08:00	23.76	kWh	69	62	0	0.000	23.76
2022-01-01 09:00	22.92	kWh	70	62	0	0.000	22.92
2022-01-01 10:00	23.64	kWh	71	62	0	0.000	23.64
2022-01-01 11:00	23.28	kWh	73	62	0	0.000	23.28
2022-01-01 12:00	23.52	kWh	75	62	0	0.000	23.52
2022-01-01 13:00	23.52	kWh	78	62	0	0.000	23.52
2022-01-01 14:00	23.88	kWh	79	62	0	0.000	23.88
2022-01-01 15:00	23.88	kWh	79	62	0	0.000	23.88
2022-01-01 16:00	23.76	kWh	79	62	0	0.000	23.76

to become degree hours, which is converted into a degree day by dividing by 24. This is the degree days recalculated at the new base temperature of 62°F. We add the column of usage adjacent to that column of degree days to simplify the plotting process. The scatter plot is shown in Figure A2.7 with the formula for the HDD trend line. To calculate the new usage, we use the trend line formula to calculate the usage based on the revised HDDs. This generates a calculated usage based on that degree base. The pattern shown for all the usage points in this figure's plots is all over the spectrum. Remember, this is plotting electric usage and comparing that to HDDs. The only electric load supporting the heating system or responding to the change in HDDs will be fan/pump systems with no electric heat. So, this particular graph in Figure A2.7 appears broken into two distinct patterns. The lower pattern will cover those items that are minor electric loads and not associated with heating. The upper pattern is the usage associated with the fan and pump systems.

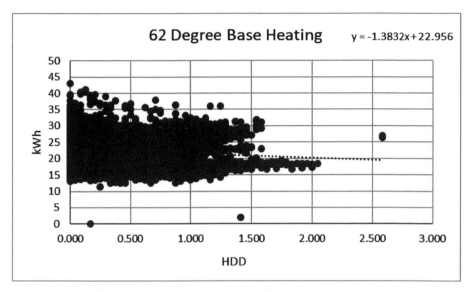

Figure A2.7   Scatter plot using 62°F for base on formula.

Table A2.8   Comparing the impact of the base degree day against the actual.

Base Temp Heating °F	Heating Degree Hours	Heating Degree Days	Actual Usage	Calculated Usage by Formulae	Base Temp Variance vs Actual	% Difference
62	41,235	1,718	97,331	97,331	100.0000%	0.0000%
63	44,282	1,845	97,331	97,332	100.0015%	0.0015%
64	47,418	1,976	97,331	97,331	100.0002%	0.0002%
65	50,659	2,111	97,331	97,332	100.0015%	0.0015%
66	54,019	2,251	97,331	97,333	100.0021%	0.0021%

In Table A2.8, we can see those various base temperatures compared for the heating season. We approached the heating season analysis with the same range in degree increments. As we indicate from the table, the variance was the same as that reported in the previous examples.

If we look at each of these, we will find the level of error introduced by the different base temperatures. In this particular climate zone, there was an insignificant variance. Therefore, the error was so small that it would not be a factor in any calculation performed on the data.

We plotted the differences in Figure A2.8, and we show the base degree crossed zero at 62°F. Even with 62°F as the zero point, the error is

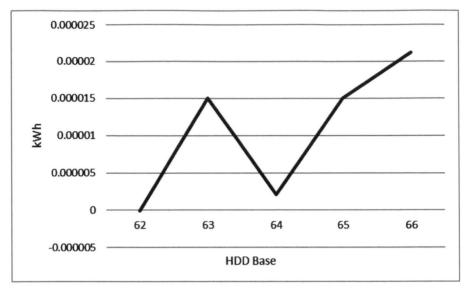

Figure A2.8   Plot of various base degrees showing where the data has zero errors.

insignificant. Therefore, we will stick with the standard 65°F in this case. The error introduced by the small variances for each degree analysis does not warrant expanding the analysis.

A2.5 Summary

In summary, this academic discussion does not impact EM's day-to-day energy management. We have found that each degree day's base change impacts 7%–8% of the degree days. The overall usage for cooling or heating based on those degree days is insignificant compared to the overall usage for electricity. Suppose we did this same analysis for gas usage. In that case, it might change the results, as the gas impact for heating is probably close to 85%, which is much higher than our analysis for the ratio of cooling and heating on electricity.

The analysis shows that each base degree day increment produced a maximum impact of 0.0021% over the example range. That impact is so insignificant that it would not be considered relevant to the degree of error involved in any scenario. We decided to continue with a 65°F base for all degree-day equations.

Appendix 3

Determine the Variance of Each Energy System in the Scatter Plot and the Overall Impact

Abstract

This appendix shows the calculations for each system's variance in the energy subsets in a scatter plot. The variances in each subset will be taken collectively for the overall impact on energy usage. We will show how much each variation in a subset affects the overall scatter plot analysis.

A3   Determine the Variance of Each Energy System in the Scatter Plot and the Overall Impact

This appendix will discuss the range of variance possible in each energy subset. The analysis will cover the impacts of the energy subsets for each energy system with variables. Those ranges will be calculated into the impact of the overall numbers to show the range that each energy system can vary and what that impact is on the overall building usage.

- Where are the variables?
- Variance in plug loading
- Variance in fan/pump system vs. AC system loading
- Impacts on each energy system on the whole building analysis
- Summary ˎ

A3.1 Where are the Variables?

The variables are divided into three areas by the energy subset they affect. Remember, the overall usage is determined by the subsets of energy that

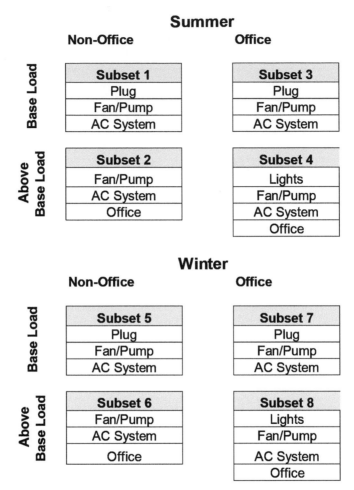

Figure A3.1   Breaking down the energy subsets.

make up its composition. Each subset is defined by a season and time (when space is occupied). As shown in Figure A3.1, there are four energy subsets for summer and four for winter. Then there are two energy subsets for non-office hours and two for office hours each season.

The plug load can impact four energy subsets in the baseload. This seems like a lot, but it is simple to calculate and only affects one other parameter when it occurs. Since the plug load is a portion of the baseline, a variance in the plug load will impact the baseline. The plug load is calculated; so it can vary depending on the impact of plug variance from an average normal layout. The plug load is averaged as 1.3 kWh/sf/yr, broken down between office and non-office hours. These endpoint extremes can vary between 0.5 and 2.1 kWh/sf/yr (based on actual field measurements).

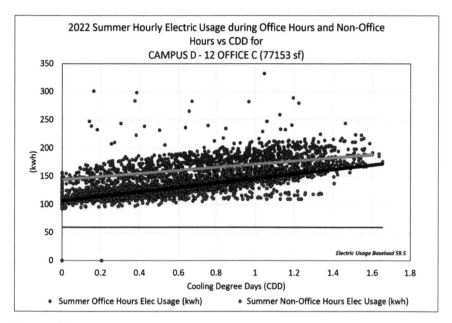

Figure A3.2   Building where the points between office hours and non-office hours mix.

These variances will impact the lighting usage in some cases, and the fan/pump's usage in others, as explained below. In those instances, the variance will be distributed between the plug and those two systems.

The second variance will be related to the fan/pump systems load ratio to AC systems. This will occur in energy subsets 2 and 4, which are summer non-office hours above the baseline and summer office hours above the baseline. These are the only energy subsets where AC systems run; so that the ratio between those can impact the overall usage. The mix is determined by the type of AC and fan/pump systems. We use a 48% fan/pump systems ratio, but the fans can be as high as 55% and as low as 45%, which is the overall variance in the results.

It is important to note that the scatter plot will fail if the data does not meet certain conditions. Failure in the scatter plot model will appear first in the lighting calculation results for three reasons. Failure will occur if the meter is bad or there is a data gap approaching 10% of the hours. Failure will occur when the lighting load drops below 0.2 watts/sf. It will also occur if the hours are off from a normal one-shift operation. The program is set up to evaluate a 1–2 shift operation. As it gets beyond that or if the office hours occur at night or beyond the boundaries of normal office hours of 4:00 AM to 10:00 PM, we can tell from the graphs as shown in Figure A3.2 where the orange points and the blue points comingle, preventing the program from

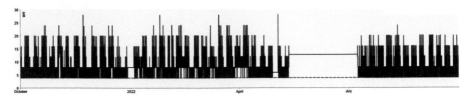

Figure A3.3   Building with a two-month gap in readings.

differentiating office and non-office hours. These are also caused by large data gaps, which smoothen to flat lines. If units are too large or too small for systems, the multiplier for adjusting the data as it is being submitted is wrong. That is depicted in Figure A3.3, where the two-month gap is too long, making the data crossover between office and non-office hours. That will cause the model to fail. The final reason for failure is a base load that is too high. A large amount of constant equipment loadings can cause that. That loading throws off the model as it differs from normal 1–2 shift building operations. Other equipment loading issues could be a charging operation, such as a type-3 EV station being added to a building load at night. That will skew the results to failure.

A3.2 Variance in Plug Loading

To check the variance in the plug loading would be difficult in most circumstances. As discussed above, we calculate this based on an average we determined and covered in the benchmarking chapters (Chapters 10 and 11). Since this is calculated, and we have actual data, we know that this also is the area where we will have the largest variances against that specific energy system. We use 1.3 kWh/sf/yr as the average, which seems to be a good point after years of analysis. As we discussed in Chapter 10, "Basic Benchmarking (First Level)," many things can change the plug loading in a facility. Those notables are network servers, data center closets, and other network equipment. Other equipment includes elevators, office machines, vending machines, personal refrigerators, and space heaters.

In the PNNL study in Chapter 11, "Second-level Benchmarking (Base Load with Plug Load)," we noted that the range they found ran from 0.54 to 2.41 kWh/sf/yr. We noted that the highest was an anomaly; so the top of the range should be around 1.87 kWh/sf/yr. Let us take two examples and calculate the variance from the actual plug loading on each building.

The first example is an office building in Category Type C, building number 704. The building had a scatter plot analysis with the plug load

Table A3.1   Breakdown of the loading into the four energy systems.

System	kWh/sf/yr	Annual kWh	% of Load
Plug	0.78	25,168.32	12.01%
Lights	1.23	39,904.09	19.04%
Fan/Pump	3.55	114,758.17	54.75%
AC System	0.41	13,155.97	6.28%
Office	0.51	16,602.20	7.92%
Total	6.48	209,588.75	100.00%

calculated at 1.3 kWh/sf/yr. That 1.3 kWh/sf/yr load is broken down into the office loading (0.513) and the basic "plug" load (0.778) during non-office hours. The results of the analysis are shown in Table A3.1. There we calculate the total usage of the building at 6.48 kWh/sf/yr. That is a good usage rate for a Category Type Office C building. The actual measurements on the building revealed the plug load to be at 0.51 kWh/sf/yr. So, the first analysis will compare the differences and impact of 1.3 vs. 0.51 kWh/sf/yr. To do that, we want to understand where the plug load affects the usage and what systems are affected in that energy subset. Figure A3.4 shows that the plug loading impacts four energy subsets.

Every subset in a base load is affected by the plug load. In four subsets, the other loading is a mix between the fan/pump and AC system load, which is shared with the plug load. In energy subset 4, there are several loadings, but the plug is segregated along with the lighting load to be differentiated easily. Understanding this relationship makes this calculation easier. Instead of looking at each energy subset to calculate the impact, we will take them as a group, as the impact of the ratios is the same across each energy subset. Therefore, if the energy for the plug cuts from 1.3 to 0.51 kWh/sf/yr, then the energy loss can be calculated by that delta. It is easier to see this on a table. So, in Table A3.2, we calculated the projected kWh/sf/yr from the scatter plot in the first column. The office load is the plug load in energy subset 4 during office hours. As discussed above, those two energy systems, the plug (office) and the lights, are easily segregated from the loads by the intercept of the office and non-office hours intercept graph, as covered in Chapter 12, "Third-level Benchmarking (Lights and Scatter Plot Modeling)." So, since we know the energy in this subset to energy subset 4, we just need to calculate the impact and move it from one system to the other. So, that difference with the office load is added to the lighting.

That can be seen in Table A3.3, with the delta for the office being 0.31 kWh/sf/yr coming off the office plug load and being added to the lighting load. The other plug loads will add the load directly into the fan/pump systems

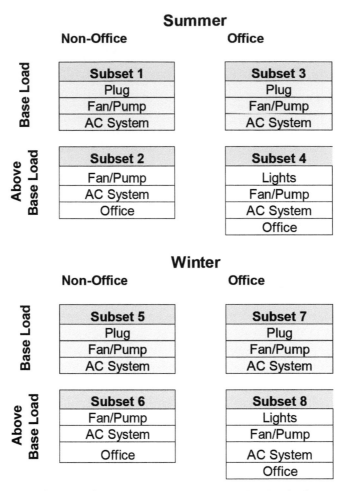

Figure A3.4   Energy subsets impacted by the plug load.

Table A3.2   Revised load on energy systems for building 407 based on variance.

System	kWh/sf/yr	Annual kWh	% of Load	Revised % of Load	Revised kWh/sf/yr
Plug	0.78	25,168.32	12.01%	4.71%	0.31
Lights	1.23	39,904.09	19.04%	23.85%	1.55
Fan/Pump	3.55	114,758.17	54.75%	62.05%	4.02
AC System	0.41	13,155.97	6.28%	6.28%	0.41
Office	0.51	16,602.20	7.92%	3.11%	0.20
Total	6.48	209,588.75	100.00%	100.00%	6.48

Table A3.3   Impact of the revised plug load variance on the other systems for building 407.

System	kWh/sf/yr	Annual kWh	% of Load	Revised % of Load	Revised kWh/sf/yr	Delta
Plug	0.78	25,168.32	12.01%	4.71%	0.31	(0.47)
Lights	1.23	39,904.09	19.04%	23.85%	1.55	0.31
Fan/Pump	3.55	114,758.17	54.75%	62.05%	4.02	0.47
AC System	0.41	13,155.97	6.28%	6.28%	0.41	
Office	0.51	16,602.20	7.92%	3.11%	0.20	(0.31)
Total	6.48	209,588.75	100.00%	100.00%	6.48	

Table A3.4   Usage by energy system in building 1021.

System	kWh/sf/yr	Annual kWh	% of Load
Plug	0.79	11,245.17	10.06%
Lights	2.07	29,562.80	26.44%
Fan/Pump	3.62	51,604.16	46.15%
AC System	0.86	12,241.79	10.95%
Office	0.50	7,176.22	6.42%
Total	7.84	111,830.14	100.00%

as that is the only place that load can be added in that energy subset. Since these systems work the same way in all three similar energy subsets, we can take them off against the whole as a kWh/sf and add that to the receiving load or fan/pump systems loading. So, in this case, we are taking away 0.47 kWh/sf/yr from the plug load and adding that to the fan/pump systems. The compartmentalized approach with the energy subsets and the other limitations dictated by each system related to the energy for each system makes this an easy calculation.

The second example is a Category Type Office N building number 1021. The building had a scatter plot analysis with the plug load calculated at 1.3 kWh/sf/yr. The results of the analysis are shown in Table A3.4. The total usage of the building is at 7.84 kWh/sf/yr. That is a good usage rate for a normal office-type building, but we will see a large portion of the increase is due to a higher plug load for buildings of this type. The measurement of the plug load on this building revealed the loading to be at 1.87 kWh/sf/yr. So, the analysis involves comparing the differences and impact of 1.3 vs. 1.87 kWh/sf/yr. To do that, we want to understand where the plug load affects the usage and what systems are affected in that energy subset. In Figure A3.4, we covered that the plug loading impacts four energy subsets. This is the same as the last building, as all energy subsets are the same in the basic building types.

As stated, the plug load affects every subset with a base load. The only other loading is shared with the fan/pump systems' load in three subsets. In

Table A3.5   Revised load on energy systems for building 1021 based on variance.

System	kWh/sf/yr	Annual kWh	% of Load	Revised % of Load	Revised kWh/sf/yr
Plug	0.79	11,245.17	10.06%	14.46%	1.13
Lights	2.07	29,562.80	26.44%	23.62%	1.85
Fan/Pump	3.62	51,604.16	47.77%	41.74%	3.27
AC System	0.86	12,241.79	9.33%	10.95%	0.86
Office	0.50	7,176.22	6.42%	9.23%	0.72
Total	7.84	111,830.14			7.84

energy subset 4, there are several loadings, but the plug is segregated along with the lighting load to be calculated easily. Understanding this relationship makes this analysis easier. So instead of looking at each energy subset to calculate the impact, we will take them as a group, as the impact ratios are the same across all energy subsets. So, if the energy for the plug increases from 1.3 to 1.87 kWh/sf/yr, then the energy loss can be calculated by that delta. It is easier to see this on a table. So, in Table A3.5, we can see the projected kWh/sf/yr from the scatter plot in the first column. The office load is the plug load in energy subset 4 during office hours. As discussed above, those two energy systems, the plug (office) and the lights are easily segregated from the loads by the intercept of the office and non-office hours intercept graph (as covered in Chapter 12). So, since we know the energy in this subset to energy subset 4, we just need to calculate the impact and add it to one system (office plug load) to subtract it from the other (lighting load). So, the row below shows the lighting load is decreased while the office load increases by that difference.

That can be seen in Table A3.6, with the delta for the office adding 0.22 kWh/sf/yr to the plug load and subtracting 0.22 kWh/sf/yr from the lighting load. The other plug loads will add the load directly into the fan/pump systems, as that is the only place to add the load. Since these systems work the same way in all three similar energy subsets, we can add them against the combined amount as a kWh/sf for the plug and subtract them from the fan/pump systems' loading. So, in this case, we are adding 0.35 kWh/sf/yr to the plug load and subtracting the same from the fan/pump systems. This is a simple calculation due to the lack of various components in each subset, and the interaction makes this an easy analysis.

A3.3 Variance in Fan/Pump System vs. AC System Loading

Now we will check the variance in fan/pump systems' loading. As discussed above, we calculate this based on an average of 48% that we determined

Table A3.6 Impact of the revised plug load variance on the other systems for building 1021.

System	kWh/sf/yr	Annual kWh	% of Load	Revised % of Load	Revised kWh/sf/yr	Delta
Plug	0.79	11,245.17	10.06%	14.46%	1.13	0.35
Lights	2.07	29,562.80	26.44%	23.62%	1.85	(0.22)
Fan/Pump	3.62	51,604.16	47.77%	41.74%	3.27	(0.35)
AC System	0.86	12,241.79	9.33%	10.95%	0.86	
Office	0.50	7,176.22	6.42%	9.23%	0.72	0.22
Total	7.84	111,830.14			7.84	

and covered in Chapter 13, "Fourth-level Benchmarking (AC Systems)." Chapter 13 also showed the boundaries of the ratios between AC systems and fan/pump systems in Table 13.4. For this analysis, we need to look at those extremes. District cooling has the highest fan ratio at 66.2%, which is accounted for in the modeling as central cooling plants are annotated, and the cooling is set to zero. The next highest is the percentage from the CEUS survey at 56%, but we are not using those surveys from 20 years ago, especially since they are regional surveys. The highest for a system in EIA is 55.7%, which EIA labels as "other" systems. For the lower end, we have the other CEUS reports, which we discounted above due to age and generic at 25% and were discounted in the Chapter 13 analysis. The lowest system analysis is 45.8% for heat pumps. So, we will show the impact of the difference for the range from 45.8% to 56% against the average of 48% used in the scatter plots. Those two extremes will be applied against the two buildings used in the plug analysis.

The first example is Category Type Office C. The building had a scatter plot analysis with the fan/pump systems' load calculated at 3.55 kWh/sf/yr. AC systems loading is 0.41 kWh/sf/yr. The results of the analysis of all the systems are shown in Table A3.1 earlier. There we notice the total usage of the building at 6.48 kWh/sf/yr. As stated earlier, this is a good range for a building of this type. The first analysis will compare the differences and impact of 48% vs. the high end of the range of 55.7% for fan/pump systems split with AC systems.

Understanding this variance requires us to understand where these ratios impact each other. While fan/pump systems have energy in all eight energy subsets, they only impact each other in two areas or two energy subsets. Those are subsets 1 and 3, as shown in Figure A3.5, and they have fan/pump systems and AC systems that interrelate in those subsets. Subsets 5,6,7 and 8 are in winter; therefore, the AC System in not used in this instance.

The issue related to the mix of fan/pump systems' energy against AC systems' energy is that the fan pump system energy exists in every energy

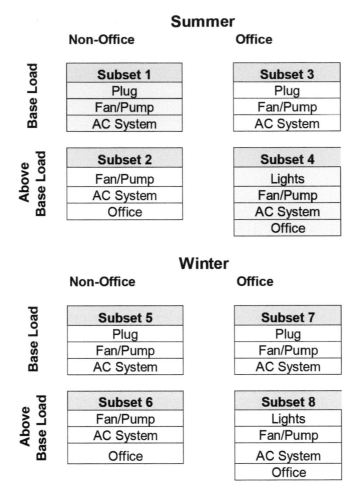

Figure A3.5   Energy subsets impacted by the ratio of the fan/pump system to the AC system.

subset. So, calculating the energy impact in the two energy subsets will require applying the results to those two subsets and then applying that differential to the overall total of the fan/pump systems and, conversely, the AC systems.

The first example will be the Category Type Office C mentioned in the plug variance section. We will address this with both extreme ranges, as discussed above. Let us first address the top end of the range for fan/pump systems using 55.7% of the energy in that subset vs. the AC systems. As discussed above, only two energy subsets affect this variance. So, we will take the energy total for these two subsets; in this case, it comes out to

Table A3.7   The transition of energy from AC system to fan/pump system.

Fan/Pump Current Usage	48.00%	12,143.97
AC System Current Usage	52.00%	13,155.97
Energy Subset Total for 1 and 4		**25,299.94**
Fan/Pump High-end Usage	55.70%	14,092.07
AC System Low-end Usage	44.30%	11,207.87
Energy Subset Total for 1 and 4		**25,299.94**

Table A3.8   Revised load on energy systems for building 1021 based on variance to the maximum ratio of fan/pump systems' load vs. AC systems' load.

System	kWh/sf/yr	Annual kWh	% of Load	Revised Annual kWh	Revised % of Load	Revised kwh/sf/yr
Plug	0.79	11,245.17	10.06%	11,245.17	10.06%	0.79
Lights	2.07	29,562.80	26.44%	29,562.80	26.44%	2.07
Fan/Pump	3.62	51,604.16	46.15%	53,416.88	47.77%	3.75
AC System	0.86	12,241.79	10.95%	10,429.06	9.33%	0.73
Office	0.50	7,176.22	6.42%	7,176.22	6.42%	0.50
Total	7.84	111,830.14	100.00%	111,830.14	100.00%	7.84

25,300 kWh/yr. If we take that and add the increased energy usage from the fan/pump system's maximum range, we can see how much the fan/pump system goes up. In Table A3.7, we see the mix on the top based on the 48% for fan/pump systems' transition to the maximum of 55.7%. The total energy for this extreme condition is shown for the fan/pump systems at 55.7% and the AC systems at 44.3%, as shown at the bottom of Table A3.7.

So, if the energy for the fan/pump systems goes up from 3.62 to 3.75 kWh/sf/yr, then the energy increase can be calculated by that delta. It is easier to see this on a table. So, in Table A3.8, we can see the projected kWh/sf/yr from the scatter plot in the first column. Conversely, the AC systems' load will decrease from 0.86 to 0.73 kWh/sf/yr.

That can be seen in Table A3.9, with the delta shown on the right for AC systems being −0.13 kWh/sf/yr and adding 0.13 kWh/sf/yr to the fan/pump systems load.

Now we will show the impact of this same building example from the other extreme. Let us address the bottom end of the range first or fan/pump systems using 45.8% of the energy in those two applicable energy subsets vs. AC systems at 54.2%. Following the same process as above, we have the same total for these two subsets, and in this case, it comes out to 25,300 kWh/yr. Let us take that total energy for the fan/pump systems and the AC systems' loading and multiply that by the fan/pump systems' minimum extreme and the

Table A3.9　Impact of the maximum ratio of revised fan/pump systems vs. AC systems plug load for building 1021.

System	kWh/sf/yr	Annual kWh	% of Load	Revised Annual kWh	Revised % of Load	Revised kwh/sf/yr	Delta
Plug	0.79	11,245.17	10.06%	11,245.17	10.06%	0.79	
Lights	2.07	29,562.80	26.44%	29,562.80	26.44%	2.07	
Fan/Pump	3.62	51,604.16	46.15%	53,416.88	47.77%	3.75	0.13
AC System	0.86	12,241.79	10.95%	10,429.06	9.33%	0.73	(0.13)
Office	0.50	7,176.22	6.42%	7,176.22	6.42%	0.50	
Total	7.84	111,830.14	100.00%	111,830.14	100.00%	7.84	

Table A3.10　The transition of energy from fan/pump systems to AC systems.

Fan/Pump Current Usage	48.00%	12,143.97
AC System Current Usage	52.00%	13,155.97
Energy Subset Total for 1 and 4		**25,299.94**
Fan/Pump Low-end Usage	45.80%	11,587.37
AC System High-end Usage	54.20%	13,712.57
Energy Subset Total for 1 and 4		**25,299.94**

Table A3.11　Revised load on energy systems for building 1021 based on variance to the minimum ratio of fan/pump systems load vs. AC system load.

System	kWh/sf/yr	Annual kWh	% of Load	Revised Annual kWh	Revised % of Load	Revised kwh/sf/yr
Plug	0.79	11,245.17	10.06%	11,245.17	10.06%	0.79
Lights	2.07	29,562.80	26.44%	29,562.80	26.44%	2.07
Fan/Pump	3.62	51,604.16	46.15%	51,086.24	45.68%	3.58
AC System	0.86	12,241.79	10.95%	12,759.71	11.41%	0.89
Office	0.50	7,176.22	6.42%	7,176.22	6.42%	0.50
Total	7.84	111,830.14	100.00%	111,830.14	100.00%	7.84

AC systems' loading maximum extreme. We get those values shown below in Table A3.10. We see the mix on the top of the table based on the average of 48% for the fan/pump system's transition to the minimum of 45.8%. The total energy for this extreme condition is shown for both energy systems next to the line items for the fan/pump systems and the AC systems.

So, if the energy for the fan/pump systems goes down from 3.62 to 3.58 kWh/sf/yr, then the energy increase can be calculated by that delta. AC systems will change from 0.86 to 0.89 kWh/sf/yr. It is easier to see this on a table. So, in Table A3.11, we can see the calculated kWh/sf/yr from the scatter plot in the first column. The right column shows the revised result that modifies the results to the minimum fan/pump systems extreme.

Table A3.12   Impact of the minimum ratio of revised fan/pump systems vs. AC systems plug load for building 1021.

System	kWh/sf/yr	Annual kWh	% of Load	Revised Annual kWh	Revised % of Load	Revised kwh/sf/yr	Delta
Plug	0.79	11,245.17	10.06%	11,245.17	10.06%	0.79	
Lights	2.07	29,562.80	26.44%	29,562.80	26.44%	2.07	
Fan/Pump	3.62	51,604.16	46.15%	51,086.24	45.68%	3.58	(0.04)
AC System	0.86	12,241.79	10.95%	12,759.71	11.41%	0.89	0.04
Office	0.50	7,176.22	6.42%	7,176.22	6.42%	0.50	
Total	7.84	111,830.14	100.00%	111,830.14	100.00%	7.84	

Table A3.13   The transition of energy from AC systems to fan/pump systems.

Fan/Pump Current Usage	48.00%	11,300.11
AC System Current Usage	52.00%	12,241.79
Energy Subset Total for 1 and 4		**23,541.90**
Fan/Pump High-end Usage	55.70%	13,112.84
AC System Low-end Usage	44.30%	10,429.06
Energy Subset Total for 1 and 4		**23,541.90**

That can be seen in Table A3.12, with the delta shown on the right in kWh/sf/yr for the fan/pump systems load being −0.04 kWh/sf/yr and adding 0.04 kWh/sf/yr to the AC system load.

The second example of the fan/pump systems' impact will be the Category Type Office N building 407 mentioned previously in the section on plug variance. As discussed in the section above, we will address this with both extreme ranges. Let us first address the top end of the range or the fan/pump systems using 55.7% of the energy in that subset vs. the AC systems. As discussed above, only two energy subsets contain both fan/pump systems and AC systems that can affect or have a variance. So, we will take the energy total for these two subsets; in this case, it comes out to 23,542 kWh per year. If we take that and add the increased energy usage from the fan/pump systems' maximum range, we can see how much the fan/pump systems go up. In Table A3.13, we see the mix on the top based on the 48% for the fan/pump systems transition to the maximum of 55.7%. The total energy for this extreme condition is shown for the fan/pump systems at 55.7% and AC systems at 44.3%, as shown at the bottom of Table A3.13.

So, if the energy for the fan/pump systems goes up from 3.55 kWh/sf/yr to 3.61 kWh/sf/yr, then the energy increase can be calculated by that delta. It is easier to see this on a table. So, in Table A3.14, we can see the projected kWh/sf/yr from the scatter plot in the first column. Conversely, the AC systems' load will decrease from 0.41 to 0.35 kWh/sf/yr.

Table A3.14   Revised load on energy systems for building 407 based on variance to the maximum ratio of fan/pump systems' load vs. AC system load.

System	kWh/sf/yr	Annual kWh	% of Load	Revised Annual kWh	Revised % of Load	Revised kwh/sf/yr
Plug	0.78	25,168.32	12.01%	25,168.32	12.01%	0.78
Lights	1.23	39,904.09	19.04%	39,904.09	19.04%	1.23
Fan/Pump	3.55	114,758.17	54.75%	116,706.27	55.68%	3.61
AC System	0.41	13,155.97	6.28%	11,207.87	5.35%	0.35
Office	0.51	16,602.20	7.92%	16,602.20	7.92%	0.51
Total	6.48	111,830.14	100.00%	209,588.75	100.00%	6.48

Table A3.15   Impact of the maximum ratio of revised fan/pump vs. AC system plug load for building 407.

System	kWh/sf/yr	Annual kWh	% of Load	Revised Annual kWh	Revised % of Load	Revised kwh/sf/yr	Delta
Plug	0.78	25,168.32	12.01%	25,168.32	12.01%	0.78	
Lights	1.23	39,904.09	19.04%	39,904.09	19.04%	1.23	
Fan/Pump	3.55	114,758.17	54.75%	116,706.27	55.68%	3.61	0.06
AC System	0.41	13,155.97	6.28%	11,207.87	5.35%	0.35	(0.06)
Office	0.51	16,602.20	7.92%	16,602.20	7.92%	0.51	
Total	6.48	111,830.14	100.00%	209,588.75	100.00%	6.48	

That can be seen in Table A3.15, with the delta shown on the right in kWh/sf/yr for AC systems being −0.06 kWh/sf/yr and adding 0.06 kWh/sf/yr to the fan/pump systems' load.

Now we will show the impact of this same building example from the other extreme. Let us first address the bottom end of the range or the fan/pump systems using 45.8% of the energy in those two applicable energy subsets vs. AC systems at 54.2%. Following the same process as above, we have the same total for these two subsets; in this case, it comes out to 23,542 kWh/yr. Let us take that total energy for the fan/pump systems and the AC systems' loading and multiply that by the fan/pump systems' minimum extreme and the AC systems' loading maximum extreme. We get those values shown below in Table A3.16. We see the mix on the top of the table based on the average of 48% for the fan/pump system's transition to the minimum of 45.8%. The total energy for this extreme condition is shown in both energy systems next to the line items for the fan/pump systems and the AC systems.

So, if the energy for the fan/pump systems goes down from 3.55 to 3.53 kWh/sf/yr, then the energy increase can be calculated by that delta. AC systems will change from 0.41 to 0.42 kWh/sf/yr. It is easier to see this on a table. So, in Table A3.17, we calculate the projected kWh/sf/yr from the scatter plot in the first column. The right column shows the revised result that modifies the previous results to the minimum fan/pump systems extreme.

Table A3.16 The transition of energy from AC to fan/pump system.

Fan/Pump Current Usage	48.00%	11,300.11
AC System Current Usage	52.00%	12,241.79
Energy Subset Total for 1 and 4		**23,541.90**
Fan/Pump Low-end Usage	45.80%	10,782.19
AC System High-end Usage	54.20%	12,759.71
Energy Subset Total for 1 and 4		**23,541.90**

Table A3.17 Revised load on energy systems for building 407 based on variance to the minimum ratio of fan/pump load vs. AC system load.

System	kWh/sf/yr	Annual kWh	% of Load	Revised Annual kWh	Revised % of Load	Revised kwh/sf/yr
Plug	0.78	25,168.32	12.01%	25,168.32	12.01%	0.78
Lights	1.23	39,904.09	19.04%	39,904.09	19.04%	1.23
Fan/Pump	3.55	114,758.17	54.75%	114,201.57	54.49%	3.53
AC System	0.41	13,155.97	6.28%	13,712.57	6.54%	0.42
Office	0.51	16,602.20	7.92%	16,602.20	7.92%	0.51
Total	6.48	111,830.14	100.00%	209,588.75	100.00%	6.48

Table A3.18 Impact of the minimum ratio of revised fan/pump systems vs. AC systems plug load for building 407.

System	kWh/sf/yr	Annual kWh	% of Load	Revised Annual kWh	Revised % of Load	Revised kwh/sf/yr	Delta
Plug	0.78	25,168.32	12.01%	25,168.32	12.01%	0.78	
Lights	1.23	39,904.09	19.04%	39,904.09	19.04%	1.23	
Fan/Pump	3.55	114,758.17	54.75%	114,201.57	54.49%	0.53	(0.02)
AC System	0.41	13,155.97	6.28%	13,712.57	6.54%	0.42	0.02
Office	0.51	16,602.20	7.92%	16,602.20	7.92%	0.51	
Total	6.48	111,830.14	100.00%	209,588.75	100.00%	6.48	

That can be seen in Table A3.18, with the delta shown on the right in kWh/sf/yr for fan/pump systems load being a −0.02 kWh/sf/yr reduction and adding 0.02 kWh/sf/yr to AC systems.

A3.4 Impacts on Each Energy System and the Whole Building Analysis

The impact on the system can be measured in two ways. The first is at the system level. For example, what percent of the system changed because of the variance? In some cases, that is large, but we will show how that affects the ability of the EM to do their job. A large impact in an area that does not affect the analysis is not as important as a large impact in an area that affects calculations for savings and proposed projects.

Table A3.19   Impact of the plug load system on the fan/pump system loads for building 407.

System	kWh/sf/yr	Revised kWh/sf/yr	Delta	Impact on Energy System
Plug	0.78	0.31	(0.47)	39.23%
Lights	1.23	1.55	0.31	125.28%
Fan/Pump	3.55	4.02	0.47	113.33%
AC System	0.41	0.41	0.00	100.00%
Office	0.51	0.20	(0.31)	39.23%
Total	6.48	6.48		

So let us examine the impact of the plug load on the fan/pumps and the lights. The variance in the plug load has the largest impact on any energy system. Look at plug loading impact for the first type building Category Type Office C building 407. One can see that the impact from the average plug load in Table A3.19 to this extreme range decreased the plug load by 39.2%, as indicated on the first row. This indicates a large impact on an energy system. Conversely, the energy system in that same energy subset is the fan/pump system. Fan/pump systems only had a 13.3% impact as an increase. So, from an energy system, the plug is not generally targeted. It certainly is not targeted in an overall project as part of a package. The plug load is targeted for specific savings initiatives, such as not powering down all the servers and laptops after office hours. In those instances, we are not looking at a general audit or energy distribution to decide what ECM we want to accomplish with the plug loads. Suppose we want to do an audit to determine the full extent and impact of the plug load; then, this tool will not accomplish that for the EM. On the other hand, this energy system impacts 13.3% of the fan/pump systems' load. This load is an important aspect of analytics. This 13.3% is large for any project we might want to do; so to mitigate that, we need to assess the major components of plug load that impact the analysis or drive it to be higher or lower than the average. We can do that by evaluating the base load in watts/sf and determining how far it is from the median for that category type. We will receive more savings for the fan/pump systems if it is lower than the scatter plot indicates. We will receive less savings if higher than the scatter plot indicates. Our rule of thumb is that if we are in the top 25% percentile over the median, we need to drop the savings to the minimum range. We will address this in the next graph. If we are in the bottom 25% percentile, we can assume that we will be near this 13% additional energy in the fan/pump systems.

Table A3.20 Impact of plug variance on fan/pump loads against the overall building load (building 407).

System	kWh/sf/yr	Revised kWh/sf/yr	Delta	Impact on Energy System	Impact on Building Analysis
Plug	0.78	0.31	(0.47)	39.23%	-7.30%
Lights	1.23	1.55	0.31	125.28%	4.81%
Fan/Pump	3.55	4.02	0.47	113.33%	7.30%
AC System	0.41	0.41	0.00	100.00%	0.00%
Office	0.51	0.20	(0.31)	39.23%	-4.81%
Total	**6.48**	**6.48**			

What is the overall impact on the building energy? Table A3.20 shows the beige highlighted impacts for those same variances to the overall energy. The overall impact will be the same for each energy system; so it will be a negative 7.3% for the plug and a positive 7.3% for the fan/pump systems. This does not help us with the impact on the system, but it relates to the total energy for the building. In our opinion, anything over 5% would be a concern, but we can mitigate this, as indicated above, which should get us into a range of less than 3% overall. This is on par or even better than most audits or modeling and certainly less than 5% of the time required for the other methods.

The other two variances are on the same energy subsets. This is for the office plug system. As indicated above, the plug is difficult to establish boundaries since it is equipment related. This is mostly driven by computers or network equipment, around 66% of the office load, as discussed in Chapters 10 and 11. The office load variance will be the same as the plug at 39.2%, shown in Table A3.21, but it is offset against the lighting component in this energy subset. While 39.2% is large, it is not a driver for the decision, nor does it impact the project analytics for the above reasons. The real impact is the 25.3% increase in the lighting. So, we must mitigate it by checking the base load, as the office load is proportional to that. We can then gauge the impact on lighting based on where the base load stands against the median.

The impact against the overall building load is smaller than discussed in the first variance, below the 5% we display in Table A3.22. We can easily mitigate this in the same way as discussed above.

Let us look at building 1021 to see how much the variances impact those results. In this instance, the plug load increased by 43.8%, which resides in the energy subset it shares with fan/pump systems. The plug has less impact here than in the last example, except that this is an increase. As

Table A3.21   Impact of office plug system on the lighting system.

System	kWh/sf/yr	Revised kWh/sf/yr	Delta	Impact on Energy System
Plug	0.78	0.31	(0.47)	39.23%
Lights	1.23	1.55	0.31	125.28%
Fan/Pump	3.55	4.02	0.47	113.33%
AC System	0.41	0.41	0.00	100.00%
Office	0.51	0.20	(0.31)	39.23%
Total	6.48	6.48		

Table A3.22   Impact of the office plug and lighting loads' variance on the overall building load for building 407.

System	kWh/sf/yr	Revised kWh/sf/yr	Delta	Impact on Energy System	Impact on Building Analysis
Plug	0.78	0.31	(0.47)	39.23%	-7.30%
Lights	1.23	1.55	0.31	125.28%	4.81%
Fan/Pump	3.55	4.02	0.47	113.33%	7.30%
AC System	0.41	0.41	0.00	100.00%	0.00%
Office	0.51	0.20	(0.31)	39.23%	-4.81%
Total	6.48	6.48			

discussed above, the increase is probably more predictable, because more equipment and computers are obvious. The mitigation logic is the same as above. The real impact is the fan/pump systems being off by 9.6%, as shown in Table A3.23, which is a reasonable range for that energy system.

What is the overall impact on the building load? We can see in Table A3.24 that the plug load variance is 4.4% of the overall usage. The fan/pump systems variance is also 4.4% of the overall usage. This can also be mitigated, as discussed previously.

The second aspect of this energy subset is the impact of the office plug load. The impact on the office plug is the same as the plug load. That has already been discussed in detail. The real impact that needs to be discussed is related to the office's impact on the lighting load. The variance in the lighting is 10.6% (Table A3.25), which greatly impacts a single system. We can mitigate that somewhat, as discussed for the previous building, to a point where it is below 5% against the system.

Table A3.23　Impact of the plug system on the fan/pump system for building 1021.

System	kWh/sf/yr	Revised kWh/sf/yr	Delta	Impact on Energy System
Plug	0.79	1.13	0.35	143.85%
Lights	2.07	1.85	(0.22)	89.36%
Fan/Pump	3.62	3.27	(0.35)	90.45%
AC System	0.86	0.86		100.00%
Office	0.50	0.72	0.22	143.85%
Total	7.84	7.84		

Table A3.24　Impact of the plug load on the fan/pump load for building 1021 compared to the building usage.

System	kWh/sf/yr	Revised kWh/sf/yr	Delta	Impact on Energy System	Impact on Building Analysis
Plug	0.79	1.13	0.35	143.85%	4.41%
Lights	2.07	1.85	(0.22)	89.36%	-2.81%
Fan/Pump	3.62	3.27	(0.35)	90.45%	-4.41%
AC System	0.86	0.86		100.00%	0.00%
Office	0.50	0.72	0.22	143.85%	2.81%
Total	7.84	7.84			

Table A3.25　Impact of office load on lights in building 1201.

System	kWh/sf/yr	Revised kWh/sf/yr	Delta	Impact on Energy System
Plug	0.79	1.13	0.35	143.85%
Lights	2.07	1.85	(0.22)	89.36%
Fan/Pump	3.62	3.27	(0.35)	90.45%
AC System	0.86	0.86		100.00%
Office	0.50	0.72	0.22	143.85%
Total	7.84	7.84		

Table A3.26   Impact of office on lights for building 1021 compared to the building usage.

System	kWh/sf/yr	Revised kWh/sf/yr	Delta	Impact on Energy System	Impact on Building Analysis
Plug	0.79	1.13	0.35	143.85%	4.41%
Lights	2.07	1.85	(0.22)	89.36%	-2.81%
Fan/Pump	3.62	3.27	(0.35)	90.45%	-4.41%
AC System	0.86	0.86		100.00%	0.00%
Office	0.50	0.72	0.22	143.85%	2.81%
Total	7.84	7.84			

Table A3.27   Calculation for the impact of high extremes on the fan/pump system ratio to the AC system 407 high extreme for fan/pump.

System	kWh/sf/yr	Revised kWh/sf/yr	Delta	Impact on Energy System
Plug	0.78	0.78		100.00%
Lights	1.23	1.23		100.00%
Fan/Pump	3.55	3.61	0.06	101.70%
AC System	0.41	0.35	(0.06)	85.19%
Office	0.51	0.51		100.00%
Total	6.48	6.48		

The impact on the overall building load is small, as seen in Table A3.26. The lights are at 2.8% variance to the overall usage, and the office plug systems are at 2.8%, but that can also be mitigated, as discussed previously.

The next variance to check is the fan/pump systems ratio for building 407 with AC systems. Let us analyze the impact of extremes on the fan/pump systems' ratio to the AC systems. We will first examine the maximum extreme variance in the fan/pump systems' ratio to AC systems. So, as we see below (Table A3.27), the fan/pump systems will increase by 0. 060 kWh/sf/yr at the maximum extreme, correspondingly decreasing the AC systems by 0.060 kWh/sf/yr. That is a 1.7% impact on the fan/pump systems' energy for the year. The offset will be a decrease in the AC systems of 14.8%, which has a large impact on one system.

Those impacts do not make a large difference in the overall building usage. As we can see from Table A3.28, those impacts are less than 1% of the

Table A3.28   Impact of the ratio of the fan/pump system to the AC system for building 407 compared to the building usage.

System	kWh/sf/yr	Revised kWh/sf/yr	Delta	Impact on Energy System	Impact on Building Analysis
Plug	0.78	0.78		100.00%	0.00%
Lights	1.23	1.23		100.00%	0.00%
Fan/Pump	3.55	3.61	0.06	101.70%	0.93%
AC System	0.41	0.35	(0.06)	85.19%	-0.93%
Office	0.51	0.51		100.00%	0.00%
Total	6.48	6.48			

Table A3.29   Fan/pump system ratio vs. AC system for building 407.

System	kWh/sf/yr	Revised kWh/sf/yr	Delta	Impact on Energy System
Plug	0.78	0.78		100.00%
Lights	1.23	1.23		100.00%
Fan/Pump	3.55	3.53	(0.02)	99.51%
AC System	0.41	0.42	0.02	104.23%
Office	0.51	0.51		100.00%
Total	6.48	6.48		

building usage. So even though the AC systems' impact is close to 15%, it does not move the needle much on the building load. That does not discount the impact on the AC systems; so that does need to be factored in when we look at the loading. Then, review Chapter 13 to see which systems will have that higher ratio and plan accordingly when we do a scatter plot to mitigate this impact.

Let us now analyze the impact of the minimum extreme on the fan/pump systems' ratio for building 407 to the AC systems. So, as we see below (Table A3.29), the fan/pump systems will decrease by 0.017 kWh/sf/yr at the maximum extreme, which will correspondingly increase the AC systems by 0.017 kWh/sf/yr. That is a 0.5% impact on the fan/pump systems' energy for the year. The offset will be an increase in the AC systems of 4.2%.

Those impacts in Table A3.29 have much less effect than those from the maximum extreme. As we can see from Table A3.30, those impacts are 0.3%

Table A3.30   Impact of the fan/pump system on the AC system for building 407 compared to the building usage.

System	kWh/sf/yr	Revised kWh/sf/yr	Delta	Impact on Energy System	Impact on Building Analysis
Plug	0.78	0.78		100.00%	0.00%
Lights	1.23	1.23		100.00%	0.00%
Fan/Pump	3.55	3.53	(0.02)	99.51%	-0.27%
AC System	0.41	0.42	0.02	104.23%	0.27%
Office	0.51	0.51		100.00%	0.00%
Total	6.48	6.48			

Table A3.31   Range of impact of ratio change between fan/pump system and AC systems for building 1021.

System	kWh/sf/yr	Revised kWh/sf/yr	Delta	Impact on Energy System
Plug	0.79	0.79		100.00%
Lights	2.07	2.07		100.00%
Fan/Pump	3.62	3.75	0.13	103.51%
AC System	0.86	0.73	(0.13)	85.19%
Office	0.50	0.50		100.00%
Total	7.84	7.84		

of the building usage. So, this variance has minimal impact on the analysis, even the AC systems.

Now we will look at the impact of the variance for the other building, 1021, between the fan/pump systems' ratio and the AC systems. We will first examine the maximum extreme of the fan/pump ratio to the AC systems. So, as we see below (Table A3.31), the fan/pump systems will increase by 0.127 kWh/sf/yr at the maximum extreme, correspondingly decreasing the AC systems by 0.127 kWh/sf/yr. That is a 3.5% impact on the fan/pump systems' energy for the year. The offset will be a decrease in the AC systems of 14.8%, which has a large impact on one system.

Those impacts do not make a large difference in the overall building usage. As we can see from Table A3.32, those impacts are 1.6% of the building usage. So even though the AC system's impact is close to 15%, it does not move the needle much on the building load. That does not discount the

Table A3.32   Chart at the maximum range for the variance ratio of fan/pump system vs. the AC system for building 1021 compared to the building usage.

System	kWh/sf/yr	Revised kWh/sf/yr	Delta	Impact on Energy System	Impact on Building Analysis
Plug	0.79	0.79		100.00%	0.00%
Lights	2.07	2.07		100.00%	0.00%
Fan/Pump	3.62	3.75	0.13	103.51%	1.62%
AC System	0.86	0.73	(0.13)	85.19%	-1.62%
Office	0.50	0.50		100.00%	0.00%
Total	7.84	7.84			

Table A3.33   Chart at the minimum range for the variance ratio of fan/pump system vs. the AC system for building 1021.

System	kWh/sf/yr	Revised kWh/sf/yr	Delta	Impact on Energy System
Plug	0.79	0.79		100.00%
Lights	2.07	2.07		100.00%
Fan/Pump	3.62	3.58	(0.04)	99.00%
AC System	0.86	0.89	0.04	104.23%
Office	0.50	0.50		100.00%
Total	7.84	7.84		

impact on the AC systems; so that does need to be factored in when we look at the loading. Then review Chapter 13 to see which systems will have that higher ratio and plan accordingly when we do a scatter plot to mitigate this impact.

Let us now analyze the impact of the minimum extreme on the fan/pump systems' ratio for building 1021 to the AC systems. So, as we see below (Table A3.33), the fan/pump systems will decrease by 0.036 kWh/sf/yr at the maximum extreme, which will correspondingly increase the AC systems by 0.036 kWh/sf/yr. That is a 1% impact on the fan/pump systems' energy for the year. The offset will be an increase in the AC systems of 4.2%.

Those impacts in Table A3.34 are much less than those from the maximum extreme. As we can see from Table A3.33, those impacts are at 0.5% of the building usage. So, this variance has minimal impact on the analysis, even on AC systems.

Table A3.34   Chart at the minimum range for the variance ratio of fan/pump vs. the AC system for building 1021 compared to the building usage.

System	kWh/sf/yr	Revised kWh/sf/yr	Delta	Impact on Energy System	Impact on Building Analysis
Plug	0.79	0.79		100.00%	0.00%
Lights	2.07	2.07		100.00%	0.00%
Fan/Pump	3.62	3.58	(0.04)	99.00%	-0.46%
AC System	0.86	0.89	0.04	104.23%	0.46%
Office	0.50	0.50		100.00%	0.00%
Total	7.84	7.84			

What is the cumulative impact of these factors? It may be confusing when we look at all these individually. If we only look at one building, 407, we see what items can be combined. Several factors play off of each other:

1. The fan/pump systems vs. the plug load (Table A3.20) indicates a 13.3% impact on the fan/pump systems and 7.3% on the building energy.

2. The lighting vs. the office loads indicate a 25.3% impact on the lighting system from Table A3.22.

3. The fan/pump system load ratio with the AC system was a 1.7% increase in Table A3.28 for the fan/pump systems and 0.9% for the building usage.

So lighting is only affected in one place. While that is the largest overall impact on a system, some mitigations can resolve most of that impact. The fan/pump systems could have a cumulative impact of 15%. As discussed in detail, the largest component of this is 13.3% against the fan/pump systems' loading, which can be mitigated to probably less than half of that impact. Therefore, we will have add 6% to 1.7% for a maximum impact if they coincide around 7.7%. Even if everything goes against the probabilities to form a worst-case scenario, this is still within our normal analytic capabilities with modeling or audits. With that, perform our due diligence with the base load as a safety factor to adjust these, if required, to ensure the tolerances stay below 7.7% for the fan/pump systems.

A3.5 Summary

In summary, the analysis covered a lot of detail related to the two major areas. The first area is that the plug was heavily impacted and can have a large variance within the specific energy system. The plug must be calculated as it is not derived from the scatter plots. Maybe in the future, we can develop a way to feed in the medians to adjust that parameter along the extremes. This impacts the plug and office load by roughly +/−40%. While this is large without mitigation, it does not impact projects or audit results. This is because the plug loads are often addressed as a standalone issue. A reduction in plug loading makes it difficult to make any real progress for savings. The only study that has addressed the plug lately was run by PNNL, as discussed in Chapters 10 and 11. They had recommendations on reducing the plug load related to various equipment pieces. The main issues are related to computer systems remaining on for updates after office hours. COVID-19 and Government pressure to reduce the energy used by computers have been forcing the energy down, and, therefore, plug load will continue to decrease. The base load test mentioned in this appendix will easily mitigate the largest portion of that load impact. Adjust it based on the additional equipment in proportion to the base load. That should get it within 10%.

The second area is the fan/pump systems' usage. That can vary around 15%, as shown in the last section. 15% in one system is a large impact, especially in the largest energy system. However, the impact with the mitigation discussed above and in the body of the appendix will drop that impact down to less than 6%. With this in mind, and as one becomes proficient in situations where an extreme condition exists, this tool becomes a lifesaver for saving EM time. Doing an audit by any method within 5% accuracy in most cases for each energy system is noteworthy, especially when it can be done in 15 minutes without mitigation and 30 with mitigation. That compares to an audit that may take 5−10 days, depending on the complexity of the equipment. Modeling will take five days and is usually within 10%. So, clearly, this tool will provide good results and save the EM precious time.

Index

About the Authors

Buster Barksdale is a Mechanical Engineer who is a Certified Energy Manager with over 44 years of energy management experience and has served at all organizational and functional levels. His service started in 1978 as an Energy Manager for the US Air Force. Since then, he has performed engineering, energy management, construction management, performance contracts, facility operations and consulted on government energy policy and procurement procedures. His experiences in the Air Force led him to evaluate and inspect maintenance for 20 installations, which developed into a study that revised how the Air Force performed maintenance. Upon retiring from the Air Force, he continued in all aspects of energy management with a specific emphasis on control systems and the development of analysis techniques. For 25 years, he has applied the techniques he learned in the Air Force to incorporate best maintenance practices into a monitoring commissioning program with meters and control systems. This experience has been poured into the Army metering program, which has developed analysis tools that the energy managers could use to do their job easier and better. Over 45 tools have been developed, with five additional in development. The professional development program led by Buster and Kecia Pierce received the International Energy Professional Develop Award for the Association of Energy Engineers in 2019. Buster is a CEM, CSDP, CDSM, Fellow Society of American Military Engineers, Fellow Association of Energy Engineers (AEE), Hall of Fame AEE, Past President of AEE, Board of Directors AEE.

Kecia Pierce is a Software Engineer and Project Manager who has over 33 years of requirements analysis, structured design, product/project management, and implementation leadership experience, thus giving her a strong technical background and a solid understanding of geospatial energy infrastructure management systems, including Outage and Incident Management. Kecia has worked with over 170 utilities and communications companies worldwide, leading to an in-depth knowledge of requirements and supporting technology in the energy geospatial software industry. Kecia has been published in various industry magazines and publications, such as Transmission

393

and Distribution World, GeoWorld, and Geospatial Today. Kecia is a Project Management Institute Certified Project Management Professional, and has served with Energy Huntsville, GEO Huntsville, the GITA conference committee, and the GITA Board of Directors. Kecia has served as the Outreach Strategist for the US Army's Meter Data Management System (MDMS) since October 2016. She provides the services of a communications strategist, technical writer, and trainer for educating US Army Energy Managers in using the MDMS to prioritize their energy conservation actions, and verify energy savings. Kecia prepares and leads the MDMS training webinars, tutorials, and the MDMS Update newsletter that notifies the Army end-user community of advancements, changes, and other pertinent facts about the Army Meter Program.